# The Warren Buffett CEO

★ ★ ★

*Secrets from the Berkshire Hathaway Managers*

Robert P. Miles

JOHN WILEY & SONS, INC.

Published by John Wiley & Sons, Inc., New York.
Published simultaneously in Canada.

This publication is designed to provide accurate and authoritative information in regard to the
subject matter covered. It is sold with the understanding that the publisher is not engaged in ren-
dering professional services. If professional advice or other expert assistance is required, the services of a competent professional person should be sought.

ISBN 0-471-44259-3

Printed in the United States of America.

10  9  8  7  6  5  4  3  2  1

*To my mother
Helen
and
my grandmother
Dorothy*

# Foreword

Consistent excellence over an extended period of time is the true test of organizational skills and philosophy. I was very fortunate to be part of a football program at the University of Nebraska that has been able to produce 39 consecutive winning seasons, and 32 consecutive teams that have won nine games or more and have gone to bowl games. Along the way, there were five national championships and numerous conference championships.

I believe that some analogies can be drawn between athletics and the business world. Some of the strategies that seemed to be successful at the University of Nebraska are common practices at Berkshire Hathaway. One of the hallmarks of Berkshire Hathaway has been an extremely long run of consistent, outstanding performance. The policies established by Warren Buffett, my friend, are at the heart of this amazing, long-lived success story.

No one is more successful at recruiting business managers than Warren Buffett. His successes stem from recruiting people instead of companies. He is loyal to his chief executive officers and, in turn, the CEOs are loyal to him.

Just as loyalty is a major hallmark of the success at Berkshire Hathaway, I found that loyalty was the most important ingredient in the success of the Nebraska football program. Bob Devaney, the head football coach at Nebraska from 1962 to 1973, established this pattern. Bob enjoyed a great deal of early success at Nebraska. However, after a 6–4 season in 1968, some people were calling for the heads of assistant coaches. Bob let it be known that there would be no sacrificial lambs; if one coach went, we all went. That loyalty factor has remained intact over the years and has been instrumental in the continuity and the success we experienced at the University of Nebraska.

Buffett buys companies and keeps the management in place—a rarity in today's world. But, this rarity is crafted by design. Buffett selects people he has confidence in, and he lets them continue running their companies just as they did before he acquired them. The CEOs do all the blocking and tackling, and Warren encourages them from the sidelines.

In dealing with assistant coaches, I found that it was important to give each coach a significant area of responsibility and to let him exercise his own discretion, as long as he operated within the basic philosophy of the football program. Micromanaging does not work in dealing with assistant football coaches, and Warren has followed this guiding principle in dealing with the managers of his various companies.

Because Berkshire has assembled an elite team, Buffett has no intention of trading anyone from his roster, and he has never lost a top executive to another enterprise. This extraordinary group of people will work forever—Buffett does not expect or want them to retire—just as he expects to work indefinitely.

Similarly, the longevity of the coaching staff at Nebraska is unparalleled. The average length of stay of an assistant coach at the University of Nebraska is 15 years, whereas the average assistant coach in major college football stays in one place for only three years. Nebraska has had only three head coaches in a span of approximately 40 years. Constant turnover, so common at most colleges and universities, disrupts recruiting, team chemistry, and a shared knowledge of the game. This process seems highly counterproductive, but it is often mirrored in the business world. Obviously, Warren Buffett has not subscribed to the idea of creating an environment that yields a huge amount of turnover. Warren's CEOs do not have to call Omaha daily or provide weekly reports. They are able to focus their attention internally because *they* are managing their companies. Of course, most of them want to talk to Buffett and check in periodically. But they don't have to.

One of the most revealing vignettes concerning Warren's management style was his handling of a crisis at a corporation a few years ago. The board of directors designated Warren, a committee of one, to select the next CEO after the top two executives had been abruptly dismissed. Warren had to make a quick decision. Instead of looking at resumes, school credentials, and peer recommendations, he based his decision primarily on qualities of character. He stated that he chose the candidate who, he felt, was an outstanding human being. Much of his success in the business world has resulted from his ability to assess the character of his managers, and his valuation of sound character above sparkling resumes or individual brilliance.

As time went by, I arrived at a similar philosophy in selecting those who worked for me. I looked for character first and foremost, often hiring people with less experience and with less impressive resumes than other candidates. If I could trust those people, if they would work hard, and if they truly cared about the people entrusted to them, they could be taught whatever specifics they needed to know. As Warren has observed, character counts.

While it is unlikely anyone will be able to replicate the success of Berkshire Hathaway, there's no doubt that everyone can learn from Buffett's management style—and that of his CEOs. This book provides an insider's view of the world of these managers—their work, their experiences with Buffett, and more—and of Omaha's unique institution, both the man and the company.

TOM OSBORNE
U.S. Congressman (R-NE)
Nebraska Head Football Coach (1973–1997)

# Preface

*T*his writing project began rather humbly and simply. After completing my first book, *101 Reasons to Own the World's Greatest Investment: Warren Buffett's Berkshire Hathaway,* I wrote to Warren Buffett and received this reply: "Be sure to give Charlie [Vice Chairman Charles Munger] and our operating managers their just due." Or, in essence, "Enough writing about me; the real story of Berkshire is the operating managers, Stupid."

He didn't say "Stupid"; he's too good a motivator and diplomat to say that. But I got the message. I then called Lou Simpson, Buffett's designated successor on the investment side of the business. His secretary said that Simpson doesn't do interviews, which was discouraging. However, much to my surprise, Simpson called back and said I could interview him and his associate, Tom Bancroft, over breakfast. That initial meeting started me off on what ultimately became a wonderful cross-country journey to meet the CEOs of most of the Berkshire Hathaway companies.

This book isn't a "How to Invest Like Warren Buffett" tome. Instead, it introduces the managers who are running the businesses that Buffett has invested in. As you read these chapters, you'll learn about different families and the beginnings of some interesting and successful businesses. You'll also learn some management and investment tenets from some of the most highly regarded CEOs around.

Warren didn't endorse my book research, but he wrote me that he would let each manager decide whether to grant me an interview. "Their time is their own," he wrote. "I'm looking forward to reading the interviews of the managers, and it could well make for an interesting book. The managers are a fascinating group of entrepreneurs, and the story of each one makes for an inspirational and educational read. Their different styles would baffle any company that thinks about getting managers in MBA cookie-cutter form."

Later, at a luncheon celebrating his seventieth birthday, Warren said he had enjoyed Lou Simpson's interview transcript (I had sent it to him as a courtesy), but he asked that no other interview transcripts be forwarded to him in advance. He didn't want to influence the book in any way.

Warren didn't encourage or discourage anyone from talking with me, but I'm reasonably certain that most of the managers called Warren to ask what he thought about my project. Would the Buffett CEOs have talked with me if they thought their boss disapproved? Probably not. He did say he was looking forward to reading the book, although he and Vice Chairman Charles ("Charlie") Munger declined to be interviewed. My access was unprecedented, but the CEOs of several Berkshire subsidiaries, including Dairy Queen, Dexter Shoes, MidAmerican, National Indemnity, and General Reinsurance, declined my request for interviews.

Most of the managers were uncomfortable when they talked about themselves but were more than happy to talk about their businesses. The founders and family managers proved to have the best stories and were more willing to share them. Nonfamily professional successors were uneasy about calling attention to themselves and their roles in the business.

I feel that I should make some disclosures here. I am a shareholder of Berkshire Hathaway, and I admit to being a biased admirer of the company and its management team. I have never worked within the financial industry or for any financial media. I am a businessman by training and a writer by passion. Furthermore, this book is not an "official" Berkshire product. I have never been on the payroll of any company that is in any way associated with Berkshire. All the expenses related to producing the manuscript—including airfare, hotels, car rentals, and transcriptions—were paid by me.

I did accept some gifts from several managers: breakfasts, lunches, dinners, a home-cooked barbecue, a television appearance, books, research material, golf balls, a T-shirt, a ball-team cap, luggage tags, and a flight simulator experience.

Some readers may be envious of my access to Buffett's team of operating managers, but I must warn you that it would cost somewhere in the neighborhood of 10 Berkshire "b" shares to meet personally with 20 Buffett CEOs—that is, if you have the time and if the managers give you the same access. Another 20 "b" shares would go toward doing the necessary research. You would spend the better part of a year reviewing 1,500 pages of transcripts and sifting through another 1,500 pages of research to pare the book down to the publisher's 400-page limit.

As part of my extensive and sometimes exhausting research, I took 10 airplane flights, one train ride, and several bus excursions, and I drove over 1,000 miles to visit 15 cities. I spent countless hours doing follow-up telephone interviews, and I made almost daily trips to various libraries.

In addition to wanting to produce a book that would appeal to as many readers as possible, I felt some pressure to provide a book that each Buffett CEO would enjoy reading. In general, the CEOs don't know one another. Each Buffett CEO is looking forward to reading about his or her counterparts and learning what qualities they share that were of interest to Warren.

Warren has said that if something should happen to him, he has chosen, from the current team, a replacement on the operating side of the business. One of these managers may become the next overall CEO, so I have tried to evaluate the Berkshire succession plan. No one told me who will replace Buffett, but after spending time with each CEO, I have made an educated guess.

Each operating manager will provide, in his or her own words, insight into the Berkshire culture and its unique management principles. For the life of me, I can't figure out why other companies do not follow Berkshire's acquisition strategy of buying a company, as one would buy a stock, and staying out of the way of management. Berkshire is about Main Street, not Wall Street.

Buffett manages his CEOs just like he manages his stock purchases. He carefully chooses them and doesn't ask them to do anything different as a result of his ownership. He is loyal to his CEOs, and they are loyal in return. No other Fortune 500 chief executive can match Buffett's for keeping his CEOs.

I also found out that Buffett is as good a manager as he is an investor. Berkshire buys the people first and the business second. Buffett would never buy a business if he didn't have complete confidence in its CEO. Buffett manages right by investing right. He is better known as an investor, but he is equally talented as a manager.

Later, I asked Warren Buffett why no other company has adopted the Berkshire culture. I thought he would say that it was because acquiring CEOs look for synergy with each new acquisition and feel compelled to impose their culture on the acquired business and its management.

Instead, he explained that the corporate culture he has established started because he took over a small enterprise at a young age (34) and, because he didn't have to retire at 65, he had enough time to establish momentum. Most CEOs inherit a culture with a short time frame in which to put their thumbprints on their organizations. In addition, these businesses are usually so large that they become resistant to change, even if the CEOs have better management methods. This concept was a major management discovery for me.

One of my favorite discoveries is the Buffett CEOs' shared trait of "giving back." Their generosity is astounding and should serve as an inspiration for managers all over the world.

Warren was right. Berkshire *is* more than Warren Buffett. The real story has everything to do with the management team behind the famed businessman and investor.

ROBERT P. MILES

*Tampa, Florida*
*September 2001*

# Acknowledgments

*T*he idea for this book really came from Warren Buffett when he responded to a letter from me and said that the real story of Berkshire Hathaway is all the operating managers who make up this company. I wish to say thanks first to him for the idea, for his artful creation of an endlessly fascinating corporate story, and for his quiet consent to having his CEOs talk openly and without advance question and transcript approval.

I also thank his partner and Berkshire Vice Chairman, Charlie Munger, for years of endless words of wisdom. He too made no attempt to influence this book in any way.

Lou Simpson, more than any other manager, made this book happen by granting me my first interview. Normally, Lou does not do interviews, so I am particularly grateful for his time spent with me, and for his insights.

In the order of their interviews, I wish to thank each Buffett CEO: Lou Simpson (Tom Bancroft, his associate), Al Ueltschi, Tony Nicely, Ralph Schey (Ken Smelsberger, Schey's successor), Stan Lipsey, Ajit Jain, Eliot and Barry Tatelman, Frank Rooney, Susan Jacques, Irvin Blumkin, Bill Child, Harrold Melton, Randy Watson, Melvyn Wolff, Jeff Comment, Chuck Huggins, Don Graham, and Rich Santulli.

The CEOs' assistants helped me with appointments, directions, research material, transcript corrections, correspondence, e-mails, photos, and chapter reviews. This group has given, collectively, 307 years (average of 15 years) of service and knows more about each business and its manager than anyone else. Listed by years of service and CEO, they are: Flora Giaccio, 33 (Ueltschi); Linda Stine-Ward, 32 (Nicely), Debbie Bosanek, 27 (Buffett), Pam Gazenski, 26 (Graham), Kris Hughes, 24 (Schey), Sherrie Bender, 17 (Wolff), Marcia Garner, 16 (Child), Barbara Urbanczyk, 15½ (Lipsey), Carrie Berman, 15 (Melton), Josephine Faiella, 14 (Rooney), Wendy Bannahan, 12 (Graham), Edith DeSantis, 12 (Smelsberger), Barbara Palma, 11 (Simpson), Nancy Bernard, 10 (Huggins), Judy Robinson, 9 (Comment), Susan Goracke, 9 (Blumkin), Karen Benson, 8 (Jacques), Lisa Lankes, 7 (Watson), Heather Copolas, 5 (Tatelman), Carol Bolicki, 3 (Santulli), Beverly Ward, 1 (Jain).

Malcolm Kim Chace, a Berkshire board member and a third-generation descendant of the original family members of the Berkshire textile mills, and his assistant, Stacey Courville, helped me to better understand the company. Former Radio Shack CEO John Roach and his assistant and partner of 30 years, Lou Ann Blaylock, gave me the inside details of one of the last acquisitions and coordinated a meeting to make my interviews with "The Newcomers" easier.

Paul Arnold of Cort Furniture made himself available for an interview that never happened. My thanks and apologies to all the other available Buffett CEOs who were not included through no fault of their own. I acknowledge the kind letters from Buffett CEOs, Terry Piper (Precision Steel), Ed and Jon Bridge (Ben Bridge Jewelers), David Sokol (MidAmerican), Brad Kinstler (Fechheimer), Ron Ferguson (GenRe), Don Towle (Kansas Bankers Surety), and Don Wurster, CEO of National Indemnity, for explaining the Buffett CEO family tree.

To all the fine folks at FlightSafety—Bruce Whitman (with 40 years of service), Jim Waugh, Tom Eff, Roger Richie, and Tom Mahoney—thank you for giving me the thrill of flying a three-engine corporate jet while safely on the ground. And thanks to United Airlines Captain Kit Darby, for giving me the pilot instruction and flight simulator statistics that he so painstaking tracked for three years. To the dedicated folks at Project Orbis, Kathy Spahn, Melanie Brandston, and Kristin Lax.

Thanks to the Bill Child family, particularly Pat, for welcoming me to her home for an old-style outdoor backyard family barbecue and Luci Schey for becoming Ralph's secretary at his retirement.

Thanks to Dave Harvey and his staff, including Bob Kemp, Lyle Dedman, Dan Dias, and Johnnie Woods for the annual See's Candies chocolate tour for shareholders. All of us who left with several boxes of chocolate are now happily addicted to their product!

Thanks to Richard Smith, III, the leader at NetJets command center in Columbus, and to Beth Ann Goettler for a catered lunch fit for a king and a personal tour of Executive Jet's state-of-the-art facility. Any prospective client/owner will become a customer of NetJets after simply visiting its world-class operation.

Thanks to Warren Buffett's online bridge partner Sharon Osberg, Jordan Furniture executive Stephen Gaskin, and Morgan Stanley Insurance analyst Alice Schroeder.

A good book is well researched, and for that work I need to thank Marlyn Pethe, director of the University of Tampa Library, and her staff. Every day I walked into her library, I found her staff and librarians ready to offer their help with online resources or research on whatever subject I needed to review.

Every book, while crafted in solitude, is the work of a dedicated team of professionals. As with every CEO highlighted in this book, an individual may get the credit but the work of a team brings about the results. Every book has to have a vision and a publisher that understands and comprehends what the author is trying to achieve. Fortunately, fellow author Janet Lowe and Wiley representative Tim Hand introduced me to publisher Joan O'Neil and my day-to-day contact editor, Debra Englander of John Wiley & Sons. Call Deb if you have a Buffett, investment, or management book in you. Nobody understands book concepts faster. She has an amazing talent to draw the book out of her authors. Her daughter Elise says that Deb is more than a mother at home. I say that Deb is more than an editor at work.

Thanks to the rest of the Wiley professional team: P. J. Campbell, Tess Woods, Greg Friedman, Robin Factor, and Mary Daniello.

Every author needs a literary agent. Andrea Pedolsky, at Altair Literary Agency, is one of the best. She carefully guided me through the business side of publishing, and she negotiated the contract, acting in her client's best interests without damaging the delicate relationship between publisher and author.

Every author needs a hand, particularly when editing 1,500 pages of interview transcripts and an equal amount of research documents. Rob Kaplan carefully edited 3,000 pages down to 300, and made this book easy to read and the whole process fun. Rob is a talented writer, editor, and decision maker. He was born for this type of work.

Most authors choose to write without the benefit of a test reader, but I found Tampa attorney and fellow shareholder Will Harrell to be the best book counselor. He read each chapter in confidence and gave me his candid review. Will suggested some major rewrites and a different line of follow-up questions for each manager. It was his idea to do a chapter on Mrs. Blumkin as the epitome of the Buffett CEO. For the cost of a weekly lunch, I got confidentiality and attorney-client privilege, an interested shareholder, grammar and sentence structure edits, an ongoing reader opinion and feedback, the ability to see whether the concepts I was trying to communicate were working, a person gifted in oral and written communication, investment knowledge, the history of Berkshire, a weekend stock analyst, a management expert, and a friend.

Steve Rymers helped me craft the original set of interview questions and shared his vision for this book. My gratitude to Eric Balandraud, Lyle McIntosh, Leslie Trvex, Joann Floyd, Mark Forster, Kristine Gerber, Rich Rockwood, Jim Chuong, Selena Maranjian, Ken Roberts, Tom Juengel, Ben Keaton, and Lee Bakunin.

Thanks to Berkshire historian and tireless author Andy Kilpatrick for dedicating his life to the chronicling of Berkshire Hathaway with his self-published books *Of Permanent Value: The Story of Warren Buffett*. His refusal to edit the bi-annual editions down has created an 1,100-page monster and bigger biceps for any other Buffett author who needs to carry his book around as "The Berkshire Encyclopedia."

Thanks to Omaha bookseller Jim Ross, Peg Hake, University of Nebraska-Omaha professors Laura Beal and Weiyu Guo whose support and encouragement are most appreciated. Thanks to Andy Cassel and Linda O'Bryon for their interview transcripts of Mrs. Blumkin. Thanks to Jack Kahn of PBS Nightly Business Report.

Encouragement, all along the long path to completion of this book, came from John Zemanovich, who boldly and enthusiastically predicted a bestseller before reading one word. Thanks to John Baum for pushing me to finish and for his belief in the law of unintended consequences.

Thanks to Whit Wannamaker for his friendship and support. Thanks to Janet Wright and her patient, thoughtful advice and emotional support during the natural ups and downs of an author's life.

Mostly thanks to my inspiration and emerging CEO, Marybeth, the best daughter a father could ever hope for.

R. P. M.

# Contents

# PART FOUR
## BERKSHIRE'S CEO FAMILY—
## CHILDREN AND GRANDCHILDREN

# PART FIVE
## BERKSHIRE'S CEO SUCCESSORS—
## THE PROFESSIONAL MANAGERS

# PART SIX
## CONCLUSION

# ★ *Part One* ★

# The Buffett CEO

# chapter one

# Introduction—
# The Warren Buffett CEO

*B*erkshire Hathaway's chief architect and CEO, Warren Buffett, receives most of the acclaim, but, to understand the company, you need to appreciate all the relatively unheralded operating managers who are part of this huge corporation. More than two dozen books have been written about the world's most famous investor, but, until now, none has thoroughly explored Buffett's management team and its unique culture. This book attempts to capture the essence of Berkshire Hathaway by profiling CEOs who are entrusted with management of its underlying wholly owned businesses.

Berkshire Hathaway (nyse:brka) is a conglomerate known most for its partly owned businesses like Coca-Cola (8 percent), Gillette (9 percent), and American Express (11 percent). Buffett's company is the largest owner of Coke stock.

Buffett made his name and wealth by growing Berkshire from $40 million in sales in 1967 to over $40 billion in sales today. Starting with shrewd common stock selections, Berkshire has transformed itself by buying wholly owned businesses like Dairy Queen (ice cream), Benjamin Moore (paint), Shaw Industries (carpets), and Johns Manville (insulation). (See Appendix Two for a complete list.)

While this book profiles one partly owned CEO (Graham of *The Washington Post*), the main focus is on the CEOs and businesses that are owned in their entirety.

This perspective is significant for several reasons:

★ Berkshire Hathaway is an investment vehicle created by a financial and management genius, but it has now become larger than Warren Buffett. Its diversified units are run by financially independent managers within a flat organizational structure. Berkshire Hathaway has over $140 billion in assets *without* a typical corporate infrastructure.

★ Although long known as Warren Buffett's holding company of publicly traded stocks, Berkshire Hathaway's present collection of wholly owned subsidiaries supersedes its image as a quasi-mutual fund. Not long ago, Buffett's holding company was composed of 90 percent equities and 10 percent operating companies, and everyone was eager to learn what stocks Buffett was buying. Today, Berkshire Hathaway is 70 percent operating companies and 30 percent equities and is striving to be 90 percent wholly owned and 10 percent marketable securities. When it was a much smaller insurance company (it now owns over 30 separate insurance firms), Buffett chose to own parts of large businesses via the stock market so that Berkshire's assets were liquid enough to pay insurance claims. As his company grew, Buffett acquired more wholly owned companies because there was less risk of having to sell them if claims were made.

★ Management can easily make a mistake in purchasing common stock. If the CEO has not acted in the best interests of the shareowners, the newly acquired business can be sold fairly quickly on the open market. On the other hand, buying a whole company that has incompatible management in place is difficult and expensive to reverse. Buffett has written: "[We] try to buy not only good businesses, but ones run by high-grade, talented and likeable managers. If we make a mistake about the manager we link up with, the controlled company offers a certain advantage because we have the power to effect change. In practice, however, this advantage is somewhat illusory: Management changes, like marital changes, are painful, time-consuming and chancy."[1] Over 35 years, some Buffett CEOs have chosen to retire, but none has left to join a competing enterprise. All Buffett CEOs are considered partners for life. This remarkable record alone is worth examining. How are the managers selected, managed, evaluated, compensated, and assigned within the corporate parent's structure to ensure such devotion and loyalty? Berkshire has a select group of managers. Primarily, they are centimillionaires who work hard for groups of billionaire board members and long-term millionaire shareholders.

★ Most CEOs allocate their own capital and expand their business whenever they can. Berkshire has centralized this function in the hands of its most talented capital allocator. This unique management structure has led to superior investment and management successes and has proven to be Buffett's finest cultural and structural strategy. It may also account for the low CEO turnover. Most, if not all, of Berkshire Hathaway's underlying businesses have enjoyed steady and increasing employment. Except for its early textile ventures and the current competition from overseas shoe manufacturers, few, if any, divisions have suffered from major layoffs.

★ Technology—particularly the Internet and its impact on Berkshire—is worth exploring from the inside. Long a technophobe and bearish on anything that he can't value, including most "new economy" stocks, Buffett has carefully avoided technology-based businesses. FlightSafety is an exception. Recent market performance has shown how difficult it is for Internet companies to devise a successful business model. Still, like the invention of the wheel, the Internet has continued to lower the costs of doing business. Among Berkshire's businesses, it has helped GEICO and See's Candies and hurt World Book. Eventually, it may threaten the *Buffalo News* and the *Washington Post*. Indirectly, the Internet has created more customers for its NetJets fractional jet business. The Buffett CEOs discuss the impact of technology on their various businesses.

What will Berkshire look like after Warren Buffett? The chairman is not anywhere near "retirement," which he defines as five years after his death, but most shareholders are curious about how the company will look when Buffett is no longer running the show. For clues, if not a definitive answer, this book spotlights the current Berkshire businesses and their managers, one of whom will someday become the CEO of the CEOs. You will learn who these managers are, what business and management principles they endorse, how they have handled the succession issue within their own businesses, and how their companies fit into the Berkshire mosaic.

One fact unearthed during the interviews may surprise you: The operating managers don't know much about the other wholly owned subsidiaries, beyond what is revealed in the chairman's annual letter to shareholders or in media reports. To some degree, you will learn, as did some of the Berkshire interviewees, what their counterparts are doing.

There is no "average" Buffett CEO, but the persons profiled here tended to be white males in their sixties, who were already managing third-generation businesses that are 100 years old. All but one of the managers were promoted from inside the business. Most Buffett CEOs manage "old economy" businesses: bricks, candy, furniture, jewelry, encyclopedias, vacuums, air compressors, newspapers, footwear, and insurance.

Each individual profiled exhibits traits that are uncompromising to Buffett: high ethical standards and integrity. When he put his reputation on the line to save Salomon Brothers, Buffett told a Senate subcommittee: "Make an honest mistake and I will be understanding, but lose the reputation of the enterprise and I will be ruthless." He has often said, "Never do anything that can't be printed on the front pages of your local newspaper."

This book has exclusive interviews with Lou Simpson, the designated backup to Warren Buffett on the capital allocation side. No one at Berkshire will reveal who will succeed Buffett on the operational side of the business, but somewhere in this book is an interview with the person who may one day inherit that major responsibility. Berkshire hires its CEOs exclusively from within, so its future CEO of operations will be a long-term employee.

After Buffett "retires," his job is to be split among three persons. One family member, most likely his son Howard, will become Chairman of the Board and continue the "Buffett family" atmosphere, influence, and culture. One manager will handle the capital allocation (buying pieces of publicly traded companies and buying wholly owned operating companies), and another manager will head the management team. Essentially, Berkshire will have a Chairman, a CEO/President in charge of capital operations, and a CEO/President in charge of operations.

According to Lou Simpson, the future management of Berkshire will be very similar to GEICO's present management structure (Lou Simpson is GEICO's CEO and President in charge of capital operations, and Tony Nicely is GEICO's CEO and President in charge of operations). This projection describes only the proposed structure, not the individuals who will fill those posts.

Simpson sees himself as a backup to Buffett, not an actual successor. With just six years separating the two men in age, it is unlikely that Lou will succeed Warren. And nobody on the inside has suggested Tony Nicely as the successor on the operational side of Berkshire, but his profile gives shareholders a vision of how things will look in the future.

Berkshire has never sold an operating company or fired an original entrepreneur after buying his or her company. A few have chosen to retire, but most have a passion for the business that continues today and into the future.

Most publicly traded companies force out brilliant managers (like Jack Welch of GE) when they reach 65 years of age, but each one of Buffett's managers, like Mrs. B, can continue to run his or her business unit until age 104 and can then "retire." Like good soldiers, the Berkshire management team is permitted and encouraged—and may prefer—to die with their boots on. Maybe that's why all the Buffett CEOs are smiling.

In the case of FlightSafety's 80-something founder and president, Al Ueltschi, Warren won't split Berkshire's stock but does intend to split Al's age when he reaches his hundredth birthday.

Buffett CEOs do not deal with the responsibilities of typical chief executives. There are no meetings with analysts or with shareholders, no press interviews, no expansion requirements, no limitations on available capital, and no headquarter mandates. These CEOs instantly obtain the highest credit rating and the financial strength enjoyed by only seven other corporations in the world.

Buffett CEOs have the unique ability to focus completely on internal affairs and completely on the long-term success of their business, with no outside distractions. Berkshire managers can report into headquarters as often or as seldom as they choose. One manager never set foot in Omaha until 20 years after being purchased.

Berkshire's unique management compensation system has been led by its chief executive. With a salary of $100,000 and no stock options, Buffett is the lowest paid of all the Fortune 500 CEOs. All of his managers have higher salaries, and all Buffett CEOs have a direct financial interest in their business. Their compensation plans are simple and are directly tied to the results of their own enterprise.

Don't expect outrageous stories or elaborate business strategies here. The business and management principles are simple:

★ Buy pieces of wonderful companies that you intend to keep forever.
★ Only consider managers that you admire and trust. Then slowly buy whole companies with phenomenal management in place.

★ Manage your companies exactly as you would a small portfolio of stocks.

★ Let the managers continue to do what attracted you to them in the first place.

Even though Buffett CEOs do not know one another and are independently wealthy enough to speak their minds, each CEO, to a person, described Buffett and his influence on them almost identically. If their responses seem repetitive, its because 20 very independent CEOs came to the same conclusions on their own.

This is a fascinating story of outstanding individuals who are led by an extraordinary man. Of Berkshire Hathaway and the Warren Buffett CEOs, Buffett wrote in his 1987 letter to shareholders, "This divine assemblage— . . . is a collection of businesses with economic characteristics that range from good to superb. Its managers range from superb to superb. Most of these managers have no need to work for a living; they show up at the ballpark because they like to hit home runs. And that's exactly what they do. When I call off the names of our managers—the Blumkins, . . . Chuck Huggins, Stan Lipsey, . . . Ralph Schey—I feel the same glow that Miller Huggins must have experienced when he announced the lineup of his 1927 New York Yankees."[2]

# chapter two

# Buffett CEO Selection

*H*ow does someone become a Buffett CEO? Berkshire Hathaway's unique acquisition process follows specific published and some proprietary criteria. Unlike the rest of those in the marketplace for quality businesses, whether it owns part or all of a business, Berkshire's approach is the same. Berkshire may be the only active investor, private or corporate, that purchases companies and their managers, either in part or whole, in the same manner.

The Buffett CEO selection and management parallels its approach to stock selection and management. Deciding to purchase a company also involves a decision to select its managers. Knowing that it will not replace management, it wouldn't buy part of a company through the stock market without considering the manager. Buffett and Company does not buy a whole company any differently. Berkshire never has invested (and never will) in a company if the manager doesn't meet the same exacting standards.

Berkshire's selection of CEOs is worth studying because Berkshire Hathaway has never lost a CEO to a competing enterprise. To best understand the CEO selection process, you need to understand Berkshire's acquisition beliefs, objectives, and methods.

## THE BERKSHIRE HATHAWAY WAY

Perhaps Buffett CEO Terry Piper, President and CEO of Berkshire's wholly owned Precision Steel Warehouse, Inc., summarized it best. "Mr. Buffett bought Precision Steel in 1979, and every manager that was here at that time is still with us today, unless they retired. He is just a terrific person to work for and we are proud to be part of Berkshire Hathaway.

I feel so lucky to be able to pick up the telephone and discuss things with one of the nicest, smartest, and most honest people you could ever think of knowing on this planet. He treats everyone with respect and is more than willing to listen than anyone I know. I learn more each and every time I have a conversation with him."[1]

Berkshire's method of acquiring CEOs and their businesses is a capitalist's dream. Several years ago, Buffett explained his approach: "At Berkshire, our managers will continue to earn extraordinary returns from what appear to be ordinary businesses. As a first step, these managers will look for ways to deploy their earnings advantageously in their businesses. What's left, they will send to Charlie and me. We then will try to use those funds in ways that build per-share intrinsic value. Our goal will be to acquire either part or all of businesses that we believe we understand, that have good, sustainable underlying economics, and that are run by managers whom we like, admire and trust. . . . "[2]

Buffett continued to simplify the business and CEO selection process. "If my universe of business possibilities was limited, say, to private companies in Omaha, I would, first, try to assess the long-term economic characteristics of each business; second, assess the quality of the people in charge of running it; and, third, try to buy into a few of the best operations at a sensible price. I certainly would not wish to own an equal part of every business in town. Why, then, should Berkshire take a different tack when dealing with the larger universe of public companies? And since finding great businesses and outstanding managers is so difficult, why should we discard proven products? (I was tempted to say 'the real thing.') Our motto is: 'If at first you do succeed, quit trying.' "[3]

## BUFFETT CEO ACQUISITION CRITERIA

The criteria have been published in every Berkshire annual report starting in 1982, when there was a $5 million pretax earnings requirement. The criteria have stayed the same over the past 20 years, except that the annual earnings criterion has gradually increased to $50 million. One major Berkshire criterion is not typical: management *must* come along with the deal.

"We are eager to hear from principals or their representatives about businesses that meet all of the following criteria:

1. Large purchases (at least $50 million of before-tax earnings).
2. Demonstrated consistent earning power (future projections are of no interest to us, nor are 'turnaround' situations ['turnarounds seldom turn']).
3. Businesses earning good returns on equity while employing little or no debt.
4. Management in place (we can't supply it).
5. Simple businesses (if there's lots of technology, we won't understand it).
6. An offering price (we don't want to waste our time or that of the seller by talking, even preliminarily, about a transaction when price is unknown).

"The larger the company, the greater will be our interest: We would like to make an acquisition in the $5 to $20 billion range. We are not interested, however, in receiving suggestions about purchases we might make in the general stock market.

"We will not engage in unfriendly takeovers. We can promise complete confidentiality and a very fast answer—customarily, within five minutes—as to whether we're interested. We prefer to buy for cash, but will consider issuing stock when we receive as much in intrinsic business value as we give.

"Charlie and I frequently get approached about acquisitions that don't come close to meeting our tests: We've found that if you advertise an interest in buying collies, a lot of people will call hoping to sell you their cocker spaniels. A line from a country song expresses our feeling about new ventures, turnarounds, or auctionlike sales: 'When the phone don't ring, you'll know it's me.' "[4]

## BERKSHIRE ACQUISITION TECHNIQUE

While the rest of the business world is hiring staff, transaction agents, and brokers to find them businesses without CEOs attached, Buffett waits for the phone to ring. The best deals have a way of finding their way to Omaha. Also, Berkshire's tentacle reach is vast, with 300,000 shareholders and relationships with most captains of industry. The most ideal situation for Buffett occurs when an interested CEO who meets all the published criteria picks up the phone and calls him directly.

Buffett employs a few more unique acquisition techniques. He enlists the help of his existing CEOs, who are the best sources for new leads, and he shamelessly advertises in his annual report. More than 300,000 copies are printed and distributed, and hundreds more people read it on the Internet.

## PURCHASING FOR TOADLIKE PRICES

Berkshire will never lose its appetite for acquiring businesses that present excellent economics and also have superior management. The key is to buy them at excellent prices whether they deliver total ownership of a business or marketable securities representing small portions of businesses.

"Our acquisition decisions," stated Buffett, "will be aimed at maximizing real economic benefits, not at maximizing either managerial domain or reported numbers for accounting purposes. (In the long run, managements stressing accounting appearance over economic substance usually achieve little of either.)

"Regardless of the impact upon immediately reportable earnings, we would rather buy 10% of Wonderful Business T at X per share than 100% of T at 2X per share. Most corporate managers prefer just the reverse, and have no shortage of stated rationales for their behavior.

"However, we suspect three motivations—usually unspoken—to be, singly or in combination, the important ones in most high-premium takeovers:

1. Leaders, business or otherwise, seldom are deficient in animal spirits and often relish increased activity and challenge. At Berkshire, the corporate pulse never beats faster than when an acquisition is in prospect.

2. Most organizations, business or otherwise, measure themselves, are measured by others, and compensate their managers far more by the yardstick of size than by any other yardstick. (Ask a Fortune 500 manager where his corporation stands on that famous list and, invariably, the number responded will be from the list ranked by size of sales; he may well not even know where his corporation places on

the list *Fortune* just as faithfully compiles, ranking the same 500 corporations by profitability.)

3. Many managements apparently were overexposed in impressionable childhood years to the story in which the imprisoned handsome prince is released from a toad's body by a kiss from a beautiful princess. Consequently, they are certain their managerial kiss will do wonders for the profitability of Company T(arget).

"Such optimism is essential. Absent that rosy view, why else should the shareholders of Company A(cquisitor) want to own an interest in T at the 2X takeover cost rather than at the X market price they would pay if they made direct purchases on their own?

"In other words, investors can always buy toads at the going price for toads. If investors instead bankroll princesses who wish to pay double for the right to kiss the toad, those kisses had better pack some real dynamite. We've observed many kisses but very few miracles. Nevertheless, many managerial princesses remain serenely confident about the future potency of their kisses—even after their corporate backyards are knee-deep in unresponsive toads.

"In fairness, we should acknowledge that some acquisition records have been dazzling. Two major categories stand out.

"The first involves companies that, through design or accident, have purchased only businesses that are particularly well adapted to an inflationary environment. Such favored business must have two characteristics: (1) an ability to increase prices rather easily (even when product demand is flat and capacity is not fully utilized) without fear of significant loss of either market share or unit volume, and (2) an ability to accommodate large dollar volume increases in business (often produced more by inflation than by real growth) with only minor additional investment of capital. Managers of ordinary ability, focusing solely on acquisition possibilities meeting these tests, have achieved excellent results in recent decades. However, very few enterprises possess both characteristics, and competition to buy those that do has now become fierce to the point of being self-defeating.

"The second category involves the managerial superstars—men who can recognize that rare prince who is disguised as a toad, and who have managerial abilities that enable them to peel away the disguise.

"Your Chairman, unfortunately, does not qualify for Category 2. And, despite a reasonably good understanding of the economic factors compelling concentration in Category 1, our actual acquisition activity in that category has been sporadic and inadequate. Our preaching was better than our performance. (We neglected the Noah principle: Predicting rain doesn't count, building arks does.)

"We have tried occasionally to buy toads at bargain prices with results that have been chronicled in past reports. Clearly our kisses fell flat. We have done well with a couple of princes—but they were princes when purchased. At least our kisses didn't turn them into toads. And, finally, we have occasionally been quite successful in purchasing fractional interests in easily-identifiable princes at toadlike prices."[5]

"Of all our activities at Berkshire, the most exhilarating for Charlie and me is the acquisition of a business with excellent economic characteristics and a management that we like, trust and admire. Such acquisitions are not easy to make but we look for them constantly. In the search, we adopt the same attitude one might find appropriate in looking for a spouse: It pays to be active, interested and open-minded, but it does not pay to be in a hurry.

"In the past, I've observed that many acquisition-hungry managers were apparently mesmerized by their childhood reading of the story about the frog-kissing princess. Remembering her success, they pay dearly for the right to kiss corporate toads, expecting wondrous transfigurations. Initially, disappointing results only deepen their desire to round up new toads. ('Fanaticism,' said Santayana, 'consists of redoubling your effort when you've forgotten your aim.') Ultimately, even the most optimistic manager must face reality. Standing knee-deep in unresponsive toads, he then announces an enormous 'restructuring' charge. In this corporate equivalent of a Head Start program, the CEO receives the education but the stockholders pay the tuition.

"In my early days as a manager, I, too, dated a few toads. They were cheap dates—I've never been much of a sport—but my results matched those of acquirers who courted higher-priced toads. I kissed and they croaked.

"After several failures of this type, I finally remembered some useful advice I once got from a golf pro (who, like all pros who have had anything to do with my game, wishes to remain anonymous). Said the pro:

'Practice doesn't make perfect; practice makes permanent.' And thereafter I revised my strategy and tried to buy good businesses at fair prices rather than fair businesses at good prices."[6]

## BERKSHIRE ADVANTAGES

Because the seller always knows more of what he is selling than the buyer knows of what he is buying, the seller has the advantage. Buffett has never fallen prey to a seller's representative who prepares a "book" to project the rosiest scenario for the business of the seller in the future. Also, because Berkshire doesn't have a specific or strategic acquisition plan, it regains the advantage of considering deals in a wide range of industries and taking a pass on those that don't make economic sense. Buffett has the further advantages of experience, deep pockets, and selecting the best one or none at all. Unlike other acquirers, Berkshire compares each wholly owned deal with what pieces of some of the best businesses in the world it could buy via the stock market. It is the buyer of choice, so just about every deal is presented to Berkshire first. One of the true secrets to acquiring a Buffett CEO is the built-in fact that because Berkshire is acquiring both the business and the manager, the CEO is more likely to put a fair price on the deal than a top price. Fair prices don't come back to embarrass the seller; they create more trust from the buyer.

If a deal is struck while the business owner is alive, the owner can pick the home for the business. By controlling the business succession process, the owner shows a loving concern for heirs, employees, suppliers, and, most importantly, his or her customers.

In 1995, Buffett wrote about more Berkshire advantages. "In making acquisitions, we have a further advantage: As payment, we can offer sellers a stock backed by an extraordinary collection of outstanding businesses. An individual or a family wishing to dispose of a single fine business, but also wishing to defer personal taxes indefinitely, is apt to find Berkshire stock a particularly comfortable holding.

"Beyond that, sellers sometimes care about placing their companies in a corporate home that will both endure and provide pleasant, productive working conditions for their managers. Here again, Berkshire offers something special. Our managers operate with extraordinary autonomy. Additionally, our ownership structure enables sellers to know that when I say we are buying to keep, the promise means something. For our part, we like dealing with owners who care what happens to their companies and people. A buyer is likely to find fewer unpleasant surprises dealing with that type of seller than with one simply auctioning off his business."[7]

## BUY WITH CASH

Berkshire prefers to buy companies with cash, and its shareholders are better off as a result. The majority of its deals are done that way. Although some sellers insist on stock, Berkshire does attempt to give them an incentive to accept cash. The *Buffalo News,* See's Candies, Scott Fetzer, GEICO, Nebraska Furniture Mart, Jordan's, FlightSafety, the *Washington Post* (18 percent), Borsheim's, H.H. Brown, Justin Boot, and Acme Brick were all acquired for cash.

## SELECTING A CEO WHO LOVES THE BUSINESS

Writing in his most recent annual report, Warren Buffett described his aversion to auctionlike business sales:

> We find it meaningful when an owner cares about whom he sells to. We like to do business with someone who loves his company, not just the money that a sale will bring him (though we certainly understand why he likes that as well). When this emotional attachment exists, it signals that important qualities will likely be found within the business: honest accounting, pride of product, respect for customers, and a loyal group of associates having a strong sense of direction. The reverse is apt to be true, also. When an owner auctions off his business, exhibiting a total lack of interest in what follows, you will frequently find that it has been dressed up for sale, particularly when the seller is a "financial owner." And if owners behave with little regard for their business and its people, their conduct will often contaminate attitudes and practices throughout the company.
>
> When a business masterpiece has been created by a lifetime—or several lifetimes—of unstinting care and exceptional talent, it should be important to the owner what corporation is entrusted to carry on its history. Charlie and I believe Berkshire provides an almost unique home. We take our obligations to the people who created a business very seriously, and Berkshire's ownership structure ensures that we can fulfill our promises. When

we tell John Justin that his business will remain headquartered in Fort Worth, or assure the Bridge family that its operation will not be merged with another jeweler, these sellers can take those promises to the bank.

How much better it is for the "painter" of a business Rembrandt to personally select its permanent home than to have a trust officer or uninterested heirs auction it off. Throughout the years we have had great experiences with those who recognize that truth and apply it to their business creations. We'll leave the auctions to others.[8]

## THOUGHTS ON SELLING YOUR BUSINESS

Many of the Buffett CEOs profiled here may have received the following letter or heard these words over the phone during initial negotiations:

Excerpt from Berkshire's 1990 Annual Report:

### Some Thoughts on Selling Your Business*

* This is an edited version of a letter I sent some years ago to a man who had indicated that he might want to sell his family business. I present it here because it is a message I would like to convey to other prospective sellers.—W.E.B.

Dear _____ :

Here are a few thoughts pursuant to our conversation of the other day.

Most business owners spend the better part of their lifetimes building their businesses. By experience built upon endless repetition, they sharpen their skills in merchandising, purchasing, personnel selection, etc. It's a learning process, and mistakes made in one year often contribute to competence and success in succeeding years.

In contrast, owner-managers sell their business only once—frequently in an emotionally-charged atmosphere with a multitude of pressures coming from different directions. Often, much of the pressure comes from brokers whose compensation is contingent upon consummation of a sale, regardless of its consequences for both buyer and seller. The fact that the decision is so important, both financially and personally, to the owner can make the process more, rather than less, prone to error. And, mistakes made in the once-in-a-lifetime sale of a business are not reversible.

Price is very important, but often is not the most critical aspect of the sale. You and your family have an extraordinary business—one of a kind in your field—and any buyer is going to recognize that. It's also a business that is going to get more valuable as the years go by. So if you decide not to sell now, you are very likely to realize more money later on. With that knowledge you can deal from strength and take the time required to select the buyer you want.

If you should decide to sell, I think Berkshire Hathaway offers some advantages that most other buyers do not. Practically all of these buyers will fall into one of two categories:

1. A company located elsewhere but operating in your business or in a business somewhat akin to yours. Such a buyer—no matter what promises are made—will usually have managers who feel they know how to run your business operations and, sooner or later, will want to apply some hands-on "help." If the acquiring company is much larger, it often will have squads of managers, recruited over the years in part by promises that they will get to run future acquisitions. They will have their own way of doing things and, even though your business record undoubtedly will be far better than theirs, human nature will at some point cause them to believe that their methods of operating are superior. You and your family probably have friends who have sold their businesses to larger companies, and I suspect that their experiences will confirm the tendency of parent companies to take over the running of their subsidiaries, particularly when the parent knows the industry, or thinks it does.

2. A financial maneuverer, invariably operating with large amounts of borrowed money, who plans to resell either to the public or to another corporation as soon as the time is favorable. Frequently, this buyer's major contribution will be to change accounting methods so that earnings can be presented in the most favorable light just prior to his bailing out. I'm enclosing a recent article that describes this sort of transaction, which is becoming much more frequent because of a rising stock market and the great supply of funds available for such transactions.

If the sole motive of the present owners is to cash their chips and put the business behind them—and plenty of sellers fall in this category— either type of buyer that I've just described is satisfactory. But if the sellers' business represents the creative work of a lifetime and forms an integral part of their personality and sense of being, buyers of either type have serious flaws.

Berkshire is another kind of buyer—a rather unusual one. We buy to keep, but we don't have, and don't expect to have, operating people in our parent organization. All of the businesses we own are run autonomously to an extraordinary degree. In most cases, the managers of important businesses we have owned for many years have not been to Omaha or even met each other. When we buy a business, the sellers go on running it just as they did before the sale; we adapt to their methods rather than vice versa.

We have no one—family, recently recruited MBAs, etc.—to whom we have promised a chance to run businesses we have bought from owner-managers. And we won't have.

You know of some of our past purchases. I'm enclosing a list of everyone from whom we have ever bought a business, and I invite you to check with them as to our performance versus our promises. You should be particularly interested in checking with the few whose businesses did not do well in order to ascertain how we behaved under difficult conditions.

Any buyer will tell you that he needs you personally—and if he has any brains, he most certainly does need you. But a great many buyers, for the reasons mentioned above, don't match their subsequent actions to their earlier words. We will behave exactly as promised, both because we have so promised, and because we need to in order to achieve the best business results.

This need explains why we would want the operating members of your family to retain a 20% interest in the business. We need 80% to consolidate earnings for tax purposes, which is a step important to us. It is equally important to us that the family members who run the business remain as owners. Very simply, we would not want to buy unless we felt key members of present management would stay on as our partners. Contracts cannot guarantee your continued interest; we would simply rely on your word.

The areas I get involved in are capital allocation and selection and compensation of the top man. Other personnel decisions, operating strategies, etc. are his bailiwick. Some Berkshire managers talk over some of their decisions with me; some don't. It depends upon their personalities and, to an extent, upon their own personal relationship with me.

If you should decide to do business with Berkshire, we would pay in cash. Your business would not be used as collateral for any loan by Berkshire. There would be no brokers involved.

Furthermore, there would be no chance that a deal would be announced and that the buyer would then back off or start suggesting adjustments (with apologies, of course, and with an explanation that banks, lawyers, boards of directors, etc. were to be blamed). And finally, you would know exactly with whom you are dealing. You would not have one executive negotiate the deal only to have someone else in charge a few years later, or have the president regretfully tell you that his board of directors required this change or that (or possibly required sale of your business to finance some new interest of the parent's).

It's only fair to tell you that you would be no richer after the sale than now. The ownership of your business already makes you wealthy and soundly invested. A sale would change the form of your wealth, but it wouldn't change its amount. If you sell, you will have exchanged a 100%-owned valuable asset that you understand for another valuable asset—cash—that will probably be invested in small pieces (stocks) of other businesses that you understand less well. There is often a sound reason to sell but, if the transaction is a fair one, the reason is not so that the seller can become wealthier.

I will not pester you; if you have any possible interest in selling, I would appreciate your call. I would be extraordinarily proud to have Berkshire, along with the key members of your family, own _____; I believe we would do very well financially; and I believe you would have just as much fun running the business over the next 20 years as you have had during the past 20.

Sincerely,

/s/ Warren E. Buffett

## BUFFETT CEO PHILOSOPHY

Perhaps the best definition of Warren Buffett's CEO philosophy was written by Buffett himself in his 1998 "Chairman's Letter to Shareholders." No micro management from headquarters. No one looking over your shoulder. Complete loyalty. Ample recognition. Buffett learned, early on, to manage his CEOs from his marketable security purchases. He manages the CEO of the *Washington Post,* Don Graham, just like he manages the CEO of GEICO, Tony Nicely.

"At Berkshire we feel that telling outstanding CEOs, such as Tony [Nicely, GEICO'S CEO], how to run their companies would be the height of foolishness. Most of our managers wouldn't work for us if they got a lot of backseat driving. (Generally, they don't have to work for *anyone,* since 75% or so are independently wealthy.) Besides, they are the Mark

McGwires of the business world and need no advice from us as to how to hold the bat or when to swing.

"Nevertheless, Berkshire's ownership may make even the best of managers more effective. First, we eliminate all of the ritualistic and nonproductive activities that normally go with the job of CEO. Our managers are totally in charge of their personal schedules. Second, we give each a simple mission: Just run your business as if: (1) you own 100% of it; (2) it is the only asset in the world that you and your family have or will ever have; and (3) you can't sell or merge it for at least a century. As a corollary, we tell them they should not let any of their decisions be affected even slightly by accounting considerations. We want our managers to think about what counts, not how it will be counted.

"Very few CEOs of public companies operate under a similar mandate, mainly because they have owners who focus on short-term prospects and reported earnings. Berkshire, however, has a shareholder base—which it will have for decades to come—that has the longest investment horizon to be found in the public-company universe. Indeed, a majority of our shares are held by investors who expect to die still holding them. We can therefore ask our CEOs to manage for maximum long-term value, rather than for next quarter's earnings. We certainly don't ignore the current results of our businesses—in most cases, they are of great importance—but we *never* want them to be achieved at the expense of our building ever-greater competitive strengths.

"I believe the GEICO story demonstrates the benefits of Berkshire's approach. Charlie and I haven't taught Tony a thing—and never will—but we *have* created an environment that allows him to apply all of his talents to what's important. He does not have to devote his time or energy to board meetings, press interviews, presentations by investment bankers or talks with financial analysts. Furthermore, he need never spend a moment thinking about financing, credit ratings or 'Street' expectations for earnings per share. Because of our ownership structure, he also knows that this operational framework will endure for decades to come. In this environment of freedom, both Tony and his company can convert their almost limitless potential into matching achievements."[9]

★ *Part Two* ★

# Berkshire's Capital Source—The Insurers

# chapter three

# The Administrator—
# Tony Nicely, GEICO Insurance

*B*efore I flew to GEICO headquarters, its CEO, Tony Nicely, al-though he had already agreed to and scheduled the interview, called to lower my expectations. He said the real story is all the men and women who work for GEICO; besides, he didn't think he would be a very good interviewee and wasn't about to give his competitors any locker-room quotes or any competitive secrets. I assured him that, as a shareholder, I didn't want to reveal or give away anything that would be a competitive advantage.

On the phone, and also in person, I got an immediate impression that this chief executive is without ego, thinks he has the best CEO job in the world, and is passionate about his company. He wanted the interview to focus on his company, the associates, the customer, and Berkshire. Later, when I requested a photo, rather than send the typical individual photo, this CEO sent a group shot of 22 GEICO managers. He was the only Buffett CEO who tried to talk me out of an interview and was clearly uncomfortable drawing attention to himself. He is happier helping share-holders and other interested parties to better understand GEICO and how it fit into the parent company. Nicely lowered my expectations, so let me lower your expectations about this chapter. As much as I wanted this to be about the CEO of GEICO, I was at the mercy of what he was willing to talk about. Therefore, this chapter is more about the business than about the manager.

As I approached GEICO headquarters, I was surprised to see the company sign, on top of its campus of office buildings, illuminated in yel-low letters instead of blue letters on a white background, the color combi-nation in its frequent advertising messages. It's difficult to miss an ad by GEICO, which is the number-one advertiser on cable television. Later, *for the same reason, I was surprised to see red mailing labels on GEICO correspondence from the corporate headquarters.*

*Within the office complex, one street is called Leo Goodwin Drive and another is Lillian Goodwin Drive, named appropriately after GEICO's founders. Signs indicating "Associates" parking areas tell all who visit headquarters how to address GEICO employees. Inside the main administration building, I noted office furniture and décor from the 1960s: metal desks, old reception counters where payments on auto insurance were made in person, and a security guard who buzzes visitors in after proper registration and clearance. Like the culture at many of the Berkshire subsidiaries, an old-style administration building says silently that the cost savings are passed on to customers in lower premiums and to shareholders in greater value. The offices must have looked the same when Warren Buffett arrived by train in 1951, when he was a student of Benjamin Graham at Columbia University School of Business.*

*At the seventh-floor administrative offices, I was greeted by Linda Stine-Ward, Tony Nicely's assistant, and ushered into a conference room adjacent to his corner office. Tony greeted me with southern graciousness. As the interview started, the tape recorder failed, which is the worst thing that can happen to any interviewer. Prepared with backup batteries and extra cassette tapes, I rifled through my briefcase and attempted to fix the motionless recorder, but the new batteries didn't work. Tony could not have been more understanding. He simply pointed out a nearby drug store that was visible from his window, and said he had plenty of work to do while I chased down a recorder that worked.*

*I sped through suburban Washington, bought a replacement, found Tony waiting patiently, and decided his name was appropriate—he's "nicely" to everyone. It also seemed appropriate that the nearby subway station stop was Friendship Heights.*

*Tony Nicely is about GEICO and is totally dedicated and loyal to his company. He can't understand all the job-hopping that today's employees seem to do. He knows one wife, one family, one company, one job, and when you talk with him, it is obvious he loves them all. If you were to define the ultimate and perfect CEO, Tony Nicely would fit the description.*

*GEICO has more than 18,000 employees, so Tony manages more people than any other Buffett CEO profiled here. One out of every five Berkshire employees is under Tony's leadership, but the percentage goes down*

*each time Berkshire makes a new acquisition. In fact, a recently acquired*
*CEO, Bob Shaw of Shaw Industries, now manages the most employees.*
*The most interesting discovery I made is that GEICO is already set up as*
*an example of how Berkshire's parent will operate after Warren "retires."*
*One CEO manages operations; the other chief executive, Lou Simpson,*
*manages investments.*

*As I asked each question, Tony reflected before answering. He looked*
*out over Washington, perhaps recalling that GEICO was originally char-*
*tered to insure the government workers. With the tape recorder setback,*
*the interview ran long into a lunchtime meeting. Tony gave me some*
*extra time in the afternoon, stayed late after all his associates had left,*
*and permitted me to call him later, in between other Buffett CEO inter-*
*views, to finish over the phone. Tony is appropriately named.*

Tony Nicely's portrait does not hang in the lobby of GEICO's corporate
headquarters in Chevy Chase, Maryland, a suburb of Washington, as do
those of former CEOs of the insurance giant. The label on the portrait of
William B. Snyder—Nicely's immediate predecessor—has a date indicating when he became CEO but has none to indicate, or even suggest, that
he no longer holds the position, even though Nicely was appointed to the
office in 1993. "That goes back to my dad," Nicely says. "I never knew
him to brag on anything. He believed that your deeds should speak volumes, and that nothing else should need to be said. So I doubt my picture
will ever go up on the wall. If it does, it would be after I'm gone."

Although he describes himself as "pretty boring—an ordinary person of
ordinary intelligence; a family man and a company man," his deeds as CEO
of operations *have* spoken volumes and it's extremely likely that Nicely's
portrait will eventually go on display at GEICO's headquarters. In fact, as
the quintessential company man, his portrait might have wound up in
GEICO's lobby even if he hadn't become CEO. He started working for the
company in 1961, as an 18-year-old clerk in the underwriting department
of GEICO's largest subsidiary, Government Employees Insurance Company. Nicely has been with the company for his entire working life.

Born at home, on a farm in rural Alleghany County, Virginia, in 1943,
Olza Minor Nicely was named after his paternal grandmother. His name
reflects his Austrian (Olza) and Swiss (Nusly) heritage. With traces of a
Southern accent, Tony, as he is called, said he initially intended to be an

engineer. "When I was in high school," he remembered, "I thought I wanted to be a civil engineer, and I spent my first year at Georgia College pursuing that. I grew up in the country and thought I wanted to work outdoors and build bridges and buildings." But in his second year he decided to switch to business, and to night school, and received a bachelor's degree in business administration in 1986.

Nicely started at GEICO over four decades ago—on August 17, 1961—and worked in every department of the company. Doing a little bit of everything, he rose through the ranks to become assistant vice president in 1973, vice president in 1980, senior vice president in 1985, and executive vice president in 1987. He was elected president of the company in 1989, and CEO two years later.

When Bill Snyder, CEO of the parent company, retired in 1993, Nicely was named co-CEO with Louis A. Simpson, who had been handling investments for GEICO since 1980. Simpson, based in Rancho Santa Fe, California, was to be president of capital operations, with responsibilities covering all investments and capital allocation functions. Nicely, who would remain at the company's headquarters in Washington, became president of insurance operations, with responsibility for all of GEICO's property and casualty insurance businesses.

Having been with GEICO and weathered its ups and downs for so long, Nicely has a healthy respect for the company's history. GEICO was founded in 1936 in Fort Worth, Texas, by accountant Leo Goodwin and his wife, to sell insurance to statistically proven lower-risk military personnel and federal government employees (hence the name Government Employees Insurance COmpany). The following year, it moved to Washington to be closer to its customers. In 1948, it became a public company, and, in 1952, began selling insurance to state, county, and municipal government workers. Six years later, it began selling to nongovernment workers as well. By 1966, premiums had reached $150 million.

But by the mid-1970s, as a result of insuring more risky drivers than it had in the past, opening new facilities, and taking on thousands of additional staff members, the company was in trouble. Its underwriting losses went up dramatically, operating expenses increased, claims from policyholders mounted, and customer service plummeted. Combined with double-digit inflation, higher accident rates, the removal of federal price controls, no-fault insurance, and increased competition, these factors brought the company to the brink of bankruptcy.[1]

Nicely, who was an assistant vice president at the time, has another explanation for what brought the company to that pass. "Bottom line," he says, "you'd have to say management. The economy wasn't good, but other companies went through it and survived. GEICO had grown very rapidly, and it hadn't made the changes it had to make in the way it was managed." In 1976, the company lost $126 million, was out of capital, and was virtually bankrupt. That same year, the chairman and vice chairman were fired, and John J. Byrne became CEO.

Nicely credits Byrne with saving the company. "Jack Byrne left two wonderful legacies for GEICO," he says. "The first was that he was able to save GEICO from complete destruction. There are few people, if any, who could have done it at the time. Jack was charismatic, convincing, and everything else he had to be. He also understood the business well, and was tenacious enough to accomplish things that perhaps no one else would have been able to. But, the other legacy," Nicely adds, "was that he installed a whole new management process at GEICO, much of which still exists today." Despite the changes and refinements that have taken place over the past 25 years, Nicely says, "the underlying part of that process is still at GEICO. And those of us who were survivors learned a tremendous amount from Jack—about the insurance business, about management, and about a lot of other things."

Early in 1977, Byrne took all the senior officers and department heads on a retreat and asked them to write a business plan. Over the three-day weekend, he challenged them to explain how they had let the business get into the shape it was in. The new CEO learned that one group handled pricing, reserves were decided by a different group, and another group decided claims. Byrne heard, one too many times: "I don't know and it's not my job." Not a great way to run a business and not a terrible surprise that GEICO was in financial trouble.

Nicely today, as CEO, learned an important management lesson from that weekend, even though, as a junior manager, he had not been asked to attend. "The business planning process, although changed, still exists. It's held us in good stead and it is a wonderful way to develop people."

However, there was also help from another quarter, in the person of Warren Buffett. By 1976, Buffett had been interested in GEICO for a quarter of a century, having first become a shareholder in the company in 1951, when he discovered that Ben Graham, under whom he was studying at Columbia University's business school, was both a shareholder and GEICO's chairman. Although, at the time, as he told shareholders in his 1995 "Chairman's Letter to Shareholders," GEICO was "to me an unknown company in an unfamiliar industry . . . on a Saturday in January 1951, I took the train to Washington and headed for GEICO's downtown headquarters. To my dismay, the building was closed, but I pounded on the door until a custodian appeared. I asked this puzzled fellow if there was anyone in the office I could talk to, and he said he'd seen one man working on the sixth floor.

"And thus," Buffett continued, "I met Lorimer Davidson, Assistant to the President, who was later to become CEO. Though my only credentials were that I was a student of Graham's, 'Davy' graciously spent four hours or so showering me with both kindness and instruction. No one has ever received a better half-day course in how the insurance industry functions nor in the factors that enable one company to excel over others. As Davy made clear, GEICO's method of selling—direct marketing—gave it an enormous cost advantage over competitors that sold through agents, a form of distribution so ingrained in the business of these insurers that it was impossible for them to give it up. After my session with Davy, I was more excited about GEICO than I have ever been about a stock." Over the next several months, he bought 350 shares of the company's stock, at a cost of $10,282. By the end of the year, it was worth $13,125, or more than 65 percent of his net worth.[2]

Although Buffett sold all his GEICO stock the following year, he was still following the company's fortunes 25 years later when Jack Byrne became CEO in 1976. And, despite the company's precarious position at the time, as he later told Berkshire's stockholders, "Because I believed both in Jack and in GEICO's fundamental competitive strength, Berkshire purchased a large interest in the company during the second half of 1976, and also made smaller purchases later."[3] In fact, by the end of 1980, Berkshire, in a classic value investment move, had put $45.7 million into GEICO and owned 33.3 percent of its shares, and had done so largely on the strength of the company's competitive advantage. Because of management's decision to buy back its own shares, Berkshire's one-third ownership grew to just over half, without making any additional purchases. In 1996, when Berkshire purchased the 49 percent of GEICO it didn't already own, the 51 percent it did own was implicitly valued at $2.4 billion, representing a 20-year annual return of nearly 22 percent.

"GEICO was designed," Buffett told shareholders in 1980, "to be the low-cost operation in an enormous marketplace . . . populated largely by companies whose marketing structures restricted adaptation. Run as designed, it could offer unusual value to its customers while earning unusual returns for itself. For decades it had been run in just this manner. Its troubles in the mid-70s were not produced by any diminution or disappearance of this essential economic advantage." That advantage, he said, was "still intact within the company, although submerged in a sea of financial and operating troubles."[4]

Thus, the combination of Byrne's managerial ability, GEICO's competitive strength, and Buffett's money and long-term investment horizon saved the company. But, according to Nicely, the company's survival came at a cost. "That period from 1975 to 1976," he remembers, "changed my life, at least as far as business is concerned. I started out as a young man, and in two to three years I became an old man. I had no middle age. Because of all the hours I had to put in, for a couple of years I was neither a father nor a husband. But it wasn't the long hours or the lack of time off that changed me. It wasn't even the stress of not knowing, after 15 years with the company, whether or not it would still be there at the end of the day. What made me an old man was all the times that I had to look people in the eye—people I knew well, some of whom had been with the company 20, 25, or 30 years—and say, 'I am sorry. I know you to be loyal and hardworking, but through no fault of your own, as of Monday you no longer have a job.' I don't want to ever have to do that again."

Having gotten back on its feet, through the 1980s the company had sensational investment returns and excellent underwriting results. In 1985, Jack Byrne retired. Investment and underwriting results continued, but the number of customers wasn't growing. By the early 1990s, GEICO was facing new financial difficulties. In 1992, the devastating effects of Hurricane Andrew cost GEICO more than $81 million. The company, with a majority of its customers living within 50 miles of a coastline, had to increase its rates and limit its new policies. In addition, expansion into noncore areas such as reinsurance and aviation insurance during Jack Byrne's tenure, and the purchase by Bill Snyder, Byrne's successor, of a variety of insurance subsidiaries, resulted in a blurring of the company's focus and less-than-outstanding financial results.

Warren Buffett, now the owner of more than half of the company, was not pleased. GEICO was not growing its customer base, and Buffett felt a change in management would be appropriate. It's not Buffett's custom to get involved in the day-to-day operations of Berkshire Hathaway's common stock investments, but he did get involved. Snyder decided to retire early and, in May 1993, Tony Nicely and Lou Simpson became co-CEOs of the company.

What Nicely did next was significant and provides an excellent management lesson. He understood that GEICO's durable competitive advantage—its moat—is its low-cost automotive insurance and superior customer service. The chief executive's job is to preserve and extend the existing moat, not expand into other areas. Soon after taking control, Nicely sold GEICO's nondirect marketers back to its former CEO Snyder, as well as its aviation insurance business. Nicely eventually sold the homeowners' insurance businesses as well. Next, Nicely focused on what he calls GEICO's "core competency" and made efforts to expand its automobile insurance business and grow its customer base by major increases in advertising. A little over a year later, in August 1994, Buffett told Board members Samuel Butler and Simpson that he would be interested in buying the half of the company he didn't already own.[5]

But before taking any further steps, Buffett contacted Tony Nicely. "We weren't looking to sell GEICO," he says. "Warren called me and said, 'I would like to buy the rest of the company, but only if you think it is a good idea.' There were two questions I had to take into consideration. First: Would GEICO shareholders get a fair price for the company? And second: In terms of serving the customer, would GEICO be better off continuing as a shareholder-owned company or as a Berkshire-owned company? I'd already thought about the second one, and I gave Warren a fairly quick answer—that GEICO would be better off as a Berkshire-owned company, for a lot of reasons. So then it was mainly a matter of making absolutely certain that we are doing right by the GEICO shareholders."

GEICO's senior executives were interested in making a deal, but that matter of GEICO's shareholders came to be the sticking point in the negotiations. Buffett had first suggested that Berkshire Hathaway acquire GEICO in a tax-free transaction in which the insurance company's shareholders would simply trade their shares for Berkshire common stock.

But Simpson and Butler were concerned about this proposal, both because Berkshire stock—unlike GEICO's—paid no dividends, and because they were not sure that the stock trade could be accomplished fairly. Numerous discussions followed, as did a variety of offers and counteroffers. A year later, GEICO's officers gave Buffett the choice of buying the company in a $70-per-share cash transaction, or a convertible preferred stock deal that was worth $70 in the market. Flush with cash from the sale of Berkshire's Capital Cities/ABC stock to the Walt Disney Company, which provided Buffett with a profit of about $2 billion, the head of Berkshire Hathaway agreed to the cash deal—for a total price of $2.3 billion. Although negotiations over the price had taken a year, it took only a week for the directors of both companies to approve the sale and sign an agreement. On August 25, 1995, Warren Buffett, who had first bought GEICO stock 44 years before, became the owner of the entire company.[6]

Why would Buffett want to buy the company after so many years? One reason, no doubt, was the "float." Insurance companies collect premiums today, but they only pay out claims as they're made in the future. In the meantime, they have the use of the money, or "float." GEICO would provide Buffett with $3 billion worth of "float"—money that he would be able to put to good use.[7] And indeed, GEICO's float has grown by over $1 billion since Buffett acquired the company. Another possible explanation, offered to the *Washington Post* by an anonymous analyst, was that Buffett and GEICO were "almost identical in the way in which they view the world." According to the analyst, "If you could incorporate Warren Buffett, he would be GEICO—unglamorous, unfashionable, and a gold mine." All Buffett had to say was, "It's been a long romance."[8] And when asked why it had taken so long for him to acquire all of GEICO, he responded, no doubt with a smile, "It takes money, you know."[9]

Tony Nicely was very pleased with the arrangement. "I really believe," he said at the time, "we probably are in a better position now for faster growth than perhaps we've ever been. In the insurance business," he explained, "you tend to lose money in the first year on [new] business. You have higher losses and higher expenses," which can alarm stockholders. But with Berkshire taking over, he said, "We won't have shareholders who are concerned with year-to-year [results]. We have a long-term investor who says, 'You folks . . . grow it to the best of your physical ability and I'll worry about the finances.'"[10] Now, having been part of the Berkshire

Hathaway family for five years, he still believes that he and the other GEICO executives made the right decision. "It obviously worked out well," he says. "And I feel good about the way it was done. I think both GEICO and Berkshire shareholders got a fair deal. And I think GEICO, and therefore GEICO's customers, are much better off."

At the time of the sale, the company was the seventh largest auto insurer in the country. It had 2.5 million policyholders ensuring 3.7 million cars; more than 8,000 employees; and regional offices in Georgia, New York, Virginia, California, and Texas. In 1994, it earned $207.8 million on $2.64 billion in revenues. At the time, Nicely says, "Warren told us that in 10 years, he wouldn't be surprised if GEICO had a 10 percent market share." As of this writing, the company is certainly moving in the right direction. Under Nicely's management, by 1999, GEICO had become the nation's sixth largest auto insurance company, with more than 4 million policyholders ensuring 6.3 million autos. Today, it has more than 18,000 employees around the country, as well as new service centers in Coralville, Iowa; Honolulu, Hawaii; Lakeland, Florida; and Virginia Beach, Virginia.

GEICO's advertising budget has grown seven times since Berkshire's purchase, and Buffett has said he would be willing to spend as much as $1 billion per year on ads. As a result, in 1995, 2.3 million auto policies were in force. At the end of 2000, the number had more than doubled to 4.7 million.

Even more significant, in the first five years after Buffett set his market share target, GEICO's insurance premiums earned has grown to $5.6 billion annually, and its market share rose from 2.7 percent to 4.5 percent of the $125 billion domestic personal auto insurance market.

In the past four years, GEICO has been the most profitable, with the least amount of float, of all the major insurance subsidiaries of Berkshire. Here is a simple and conservative method for calculating the profits of GEICO and comparing them to its sister insurance companies: Multiply the float by the risk-free rate to acquire money, and deduct the cost (or profit) to deliver that float. Accumulated net profits (before taxes) of nearly $1.2 billion in four years are very conservatively stated because Lou Simpson has been able to meet and exceed the S&P index rate of 18 percent over the same time period. A more realistic accumulated net profit before taxes is twice that shown and means that Berkshire paid for its GEICO purchase in four years.

# GEICO'S FOUR-YEAR PROFIT CALCULATION

| Year | Float | Risk-Free Rate of 6 Percent | Operating Profit (Loss) | Net Profit Before Tax |
|------|-------|------------------------------|--------------------------|------------------------|
| 1997 | $2,917,000,000 | $175,000,000 | $281,000,000 | $  456,000,000 |
| 1998 | 3,125,000,000 | 188,000,000 | 269,000,000 | 457,000,000 |
| 1999 | 3,444,000,000 | 207,000,000 | 24,000,000 | 231,000,000 |
| 2000 | 3,943,000,000 | 237,000,000 | (224,000,000) | 13,000,000 |
| Total | | | | $1,157,000,000 |

# BERKSHIRE REINSURANCE'S
# FOUR-YEAR PROFIT CALCULATION

| Year | Float | Risk-Free Rate of 6 Percent | Operating Profit (Loss) | Net Profit Before Tax |
|------|-------|------------------------------|--------------------------|------------------------|
| 1997 | $4,014,000,000 | $241,000,000 | $128,000,000 | $  369,000,000 |
| 1998 | 4,305,000,000 | 258,000,000 | (21,000,000) | 237,000,000 |
| 1999 | 6,285,000,000 | 377,000,000 | (256,000,000) | 121,000,000 |
| 2000 | 7,805,000,000 | 468,000,000 | (175,000,000) | 293,000,000 |
| Total | | | | $1,020,000,000 |

# GENERAL RE'S TWO-YEAR PROFIT
# (LOSS) CALCULATION

| Year | Float | Risk-Free Rate of 6 Percent | Operating Profit (Loss) | Net Profit (Loss) Before Tax |
|------|-------|------------------------------|--------------------------|-------------------------------|
| 1999 | $15,166,000,000 | $910,000,000 | $(1,184,000,000) | $(274,000,000) |
| 2000 | 15,525,000,000 | 932,000,000 | (1,124,000,000) | (192,000,000) |
| Total | | | | $(466,000,000) |

As the previous tabulations demonstrate, it's not the total amount of float available, it's the cost to deliver the float to Berkshire for investment. If your delivery costs are higher than the risk-free rate, you are in an unprofitable insurance business. Costs of doing business can be attributed to a lot of things. They include inadequate pricing, too many claims, writing low-quality business, too much capital chasing too few quality customers, or, in GEICO's case, the largest competitor willing to engage in short-term unprofitable business in order to keep its dominant market share. GEICO has been fortunate to have a business model that makes it a low-cost provider in an environment that rewards direct auto insurance marketers.

There have been other rewards as well, Nicely says. One of the most significant is the way he thinks of the company. Although he had owned GEICO stock prior to the sale, he says, "I no longer own a single share of GEICO. There is only one owner of GEICO—Berkshire Hathaway. But I feel as much like an owner now as I ever did in the past. GEICO is my company, and, next to my family, it's the most important thing in my life. My hope is that, over the years, every associate will grow to feel that way, too." Interestingly, when asked about what other changes have taken place since Buffett bought the company, Nicely says (as do most of the other Buffett CEOs), "A lot of things changed in terms of what I *don't* have to do," like meeting with analysts or finding ways to smooth earnings. Being free of such external concerns has enabled him to concentrate on the internal things that he feels are important for the company's long-term success.

Increasing brand awareness and improving market share are among them, although he says they are not ultimately the most important. "We've been able to increase our brand awareness markedly, and gained fairly significant market share. But that's not important unless you've done it well, which I think we have. You also have to make sure that you position yourself to continue the growth by providing an infrastructure for everything— people, equipment, and programs. But ultimately," he says, "the real satisfaction—what's really important—comes from doing right by the customer. It comes from saving people money and giving them excellent service. That's what keeps us going. That's what our real accomplishment is."

He also believes, though, that GEICO—and other companies that sell insurance by direct marketing—provides a benefit even for consumers who insure with other companies. "The insurance industry was truly a cartel," he explains, "and it can't be anymore. Now, it's probably as competitive as any industry. So no matter what kind of insurance you're selling, no matter what distribution system you have, in the long term, if you're not the most efficient, you're probably losing market share. The direct distribution system has not only saved consumers, and continues to save consumers, a lot of money directly, but it definitely causes all of the other providers to be better than they would be." In fact, he says, several of GEICO's competitors are beginning to move toward direct marketing of their insurance policies. He believes, though, that it will be hard for them to match his company's competitive advantages.

The company's most immediately recognizable advantage is its low operational costs. "There's nothing esoteric about GEICO's success," Warren Buffett told his shareholders shortly after the merger with Berkshire. "The company's competitive strength flows directly from its position as a low-cost operator. Low costs permit low prices, and low prices attract and retain good policyholders. The final segment of a virtuous circle is drawn when policyholders recommend us to their friends. GEICO gets more than one million referrals annually and these produce more than half of our new business, an advantage that gives us enormous savings in acquisition [of customers] expenses—and that makes our costs still lower."[11]

Nicely believes that the company also has other competitive advantages. "Unfortunately," he admits, "we don't have a Coke formula locked away in a vault. I wish we had that type of competitive advantage. What we do have is the 65-year know-how of dealing directly with customers, and the ability to continue to make the changes necessary to be a leader in our field." This has been proven with GEICO's quick adoption of the Internet to capture new business and maintain existing customers. In addition, Nicely believes that Buffett himself provides another advantage. "The greatest thing," about becoming part of Berkshire Hathaway, he says, "is being able to talk with Warren even more frequently. We have, in Warren, an owner, a manager, who takes the same outlook on insurance as he does on all of his other investments. And that is: 'Where are we going to be, and where is the world going to be, 30 years from now?' Not 'Where is it going to be tomorrow?' So he not only encourages us to take a long-term perspective on the business, but also gives us the freedom to act on the basis of that perspective. That has enabled us to create, renew, and expand our management team to make sure that the company will be strong not only next year but 30 years from now."

In fact, Nicely can become quite expansive on the subject of Warren Buffett. "When people ask me," he says, "what it's like to work for Warren, I give a pretty simple answer. No one has a better boss than I do. I don't care who they are or what business they're in. He's the best boss in the world. Period. He's absolutely the best person that you can report to in terms of support, in terms of wisdom, and in terms of encouragement. So, I'm a mighty lucky person." Nicely says with a slight southern accent, "I sincerely want to make him proud. I would run GEICO the same way if Warren wasn't there, but it's nice having Warren as the CEO, and I do want to make him proud."

Buffett has equally positive things to say about Tony Nicely. In his 1995 "Chairman's Letter to Shareholders," he referred to Nicely as "an extraordinary manager" and said, "There's no one I would rather have managing GEICO's insurance operation. He has brains, integrity, and focus."[12] The following year, he told Berkshire shareholders that Nicely was a "Superb business manager and a delight to work with. Under almost any conditions," he added, "GEICO would be an exceptionally valuable asset. With Tony at the helm, it is reaching levels of performance that the organization would only a few years ago have thought impossible."[13] And in 1998 he wrote: "Combine a great idea with a great manager . . . you're certain to obtain a great result. That mix is alive and well at GEICO. The idea is low-cost auto insurance . . . and the manager is Tony Nicely. Quite simply, there is no one in the business world who could run GEICO better than Tony does. His instincts are unerring, his energy is boundless, and his execution is flawless."[14] His year 2000 letter stated: "Tony . . . remains an owner's dream. Everything he does makes sense. He never engages in wishful thinking or otherwise distorts reality, as so many managers do when the unexpected happens."[15]

Although Nicely acknowledges that Buffett is one of *his* heroes, he says that the people who have had the greatest influence on his life have been his father and grandfather. "If I could ever be half the man my father, or his father, was, I would be quite a successful human being. There are no two people I've admired more." Conversely, when asked whose admiration he values most, he says, "My wife, and my children." He does not, however, expect to bring his children into the business. "We have a nepotism policy for officers at GEICO," he explains. "We hold ourselves to a high standard. We don't only want to *be* the fairest organization that we could possibly be; we also want to be *perceived* as the fairest organization possible. I think that's an even higher standard."

In a similar vein, when asked what ingredients he thinks make a successful operating manager, he says, "I think, certainly, honesty and integrity have to be at the top of the list. But it not only has to be there, there has to be a perception that it's there." He also believes that "the ability to communicate well, and . . . to work with people for a common cause are extremely important to success." Ultimately, though, he doesn't really believe in giving advice to others. The only advice he proffers to someone starting out in business is to "observe others, and then create your own persona. Don't try to follow someone's formula for success," he warns. "It's probably not going to work."

What aspect of his work does he get most excited about? Nicely says, "I get most excited when I'm interfacing with our associates. We are now right at more than 18,000 associates, and they are the people who make things happen at GEICO. I spend a good deal of my time with our associates and I enjoy that most." It's clear, in fact, that Nicely considers the people who work for GEICO to be its great asset. According to the *San Diego Union-Tribune,* the company has "an emphasis on opportunities for advancement, generous benefit packages, a pleasant workplace and keeping people happy until they retire." In 1999, for example, when the company built its West Coast headquarters in Poway, California, aside from the necessary office space, the building included a sand-lined volleyball court, a workout room, a cafeteria, and a store supplying staples such as milk and bread. "We want to be a company that doesn't have to worry about retention," Nicely told the newspaper.[16]

It's unlikely that Warren Buffett will ever have to worry about retaining Tony Nicely. "I have the best CEO job in America," he says. "Because, in my opinion, we have the best company—a company with a great product, a 65-year history, and a great tradition of serving the customers and giving them great value. And we have a product that is going to be needed for many, many, many, many decades to come. It's something that affects the lives of virtually every household in America, and it doesn't cause cancer or pollute our environment. The thing that I am most proud of," he says, "is what GEICO has achieved, and the fact that I have been a little part of that. It's not material possessions, or wealth, or those types of things that give you satisfaction. It's being part of creating something that is truly worthwhile."

Given such sentiments, it's not surprising that Nicely has no intention of retiring. "I think that most people who work for Berkshire do it because they love their work, not because of anything else," he says. "I would certainly put myself in that category. I try to not even think of when I may retire, although I know that a day may come when I start saying that I want to do something else. My wife Sally has been extremely supportive for 39 years, and I would like to be able to give her a little more time some day. But that day will probably come some time in the future."

Not surprisingly, when asked about hobbies and special interests, Nicely says, "My number-one hobby is GEICO. For recreation, I like to hunt, fish, and play golf, but I don't do either of those very much. Every round of golf I play probably costs me several thousand dollars because I do it so infrequently. My membership and other costs are not a very good investment on my part." Nor is he particularly interested in traveling from their home in Great Falls, Virginia. "In years past, my wife and I have made two trips with a church group—one to tour the British Isles and the other to tour Greece and the Greek Isles. We enjoyed both of those immensely, but I don't do a lot of recreational traveling."

Although he says that he is "intense while I'm working," he adds: "I've changed my work habits over the last 10 years or so, to try to do more of my work at home where I can at least be in the presence of my wife. I enjoy the company of my wife, so even though we may be in the same room and not communicating, her presence is valuable to me, and, hopefully, mine is to her. Our computer is in the library, which is next to the family room, so even if I'm working on the computer we can still carry on a conversation." It may be that he believes working at home will enable him to avoid having, in the future, regrets that are like some he has about the past. "I worked so much, both in school and at work, when my children were small, that I missed out on a lot of their early youth. Both of my children"—he has a son and a daughter—"are what they are because their mother did such a wonderful job of raising them. I have two of the most well rounded children in the world. They're both grown, married now, and I'm a grandfather. But I still regret that I wasn't as involved in raising them as I would have liked to have been."

As far as the future is concerned, Nicely describes his outlook as "very positive for the world in general. I think the best is yet to be," he says, "for this company and for our country. The last century was certainly the century with the most progress, but I think those fortunate enough to look back over the twenty-first century will say that this was the best century." In the meantime, he is taking steps to make sure that his company's future is a rosy one. "My strategy for the future," he says, "is simply to keep growing GEICO. We have a very small market share, and while I don't focus on market share, I think the results of our efforts will be to have a higher market share in the years to come. It's a pretty simple strategy—to be the low-cost provider with the best service. I don't believe that those two things are antithetical. In fact, I don't think you can be the low-cost provider without giving the best service, and I don't think you can give the best service unless you have the lowest costs in the long run, because consumers tend to view those things somewhat synonymously."

"We're going to focus," he says, "on where we have the most opportunity, and that's to grow our automobile insurance business. There are lots of people out there—lots of analysts, lots of business critics—who say that you've got to be more things to more people if you are really going to grow. I just don't believe that. I believe that automobile insurance is so important to every household, and takes such a large portion of the disposable income, that if you can give it to the customer with great service and low prices, the customer is not necessarily going to demand that you provide other products as well."

One of the ways Nicely is trying to grow the company is through extensive advertising. GEICO was scheduled to spend approximately $300 million on advertising in 2000, but cut back when results didn't pan out. It was an unusual and difficult advertising year with higher rates, greater competition, and lower results because of the summer Olympics and the fall presidential election. He believes that name recognition is extremely important because, in the future, "there will only be two or three sustainable brands. I believe GEICO will be one of those," he adds. "But who the others will be, I don't know. Perhaps Allstate and State Farm. But my ultimate objective is for GEICO to be like Coke or McDonald's. If I say 'Soft drink,' you say 'Coke.' If I say 'hamburger,' you may say 'McDonald's.' When I say 'automobile insurance,' I want you to say 'GEICO.' We're a way from there yet, but we've taken a very large step in getting there."

He also believes that the Internet will have a substantial effect on GEICO's business. "It will continue to change our distribution of both products and services," he says. "More and more people will want to communicate through the Internet, buy a policy outright, make changes to the policy. They won't want to deal with paper at all. So unless the government screws it up by overregulation, which I don't think it will, the Internet will reduce costs for everyone who takes advantage of it. Of course, it's not a unique opportunity for GEICO, but it plays into our hands better than most, because the Internet isn't the threat to GEICO that it is to most agents."

Although Nicely clearly expects to be at the helm of GEICO for many years to come, he also knows—as an insurance executive, of all people, should—that one can never tell what the future might bring. Like any good CEO, he knows he's replaceable, and says he is "trying to prepare the organization to be better after I'm no longer around." But many Buffett watchers think there might be a new job in the future for Tony Nicely— as one of the two Berkshire Hathaway co-CEOs with whom Buffett expects to replace himself. Although Buffett has already designated Nicely's co-CEO Louis Simpson as the executive who will handle the company's investments, there is much speculation about who will take over as operations manager. But when asked who he thinks will succeed Buffett in that capacity, Nicely says, "I don't think that's an important question because it's a long way off. Warren is going to live for a long, long time."

Even so, when asked about the essential elements in a working relationship among the future co-CEOs of Berkshire, Nicely refers to his own relationship with Simpson. "The most important thing," he says, "is mutual respect. Lou and I have a wonderful relationship. Neither of us has any desire at all to interfere with the other. We have total respect for each other on both a personal and a professional basis. But I'm reluctant to give anyone else business advice about what might be best under his or her circumstances. All I can tell you is the relationship at GEICO between Lou and myself is one that works quite well."

When asked if he has a vision for Berkshire's future, Nicely defers to his boss. "I don't," he says, "because I think that has to be Warren's vision. I don't know if he has a master plan, but I do know that Berkshire is evolving the way every company has to evolve if it is going to sustain success. And that Warren will figure out the best way for it to evolve. I'm quite certain of that." He does believe, though, that over the next 10 to 20 years, the company "will evolve into many businesses," rather than strictly a property casualty insurance company. "If there are good opportunities in property casualty," he says, "they will be recognized and taken advantage of. But there may be other businesses as well. Some of those companies may not seem so obvious now because the world continues to evolve, and it may not yet be clear what the good businesses of the twenty-first century will be. The real challenge is to find the businesses that are most likely to be sustainable over the next 10, 20, or 30 years—the companies that will be worth something in the future. And there's no one better at doing that than Warren."

But Nicely doesn't think Berkshire Hathaway shareholders have to worry about the company's future, with or without Buffett. "Even after Warren," he says, "Berkshire will probably be very similar to the way it is right now. The method Warren uses is a wonderful one, and my guess is that his replacement will follow the same method, or a similar one. No doubt there will be a change in the price of a share the day that Warren passes on, but it's not going to truly change the value of Berkshire. Berkshire will continue to be a good investment."

In keeping with his positive view of the future of GEICO and Berkshire Hathaway, he is also extremely positive about the future of the system under which the companies have thrived. "The free enterprise system," he says, "is a wonderful thing. If you allow the competitive system to work, it will work, and ultimately to the benefit of the consumer. There are two reasons why we in America have the highest standard of living. The first is our form of government—democracy. And the second is because we come close—not as close as I'd like, but pretty close—to having a true free enterprise system. Sometimes it seems like special-interest groups are taking over, but they can keep things going their way only so long. Eventually, the consumer will determine what the rules are, and that's the way it should be."

## TONY NICELY'S BUSINESS TENETS

- ★ Service your customers. Know what your customers want. Help them save money, and they'll stay with you.
- ★ Be honest in all your relationships.
- ★ Learn how to communicate effectively.
- ★ Don't abandon your core businesses. Look first to expand your strongest areas before trying new ones.

# chapter four

# The Back-Up Capital Allocator—
# Lou Simpson, GEICO Insurance

*T*o celebrate the new millennium, Lou Simpson journeyed to the Patagonia region of southern South America to hike in the mountains. Mountain hiking, a solitary endeavor, befits this man who maintains a very low profile. Simpson guards his privacy, doesn't do interviews (mine was a rare exception), and seeks no fame, press, or celebrity.

Why doesn't he do interviews? I can only guess that it's because Simpson doesn't want to contribute to the investment advice given to the masses. Most recent stories discuss the stocks that he is buying and/or selling—as if these decisions will reveal some hidden secret to successful investing. Despite his disdain for the financial media and their focus on "beating the market," Simpson respects those who exhibit an investigative and journalistic mind. (Two of his assistants are former journalists.)

Unlike all the other Buffett CEOs, who send their excess capital to Omaha for allocation, retain earnings, or borrow capital for the expansion of their enterprises, Simpson allocates capital on behalf of GEICO. Therefore, he is essentially Buffett's "backup."

When Lou Simpson agreed to sit down with me for an in-depth interview, his only condition was that he would not discuss any of the holdings in GEICO's equity portfolio. He then answered some 270 questions.

His office in the mountains outside San Diego is surrounded by large estates, horse trails, and golf courses. The typical California traffic congestion is absent in this quaint village of real estate brokers, banks, investment advisers, and stock brokerage firms. There is one school, one library, one fire department, and just a couple of stop signs.

Simpson works in a small freestanding office building that offers four private offices separated by window panes, wide-open reception space, and a small conference room. The office could have come right out of Architectural

Digest. *Picture a very clean, wood-floored, modern library with custom file cabinets full of annual reports and documents, and wooden magazine racks offering every available business and investment publication.*

*After a friendly greeting and an introduction to Tom Bancroft (Lou's 30-something associate), we went to the conference room. Simpson looked like the classic college professor; Bancroft looked like the prize student. I was reminded of the relationship Ben Graham might have had with Buffett years before. As the interview progressed, it became evident that Lou valued and respected Tom and treated him accordingly.*

*After the interview, Lou left us, and Tom answered a few questions solo. I commented on the great work environment they enjoyed. Tom admitted, "It's a great place to think."*

*As I was leaving, I looked back at the small but stunning building. Through the pane glass windows, I could see Lou in his office, speaking intently on the phone.*

*My hotel was across from Lou's office, so when I returned there at about 7:30 P.M., I couldn't help noticing that he was still at work in his office. The next morning, as I was leaving to catch an early-morning flight home, he was already in his office.*

*Lou Simpson is in a unique class of "superior investors." The average investor enters the investment world believing that he or she can be a superinvestor like Lou Simpson or can mimic his stock picks and get the same results. However, to mimic Lou, you would have to spend most of your life reading just about everything written in the financial press. Even if your intelligence level matches his, you probably wouldn't have the ability to do what he does instinctively.*

*I am reminded of the opening pages of Ben Graham's the* Intelligent Investor *where he asks the reader to make a decision: You can be an active investor and compete with Lou and Warren by allocating your own capital. Or, you can be a passive investor and let a computer and an index fund, or a superinvestor, do it for you.*

After literally years of speculation on the part of Berkshire Hathaway shareholders, not to mention the business community at large, to everyone's surprise, Warren Buffett let slip a suggestion of who might replace him in his "Chairman's Letter to Shareholders," in 1995. He was discussing the company's recent purchase of GEICO Insurance, and in the course of praising the performance of Louis A. Simpson, GEICO's head of investments and CEO of capital operations, Buffett wrote, "One point that goes beyond Lou's GEICO work: His presence on the scene assures us that Berkshire would have an extraordinary professional immediately available to handle its investments if something were to happen to Charlie [Munger] and me."[1]

At the time, Lou Simpson was not well known, but Buffett had already known him for quite a while. Having been a large shareholder of GEICO for many years prior to the purchase, Buffett was well aware of Lou Simpson's accomplishments. Simpson had joined the company in 1979, and had soon become a member, along with Ben Graham and Charlie Munger, of the so-called Buffett Group, a kind of "inner circle" of superinvestors who met with Buffett every other year to discuss investing. Now Buffett was allowing that, following a model already in place at GEICO, after he was gone he expected his responsibilities to be split between two executives: an operating manager to run the organization, and a capital allocator to handle the company's investments. He named one executive to manage the company, and he left little doubt that Simpson was his choice for head of investments. Five years later, perhaps as a result of his celebrating his seventieth birthday, Buffett officially announced that once he was no longer working, his son Howard would become chairman of Berkshire Hathaway, and Simpson would take over the company's investments.[2]

Of course, that assumed that Simpson would survive Buffett, who is only six years his senior, and who jokingly plans to officially retire five years after his death and communicate to Berkshire's directors via regular séances. Moreover, even though Simpson now agrees that "splitting the CEO function like they have done at GEICO into operations and capital allocation probably makes a lot of sense," he nevertheless downplays the likelihood of ever becoming Buffett's successor. "I don't see myself that way at all," he says. "I don't even think about it. I see myself as a potential backup. Warren *is* Berkshire," he asserts, "and as long as Warren is around he will be running Berkshire. He has dedicated his life to it and he's the best person to do it." Of course, taking over for Buffett would, in all likelihood, be a daunting task. Not only would Simpson be responsible for over $75 billion worth of investments, he would also have to step into the shoes of a legend. When asked why he would be willing to put himself in such a situation, Simpson simply says, "I would do it out of a sense of responsibility to the people who treated me well."

Although Simpson did not always know that he would be picking stocks for a living, it could be argued that he is ideally suited for the job. Born in the Chicago suburb of Highland Park in 1936, he graduated from high school in 1954 and enrolled at Northwestern University to study engineering. But, as he later told a reporter, "I was a misfit in engineering." After a year at Northwestern, he transferred to Ohio Wesleyan University, where, with a major in accounting and economics, he earned a bachelor's degree in 1958. Two years later, he received a master's degree in economics from Princeton and, contemplating a career in academia, remained at the university to teach. But, dissatisfied with the financial rewards of teaching, he joined the Chicago investment firm of Stein, Roe & Farnham in 1962.[3] He stayed with the firm until 1969 and then left, according to former Stein Roe colleague Richard Peterson, "in part because he thought they were too conservative and therefore missing—this is a young Lou Simpson— many great opportunities."[4]

In 1970, he joined Shareholders Management, a Los Angeles-based firm that was getting a lot of attention with its very successful Enterprise Fund. However, shortly after Simpson came on board, the climate on Wall Street changed and the fund tumbled. In addition, the Securities and Exchange Commission filed a complaint against the company for record-keeping violations. "It was a painful, searing experience for Lou," Peterson recalled. "Before then, Lou was a pure growth investor—a shoot-for-the-moon guy. I think he learned the importance of going into really good situations that are relatively low risk—that you need growth, but also low valuation."[5] Simpson stayed with the firm for only eight months. Then, in 1971, he became executive vice president of the Western Asset Management division of Western Bancorporation, and was promoted to president and CEO of the unit in 1976. Although the firm prospered under his leadership, by 1979 he had become anxious to test some of his own ideas, and realized that managing other people's money provided him with few opportunities to do so.[6]

As it happened, GEICO's chairman, John J. Byrne, Jr., was looking for a new chief investment officer, and Simpson was one of the four final candidates. In deference to Warren Buffett, who at that point owned about 30 percent of the insurance company, Byrne had agreed to have all four men go to Omaha to see Buffett. But "he called me as Lou was leaving his office," Byrne later told a *Money* reporter. "He said, 'Stop the search. That's the guy.'" Simpson's official title was senior vice president and chief investment officer. Byrne was particularly pleased that the company didn't have to pay "outlandishly" to get him to join because, he explained, "Simpson really wanted to get back to picking good stocks and being a good investor rather than managing a company."[7]

At that point, saving money and bringing in a capable stock picker were priorities for GEICO. As a result of poor management and poor invest- ment choices, the company had come close to bankruptcy in the mid- 1970s, and had racked up a $126 million loss in 1976. The economy, too, had played a role in the company's less-than-sterling performance. Like most insurance companies, GEICO's portfolio included a wide array of bonds and only a few stocks. Its managers were counting on diversifica- tion to minimize their risk. In fact, true to the typical insurance company investment model, much of the company's money was tied up in U.S. Government bonds. When Simpson took over, only 12 percent of the company's portfolio was in stocks, and the inflation of the 1970s brought sizable losses.

---

### Researching and Choosing Investments

Where does Simpson get his investment ideas? He regularly works 14-hour days. He reads every annual report and every financial publication. He also spends time talking with managers, customers, suppliers, and competitors before making a significant investment. He works with a small team that excels in filtering out the noise, asking the right questions, and examining every bottom line.

---

Given free rein by his new employers, Simpson switched from bonds to utility, energy, and industrial stocks, and also increased GEICO's holdings in food packaging and banking companies. Common stocks soon came to represent 32 percent of the company's portfolio. Although his first-year return of 23.7 percent on equities was well below the market average of 32.3 percent, in 1982, when the market's gain was 21.4 percent, GEICO's was 45.8 percent. "We gave him a broad, unfettered pasture to work in, and we allowed him to put an unusual percent of the company's assets into equities," John Byrne later said, "and Lou just knocked the cover off the ball for us."[8] In fact, Simpson continued to knock the cover off the ball. In the 17 years between his joining the company and its being sold to Berkshire Hathaway in 1996, Simpson cut the company's diversified portfolio from 33 companies to just 10, and, in the process, increased its value from $280 million to $1.1 billion. He also beat the S&P Index in 12 of those 17 years, and engineered an average return on GEICO's investments of 24.7 percent, compared with the S&P's 17.8 percent.

Holding true to one of his most defining investment principles at the time of the interview, and running contrary to most conventional investment wisdom, Simpson had $2.5 billion in equities invested in just seven stocks. By contrast, the average large-cap value mutual fund owns 86 stocks.[9] Buffett has long followed a concentrated approach that puts over 70 percent of Berkshire common stock holdings in just four stocks. Warren wrote, "Lou takes the same conservative, concentrated approach to investments that we do at Berkshire."[10]

Simpson stresses: "If we could find 15 positions that we really had confidence in, we'd be in 15 positions. We'll never be in 100 positions because we're never going to know 100 companies that well. I think the merits of a concentrated portfolio are: 'You live by the sword, you die by the sword.' If you're right, you're going to add value. If you're going to add value, you're going to have to look different than the market. That means either being concentrated, or, if you're not concentrated in a number of issues, you're concentrated in types of businesses or industries."

Although Simpson clearly has good reason to be proud of his extraordinary investment achievements by concentrating his portfolio, he's modest when speaking about it. "By managing the portfolio," he says, "I was able to add value at GEICO by creating the returns, which enabled us to buy in more of our own stock. And that created more value on a per-share basis." Keeping true to Lou's second investment principle—"Invest in high return businesses run for the shareholders"—and because of Simpson's superior equity investments, from 1979 to 1995, GEICO reduced its shares outstanding from over 34 million to fewer than 17 million. As a result, Berkshire's 33 percent ownership of GEICO, purchased for $45.7 million before 1980, grew to 51 percent by 1996 without further investment. Of course, the important words here are "managing the portfolio," something Simpson does better than just about everyone else—with the notable exception of Warren Buffett. Perhaps not surprisingly, in keeping with his low-key personality, Simpson makes it all sound very simple. He says that his investment approach, developed through "trial and error," has evolved over time.

It begins, he says, with research. Once he or Tom Bancroft, his chief assistant, has identified a possible stock purchase, a meeting with company executives is arranged. "One of the things I have learned over the years," Simpson says, "is how important management is in building or subtracting from value. We will try to see a senior person, and prefer to visit the company at their office, almost like kicking the tires. You can have all the written information in the world, but I think it is important to figure out how senior people in the company think."[11] Given his status ($2.5 billion under his control and billions more available) and the fact that Simpson can make a substantial investment on behalf of GEICO, a company's executives are, more often than not, agreeable to meeting. If they are not agreeable, he doesn't invest in the company.

This is one area where Simpson disagrees with his boss and with famed value investor Ben Graham. Instead, he follows legendary investor Phil Fisher and the qualitative approach to investing. Buffett and Graham believe in quantitative analysis: By studying the numbers, a wise investor can determine the best investment. In fact, Graham wrote that visiting management, also known as qualitative analysis, might subject an investor to management's salesmanship and charm. With a serious demeanor, straight talk, and down-to-business approach, few if any managers would have the ability to charm Simpson.

---

### Value Investing

"When you ask whether someone is a value or growth investor—they're really joined at the hip. A value investor can be a growth investor because you're buying something that has above-average growth prospects and you're buying it at a discount to the economic value of the business."—Lou Simpson

---

Lou has three qualities that are admired by Warren Buffett: intellect, character, and temperament. Buffett on Simpson, "Temperament is what causes smart people not to function well. His temperament probably isn't different than mine. We both tend to do rational things. Our emotions don't get in the way of our intellect."[12]

Even Charlie Munger, Berkshire's vice chairman, weighed in on Simpson's personality: "I would argue that good stock-picking records are held by people who are a little cranky and are willing to bet against the herd. Lou just has that mind-set and that's what impressed us."[13]

Besides concentrating his holdings in just a handful of stocks, as Buffett does, Simpson reads everything and has a very small staff. Like Warren and unlike most institutional investors, no matter the size of assets under management, compensation will be directly related to earnings, and the size of Lou's staff will stay the same. Remarkably, both men are not people-intensive but thought-intensive. They are not trading-intensive but reading-intensive.

Still, there are differences between Simpson and Buffett. They're not the same; never have been and never will be:

★ Lou, an independent thinker who has his own investment approach and principles, has a number of outside directorships and affiliations. Buffett has none.

★ Simpson chooses a whole different set of value stocks and buys pieces of companies. Buffett buys whole companies.

★ Simpson is a net buyer of stocks. In recent years, Buffett has been a net seller of publicly traded stocks.

★ Simpson is 100 percent stocks. Buffett is 30 percent stocks and 70 percent wholly owned businesses and he's aiming for a 10/90 mix.

★ Simpson's scope is focused on $500 million purchases. Buffett's appetite is for $5 billion deals.

★ Simpson works quietly alone. His boss receives over 3,000 letters annually and hosts the mother of all annual meetings each spring.

★ Simpson doesn't suffer fools gladly, seeks no celebrity or fame, and was the only manager to share his interview with an associate. Buffett, like his father, has the personality of a politician running for office and is always happy to pose for a photo and offer an autograph.

★ Simpson reads everything but doesn't write or publish. Buffett is the most widely read of all CEOs with over 300,000 annual reports distributed. Untold thousands read his writings on the Internet.

★ Simpson, like the rest of Berkshire's CEOs, makes considerably more salary and bonuses than his boss.

In managing the portfolio of stocks he does buy, Simpson says he follows five basic principles. He outlined these timeless principles in GEICO's 1986 annual report, and he explained them at greater length in an interview with the *Washington Post* the following year:

1. *Think independently.* "We try to be skeptical of conventional wisdom," he says, "and try to avoid the waves of irrational behavior and emotion that periodically engulf Wall Street. We don't ignore unpopular companies. On the contrary, such situations often present the greatest opportunities."

2. *Invest in high-return businesses that are run for the shareholders.* "Over the long run," he explains, "appreciation in share prices is most directly related to the return the company earns on its shareholders' investment. Cash flow, which is more difficult to manipulate than reported earnings, is a useful additional yardstick. We ask the following questions in evaluating management: Does management have a substantial stake in the stock of the company? Is management straightforward in dealings with the owners? Is management willing to divest unprofitable operations? Does management use excess cash to repurchase shares? The last may be the most important. Managers who run a profitable business often use excess cash to expand into less profitable endeavors. Repurchase of shares is in many cases a much more advantageous use of surplus resources."

3. *Pay only a reasonable price, even for an excellent business.* "We try to be disciplined in the price we pay for ownership even in a demonstrably superior business. Even the world's greatest business is not a good investment," he concludes, "if the price is too high. The ratio of price to earnings and its inverse, the earnings yield, are useful gauges in valuing a company, as is the ratio of price to free cash flow. A helpful comparison is the earnings yield of a company versus the return on a risk-free long-term United States Government obligation."

4. *Invest for the long term.* "Attempting to guess short-term swings in individual stocks, the stock market, or the economy," he argues, "is not likely to produce consistently good results. Short-term developments are too unpredictable. On the other hand, shares of quality companies run for the shareholders stand an excellent chance of providing above-average returns to investors over the long term. Furthermore, moving in and out of stocks frequently has two major disadvantages that will substantially diminish results: transaction costs and taxes. Capital will grow more rapidly if earnings compound with as few interruptions for commissions and tax bites as possible."

5. *Do not diversify excessively.* "An investor is not likely to obtain superior results by buying a broad cross-section of the market," he believes. "The more diversification, the more performance is likely to be average, at best. We concentrate our holdings in a few companies that meet our investment criteria. Good investment ideas—that is, companies that meet our criteria—are difficult to find. When we think we have found one, we make a large commitment. The five largest holdings at GEICO account for more than 50 percent of the stock portfolio."[14]

Warren Buffett reprinted Simpson's investment results in his company's 1986 annual report, which helps to explain why he thinks Simpson would be more than able to replace him as head of investments for Berkshire. In fact, not only are their investing approaches very similar, the results of their efforts have also been extremely close. Simpson's average 24.7 percent return between 1980 and 1996 is slightly less than Buffett's 25.6 percent over the same period, but both handily beat the S&P index of 17.8 percent. Simpson's returns have been comparable to those of famed investor Peter Lynch a decade ago, when he was managing money for Fidelity's Magellan fund.

Simpson's record is even more outstanding because his returns are based solely on equities. Buffett's annual return is calculated on changes in Berkshire's book value, which is enhanced by float and other factors, including the earnings of wholly owned businesses. On an equity selection return comparison between Simpson and Buffett, Simpson may win as the superior stock picker.

Perhaps not surprisingly, the two men share a mutual admiration that enables them to work very effectively together. In fact, even before Berkshire took over complete control of GEICO, Buffett was singing Simpson's praises. As early as 1982, Buffett called Simpson "the best investment manager in the property-casualty business."[15] And in his 1986 "Chairman's Letter to Shareholders," Buffett wrote, "Indeed, it's a little embarrassing for me, the fellow responsible for investments at Berkshire, to chronicle Lou's performance. Only my ownership of a controlling block of Berkshire stock makes me secure enough to show how successful Simpson is.[16]

A year later, Buffett told the *Washington Post:* "Lou has made me a lot of money. Under today's circumstances, he is the best I know. He has done a lot better than I have done in the last few years. He has seen opportunities I have missed. We have $700 million of our own net worth of $2.4 billion invested in GEICO's operations, and I have no say whatsoever in how Lou manages the investments. He sticks to his principles. Most people on Wall Street don't have principles to begin with. And if they have them, they don't stick to them."[17]

Simpson is positive about his boss. "He's a great guy," he says. "I doubt there will ever be another Warren. The best thing about working with him is that he is ultimately totally fair and totally rational. He gives you a lot of rope, and if you do well, he'll applaud. But he also understands if you don't do so well, and he has a long horizon."

About Buffett, Simpson has said: "I think, in terms of basic values and similarities, our investment approach is pretty similar." He also believes there are major differences—both personal and professional—between them. "Warren is a unique person who is off the charts as far as intelligence is concerned. He is focused on Berkshire, his life is his work, and he loves what he does. I love what I do too, but I probably don't have the same dedication that he has. I'm able to get away and not think about the market for a week or two. I'm not sure Warren ever does that." And, although Simpson does not point them out, there are small but significant differences in their investment philosophies. Simpson, for example, seems willing—and better able—to move more quickly than his boss, although that may be due to the relative size of their portfolios. As of this writing, GEICO owned just nine stocks: Dun & Bradstreet, First Data, Freddie Mac, GATX, Great Lakes Chemical, Jones Apparel, Nike, Shaw Communications, and U.S. Bancorp.[18] Simpson says simply, "Most investors should own no more than 10 to 20 stocks."

The stocks in GEICO's portfolio, in fact, point out another distinction between Simpson and his boss. They have both beaten the widely held market with a different lineup of stocks, further proving Buffett's theory that superinvestors all originate from the small town of Graham and Doddsville. This was Warren's way of saying that value investors like Simpson, who follow the value methods taught by Graham and Dodd, can succeed even by investing in different stocks. Using the same value principles, Simpson personally invested in Cort Furniture Rental before his boss recognized the same value and bought the whole company. Lou has invested in telephone and cable companies, which suggests that he might be more comfortable with high-technology companies than the famously tech-averse Buffett. Simpson recently accepted a seat on AT&T's board of directors.

Although the two men have known each other since Buffett interviewed Simpson for his first position at GEICO in 1979 ("We talked about the Chicago Cubs," according to Simpson), their relationship has grown somewhat closer since 1996 when Berkshire bought the 49 percent of GEICO it didn't already own. "I talk to Warren once a week, or once every 10 days," Simpson says. "But sometimes I'll talk to him two or three days in a row, and we generally always talk about stocks and companies." Another one of the changes that has taken place is in Simpson's responsibilities. Ensconced in his modest offices, Simpson says, "I don't really have a lot of day-to-day responsibilities other than the portfolio. Four times a year, I participate in internal GEICO board meetings, usually by phone, and twice a year I fly to the company's headquarters in Washington, D.C., for meetings. I do, though, talk regularly to Tony Nicely, who runs GEICO's operations, as well as other people in Washington."

Among the things that haven't changed is Simpson's ability to make his own decisions. In 1998, after it also became a wholly owned subsidiary, Buffett took over the investment portfolio of Berkshire's other major insurance company, Gen Re, but he has allowed Simpson to continue to manage GEICO's equity portfolio. By way of explanation, Simpson says, "We've known each other a long time, and he knows all of us here, so he's willing to have us do it. He's never done that, but this case is different in that we've been managing money at GEICO for a long time. Gen Re," he adds, "had a totally different [but typical] approach to their portfolio." And when it's suggested to him that being allowed by the world's best known investment manager to continue managing the portfolio is a considerable compliment, Simpson just waves his hand and says, "Well, so far. . . . You know what they say," he adds with a laugh. But when asked if GEICO has changed in other ways since being acquired by Berkshire, he turns serious again. "It will take a much longer time horizon to know," he says. "I think the necessity of generating an underwriting profit short term is less important. The ability to grow where it makes sense to grow is more important."

Equity investing for GEICO is a little different than investing for Berkshire. It's the difference between buying part of a company versus the whole company—kind of like the difference between an individual investor and a conglomerate. Smaller portfolios have more investment alternatives, or, as Lou says, "A much bigger pond to fish in." Despite the size of the portfolios, the analysis is the same but the economics of buying a whole business can ultimately create more value and can be more attractive from control, tax, and cash-flow perspectives.

Perhaps not surprisingly, although he considered other careers, Lou says, "I'm really glad I landed in investment management. It's very challenging intellectually, and it's also very practical and bottom-line." Interestingly, considering his apparent lack of interest in being involved in day-to-day operations, when asked what career he might have pursued other than investment management, Simpson said: "It would have probably been in general management. I would have been a general manager of a non–high-tech business. Not so much because of its bottom-line nature, but more because I enjoy the whole process of being part of top management, running a business, and building value. Although I have a specialty—that's been my role at GEICO—I sort of consider myself a general manager with an expertise in investments and finances."

That expertise has provided Simpson with a very handsome income, despite charging miniscule management fees. With $2.5 billion under management, the average professional manager would charge $25 million. The exact amount isn't known, but Simpson probably charges one-tenth of that. Unlike others in the professional management community, Lou is not compensated on the size of the asset base but on his actual performance. He has no incentive to advertise, boost his performance, become a talk show favorite, market forecaster, or submit to interviews. Like all the other Buffett CEOs, his focus is internal not external. And with a 24 percent annual average, Simpson can bring shareholders an additional $600 million in annual investment earnings.

Berkshire doesn't report Simpson's salary or performance bonus. In 1996, the last year before Buffett took over GEICO, Simpson was paid

$600,000. In 1999, when value investing and Berkshire itself didn't beat the broad S&P market, Lou didn't receive a bonus based on a comparison of his rolling three-year average versus the S&P 500 index. While it's true that was not in itself a munificent salary, particularly in today's world of mutual fund managers' compensation, he had in 1992 earned a $1.5 million bonus for beating the market, and the following year exercised stock options that brought him $38 million in profits. In addition, when Berkshire purchased the company, he cashed in shares worth more than $25 million. As a result, even though, like many Berkshire executives, Simpson doesn't have to work, he continues to do so because of the excitement. That excitement comes, he says, "in really understanding businesses. I get excited when we get some insights on a business that's not really well understood." In fact, he says that his sense of competence rests on that ability to understand.

That understanding only comes, though, with a great deal of study. An ideal day, he says, "would be a day when I'm here in my office, the market is closed, there are no telephone calls, and I can read all day." Reading is, in fact, the way he spends the majority of his time. "I'd say I try to read at least five to eight hours per day. I read a lot of different things, including a wide variety of filings, annual reports, industry reports, and business magazines." Among his favorite business publications: the *Wall Street Journal, Fortune, Business Week, Forbes,* and *Barron's.* "You can get good ideas from any of them. But," he hastens to add, "you also can get a lot of noise." Filtering out that noise and thinking independently are important elements in deciding which companies he might invest in.

One way he does that is by looking carefully at annual reports. "During annual report season," he says, "I probably read 15 or 20 a day. I generally read the Chairman's letter to get a flavor of the culture, then I go to the Sources and Uses of Funds, and I read some footnotes. But it's the CEO's letter that sets the tone," he concludes. He is particularly wary of CEO letters that are too personal. He admits that "Berkshire's is personal in some ways," but he hastens to add that "Berkshire *is* Warren, and Warren is the star of the company." He doesn't like it when chief executives are "too cutesy-personal" and points out that "even if Warren is personal, he does deal with substantial issues. There are a lot of CEOs' letters where you really don't have much of a clue what's happening in the business. It's all PR, marketing, and smoke."

It's no surprise that Simpson practices what he preaches. In 1993, the *Washington Post* singled out GEICO's annual report—and its investment chief—for praise. "Over the years," staff writer Stan Hinden explained, "we've discovered that reading annual reports, as tedious as that may sound, is an excursion into the land of corporate doublespeak. But it's also a chance to search for an unusual idea, for a refreshing approach to bad news, or for a rare bit of business candor." Because the paper considered GEICO's report to be an excellent example of business candor, it awarded the company its "Straight-Talk Award." "When Simpson does well," the *Post* noted, "he tells you. And when he does poorly, he also tells you." Quoting from the annual report, Hinden showed how Simpson had explained the company's relatively poor performance in the early 1990s by candidly admitting, "There are two obvious reasons for the lessened performance. First, we have not been as successful in identifying good investment ideas, and second, the stock market's appreciation has been lower than in the 1980s."[19]

Simpson is, in fact, refreshingly open about admitting his own weaknesses, limitations, and mistakes. He considers his greatest fault as an investor to be a "lack of understanding of technology, because certain technology is crucial to the economy of the world." Moreover, he faults himself on not "taking the time to understand technology," at the same time admitting that "I don't know if it would have done any good. I kind of block that area out." Interestingly, he admits that technology presents "a great opportunity to make money," but he is not apologetic about not getting more involved in it. "I think that dealing in a circle of competence," he says, "dealing with companies that you have the ability to understand, being able to come up with a good analysis of a company's value and earning power, is fundamental." For example, he explains, "I don't understand AOL's valuation. I understand AOL's business—I think it's extremely well run in terms of building value, but I don't understand the valuation versus the business prospects." Then, thinking again, he adds, "Maybe I don't understand the business. In fact, I'm sure I don't."

About taking risks that have resulted in failures, Simpson says, "We have made very concentrated bets in the past, and I think those have been our greatest risks. In some of those cases it's worked out great, but in others it hasn't worked out very well. We've also made some inaccurate assessments of people, particularly management and owners.

"We're trying to get more competent. It's really a combination of understanding businesses *and* understanding people. We've probably done a better job of understanding businesses, but we're still learning about both of them. And," he adds, "when we make mistakes, we always try to do postmortems. I think it is very important to look at your mistakes and determine why you made them."

Simpson's biggest mistake wasn't selling too soon, nor investing in technology, trading excessively, or blindly following a stock tip. Rather, he listened to inside information on a company in which he had an ownership position. "This in effect froze our position since we became an insider," explained Simpson, "And we lost some money, and we couldn't either buy or sell because we had the information. We'll never do that again. We don't want any insider information. We want to be as flexible as we can be."

Characteristically, when asked about his greatest strength, Simpson says, "If we have any strength, it's really in understanding businesses and, hopefully, management. To be able to get the conviction, assuming that you're buying a business at a fair price, maybe a cheap price to go in and take very concentrated bets. On balance, it's worked out pretty well, although sometimes it hasn't."

Simpson says that it is important to evaluate the qualitative *and* quantitative aspects of a company. He feels that his team's in-depth analysis of industries, and the companies within them, gives him an edge in that respect. At the same time, when asked about the most important quantitative aspects of evaluating companies, his reply is: "Return on capital. That really tells you a lot. One of the basic problems is that there is so much noise around earnings that you really have to rip apart the financials to understand what the real numbers are. It's really the basic returns on equity capital [that are] important, but sometimes they're not obvious. Even so," he says, "I think you have to look at a lot of things. You have to figure out what the earnings growth rate of the company will be over an extended period of time, and then apply a discount rate to it so you can come up with the best valuation. It's easy in principle but it's extremely difficult in practice."

Although Simpson is more than willing to share his expertise, he doesn't think someone can be taught how to be a successful investor. "I think it's an art," he says. "There's a lot of psychology and emotion involved." He also believes that "a lot of people don't have the patience or temperament to really be investors," and, ultimately, "the average investor is not properly equipped to be successful." One thing that will help, he says, is familiarity with two of Benjamin Graham's classic books—his own the *Intelligent Investor,* and *Security Analysis,* which he coauthored with David L. Dodd. When asked what advice he would offer individuals who are currently in the financial industry or are thinking about a career in investment management, Simpson says, "I'd advise you to associate yourself early in your career with really good people, people who have integrity and confidence, people you can learn from. And not to be too short-term oriented." In fact, he considers his own most admirable attribute to be his ability to think long term. "One of the things I've learned," he says, "is that you cannot will the market to do what you want it to do. But, over time, the market is ultimately rational, or at least somewhat rational."

Asked for the one piece of advice he would give individual investors, he repeats some advice that he got from Warren Buffett. "When I first met him," Simpson says, "one of the things he suggested to me was to think of investing as a situation in which you are given a fare card with 20 punches. You can only make 20 investment moves, and at the end of those 20 moves you have to stay with what you have. Thinking of it that way really helps, because it focuses you on being very careful and having a lot of conviction about whatever changes you want to make. In general," he adds, "people are just churning their portfolios. Ben Graham once told me that the way a lot of individuals and institutional investors invest reminded him of people who traded their dirty laundry with each other. They were just trading for the sake of trading, and they didn't really own businesses. Investors are going to make out a whole lot better if their whole emphasis is on owning businesses and having a reasonable time horizon."

Even at the age of 64, Simpson sees retirement as being a long way off. He still arrives at the office every day at 6:00 in the morning—before any of his three assistants—and usually doesn't leave until 7:30 in the evening. He recently renewed his office lease for another five years. "I really like what I'm doing," he says. "We have a very good, compatible, small group that works well together, and the surroundings couldn't be nicer. I don't know what I'd do with myself if I retired." Newly remarried, and with three grown sons, he has few outside interests, except for an occasional hike in the mountains. One of those interests, though, is a commitment to civic pursuits. For example, although his sons graduated from the Cate School several years ago, Simpson continues to be a trustee and to provide the school with investment advice. He has also set up a financial aid fund for the school that gives away over $1 million every year. "Typical of Lou," Meg Bradley, the school's director of development recently told *Money* magazine, "he gave the most generous gift in the world of development—one with no conditions. He is a remarkably good and generous man."[20]

In keeping with his lack of interest in retirement, Simpson says that he's not training anyone to take over for him at GEICO's capital operations. "I don't think it's the kind of business where you build a succession of management," he says. "We have a collegial environment where we're working together, and I'd like to continue to do that into the indefinite future." When asked whether he has a vision for GEICO, he defers to co-CEO Tony Nicely, but adds, "GEICO is probably the future of automobile insurance. Insurance is going to be more and more direct response, probably more and more the Internet. And I think that GEICO is, and will be, a combination of very good prices and excellent service."

He's equally—if not more—reticent about discussing the future of Berkshire Hathaway. As with his response to the question about GEICO's future, when asked if he has a vision for Berkshire he will only say, "That's really Warren's call. But I do think it's going to be opportunistic." He doesn't believe that Buffett has a master plan for the company ("I think it's more of an ever-evolving painting," he says) nor is he willing to forecast what that painting may look like in 10 or 20 years. "It's going to depend on what the opportunities are. So I think it's going to be very, very interesting." He also thinks that there's little reason for shareholders to be concerned about Buffett's retiring. "As long as Warren remains mentally sharp—and he's as sharp now as when I first met him over 20 years ago—he's going to continue doing what he's doing."

Associates say that Simpson is very pleased with the recognition he received when Buffett named him as one of the two individuals to replace the boss as co-CEOs of Berkshire Hathaway, but Simpson doesn't seem concerned about it.[21] "By the time he steps down," Simpson says, "there will be younger people around to take over."[22] Nor is he willing to discuss who might be chosen as the operational CEO of the company. "There are a number of people at Berkshire who are possibilities," he says. "I don't know who else I would pick." Company insiders believe that the three most likely contenders are Ajit Jain, who runs Berkshire Reinsurance,

Rich Santulli, founder and president of Executive Jet, and Simpson's present co-CEO at GEICO, Tony Nicely.[23] Of course, only the future will tell which—if any—of these men will take over for Warren Buffett.

In the meantime, Lou Simpson plans to simply continue doing what he has always done. "There are no secrets—or surprises—in the way we do things," he says. "We are all very clear on what we're trying to do. We have a very good approach. It's just a question of doing it. Of course, the implementation of our approach is not easy. We know that we're in a long race, but we're convinced that our approach will work."

## PETER LYNCH VERSUS LOU SIMPSON

Perhaps the best way to understand Lou Simpson and his investment principles and practices is to compare him to the second best-known investment manager, Peter Lynch. The contrast is striking.

| Peter Lynch | Lou Simpson |
| --- | --- |
| Famous media darling, three books published, magazine articles, advertising spokesman. | Unknown. Doesn't do interviews. Doesn't write or publish. No interest in publicity. |
| Retired from managing money at age 46, over a decade ago. | Still actively managing money at age 64. |
| "Invest in stocks that you and your family are familiar with. Invest in what you know." | "Invest in value stocks. Invest in what others don't know and are uncovered by research and independent thought." |
| "Everyone can be an above-average investor." | "The average investor is not properly equipped to be successful." |
| $14 billion under management, diversified into 350 stocks. | $2.5 billion under management, concentrated into seven stocks. |
| Made money for the Johnson family, owners of Fidelity Funds. | Made money for the shareholders of GEICO and Berkshire Hathaway. |
| Thirteen-year career (1977–1990). | 38-year-plus career (1962–    ). |
| One million shareholders. | 300,000 shareholders. |

*(continued)*

| Peter Lynch | Lou Simpson |
|---|---|
| Best stock returns after three or four years of ownership. | Invest with a 20-investment-decisions-in-a-lifetime method. |
| Consider a turnaround a special situation. | Consider out-of-favor value stocks. |
| Personal earnings based on assets. | Personal earnings based on earnings and on adding to shareholder value with share repurchases. |

## SIMPSON'S EQUITY RETURNS COMPARISON

| Year | Simpson | Buffett | Lynch | S&P 500 |
|---|---|---|---|---|
| 1980 | 23.7 | 19.3 | 69.9 | 32.3 |
| 1981 | 5.4 | 31.4 | 18.5 | (5.0) |
| 1982 | 45.8 | 40.0 | 48.1 | 21.4 |
| 1983 | 36.0 | 32.3 | 38.6 | 22.4 |
| 1984 | 21.8 | 13.6 | 2.0 | 6.1 |
| 1985 | 45.8 | 48.2 | 43.1 | 31.6 |
| 1986 | 38.7 | 26.1 | 23.7 | 18.6 |
| 1987 | (10.0) | 19.5 | 1.0 | 5.1 |
| 1988 | 30.0 | 20.1 | 22.8 | 16.6 |
| 1989 | 36.1 | 44.4 | 34.6 | 31.7 |
| 1990 | (9.1) | 7.4 | (4.5) | (3.1) |
| 1991 | 57.1 | 39.6 | | 30.5 |
| 1992 | 10.7 | 20.3 | | 7.6 |
| 1993 | 5.1 | 14.3 | | 10.1 |
| 1994 | 13.3 | 13.9 | | 1.3 |
| 1995 | 39.7 | 43.1 | | 37.6 |
| 1996 | 29.2 | 31.8 | | 23.0 |
| Average | 24.7 | 26.8 | | 16.9 |

*Note:* Simpson's (GEICO) and Lynch's (Fidelity Magellan) returns are before tax and before management fees, and are stated as a return on equity. Lynch's returns are before a 3 percent load to buy into the fund. Berkshire's returns are after tax and after management fees, and are stated as increases in book value, not market price. The S&P 500 returns are before tax and before management fees, and include reinvested dividends.

Simpson's and GEICO's annual returns have not been made public since 1996, when GEICO became a wholly owned subsidiary of Berkshire Hathaway. *Forbes* magazine estimated Simpson's 1999 return to be 17 percent.[24]

*Scorecard Facts on Lou Simpson*

1. Beat Buffett in 7 out of 17 years.
2. Beat the S&P 500 in 12 out of 17 years.
3. Beat Lynch in five of the last seven years of Lynch's management.
4. Beat Lynch's total return in the last 10 years of Lynch's management.
5. Comparison of Simpson's market price returns with Buffett's changes in book value does not yield a fair comparison.
6. Number of years of public performance = 17 years.
7. Number of years of underperformance = 4 years.
8. Number of consecutive years of underperforming the S&P 500 = 1 year.
9. 1980: GEICO's equities represented just 12 percent of the portfolio.
10. 1983: GEICO's equities represented 32 percent of the portfolio.
11. 1982: GEICO had $280 million invested in 33 companies.
12. 1995: GEICO had $1.1 billion invested in just 10 companies.

## LOU SIMPSON'S BUSINESS TENETS

★ Read the financial press voraciously.
★ Research any company extensively before making an acquisition.
★ Don't overpay for acquisitions.
★ Think independently.
★ Invest for the long term.
★ Hold only a few stocks.

# chapter five

# The Accidental Manager—
# Ajit Jain, Berkshire Hathaway
# Reinsurance Division

*A*jit *(pronounced Á-gheet) Jain was born half a world away. He is a native of India and was raised south of Calcutta in the State of Orissa, in a coastal town known for frequent cyclones and other weather-related disasters. Little did he know that these extremes of nature in his home country would one day assist him in his "accidental" profession.*

*Speaking English as a second language, Ajit has single-handedly generated more revenue and earnings than any other individual Berkshire employee.*

*Ajit Jain is part of a diverse CEO team of Christian and Jewish managers. Jain gets his name from and belongs to a small religious group from India called Jainism. Management's cultural, religious, political, and educational diversity isn't a directive or a master plan by Warren Buffett. It is simply based on applied intelligence, hard work, and merit.*

*Like Rose Blumkin of Nebraska Furniture Mart (Chapter Six), Ajit is foreign-born and a salesperson at heart. He traveled great distances to get where he is. He quickly adapted to his new environment and is highly regarded by his boss. Unlike Mrs. Blumkin, who never received a day of formal education, Ajit is one of the most educated of the Buffett CEOs. Excluding his boss, Jain is Berkshire's most profitable employee. In just 14 years, he has built a $7.8 billion insurance float business staffed with only 14 people. He is now known for closing the largest sale in reinsurance history, but no deal is too small for him. He will still get in his car to capture a $1 million insurance agreement.*

*Situated in Stamford, Connecticut—home of the University of Connecticut, General Re (a wholly owned Berkshire subsidiary), and Xerox— Ajit's cluttered office is full of papers and documents.*

*Ajit is very frugal—maybe even more so than Buffett. At the time of our interview, he hadn't replaced his secretary in three months, and was retrieving his own e-mail and booking his own travel reservations. Although an Executive Jet could be made available to assist him in capturing more business, he is too cost-conscious to take advantage of it.*

*Jain is funny, humble, self-effacing, conversational, open, modest, and, by all appearances, a regular kind of guy—all the things you wouldn't expect in someone who has traveled so far and done so much. But maybe that's why he has come so far so successfully.*

In the spring of 2001, a small tremor ran through the ranks of the Berkshire faithful—as well as the merely curious—when Warren Buffett released his annual "Chairman's Letter to Shareholders." In discussing Ajit Jain, head of Berkshire's Reinsurance Division, and referring to the considerable amount of recent talk about his own health, Buffett wrote, "It is impossible to overstate how valuable Ajit is to Berkshire. Don't worry about my health; worry about his."[1] This apparently almost offhand remark caused a tremor because those in the know—including Berkshire Hathaway employees and board members, and Buffett family confidants—believe that Jain is one of the three candidates, along with Executive Jet's Richard T. Santulli and GEICO's Tony Nicely, most likely to take over as Berkshire's operating co-CEO after Buffett is gone.[2] As of this writing, Buffett is in reasonably good health for a man of his age. Jain, the youngest of the rumored candidates, has more than 20 years on his boss, and it's entirely possible that he will succeed him as head of operations for the company. If so, he will have come a long way from his modest beginnings.

*Business Week* has reported that, during a recent trip to Paris to promote Executive Jet, another expanding Berkshire division, Warren Buffett checked into his Paris hotel room and kept a large group of France's finest civic and business leaders waiting as he slipped away to talk with his daily phone companion—Ajit Jain.[3]

Born in India in 1951, Jain began his professional life as an engineer, having earned an undergraduate degree in engineering from the Indian Institute of Technology (IIT) in Kharagpur in 1972. In 1956, the Parliament of India passed the IIT Act, declaring IIT as an institute of national importance. Entry based solely on merit and widely known among the worldwide engineering and technological community, IIT is believed by many to be one of the world's premier places for technological education. Less than

4,000 new undergraduate students are accepted each year among six regional campuses, from a population base of 900 million.

In 1991, Bill Gates told Buffett if he could recruit technology talent from one school in the world it would be IIT.

However, Jain says, "Even though I enjoyed being an engineer and looked forward to engineering as a profession, I very quickly realized that engineers—certainly in India, but also here in the United States—end up being shortchanged. I was working six days a week and making a quarter of what the people in sales and marketing were getting paid. So I figured that if I couldn't beat them, I'd join them."

As it happened, at that time (1973), "IBM was looking for people for sales and marketing for their data-processing operations, so I joined them to sell computer systems in India." Jain displayed his natural salesmanship by being named IBM's "Rookie of the Year" for his region. But then, in 1976, the Indian government passed some laws that required multinationals operating in India to have some Indian ownership. Most of the multinationals caved in, but Coca-Cola and IBM drew a line in the sand and said, "As far as we're concerned, either the Indian operations are going to be 100 percent owned by the American parent or we're going to walk out of the market." And both firms did walk out, so Jain suddenly found himself jobless.

In the meantime, one of Jain's supervisors had been urging him to consider going to business school in the United States. "Even though I told him that I didn't want to go," Jain says, "that it was too tough in the States, he literally pushed me to take the exam to see how well I could do. Fortunately," he adds, "I did okay on the exam." Saying he did okay, however, is clearly an understatement. In fact, he applied to and was admitted to the Harvard Business School. He did not, however, enjoy the experience. "It was the first time I'd been abroad," he says. "I was a strict vegetarian, so food was a problem. I was also convinced I wouldn't get a job. I kept thinking: 'What am I doing in a place like Harvard with all these superstars?' I was sure I was going to flunk. So there was a lot of fear, and I never enjoyed it." At the same time, he says, "I was a little disappointed with what they taught us in business school. A lot of it seemed so obvious, and I felt like they were making a big deal out of something that was really very natural and intuitive."

After receiving an MBA in 1978, he immediately got a job befitting a graduate of IIT and the Harvard Business School: a management consultant with McKinsey and Company. "I was delighted to join McKinsey," he says. "The pay was great, the first-class travel to Europe was great, and it was nice to have the name on my resumé. But I never really enjoyed the job. Playing consultant, drawing charts in the middle of the night, wasn't as much fun as being a salesman for IBM. So, one fine day in 1981," he explains, "I just felt like I'd been there and done it, so I pulled the plug." He returned to India, where he remained for the next two and a half years. Jain had an arranged marriage with his parents selecting his bride and strongly suggesting he marry within their Jainism religion. After a one-month courtship, he fulfilled his parent's wish. "I probably wouldn't have come back [to the United States]," he says, "but for the fact that when I was in India I got married, and even though I'd gotten the western world out of my system, my wife hadn't." When he returned to the United States, McKinsey, as he put it, "made the same mistake twice" and rehired him.

During his first stint at McKinsey, he had worked for Michael Goldberg, who had left the consulting firm for Berkshire Hathaway in 1982. In 1986, Jain was invited by his former boss to join Warren Buffett's company. "When I joined Berkshire," he recalls, "I didn't know how to spell insurance, or reinsurance, but I was hired to do a job in the reinsurance operations of National Indemnity. Fortunately," he adds, "that was at a point in time when it was raining gold in the insurance industry, and you really didn't need to know much about the business as long as you could understand some basic numbers. Of course, the industry does go through cycles, and I was very lucky in terms of having gotten into the industry at one of its peaks.

"There was a huge shortage of capital in the business at the time," he says, "and we were one of the few entities that actually had capital. So we'd get bombarded with deals and phone calls from people wanting insurance. Being new, I didn't understand most of it, but, every now and then, I would see something where I would look at the numbers and say, 'This looks interesting.'" Initially, Jain had been hired to handle the specialty insurance division, which is dedicated to underwriting large unique risks and difficult-to-place product liability coverages, like all-terrain vehicles. But within six months, he was asked to take over all of the reinsurance operations.

National Indemnity and its Reinsurance Division were, even then, only a part of Berkshire's large—and growing—insurance group. National Indemnity had been founded in Omaha in 1940 by Jack Ringwalt. Buffett purchased it in 1967, along with National Fire & Marine Insurance, for $8.6 million. Two years later, Buffett hired George Young, whom he had met at a financial seminar, and together they started Berkshire's reinsurance operation. Reinsurance is the business of supplying insurance to the insurance industry in exchange for some of the premium or the act of wholesaling insurance. Buffett continued to oversee the entire insurance business himself until 1982, when he hired Michael Goldberg to take over management of the various operations. Goldberg served essentially as chief operating officer of the insurance group until 1993. He was then reassigned to special projects in the Omaha office, and the operating managers who had reported to him began reporting directly to Buffett. When Jain joined National Indemnity, its reinsurance operation was based in Philadelphia. It was moved to New York City in 1987, and to its current headquarters in Stamford, Connecticut, in 1992.

When asked how his responsibilities have changed since becoming head of the reinsurance operation, Jain says, "I was responsible for the operation then, I'm responsible for the operation now. My responsibilities haven't changed. It's just that we're doing a lot more now than we did back then. We cover a broader spectrum of deals, and we're making bigger deals. But I wouldn't say that my responsibilities have increased. They are what they were then." His title has also remained the same. "I have a business card that says 'President, Reinsurance Division,' but it doesn't mean anything."

The operation that Jain oversees is relatively unique. There are not many companies in the business, largely because such operations require an enormous amount of capital. "That's what you need to get into this business," he says, "Capital. Lots of capital, patient capital, and a real stomach to put that capital to risk." Although in 2000, the worldwide insurance market was $2.13 trillion and non-life insurance business in the United States represents approximately $289 billion a year, only a small percentage of that is passed on to reinsurers, and Jain estimates that Berkshire Reinsurance has about 10 percent of that market. He points out, however, that because of the inherent risks of the business, "That number could very easily fluctuate from less than 5 [percent] to more than 15 percent at the drop of a hat." He is clearly aware that, as his boss has pointed out, "In insurance, it is essential to remember that virtually all surprises are unpleasant."[4]

Nevertheless, under Jain's guidance, the company has become the nation's largest reinsurer in terms of capital, as well as the third or fourth in terms of premiums. It is also, as a result, extremely profitable. The numbers, however, can be somewhat misleading because, like all insurance companies, in good years, Berkshire Reinsurance can actually have two sources of income: (1) the money it receives from selling policies, and (2) the money it makes from investing in what Warren Buffett refers to as the "float."

The existence of "float" is a result of the way insurance companies do business. They receive premiums before they have to pay out any losses, so they have what is essentially free use of the money for the interim. Berkshire—like other insurers—invests that money. The float is, in fact, one of the things that make insurance companies so attractive to Warren Buffett. He became the controlling stockholder in what is now called Berkshire Hathaway Reinsurance in the mid-1960s. Since then, the size of the float has increased substantially. In 1967, it was $17 million; in 2000, it was $7.8 billion (company-wide, the float exceeds $30 billion). Float has been and continues to be the way Berkshire buys businesses with low-cost money.

In 2000, Jain's Reinsurance Division was the most profitable of Berkshire's insurance companies. His division delivered a record $7.8 billion in float at a cost of $175 million, or 2.2 percent of the cost of the money. If the float of $7.8 billion is reinvested at the risk-free rate of 6 percent, the $468 million in earnings, less the $175 million in costs, brings pretax earnings of $293 million. Jain's most profitable year came in 1997. With far less float, and using the same conservative risk-free rate, his division generated $369 million in pretax profit, or 13 percent of Berkshire's total pretax earnings. If Buffett and company can generate more than the risk-free rate by investing in the ownership of other businesses, as it often does, then the profit potential on other people's money is enormous.

By comparison, GEICO delivered $3.9 billion in float in 2000 at a net cost of $224 million or 5.7 percent of the cost of the money. Using the risk-free rate, the net pretax earnings were just $10 million, although it should be noted that in each of the previous three years, GEICO, with less float, out-earned Berkshire Reinsurance by an average of $140 million per year.

As a further comparison to the recently purchased General Re, profits from Jain's division have been positive and consistent whereas GenRe has delivered only losses. In 1999, GenRe generated $15 billion in float but had a net $274 million in losses using the risk-free rate. Again in 2000, GenRe's $15 billion in float cost an additional $292 million in net losses. Year 2001 should be the turnaround year for GenRe, and it is showing signs that it will begin to match the cost structure of Jain's division. Because GenRe has twice the float, it should exceed Jain's division's profits.

In fact, the first-quarter results for 2001 showed early indications that GenRe was moving in the right direction.

One of the largest sources of revenue for Berkshire reinsurance is the sale of policies that have what is referred to as "super-cat" coverage. Under these policies the reinsurer covers other insurance companies—and sometimes other reinsurance companies—against major losses from catastrophes such as hurricanes or earthquakes. Not surprisingly, such policies not only entail considerably more risk than other policies but also are more complicated to calculate. Buffett did, however, provide a clear explanation of these "super-cat" policies in his 1990 letter to Berkshire Hathaway shareholders: Although a typical super-cat contract is complicated, he wrote: "[In] a plain-vanilla instance we might write a one-year, $10 million policy providing that the buyer, a reinsurer, would be paid that sum only if a catastrophe caused two results: (1) specific losses for the reinsurer above a threshold amount; and (2) aggregate losses for the insurance industry of, say, more than $5 billion. Under virtually all circumstances, loss levels that satisfy the second condition will also have caused the first to be met.

"For this $10 million policy," he continued, "we might receive a premium of, say, $3 million. Say, also, that we take in annual premiums of $100 million from super-cat policies of all kinds. In that case, we are very likely, in any given year, to report either a profit of close to $100 million or a loss of well over $200 million."[5] As he also pointed out in a later shareholders' letter, "Since truly major catastrophes are rare occurrences, our super-cat business can be expected to show large profits in most years—and to record a huge loss occasionally." But, he cautioned, "What you must understand . . . is that a truly terrible year in the super-cat business is not a possibility—it's a certainty. The only question is when it will come."[6]

Asked to name his biggest success in 14 years with Berkshire Reinsurance, Jain quickly names the recently expired California earthquake deal. Jain's division agreed in 1997 to insure the State of California against $1.5 billion in losses after the first $5 billion in earthquake losses for a $590 million premium paid annually over four years.[7]

Another major source of premium revenues is what Jain refers to as "one-of-a-kind deals," in which he says his company leads the field domestically. An example of this kind of deal is the policy the company wrote in 2000 for the Texas Rangers baseball team, to protect the organization from the possibility that its star player, Alex Rodriguez, might become permanently disabled. The team had signed Rodriguez for a record-setting $252 million, and clearly felt a need to protect its investment. "We think," Warren Buffett said of the deal, "that our policy probably also set a record for disability insurance."[8] Another example is the policy Jain arranged for Grab.com in the fall of 2000. The Internet company wanted to attract millions of people to its Web site so it could gather information about them that would be useful to marketers. To do so, it offered the possibility of a $1 billion prize, and Berkshire, with $136 billion in assets, insured its payment. *USA Today* reported that the $1 billion guarantee required a seven-figure premium payment to Jain's division.[9] Although it was explained on the company's Web site that the chance of anyone winning was low (1 in 2.4 billion), Jain was nevertheless taking a real risk—someone might have won the prize. Fortunately for Berkshire, no one did.[10]

Substantial premium revenues are also generated by transactions in which the company assumes past losses of a company that wants, as Buffett put it, "to put its troubles behind it. To illustrate," he explained in his 2000 shareholders' letter, "the XYZ insurance company might have last year bought a policy obligating us to pay the first $1 billion of losses and loss adjustment expenses from events that happened in, say, 1995 and earlier years. These contracts can be very large, though we always require a cap on our exposure." Among several such deals the company made in 2000 was one that retroactively covered a major British firm and brought Berkshire Reinsurance a $2.4 billion premium, which Buffett suggested might be the largest in history.[11]

Although Buffett admits that the company will lose some money on these retroactive policies every year, when the premiums from all of Berkshire Reinsurance's policies are combined, they provide not only substantial revenues but substantial profits. At least as important, if not more so, these policies also provide the company with a substantial amount of "float."

Jain believes that several factors have contributed to the company's success. The most obvious is Berkshire's net worth, which, as of the end of 2000, was almost $62 billion, and which has helped toward the company's AAA rating. But, Jain says, "In addition to the capital, you need that brand name or franchise value. People know if they're going to buy something from Berkshire, and they're buying it for something, that we will give back to them 15 or 20 years from now. The Buffett name, the Berkshire name—that lends us a lot of credibility." Jain also considers

Buffett himself to be a contributing factor to the company's success. "Given the mindset and the orientation that Warren has," he says, "we have an unfair advantage over our competition." That mindset, as Buffett has put it, lies in the company's willingness to "accept more reinsurance risk for our own account than any other company," partly because "we simply don't care what earnings we report quarterly, or even annually, just as long as the decisions leading to those earnings (or losses) were reached intelligently."[12] Jain even suggests that, as a result of Buffett's mindset, "the operating manager, which fortunately happens to be me, ends up getting more than his share of credit than the situation does."

Like virtually all of Warren Buffett's operating managers, Ajit Jain has nothing but positive things to say about his boss. "He's smart," Jain says, "he's quick, he's decisive, and he's supportive. I can take a deal that I've spent 10 days trying to analyze and give it to him, and in five minutes he's two steps ahead of me. And he'll give you an answer; he won't send you back to the drawing board and say, 'Do these three other things and then come and talk to me.'" Perhaps even more important, Jain says, Buffett is "a boss who not only understands the business, but could teach it to me and everyone else in the business. He's just a unique individual. To have a boss like Warren," he concludes, "is even better than having no boss at all."

Buffett has equally positive things to say about the head of Berkshire Reinsurance. "Our ability to choose between good and bad proposals reflects a management strength that matches our financial strength," he told the company's shareholders in 1992: "Ajit Jain . . . is simply the best in this business."[13] Two years later, he said, in discussing writing catastrophe policies: "Super-cat policies are small in number, large in size and non-standardized. Therefore, the underwriting of this business requires far more judgment than, say, the underwriting of auto policies, for which a mass of data is available. Here Berkshire has a major advantage: Ajit Jain, our super-cat manager, whose underwriting skills are the finest. His value to us is simply enormous."[14]

In 1996, Buffett compared Jain favorably to himself. "What I can state with certainty," he wrote, "is that we have the best person in the world to run our super-cat business: Ajit Jain. . . . In the reinsurance field, disastrous propositions abound. I know that because I personally embraced all too many of these in the 1970s and also because GEICO has a large runoff portfolio made up of foolish contracts written in the early-1980s, able though its then-management was. Ajit, I can assure you, won't make mistakes of this type."[15] And in 1999, Buffett wrote: "In Ajit, we have an underwriter equipped with the intelligence to properly rate most risks; the realism to forget about those he can't evaluate; the courage to write huge policies when the premium is appropriate; and the discipline to reject even the smallest risk when the premium is inadequate. It is rare to find a person possessing any one of these talents. For one person to have them all is remarkable."[16]

Partly due, no doubt, to their mutual admiration, and Buffett's own longtime interest in the insurance industry, the two men work considerably more closely than Buffett does with his other operating managers. In fact, they speak on the phone every day. "I do it as much for enjoyment as anything else," Buffett says. "He could do it just as well without me."[17] Even so, in regard to those conversations, Jain says, "Warren and I might have had a 30-second conversation or a 30-minute one, but he has been involved in every piece of business I have done." Despite—or perhaps because of—the closeness of their relationship, Jain is uncomfortable with any comparisons being made between himself and his boss. "There is no comparison," he says. "Warren is a lot smarter, he has a lot more experience, and he can make judgment calls. There is no dimension I can think of where I think I'm anywhere close to where he is." Jain readily admits, too, that he has been influenced by his boss. "Warren has shown me," he says, "how to look at deals in terms of their fundamental economics, as opposed to getting lost. But he's also influenced me in terms of how you do business. He has discouraged me from getting too close to the line when it's a close call. He's taught me this whole notion of doing first-class business in a first-class way."

Jain also feels that Buffett has influenced his management style, his beliefs, and his management philosophy, although, he says, "probably not enough. This is probably one of my weaknesses," he admits. "I probably haven't treated the people who work for me in the same way that Warren treats the people who work for him. But," he adds, "it's a little bit like comparing apples and oranges. Warren's inheriting people like Ron Ferguson [General Re] and Rich Santulli [Executive Jet], who built up businesses of their own. We're recruiting kids out of business school, and even though some of them have been with us for 10 or 12 years, I still don't end up giving them the same degree of freedom and authority that Warren gives the people who work for him."

He also readily admits to another weakness. "I probably don't do as good a job as I should in terms of maximizing the upside," he says, "because I spend more time trying to minimize the downside. Ideally, you want somebody—and I think Warren is a lot better at it than anyone else I know—who is truly risk-neutral and rational about that. You make a decision looking at the upside and the downside, and you balance the two. But I probably assign more value to minimizing the downside. Of course," he adds, "that isn't all that bad if you have somebody who is risking capital on your behalf." He denies, though, that he could accordingly be considered more conservative than his boss. "It's difficult to say," he explains, "because we talk so much that ultimately we converge one way or the other."

Risk is obviously the major factor in his operation. "We're taking huge bets," he says, "and you want to make sure you're not missing something that's fundamental. The insurance business lends itself to what we call adverse selection. The reason that occurs is that, more often than not, the person who is buying the product from us knows more about the cost of goods sold than we ourselves, the sellers, know about it. And that's a very scary position to be in. But you can't let that keep you up at night," he adds. "Once we've made a deal, we've made our bed and we have to lie in it. Unlike any other company, we have an organization that takes risks, and we go into it with our eyes wide open, knowing that someday there will be a loss.

"It's a unique situation," he continues, "a unique opportunity. And because of that, we get to see a number of very interesting deals. Unlike any other reinsurance operation, this little operation is not a factory. We don't have clients who need products that we keep supplying year after year. If there's someone who has that kind of problem, they'll find a traditional solution that will be a lot cheaper than what we have to offer, and we won't even get a phone call. What we're looking at are unique, one-of-a-kind deals that few people have the risk appetite for. It's only when large sophisticated clients have that kind of problem, want it solved fairly quickly, and capital is a key element of the solution, that we get the phone calls. So we get to see a lot of interesting, unique, one-of-a-kind situations."

The company's size is another factor that makes the business unique. There are usually fewer than 15 people working for Berkshire Reinsurance at any given time; this is one of the elements that enables Jain and his staff to move quickly. "Somebody can call us," Jain explains, "and say,

'Here's the situation. We need a billion-dollar deal and we need an answer in the next 48 hours,' and depending on whether we can put our arms around what the risk is, we'll put a number on it. And because we're so small here, even if I don't get the phone call directly, I hear about it real-time. I pick up the phone and talk to Warren. We do our work, and we do our analysis, and we give them an answer. We don't need to syndicate and bring other people into the deal. If we understand it and price it, we can do the whole deal ourselves."

"But," Jain is quick to point out, "it's not just rolling the dice and hoping we get lucky every year. We do whatever we can to make sure that we're aware of all the possible risks when we sign onto a deal." In fact, he says, his biggest challenge is "avoiding dumb mistakes. It's so easy to make dumb mistakes in this business. And even though you can do a lot of good deals, if you do one lousy deal you give it all back. It's that one rotten apple, that's what you've got to guard against." When asked exactly how he would define a dumb mistake, Jain says, "It's something that you hadn't thought through when you underwrote the deal, and later [it] comes back to haunt you. Those . . . mistakes will paralyze you; they'll make you feel like jumping out of the window." In fact, he measures his success by "how well we have avoided doing dumb things."

But just avoiding dumb mistakes is, obviously, not enough. "I used to think," Jain says, "that IQ was the answer to a lot of questions in the world of business; that knowing what to do was the biggest challenge. But now there's a part of me that says there's a lot more to business decision making than just sheer, raw IQ; that actually getting it done is an equally important part of the equation, and one that a lot of people—including myself—overlook. It's the ability to make a decision in spite of the uncertainty, to act and move on, that you really need to be a good operating manager." He says the easiest decisions for him are "saying 'No' to deals I don't like," and the hardest are "saying 'Yes' to deals that I'm on the fence about. My starting hypothesis," he explains, "is that if you're on the fence about it, you should just say 'No.' Why screw around? But every now and then, you get sucked into it, and find some rationale why you need to do it. These are very subjective trade-offs, and you may end up on a slippery slope without realizing it. Reminding yourself about that slippery slope is what makes these decisions difficult."

Difficult though those decisions might be, Jain has no interest in doing anything else. "I enjoy what I do," he says, "Being in on the different deals we do is a lot of fun. Working for Warren is a lot of fun. We also have a small group of people here that has been fairly stable for a long period of time, and I enjoy working with them." Unless he has to travel from his Stamford headquarters into New York City for meetings or business lunches, which he does about three days a week, he normally gets into his office at 8:00 or 8:30 every morning, and works until 6:30 or 7:00 in the evening. He also, though, spends "a lot of time over the weekends on the phone with people who work for me. I try not to use 9:00 to 6:00 during the week on internal affairs," he says, "because that's prime time that I want to reserve for customers and making deals."

In fact, other than his work and his family—he, his wife Tinku, and twin sons Akshay and Ajay live in Rye, New York—he has few other interests. And he, at least, thinks that his lack of other interests shows. When asked about his most marked characteristic, he says, "I'm probably a very boring dinner companion. I feel sorry for a lot of people I go out to dinner with because I don't drink, I don't eat meat, and I'm not very good at small talk. I'll order something like a diet soda and talk about business, and then want to get the hell out of there and go home." Not surprisingly, he has no interest in retiring, and expects to be involved in Berkshire's reinsurance business for many years to come.

"I'm very positive about what we've done," he says, "and I'm very positive about what I think we'll end up doing in the next several years." He does not, however, have specific plans for exactly what the company will end up doing in the foreseeable future. "I don't think I've done a lot of stepping back and doing what the business schools and the consultants teach you: asking yourself where you want to be five years from now, and how you're going to get there. That really hasn't been the focus, because we tend to be very transaction-oriented, and, fortunately, the phone rings. Once the phone rings, the focus is on that transaction." When asked, in fact, if he has a vision for the future of Berkshire Reinsurance, he says his hope is that "when it comes to those unique, large, one-of-a-kind deals, we get the first phone call. That's our biggest challenge. What happens after that," he adds, "whether we can translate it into a transaction or not, is important, but not that important."

Not surprisingly, considering the nature of his business, when Jain is asked whether his company's sales and earnings will increase, decrease, or stay about the same, he says, "A lot will depend on whether or not there are any major physical or financial catastrophes. If the earth shakes in California tomorrow, we'll take a big loss. But I do think that, over the next 10 years, we'll probably see a lot of growth, both in earnings and revenues. I think that the next 10 years will be better than the last 10." He is, understandably, even less specific about the future of the reinsurance industry. "There are investment banks," he says, "that are trying to see if they can put together alternative pools of capital that can be mechanisms for risk transfer. If that were to take off, that will make the world of reinsurance come under a lot of pressure. Even without it, though, it's not going to be a great growth business. We'll just grow along with the economy."

A few years ago, when Berkshire made its largest acquisition to date and bought Jain's largest customer and neighbor, General Re, for $22 billion, he had to do some scrambling. First, he was losing his largest customer; GenRe no longer had a need to buy reinsurance because it was now part of the parent company. Second, he needed to call, and sometimes visit, his other major customers that compete against GenRe, to assure them that business was same as usual even after the merger. Berkshire Reinsurance and GenRe, like all of the other Berkshire subsidiaries, would continue to run competitively, autonomously, and without any synergy directives from the head office.

Jain is equally—if not more—reticent about discussing the future of Berkshire Hathaway. He is willing to say, though, that "with the kind of capital it has," over time the company "will end up making a few other big acquisitions. We have a first-class reputation," he points out, "and I think that will continue to build. I also think we will get to see deals just because of who we are. Not just because of the size of the capital, but because of the quality of the company." When asked if he thinks the company will be different after Warren Buffett is gone, he says that though he expects it will, it's not possible to predict exactly how. "I think it will be a conglomerate," he says, "but I also think we might not end up getting the 'first phone calls' if there's some business that's up for sale. Given how we're set up, I think we'll still get some, but not as many as we might if Warren was around."

Although he is aware that his name has been prominently mentioned as a possible successor to Buffett on the operational—as opposed to investment—side of Berkshire's business, when asked who he thinks will get the position he just answers, "I have no idea." He points out that his biggest mistake may be a management one: His failure in not developing a big enough organization, including opening a Tokyo office, to see all the big reinsurance deals. And Jain hasn't really cultivated a successor, which is a basic requirement for a move up. In addition, as if to further distance himself as a contender for the job, he is quick to downplay his achievements. In regard to the success Berkshire Reinsurance has enjoyed under his direction, he says, "It's very difficult to distinguish between the hand one is dealt and the person playing the hand. I think this is a unique opportunity, and I just happened to fall into it. Of course there are some people who are dummies and who would have screwed things up, but I think that most people who had this opportunity would have done a great job at it."

Others, however, are considerably less critical. In fact, even one of the other leading candidates for the job—Tony Nicely, GEICO's co-CEO in charge of operations—claims to consider Jain to be an excellent candidate. "In a mathematical way," he says, "Ajit is as close to Warren as you can get," and, he adds, "might make as much money for Berkshire Hathaway as any single person."[18] Another positive attribute Jain possesses is his knowledge of insurance, which Buffett has said would be an essential element of the future CEO's background, although it must be noted that Nicely has such knowledge as well. In the end, though, it's also entirely possible that Jain might not consider the position desirable. "I enjoy what I do," he insists. "I have no interest in trying to take on something that I know nothing about."

## AJIT JAIN'S BUSINESS TENETS

★ When you take risks, you have to accept that you have some losses. You can't let this keep you up at night. When we make a deal, we stick with it.

★ We have the ability to make quick decisions because we're small. If there's a large potential deal, I get involved right away. We do our research and we make our decision.

★ Avoid dumb mistakes—do everything possible to anticipate the risks in a deal. The worst thing is when something you hadn't even considered comes back to haunt you.

★ A good manager must quickly make a decision and move on. If you're on the fence about a particular deal, then you probably should decline and move on to the next opportunity.

★ *Part Three* ★

# Berkshire's Founders

# chapter six

# The Natural—Rose Blumkin,
# Nebraska Furniture Mart (NFM)

*F*or over 100 years, Mrs. Rose Blumkin lived an extraordinary life of *unyielding principles, hard work, determination, brains, and focus. This female Horatio Alger, "Mrs. B," met every challenge—as an immigrant, a wife and mother, a manager, and a businesswoman—with a resolve to overcome. Mrs. B faced poverty, war, invasion, discrimination, persecution, annihilation, family separation, relocation, supplier boycotts, court battles, illiteracy, a middle-age career start, and a major weather-related disaster. Not only did she overcome these obstacles, she succeeded in what many considered a man's world.*

*Mrs. Blumkin made it to the top of her chosen career, and her company was acquired by America's premier captain of business, Warren Buffett. She is one of two women among this book's elite group of CEOs.*

*Buffett has often said that business students should study the life and times of Mrs. B because her life demonstrates some old Ben Franklin virtues. Buffett has also commented: "If I had a choice of going to some business school for a couple of years or apprenticing with her for a few months—it would be a tough couple of months, incidentally—but you would know how to run a business when you got through . . . . You don't need to know anything except the kind of things she does."*[1]

*Rose Blumkin's life is the quintessential "rags to riches" story. It contains human interest, business success, inspiration, a family, and an extraordinary investment tale. She became one of the most significant and accomplished retailers in the nation, the female equivalent of Sam Walton of Wal-Mart.*

*Rose Blumkin passed away in 1998. She is the only Warren Buffett CEO who wasn't available for an interview. Fortunately, Andrew Cassel, then a reporter and now a columnist for the* Philadelphia Enquirer, recorded and transcribed an interview with Mrs. B on December 14, 1989. At that time, she had split from her family and was starting a competing carpet business. Cassel followed her on her electric cart, and tape-recorded her candid comments and brief oral history. In her own words, in broken English, we come to understand the life of this extraordinary entrepreneur and to know the type of person who ends up selling his or her business and working for Berkshire Hathaway. Contrary to popular myths, Warren Buffett invests in people first, businesses second. If the management of the business doesn't meet his very high standards, then, no matter how appealing the business is, he won't invest.

Like those of other Buffett CEOs, Mrs. B's story is about Main Street, not Wall Street. Indeed, the Nebraska Furniture Mart is located just off Omaha's main thoroughfare, Dodge Street, and is in the heart of Omaha, the heart of Nebraska, the heart of the Midwest, and the heart of America. Mrs. B, the first inductee into the Berkshire Manager Hall of Fame, has set the standard for the other Berkshire operating managers.

To understand Berkshire's phenomenal success, it is important to study Buffett's investments, particularly his investment in the Blumkin business. Nebraska Furniture Mart (NFM) is a simple business run by a dedicated family. With no debt or rent expenses, the NFM has been able to pass the savings along as lower prices to its customers, and therefore to command a huge market share and a durable competitive advantage. The business was purchased at an excellent value and, most importantly, came with layers of family management. Mrs. B's son Louie succeeded her, and his sons, Ron and Irv, succeeded him. Sales and profits have increased year after year. Mrs. B's greatest contribution may be the new Berkshire retirement age: 104. Despite starting her business at the age of 44, she served it for 60 years, and her business principles remain the very core of her business.

Mrs. B's business model consists of very high volume and inventory turns driven by very low profit margins. Like most of the Berkshire managers, she discovered the model naturally and instinctively, not in a textbook or classroom or even from copying other retailers.

On Tuesday, August 11, 1998, Rose Blumkin, 104 years of age, widow of the late Isadore, mother of Louis, Frances, Cynthia, and Sylvia, grandmother of 12, great-grandmother of 21, and founder of the Nebraska Furniture Mart (NFM), was buried at Golden Hill Cemetery in Omaha.[2] So respected was she by her family, friends, and neighbors that more than 1,000 people attended her funeral.[3] But the store in Omaha, which by then was being run by two of her grandsons, Irv and Ron, didn't close for the day. "I don't think she would want us to close," her daughter, Frances Batt, told a reporter for the *Omaha World-Herald*.[4]

Thanks to Rose Blumkin's perseverance, the Nebraska Furniture Mart, which she founded at the age of 44, in 1937, with $500 borrowed from her brother,[5] now occupies a 77-acre campus in the heart of Omaha, Nebraska, employs 1,500 people, and sells annually $365 million worth of furniture, floor coverings, electronics, and appliances. It completely dominates its market; NFM sells almost three-quarters of the furniture sold in the Omaha area, at 10 percentage points below the typical margin in the industry. It's also the largest-volume home furnishings retail operation in the United States.[6] Over NFM's six-decade history, it has always recorded an annual increase in sales revenue. NFM sells 40 percent more per employee than other national retailers, and enjoys nearly twice the net profit margin. Its annual sales are more than eight times the average Wal-Mart store. What is most impressive, NFM's sales of $865 per square foot is nearly a full $100 more than Costco, the premier wholesale club and discount leader. That's a long way from Mrs. B's humble beginnings in czarist Russia.

Born Rose Gorelick, on December 3, 1893, in Schidrin, a Jewish *shtetl* (village) near Minsk, Russia, she was one of eight children of Solomon and Chasia Gorelick. The family lived in a two-room log cabin and slept on straw mattresses. As was often the case in the Jewish settlements at that time, her father spent his days in study, and her mother supported the family by operating a grocery store. Rose never had any formal education, not even grammar school.[7] Many years later, she remembered helping her mother in the store when she was no more than six years old.[8] She also remembered one time when she "woke up in the middle of the night, and my mother was mixing bread. I said, 'Ma, it breaks my heart how hard you work. Wait 'til I grow up; I'll find a job and I'll go to America. And I'll bring you over.[9] I'll go to a big town and find a job. You'll be my princess.'"[10]

By the time she was 13, she was ready to leave Schidrin. She walked barefoot—with her shoes over her shoulder to preserve the soles—18 miles to the nearest train station. Taking a train, she visited 25 stores looking for work. Finally, the owner of a dry goods store was willing to give her a job. Within three years, she was managing the store and all six of its male employees.[11]

In 1913, at the age of 20, she married Isadore Blumkin, a shoe sales-man. But when the First World War broke out the following year, Isadore, having no desire to fight for the czar, left Russia to avoid being drafted.[12] Three years later, in 1917, Rose decided it was time to follow her husband to America. Traveling on the Trans-Siberian Railroad, she was stopped by a soldier at the Russian–Chinese border in Siberia.[13] "I'm buying leather for the army," she later recalled telling the soldier. "'When I'll come back, I'll give you a big bottle of vodka.' So he let me through."[14]

She traveled by ship across the Pacific and landed—unable to speak En-glish, and with no entry visa—in Seattle, Washington. Fortunately, the He-brew Immigrant Aid Society and the American Red Cross helped her cut through the Immigration and Naturalization Service's red tape so that she could join her husband in Fort Dodge, Iowa,[15] a city she pronounced "Fort-dotch-ivie" until the day she died.[16] Leaving Russia, in all likelihood, saved her life. Of the 2,000 Jews in her native village, as she later told the story, "Hitler killed 1,900 on a Jewish holiday, Rosh Hashanah. They dig their own graves, and [the Nazis] put on kerosene and buried them. They killed everybody. The whole town."[17]

Because of their inability to speak English, the Blumkins found life dif-ficult in Fort Dodge. One day, Mrs. Blumkin was trying to have a conver-sation with a neighbor who had said, "My father is dying." Unable to understand what the woman was saying, Mrs. Blumkin simply "smiled real big and said, 'That's all right.'" Later, when she learned what the woman had said, she was thoroughly embarrassed. "I couldn't talk English," she told a reporter many years after the incident. "I was a dummy.[18] I knew I had to go somewhere that was bigger so I could communicate." "Some-where that was bigger" was Omaha, which had a small community of Jew-ish immigrants who spoke both Yiddish and Russian.[19]

Settling in Omaha in 1919, Isadore and Rose Blumkin opened a sec-ondhand clothing store, and the family did reasonably well.[20] Within four years, in fact, they were doing well enough to enable Mrs. Blumkin to ful-fill her childhood promise to her mother. "I brought over my mother, my father, with the seven kids," she later recalled. "I sent 'em to school. They lived with me because I had a big house. And when they got married, I put 'em in business. And my mother was the queen of America."[21]

In addition to taking care of Mrs. Blumkin's parents and siblings, the Blumkins had four children of their own. When the stock market crashed in 1929 and set off the Depression, the need to feed all the family led to Mrs. Blumkin's assisting her husband in his business—encouraging him to cut prices and helping him to expand his product line. She also developed some innovative advertising ideas,[22] one of which came to her after she had checked the prices in Omaha's other clothing stores. Money was tight for everyone, and Mrs. Blumkin was sure that business would pick up if they offered to dress any man, from head to foot, for five dollars. She had 10,000 fliers printed, announcing the five-dollar offer. The day after it was circulated, the used clothing store took in $800.[23]

But the most important effort she made on behalf of her family was to borrow $500 from a brother, in 1937, to open a furniture store in the basement of a pawnshop across the street from her husband's clothing shop.[24] To stock her store, she traveled to Chicago—the center of the country's wholesale furniture business at that time. "I'm from Omaha," she told the manufacturers. "I'm starting up a business. I don't have any money. But you can trust me. I'll pay you."[25] As she recalled it many years later, their response was: "Talking with you, we'll trust you anything,"[26] and she returned to Omaha with $12,000 worth of furniture. She also returned with a name for her store. Having seen the American Furniture Mart in Chicago, she decided to name her own 30-by-100-foot showroom the "Nebraska Furniture Mart."

The store opened on February 7, 1937, and, as she told the story, "I put in one ad and I had customers right away."[27] Having bought the furniture at 5 percent above wholesale, she resold it at a 10 percent markup, thus establishing the one basic rule that she continued to follow for the rest of her life: "Sell cheap and tell the truth."[28] This established Mrs. B as an early discount retailer long before the other well known national store chains. But, times being what they were, there were financial difficulties along the way. At one point shortly after opening the store, she had to sell off the furniture and appliances in her own home to pay off her suppliers.[29]

"We came home from school, walked in our house and the house is totally empty," recalled Mrs. B's daughter, Frances Batt. "All of us, the four children, we cried and we cried. And she says, 'Don't worry, don't worry, I'll buy you better beds. We'll have another kitchen table. But I owe this person money and that's what's most important.' We finally calmed down. And you know what—we understood, because her word was her bond."[30]

Mrs. Blumkin's competitors were, not surprisingly, unhappy about being undersold. In an effort to stop her, they pressured the furniture and carpeting manufacturers to not sell their merchandise to her.[31] As she later recalled, "Up to 1942, nobody would sell me nothing—the leading lines. I wasn't good enough for them. And the banks never loan me a penny. So I was so smart, I outsmarted the bankers. Anything the manufacturers didn't sell me, I went to different towns."[32] Those different towns included Chicago, Kansas City, Missouri, and New York, and even with the additional costs incurred by buying so far away, she was still able to undersell her rivals.[33]

The Korean War, which began in 1950, seriously disrupted the U.S. economy and brought furniture sales to a standstill. As usual, though, Mrs. Blumkin found a way around the problem. "I went to Marshall Field in Chicago," she recalled later. "I tell them I need 3,000 yards of carpet for an apartment building—I got, actually, an apartment building. I buy it from Marshall Field for $3 a yard; I sell it for $3.95 a yard. Three lawyers from Mohawk take me into court, suing me for unfair trade—they're selling for $7.95. Three lawyers and me with my English. I go to the judge and say, 'Judge, I sell everything 10 percent above cost, what's wrong? I don't rob my customers?' He throws out the case. The next day, he comes in and buys $1,400 worth."[34]

The turning point for the Nebraska Furniture Mart was also in 1950. Although she had a considerable amount of paid-for furniture in the store, Mrs. Blumkin was short of cash. "I can't pay my bills," she later remembered, "and I worried to death." One day in July, while talking with Wade Martin, a vice president of a local bank, Mrs. Blumkin mentioned her cash problem. "I've got a store full of furniture," she told him, "but I can't eat it. Nothing's moving. I don't know what to do."

Much to her surprise, Martin offered her a $50,000 loan for 90 days, with the paid-for merchandise as collateral. Once she sold the furniture she would be able to repay the bank. Although Mrs. Blumkin accepted the offer and signed for the loan, she couldn't sleep that night. "I got so excited," she later recalled. "What I'm gonna do if I couldn't repay it." Again, though, she found a way. Renting the city auditorium, she filled it with furniture, and then placed an ad in the *Omaha World-Herald*. In three days, she sold $250,000 worth of merchandise, and was able to pay off both her old debts and the $50,000 loan. She never borrowed money again.[35]

In 1950, Isadore Blumkin, Rose's husband of almost 40 years, passed away. Mrs. B's only son, Louis, had started in the business in 1948, assumed management control, and quickly became a nationally recognized retailer in his own right. After turning over the reins to her son, Mrs. B took over the carpeting department as her private bailiwick. Having never borrowed money, the Furniture Mart had no rent or interest to pay, so it was able to keep its overhead low and still offer its furniture at 20 to 30 percent below what other retailers were charging.[36] As a result, over the next 30 years, the store continued to grow. In 1975, it even weathered a tornado that nearly destroyed the store and caused millions of dollars of damage.[37]

Mrs. B was way ahead of the retailing trend of the past two decades—offering permanent value to the customer—which has contributed to the growth of mass discount merchandise stores and warehouse and whole-sale clubs. As an innovator and originator, she was a match for Sam Walton of Wal-Mart, but she lacked the ability or inclination to take her concept national and international. Her whole focus was to satisfy her customers with great selection and excellent value. Her lean management team spent more time on the sales floor, face-to-face with customers, than at any other major retailer. Her ultimate success was determined by how much time she spent on the sales floor—about 100 percent. "She was about as close as any major retailer can be to the customer," according to her grandson, Irv Blumkin. Mrs. B was legendary for not spending money unless it was in the best interest of her customer. Every expense was audited, and there were no hired buyers. She and her son Louie did all the buying—once again passing the savings on to the customer via lower furniture prices.

One day in 1983, Warren Buffett walked into the Nebraska Furniture Mart. The store was then grossing $88.6 million and a remarkable $443 per square foot in sales. Buffett announced to Mrs. Blumkin that he wanted to buy the store. "I got tired of the kids' bossing me," she later told a reporter. "So I thought, 'I'll sell it and he'll be the boss.' He didn't bother me."[38] And without even auditing either her books or her inventory,[39] "She just told me," said Buffett, "that everything was paid for, how much cash was in the bank, and shook my hand."[40] In regard to that handshake, he later said, "I would rather have her word than that of all the Big Eight auditors—it's like dealing with the Bank of England."[41] Later, Buffett would confide in Mrs. B's son Louie that he sometimes had a hard time understanding his mother's broken English. "Don't worry," said Louie, "she understands everything you say."

Although Mrs. Blumkin later said that the company was worth $100 million,[42] she agreed to sell 90 percent of it to Buffett for $60 million. (Members of the Blumkin family subsequently exercised an option to buy back an additional 10 percent, so, in the end, Berkshire shareholders got 80 percent of the company for $55 million.[43]) When the time came for formal contracts to be signed, Mrs. Blumkin simply put her mark on the paper. She had never learned to read or write.[44] And when Buffett handed her the check, she simply folded it and said, "Mr. Buffett, we're going to put our competitors through a meat grinder."[45] As simple and quick as that, the total legal and accounting fees for the NFM acquisition were $1,400.[46] The sale was cheaper and faster than a typical house purchase.

Why did Mrs. B sell? Probably for the same reasons that most, if not all, other family businesses sell: to reduce estate tax considerations and to ensure the continuation of the business for family, management, employees, and customers. According to Buffett, Mrs. B had given each of her four children 20 percent of the business and kept 20 percent herself. At the age of 89, she felt that a sale of the business would give her family cash.[47] She also gained a hands-off partner who had plenty of capital and practiced expansion by acquisition, and she managed to keep a 20 percent interest in the business for her family.

In his 1983 letter to the stockholders of Berkshire Hathaway, Buffett explained why he had purchased the Nebraska Furniture Mart: "One question I always ask myself in appraising a business," he wrote, "is how I would like, assuming I had ample capital and skilled personnel, to compete with it. I'd rather wrestle grizzlies than compete with Mrs. B and her progeny. They buy brilliantly, they operate at expense ratios competitors don't even dream about, and they then pass on to their customers much of the savings. It's the ideal business—one built upon exceptional value to the customer that in turn translates into exceptional economics for its owners."

By way of further explanation, he added: "And what managers they are. Geneticists should do handsprings over the Blumkin family. Louie Blumkin, Mrs. B's son, has been President of Nebraska Furniture Mart for many years and is widely regarded as the shrewdest buyer of furniture and appliances in the country. Louie says he had the best teacher, and Mrs. B says she had the best student. They're both right. Louie and his three sons all have the Blumkin business ability, work ethic, and, most important, character. On top of that, they are really nice people. We are delighted to be in partnership with them."[48]

The following year, at the age of 91, Mrs. Blumkin was still working full time in the store. "I come home to eat and sleep," she told a reporter, "and that's about it. I can't wait until it gets daylight so I can get back to the business."[49] That same year, another reporter described her as being "just under five feet tall, with the compact, bright-eyed and intense look of a Jewish Yoda."[50] And her new boss said, "Put her up against the top graduates of the top business schools or chief executives of the Fortune 500 and, assuming an even start with the same resources, she'd run rings around them."[51]

Describing Mrs. B's business skills, Buffett has said: "She figures out how to deliver the best value to the customer. She outworks everyone else. She knows what she knows, and she knows what she doesn't know. She defines what I call her 'circle of competence' perfectly." Buffett went on to explain a very important investment lesson. "If you want to sell her 10,000 throw rugs or end tables or something like that, she knows how to buy 'em. If you want to try and sell her 100 shares of General Motors stocks, she says, 'Forget it,' because she doesn't know anything about General Motors stock."[52]

In 1984, she also received an honorary Doctor of Law degree from Creighton University in Omaha. The Nebraska Society, in Washington, D.C., gave her a Distinguished Nebraskan Award, and she was inducted into the Nebraska Business Hall of Fame.[53] She was also given an honorary doctorate in commercial science by New York University, the first woman ever to receive a prize reserved for captains of industry.[54] Among previous recipients of the honorary degree are Clifton Garvin, Jr., CEO of Exxon Corporation; Walter Wriston, then CEO of Citicorp; Frank Cary, then CEO of IBM; and Tom Murphy, then CEO of General Motors. Although Buffett later commented that "They are in good company,"[55] Mrs. Blumkin's reaction was typical: "That doesn't mean nothing."[56]

Five years later, at the age of 96, Mrs. Blumkin was still going strong. She got up at 6:00 in the morning, was in the store by 9:00, and worked until 5:00.[57] Although she had long since developed difficulty walking, she had solved the problem by buying an electric cart—nicknamed the "The Rose B"—in which she sped around the store, as she put it, "like a Russian Cossack."[58] At the end of the workday, she would have her driver take her around Omaha so she could check the parking lots and stores of her competitors—sometimes until as late as 9:00. "To me," she told a reporter, "it's the biggest punishment when I'm home."[59]

She was going so strong, in fact, that she was on a collision course with her family. Although Mrs. Blumkin was still running the carpeting department in 1989, her son Louis had already retired as CEO and had become Chairman of the Board. He had been succeeded by his son Irvin, who ran the company with his brother Ronald, the Chief Operating Officer. Mrs. Blumkin's grandsons had an enormous amount of respect for her, but they wanted to run the company *their* way, and found themselves in conflict with the family matriarch.

Backing away, after being so hands-on for so long, is the challenge of every creator and entrepreneur. To turn over her creation to someone else, even her own family, may have been Rose's most difficult assignment. This orderly act of succession in order for the business to survive from one generation to the next—or, in her case, from first-generation to third-generation management—often brings a troublesome decline or even an end to the business.

In fact, in May, when Mrs. Blumkin thought that the "boys" were interfering too much in her operation of the carpeting department, she quit. Like any strong-willed successful entrepreneur, she hated being told she was wrong and having bosses, even if they were her grandsons. As she later recounted the story to a reporter, "The last couple months they took away my rights. I should not be able to buy anything. They wouldn't pay, they told the manufacturers if the salesman talk to me, they not gonna buy from him nothing. And that made me awful mad. They don't know nothing," she added, referring to her grandsons, "and they are the big shots. So one morning I got mad and I walked out of there. And Warren Buffett [who had] acted like he's an angel—said there's nobody like me, I don't care how old you are, you are doing a terrific job—he stuck up for them. He never came to say he's sorry. Never. I got fooled with him. I thought he's an angel."

But, true to form, Mrs. Blumkin didn't just quit. As she later told the story, "I went home, cried for a couple months. Too lonely, I'm so used to being with people. And then mine daughters told me, 'Momma, you gotta start another. Open up. Even if you lose money, you're gonna lose your mind if you sit home always worried by what happened to you.'"[60] So, at the age of 95, investing $2 million of her own money, in October of 1989 she opened up Mrs. B's Warehouse right across the street from the Nebraska Furniture Mart.[61]

"I wish to live two more years," she told a reporter at the time, "and I'll show them who I am. I'll give them hell." "Them," of course, were her grandsons. "They told me I'm too old, too cranky," she said. "I gave my life away for my family. I made them millionaires. I was chairman of the board and they took away from me my rights . . . my high-class grandsons . . . who only know fancy things and to always take vacations. Now there are too many executives," she added, comparing her grandsons' management to her leaner style, "too many meetings, too many vacations, and all that is costing them money. I told Buffett, when I ran it, expenses were $7 million. Now they are $27 million. Now every stupe is a president, a vice president."[62]

Ironically, when she opened up her new store to compete with her grandsons, Mrs. Blumkin found herself in the same situation she had been in when she'd first opened the Furniture Mart. "I'm under a boycott," she told a reporter. "All the leading manufacturers from Nebraska Furniture Mart shouldn't sell me nothing. They [her grandsons] told them if they'll sell me they're not gonna buy. They do 155 million dollar a year. I built them the biggest business in the country. So they don't want mine competition."[63]

"They are the elephant. I am the ant," she told her granddaughter, Claudia Boehm, who was helping her in the new store. Even so, despite having only a small inventory, despite the fact that major manufacturers were refusing to sell her merchandise, and before she ran a single ad or had even "officially" opened, in her third month of operations, Mrs. B's grossed $256,000. "I'm a fast operator," Mrs. Blumkin explained. "Thank God, I still got my brains, my know-how, my talent. . . ."[64]

By 1991, after just two years of operation, Mrs. B's had not only become profitable but was Omaha's third-largest carpet outlet.[65] And on December 1, 1991, two days shy of her ninety-eighth birthday, Warren Buffett walked into Mrs. B's hoping to effect a truce. He carried with him two dozen pink roses and a five-pound box of See's chocolates. Buffett and Mrs. Blumkin had not spoken since she had opened Mrs. B's, so she appreciated the effort he'd made. "He's a real gentleman," she said. A few months later, Mrs. Blumkin sold Mrs. B's Warehouse to the Nebraska Furniture Mart for $4.94 million.[66]

Although embarrassing to her family and confusing to customers, her move across the street actually made the business stronger overall and highlights the classic struggle between multigenerational family managers. Mrs. B's grandsons were able to prove that they were very capable of managing the business; NFM proved just how strong its competitive advantage is, even with the stiff competition of its very founder; their grandmother found out that she could be replaced and the business would still go on and grow; and all the carpet sales she was able to cannibalize eventually became part of and added to the bigger enterprise when they were reunited.

"I am delighted that Mrs. B has again linked up with us," Buffett later told his shareholders. "Her business story has no parallel and I have always been a fan of hers, whether she was a partner or a competitor. But believe me, partner is better. This time around, Mrs. B graciously offered to sign a non-compete agreement—and I, having been incautious on this point when she was 89, snapped at the deal. Mrs. B belongs in the *Guinness Book of World Records* on many counts. Signing a non-compete at age 99 merely adds one more."[67]

A year later, at the age of 100, Mrs. Blumkin was still working 60 hours a week in the Furniture Mart, and the birthday celebration—held in the store, of course—included among its guests Nebraska Governor Ben Nelson, Senator Bob Kerrey, Representative Peter Hoagland, and Omaha Mayor P. J. Morgan. "I live alone now and so that's why I work," she said at the time. "I hate to go home. I work to avoid the grave."[68]

At 100 years of age, she summed up her life. "I come from Russia 75 years ago, started a business, never lied, never cheated, never been a big shot."[69] Her grandson, Irv Blumkin, spoke about how she was able to build such a huge dominating enterprise: "She was focused and she had a vision." And echoing her business motto that continues to this day, "We improve people's lives one purchase at a time, generation after generation. Cash is king and stay away from debt."

As she approached age 104, Mrs. Blumkin finally began to slow down. Afflicted with pneumonia, heart problems, and chronic bronchitis, she was no longer able to work long hours, as she had before. Day-to-day operation of the newly acquired Mrs. B's Warehouse was turned over to her grandchildren, Claudia Cohn Boehm and Barry Cohn. She did, however, keep in touch. Her nurse drove her to the store once or twice every day to find out how business was going. On some days, she actually got out of the car and visited with employees and customers for a while, but more often she waited for her granddaughter to come out and report on sales. She also checked-in by phone four times a day. "She has to know what's going on," Boehm said. "She has her finger in the pie all the time." And, she added, "We try to run the business exactly like she wants it run."[70]

Mrs. Blumkin died on August 9, 1998, four months short of her 105th birthday. She left behind an extraordinary legacy—not just in the Nebraska Furniture Mart and a talented management team, but in her numerous philanthropic efforts. She donated $1.5 million to the Jewish Federation of Omaha, which enabled the building of a 119-bed nursing home. When asked why she had donated so much money to the Federation, she explained that when she'd arrived in the United States, she had been given a meal by the Hebrew Immigrant Aid Society, and had promised herself that she would one day do something for the Jewish people who had been so kind to her.[71]

She also paid over $200,000 for the Astro, an old theater in downtown Omaha, because she didn't want the building to be razed, and she was instrumental in raising $9 million for the building to be remodeled. Warren Buffett's daughter Susan led the drive, and the Blumkin and Buffett families each donated $1 million. The theater was subsequently reopened as the Rose Blumkin Performing Arts Center, commonly referred to simply as "The Rose."[72]

It is, however, the extraordinary success of the Nebraska Furniture Mart that endures as Mrs. Blumkin's most outstanding legacy. She was a natural businessperson who instinctively knew what she had to do to ensure success. To her, that meant being willing to devote one's life to the business. "What every business needs is a good manager," she said, "someone with his whole heart in his work—not someone who takes three-and-a-half hours for lunch, or goes to Las Vegas or Hawaii or a bowl game."[73]

Most important, of course, were her customers. "All the things you read about putting the customer first and all that," Warren Buffett said of her, "she invented it as far as I'm concerned."[74] And she was truly charming with those customers. "Honey," she would say, "what are you looking for? Whatever you want, I'll give you a real bargain . . . the best deal."[75] Her customers loved her for it, and kept coming back.

At the same time, she rode her staff hard, especially those who were members of her family. Racing around in her electric golf cart, she would shout, "You worthless *golem!* You dummy! You lazy!" Fortunately, her son Louis was a gentler soul and was able to soothe the employees' ruffled feathers. When the matriarch tore into a salesman, Louis would placate him. And when she fired employees, Louis would hire them back.[76]

While Mrs. Blumkin was quite demanding of her family and employees, she was also sure that she knew what it took to make a person happy. "The only way you're successful and happy," she told a reporter when she was 96, "is when you do an honest life—across 50 years, 60 years—nobody's mad at you, and you're feeling good. That's what your happy life is." And as far as her own success was concerned, she understood it perfectly. "The reason [for] mine success," she said, "I was honest with the customers. I told 'em the truth. I sold cheap. And if anything was wrong, I made it right."[77]

## ROSE BLUMKIN'S BUSINESS TENETS

★ The customer is always first. Give them what they want and they'll keep coming back.
★ Spend 100 percent of your time with the customer—on the sales floor.
★ Don't spend on anything unless it's going to help the customer.
★ Pass on your savings to the customer.
★ Don't take on any debts.

# chapter seven

# The Visionary—Al Ueltschi, FlightSafety International

*At New York's LaGuardia Airport, directly across from what was Pan Am's marine terminal and is now Delta's Shuttle Terminal, are the executive offices of FlightSafety International (FSI). The building is literally a stone's throw from where Al Ueltschi (pronounced Yule-chee) spent 25 years flying Pan Am's first corporate plane and where FSI got its humble beginnings.*

*This 36,000-square-foot former Pan Am building has no elevator, sports 20-year-old carpeting, and offers dated but functional office furniture. This is home to Al Ueltschi, an aviation legend and a business and medical hero, who now oversees one of Berkshire's most profitable divisions: FlightSafety.*

*Despite spending most of his adult years in New York, Al still has a distinct southern accent and is a delightful storyteller. This day, he sounded like a man half his years; only his fading memory for precise dates indicated his true age. Waiting outside the conference room was a delegation from Brazilian airlines. These visitors gave me the impression that they would have waited all day just to meet the legendary Mr. Ueltschi and shake his hand.*

*As the interview ended, there was a brief struggle over whether Mr. Ueltschi or I would carry my briefcase full of research material, recorded tapes, and interview notes. I am sorry to say that this man, twice my age, won the tug of war. Later, Jim Waugh, Vice President of Marketing, explained that, not long ago, Al carried the bags for all his distinguished passengers. He put them on Pan Am's corporate plane, and he carried them off. Carrying someone's bags is just one Ueltschi trademark. It's his way of showing respect for others, regardless of their station in life.*

After our interview and lunch, I was taken over the Hudson River to FSI's Teterboro training center, where I experienced the simulated flight of a Falcon 900EX, a three-engine, transatlantic, $34 million business aircraft. The stark corporate offices are in sharp contrast to the latest and greatest training equipment, flat-screen computer monitors, and technologically advanced classrooms. Shareholders should be pleased to know that Al Ueltschi's company spends its money on its customers, not on comforts for its executives.

The FAA-approved and highest rated Level D simulators are manufactured by FSI's simulator division and sold internally, without markup, with the actual airplane cockpit (including a $25,000 pilot seat). All simulators manufactured by FSI are to Level D, which is the highest standard in simulator technology. When the flight instructor turned on the visual display, it wasn't difficult to imagine that I was in the cockpit of a brand new corporate jet on Teterboro's runway 6. The Manhattan skyline was in the distance, and I was ready for takeoff. This $15 million state-of-the-art quasi-airplane had more advance avionics (pilots' term for instruments) than NASA's lunar lander.

After getting clearance from the control tower, I accelerated down the runway, pulled back, and was airborne. As I flew through the clouds, the plane shook with typical turbulence. With sweaty palms, I attempted to land, something people in their right mind would never let me do with a jet they owned or were passengers in. I had clocked some 400 hours of single-engine/propeller flying time, so, with my copilot Jim Waugh coaching me, I managed a somewhat controlled crash on the first attempt. On the second and third tries I was able to land with surprising ease. By touching a computer screen behind me, the flight instructor was able to let me take off at dawn and, a minute later, land at dusk. "Let's make this interesting. Give me some low visibility," I suggested. Just like that, I was looking at 50 feet of visibility, snow on the ground, and ice on the runway.

Over 200 combinations of errors and life-threatening problems can be introduced in a controlled environment, and all of the simulation and response is videotaped so that, later, the pilots can review how, when, and if he or she reacted.

As I left the state-of-the-art simulator, I felt like I had just spent the whole day flying. My sweat-soaked shirt attested to the realism of Flight-Safety's training program.

"I don't know why," Al Ueltschi remembers, "but even as a kid I was fascinated by airplanes. There weren't many of them around back then, but I'd read everything I could about them and about the men who flew them."[1] And then, one day, in the spring of 1927—a few days after Al's tenth birthday—a young mail pilot named Charles Lindbergh took off from Roosevelt Field in New York in an attempt to be the first man to fly the Atlantic alone.

"Many others had tried, but none had done it alone," Ueltschi recalled. "My ear was glued to our vacuum-tube RCA radio, listening for every scratchy-sounding news report on the progress of his flight. When the bulletin came announcing that he had landed in Paris and was carried off the field on the shoulders of thousands of cheering Frenchmen, I was hooked. There was no question in my mind that I would be a pilot, just like Lindbergh. I was certain of it."[2]

Al Ueltschi did become a pilot. But his flying experience and his ability to recognize an opportunity when he saw one led him to almost single-handedly create the aviation training industry. And, in founding, nurturing, and building FlightSafety International, he made flying safer for thousands of pilots and millions of their passengers.

Born Albert Lee Ueltschi on May 15, 1917, on a dairy farm near Frankfort, Kentucky, he was the youngest of seven children. His first four years of education were in a single-room schoolhouse in Choateville, Kentucky. He then transferred to a school in Frankfort, a "big" city by comparison, boasting some 15,000 residents. "The school was on a hill," he remembered, "and when class let out I'd step outside and look out over the valley and think this must be what pilots see all the time. I wanted to see the world that way as well."[3]

Surprisingly, even though it was the middle of the Depression and the state of the family's finances was uncertain, both his parents were very supportive. "My Dad and Mom were great. They never discouraged my dreams about flying, even though the idea must have seemed preposterous. Here we were, a family of nine living on a farm out in the sticks and barely able to keep a roof over our heads, and I was jabbering on about flying airplanes."[4]

Even with his parents' support, becoming a pilot wasn't going to be easy. Flying lessons cost money and he could not earn enough, working on the farm, to pay for them. But shortly after he graduated from high school in 1934, he found a way. "Just about that time," he later recalled, "a new outfit called White Castle opened a hamburger place in Frankfort, and it was drawing a lot of customers. The business seemed pretty simple, so I opened my own hole-in-the-wall hamburger stand in Frankfort, but on the opposite side of the Kentucky River from my competitor." Ueltschi named his business "Little Hawk" because he thought the name had "an aviation ring to it."

"Business was good almost from the start. By pricing burgers and Cokes at a nickel each, I sold a lot of them. Trouble was, I wasn't making any money. So I doubled my prices (there was a volume discount, of course— a dozen burgers for a buck), and suddenly I was making money."[5]

He saved all the profits from the hamburger stand and, within a year, had earned enough to begin taking flying lessons. Two years later, he soloed for the first time. At 18, having established a successful business, Ueltschi approached the president of the Farmers Bank in Frankfort, one of his customers, and asked him for a loan to buy an airplane. Using the hamburger stand as collateral, he was able to borrow $3,500, and soon was flying his own Waco 10,[6] a classic open-cockpit bi-wing airplane that required a pilot to wear goggles.

His parents had hoped that he would attend the University of Kentucky, but their youngest son spent his time at the airport. In 1937, Ueltschi sold the hamburger stand to his brother Bob for one dollar and the unpaid loan balance, and devoted himself, full time, to his flying passion. The country was still in the grips of the Depression, and making a living as a pilot was hard. "There weren't any flying jobs to speak of," Ueltschi remembers. "Even the military had just a handful of airplanes. So I did what many other aviators did: anything and everything. I took people up for a dollar a hop, gave lessons, and even put on air shows. Folks came out to see if the fool kid would kill himself, and like a fool, on several occasions I almost obliged."[7]

One of the most memorable of those occasions occurred after Ueltschi had been hired as chief pilot for Queen City Flying Services in Cincinnati. One day in 1939, the chief pilot was instructing a Civil Aeronautics Administration [the CAA was the predecessor of the Federal Aviation Administration (FAA)] pilot in how to do snap rolls in an open-cockpit plane—that is, rolling the plane into an inverted position and continuing to fly straight and level while upside down. The CAA pilot, as Ueltschi remembered the incident, "began the roll sharply, and the airplane quickly twisted onto its back when, suddenly, the whole airplane was missing!"[8]

Ueltschi's seat had broken free of the cockpit, and he was falling straight to the Ohio farmland below.

Pulling off his heavy leather gloves (Ueltschi still remembers how cold the air was), he yanked the rip cord of his parachute. At about 150 feet, seconds before he would have hit the ground, the parachute opened, and he walked away unharmed. It took him some time to recognize that the experience led to several significant realizations:

★ "Training in an airplane can be hazardous."
★ "When the unexpected occurs, take appropriate action in a timely fashion."
★ "If at all possible, be lucky."

He later said that the first two realizations "had a strong influence on my career choices and business dealings over the years. And as for luck, it's been with me my whole life."[9]

In 1941, Ueltschi signed on with Pan American World Airways, which, even at that time, was a major carrier. Pan Am had begun operating between Havana, Cuba, and Key West, Florida, in 1928. By the time Ueltschi joined the airline 13 years later, its routes covered the globe. As Ueltschi remembered it, "Pan Am was America's flag carrier to the world. There was nothing else like it. Its flight crews were the most experienced and the most respected in all of aviation. To be a part of that operation at that moment in history was an experience without equal, and one probably never to be known again."[10]

Paradoxically, although Pan Am was America's only international carrier, it was not allowed any domestic routes. When its founder and president, Juan Trippe, traveled within the United States, he had to use other airlines. To avoid this, Pan Am converted one of its twin-engine propeller planes (the same type flown by Amelia Earhart) into an executive aircraft for Trippe's use. In 1943, Ueltschi was chosen to pilot it. The assignment was supposed to be for six months, but it lasted until Ueltschi retired from Pan Am 25 years later.[11]

Given his boss's stature in the business world, Ueltschi found himself flying and carrying the bags for many business executives and numerous other luminaries: General Dwight D. Eisenhower, George Marshall, financier Bernard Baruch, Francis Cardinal Spellman, and Prescott Bush, whose son and grandson became American presidents. Flying Charles Lindbergh, his boyhood hero, was a particular thrill for him. "For a Kentucky farm boy, it was like stepping into a wonderland," he later said. "What I especially valued was the time spent just observing Mr. Trippe and his associates. Listening as these men—some of the most successful businessmen alive— negotiated business deals, argued politics, forgave slights, planned new ventures, and worked out financing strategies was a business-school education of the highest order."[12]

One potential venture that seemed promising to both Juan Trippe and his pilot was business aviation. Each year, more and more of the country's top executives were discovering the advantages of having their own corporate airplanes, and as their numbers grew larger, Al Ueltschi began to see possibilities that no one else was able to see at the time. Most of the business pilots he knew—and he knew many of them—were excellent, having been trained during World War II by the Navy or the Army Air Corps. But once they left the military and began flying corporate jets, their training essentially came to an end.

Pressurized, high-performance planes were beginning to enter the commercial fleets, and, for pilots accustomed to older aircraft, the transition could be a challenge. The airlines were capable of handling the challenge—Ueltschi himself was involved in helping older pilots make the transition to DC-6s and Constellations. In addition, the federal government required all airline pilots to demonstrate their proficiency every six months. But business pilots were under no such obligation, and it was clear to Ueltschi that this lack of additional training would become more and more of a problem.

Moreover, even if corporate pilots wanted to get additional training, there was no one to provide it. "I thought about that a good long while," Ueltschi says, "and figured that there might be an opportunity in giving those guys a training system similar to what the airlines had." In 1951, with his boss's blessing, Al Ueltschi took a $15,000 mortgage on his house and opened FlightSafety's office in the Marine Air Terminal at LaGuardia Airport in New York. Inside the company's single 200-square-foot room were a wooden desk, a telephone, and an electric typewriter, behind which a secretary—FlightSafety's only full-time, paid employee—typed her boss's letters soliciting business.[13]

Ueltschi had married Eileen Healey in 1944. By the time he founded the company seven years later, they had four children. To support his family, Ueltschi kept his job at Pan Am. In fact, he continued working full time as Juan Trippe's pilot for 17 years—until 1968—after he started FlightSafety. He never asked his boss—nor did Trippe ever offer—to invest in the new company; nevertheless, Pan Am's chief continued to be very supportive of Ueltschi's efforts. "Many of his friends were CEOs of companies that operated airplanes," Ueltschi says of his mentor and former employer, "and he urged them to have their pilots get training at FlightSafety. In many ways, he was FlightSafety's original ambassador to the Fortune 500."[14]

When Al Ueltschi's company began training pilots, all the training was done in the air; there were no flight simulators. In fact, there was a considerable amount of resistance to the idea of training pilots on the ground. Nevertheless, there were some visionaries—including Al Ueltschi—who were convinced that realistic simulator training was an efficient and economical way for pilots to not only maintain proficiency but also to make transitions from one type of aircraft to another. Moreover, as Ueltschi has pointed out, "If you can fly a simulator, you can fly a plane, but the opposite isn't necessarily true. The simulator can safely put you in 'dangerous' combinations of situations that are unlikely—but not impossible—to come up during a real flight, so you can be prepared for them." And, as the National Business Aircraft Association (NBAA) put it, "With missionary zeal, Ueltschi set about convincing a skeptical industry that he and FlightSafety could fulfill most of aviation's flight proficiency training needs with technologically advanced simulators and professional instructors using carefully planned curricula."[15]

Simultaneously, Ueltschi created a brand new company and a brand new industry. FlightSafety used whatever little ground training equipment was available almost as soon as it opened its doors, but only got the opportunity to contract for its first modern simulator in 1954. However, the simulator, which had been built by Ed Link, from whom FlightSafety had earlier bought used Link Trainers, was $150,000, a good deal more money than the fledgling company had, and a good deal more than any bank was willing to lend. Fortunately, as Ueltschi recounts the story, "Some of our best customers not only agreed with the value of simulator training but also backed their convictions with hard cash. A nucleus of flight departments, including those at Eastman Kodak, National Dairies, Coca-Cola, Gulf Oil, and Olin Mathieson, agreed to advance us a total of nearly $70,000 to guarantee training for their pilots within five years of simulator delivery.

With those checks in hand, we got our simulator. And with that acquisition, it looked like we were going to succeed."[16]

However, not until the mid-1960s, when turbine-powered aircraft started being built, did FlightSafety's future begin to look secure. One important factor was the result of a deal Ueltschi's boss made with Marcel Dassault, who was responsible for building France's Mystère jet. Trippe and Dassault had agreed that Pan Am would start a new division—Pan Am Business Jets—to handle North American marketing for the Mystère, which Trippe named the Falcon Jet. And, as Ueltschi tells the story, "Shortly thereafter, I persuaded Mr. Trippe to include pilot and maintenance-technician training at FlightSafety as a part of the purchase price of every new Falcon, which established FlightSafety's simulator training as an integral part of modern business aircraft operation. FlightSafety training became the standard."[17]

This development was a critical step in building the FlightSafety International (FSI) name, reputation, recognition, exposure to the customer, and loyalty. Including FlightSafety training in the purchase price would become its durable competitive advantage.

But there were other factors as well. "When JetStars, Sabreliners, Gulfstreams, and Learjets started coming on the scene," Ueltschi explains, "the whole tenor of business aviation changed. These were not military hand-me-downs. These were sophisticated, high-altitude, high-speed machines with price tags to match." Although enthusiasm for these jets was far from universal, no one could deny that they were the wave of the future. When a series of accidents made it painfully clear that these aircraft were substantially different from their predecessors, "pilots, owners and insurers all arrived at the same conclusion: the best place to learn about such things and to master this new breed of business aircraft was inside a simulator. It was then that business at FlightSafety took off."[18]

By 1968, at the age of 50, Ueltschi had taken FlightSafety public and felt that the time had come for him to retire from Pan Am. "Leaving Pan Am was probably both the hardest and the most exciting moment of my career," he says. "I loved that airline and my job, and I thought the world of Juan Trippe. Still, the prospect of leading my own company, full time, thrilled me. And so the day finally arrived. After returning from a flight, I proudly carried Mr. Trippe's luggage from the airplane, shook his hand, and thanked him from the bottom of my heart for the wonderful career he'd given me. Then I crossed the ramp, climbed the stairs, and became the full-time CEO of FlightSafety. It was only then, 17 years after I started the company, that I began collecting a paycheck from FlightSafety. I had to. I had just quit my regular job."[19]

Collecting a paycheck from FlightSafety was never a problem. As the years passed, with something close to a monopoly on aviation training, FlightSafety thrived, and Al Ueltschi amassed a personal fortune of over $500 million. He became a member of the *Forbes Richest 400* in 1983. But, in 1996, as he approached his eightieth birthday—a widower now, with four grown children and 12 grandchildren—he began to worry about what would happen, after he was gone, to the company he'd spent so many years building. He had received offers from several large companies over the years, but he was opposed to having the ownership of the company broken up, and was determined to keep that from happening.

Ueltschi had a general disdain for Wall Street, green-mailers, leverage buyout artists, and corporate raiders. "Fortunately," as he tells the story, "my good luck held once again. Warren Buffett called. Although Warren had been sending his pilots to us for training, he and I had never met, so the contact came as a surprise. He wanted to know if I'd be interested in discussing FlightSafety's future. I was."[20]

Buffett's call was the result of a suggestion made by a FlightSafety and Berkshire stockholder. Richard Sercer, an aviation consultant based in Tucson, Arizona, had been persuaded by his wife, Alma Murphy (a Berkshire shareholder and a Harvard-trained ophthalmologist), to purchase some Berkshire stock. And as Buffett subsequently told his stockholders, "Fortunately, Richard had also been a long-time shareholder of FlightSafety, and it occurred to him that the two companies would make a good fit. He knew our acquisition criteria, and he thought that Al Ueltschi might want to make a deal that would both give him a home for his company and a security in payment that he would feel comfortable owning throughout his lifetime. So Richard wrote Bob Denham, CEO of Salomon Inc., suggesting that he explore the possibility of a merger. Bob took it from there."[21]

All of this took place despite Buffett's alleged aversion to high-tech companies. In fact, if Buffett has seemed to avoid such companies, it is less because of their use of technology than it is because of the uncertainty of the future of such organizations. Buffett had no such concern about FlightSafety, and he and Ueltschi met in New York City in September.

They had a lot in common: spartan corporate offices, well-known frugal and self-made natures, concern for the shareholder, disdain for short-term analysts, long-term membership on the Forbes 400 Richest list, and part-ners named "Charlie." Warren's partner is Berkshire Vice Chairman Charles Munger. Al's "Charlie" is a golden retriever that beds down be-tween the pilot's and the co-pilot's seats, below the throttles, when Al flies his own jet. Charlie even sleeps with him.

"We got to know each other over a couple of hamburgers and Cherry Cokes," Ueltschi says, "and I liked what I saw and heard. Warren said he'd like FlightSafety to be a part of Berkshire Hathaway, but he wanted it to remain an independent subsidiary, to continue on its same course of busi-ness, and to be run by the same people as before. At the end of the meal—the best burger I'd eaten since selling Little Hawk—we shook hands on the deal, and by the end of December, 1996, it was done. FlightSafety be-came a wholly owned subsidiary of Berkshire Hathaway."[22]

Buffett had offered Ueltschi $1.5 billion for the company, and Flight-Safety stockholders were given a choice of taking either $50 in cash for each FlightSafety share or $48 a share of Berkshire's Class A or Class B common shares. Ueltschi, who, along with his family, owned 37 percent of the stock, chose Berkshire stock in a tax-free exchange, noting, "I per-sonally consider Berkshire shares to be one of the finest investments that I could make and anticipate holding the shares indefinitely."[23] By the time the merger was complete, 49 percent of FlightSafety's stockholders had also taken stock; the remainder took cash. And Ueltschi reported, "I could not be more pleased."[24]

Warren Buffett was equally pleased. At the time, all he said was: "FlightSafety is a business that I like, run by a man I like and admire."[25] But as he later explained, "He [Al] understood what I was about. I under-stood what FlightSafety was all about, and I could tell that he loved his business. The first question I always ask myself about somebody in his po-sition is: Do they love the money or do they love the business? But with Al, the money is totally secondary. He loves the business and that's what I need, because the day after I buy a company, if they love the money, they're gone. If they love the business, they are there to run the company, just like before."[26]

FlightSafety has flourished as part of the Berkshire Hathaway family. At the time of the merger, the company had annual revenue of approximately $365 million. Four years later, that figure had grown to an estimated $645 million in sales. As a result, the company has already provided Berkshire Hathaway with estimated accumulated pretax profits of $700 million—half of the $1.5 billion it paid for FlightSafety. Moreover, the company now has an estimated value at 20 times earnings, or $3 billion—twice the original purchase price. The pretax profits, combined with the substantial increase in value, represent a 25 percent annual internal rate of return and provide a specific measurable example of why Buffett prefers buying the whole company instead of part of a publicly traded one.

These increases are partially the cause and partially a result of an expansion of the company's operations. In 1996, FlightSafety had 2,500 employees managing 175 simulators in 41 training centers in the United States, Canada, and Europe. Today, it has 4,000 employees managing more than 200 simulators in 44 locations. It now trains about 60,000 pilots every year and has estimated annual revenues over $600 million, the vast majority of which comes from training corporate and regional airline pilots. In fact, almost every new business airplane sold in the United States and Europe includes a FlightSafety pilot and technician training program as part of the sale.[27]

The company also provides pilot training for the government and the military, including the FAA, the DEA, Coast Guard Search and Rescue, Air Force pilots, and Army liaisons. They also train the pilots who fly the Gulfstreams assigned to the White House.[28] As a result, FlightSafety is the largest nonairline nongovernment aviation training company in the world, and the world's second-largest maker of flight simulators.[29] It is significantly larger than its nearest competitor.

In 1997, FlightSafety entered into a long-term partnership with Boeing, the world's largest manufacturer of airplanes, to operate FlightSafety Boeing training centers. Independently owned and operated, this joint venture is devoted to aircraft of 100-seat-capacity (or more) Boeing, Airbus, and Fokker models. Twenty training centers are checkered throughout the world, with locations in England (London and Manchester), China, Brazil, South Africa, France (Paris), Spain, Mexico, and South Korea. An additional 600 employees staff these centers and offer 65 full-flight simulators. The newly opened $100 million Miami center will soon train 7,000 pilots and 3,000 maintenance technicians annually.[30]

Although Ueltschi recognizes that this gives the company a distinct competitive advantage, he insists, "We have a lot of competition. Many airlines compete with us, selling their excess capacity. There are also other companies getting into the business. All I can say is that we're going to do our best. We want to be the leader in this business. Every day, that can change, but we do our best—that's our mission." Even so, he adds, "We can only do so much. There's a big demand for pilot training out there right now, and I'm not saying our mission is to take everything away. My Daddy used to say, 'If you win all the marbles, no one will be able to play with you.'"

Possibly initiated by the acquisition of FSI by Berkshire Hathaway, other major simulator manufacturers, notably CAE and GE, have entered the aviation training business. There is not likely to be a great deal of competition coming from new-training companies. Not only would starting such a company be extremely expensive—one flight simulator can cost as much as $19 million—but Ueltschi also believes: "It would take more than money. It would take an organization to be able to do the thing." Even so, according to AVweb, an aviation data consulting firm, Ueltschi's company is not alone in the field. "Until about ten years ago," they said in 1998, "FlightSafety was pretty much the only game in town for professional-caliber simulator-based recurrent training for piston-powered aircraft. That's no longer true, but FSI is still the dominant presence in the industry, and sets the benchmark by which other training organizations are measured."[31]

FlightSafety is considered the benchmark because of its extraordinary record. For example, Executive Jet, which is FlightSafety's biggest customer (and, coincidentally, another Berkshire Hathaway company) has never had a fatal accident. More than any other and more than required by law, Executive Jet pilots train 22 days a year exclusively with FlightSafety.

Of course, being measured against that benchmark can't be easy for any company. Al Ueltschi and the people at FlightSafety sincerely believe in what they do. "The best safety device on any aircraft," Ueltschi says, "is a well-trained pilot. That's our motto and I believe it. When jets were first put into service, there were no simulators and all training was done in the aircraft. There were more accidents in the training flights than there were in passenger flights because pilots didn't have the opportunity to practice in the simulator. And today's airplanes are so complicated that there's no way to practice normal or emergency procedures in the actual aircraft. It doesn't make sense to train in aircraft when you can train under controlled conditions in a simulator."

In fact, Ueltschi and the people at FlightSafety don't only talk about the importance of training—they're also willing to back their training up. "FlightSafety trains pilots flying for over 2,500 corporate aviation departments," Ueltschi says. "They train twice a year. We stand behind our service by providing accident insurance—$100,000 worth—to pilots who've earned a current Certificate of Professional Pilot Proficiency as Pilot in Command and/or who have successfully completed FlightSafety's training program as a Co-Pilot. FlightSafety pays the premiums, and the pilots name their beneficiaries."

Paying insurance premiums for those who have completed Flight-Safety's program is something that the company did long before it became a part of Berkshire Hathaway. Little else has changed since the merger. "I'm still president," Ueltschi says, "and my responsibilities are the same. The only difference is that everything is better. Before we became part of Berkshire, when we were on the New York Stock Exchange, I was constantly questioned about how much money we were going to make the next quarter and why we didn't make more the last quarter. Now we run the company for the long term without worrying about the next quarter. That's one of the best things about working with Warren."

When asked what he considers *the* best thing about working with Warren Buffett, Ueltschi immediately cites his leadership abilities. "Leadership is really what being a good manager is about," he says. "And the letters of the word represent the qualities that a good manager should have. **L** is for loyalty and **E** is for enthusiasm. **A** stands for attitude, and **D** is for discipline. **E** stands for example—you have to set a good example—and **R** is for respect. **S** represents scholarliness, and **H** is for honesty. And **I** and **P** stand for integrity and pride. The thing I like the best about Warren Buffett is that he possesses all these qualities."

Not surprisingly, he has no regrets about agreeing to the merger with Berkshire Hathaway. "It's the best thing I could have done," he says. But even though the deal made him one of Berkshire's largest shareholders, he neither expects nor gets any special treatment. "I don't think it makes any difference," he says. "I have to sit in the bleachers at the annual meeting like everybody else." Even so, he admits to caring about how Buffett views him. "I try to make him proud," he says, "and I try to make every shareholder proud. I feel very obligated to try to do that. I don't want to run a company that you read bad things about in the newspaper."

Ueltschi obviously admires and respects Buffett, but the people who influenced him the most are his parents. "My mother and father were my biggest influences," he says. "They probably did more for me than anybody. We didn't have much money on that farm down in Kentucky, but we were rich in a lot of other ways." When asked if his parents would be proud of his success, he says, "I don't really consider my success. I never think of that." In fact, although he has been a pilot, air showman, restaurateur, corporate pilot, trainer, entrepreneur, medical philanthropist, and billionaire, he describes himself as "just a lucky person, born at the right place and the right time."

"The secret to making money," he says, "is controlling costs and being productive. It's not very complicated."[32]

"You have to figure out how you're going to make more in revenues than expenses. That's the biggest thing to do." Perhaps not surprisingly, he considers discipline to be an important factor in one's success. "Running a business is like being a pilot," he explains. "You can get yourself killed if you're not careful."[33]

Ueltschi is very optimistic about the future of the aviation training industry and FlightSafety's position. "People are traveling more," he says, "and they're going to continue to travel more. The industry has unlimited opportunity, and not only in America. There's a shortage of pilots around the world today—a greater shortage than before. A lot of pilots can only fly until they're 60, and in some countries they have to retire at 55. As these people retire, there are new ones coming on. And with all these new airplanes, there's a big demand. We're expanding all the time, but we can't do it all."

"In fact," Ueltschi says, "the next 50 years of aviation may be even more dramatic than the past 50. It seems that, every day, another border is erased, another curtain is lifted, and another closed society is opened. The movement of people and goods around the globe is expanding at amazing speed. And although there's no telling where all this will lead, I know how it will get there—on airplanes."[34]

"So we're going to continue training pilots and technicians," he says. "Our objective is to make aviation safer all the time, and we want to continue to develop and improve new procedures. The most important thing any human being has is a life, and in order for the industry to grow we must do everything possible to prevent people from getting killed. Going to a funeral is a sad thing. If you can help prevent accidents in aircraft, that's a good feeling."

One of the ways FlightSafety aims to accomplish this goal is by reaching out to students. "They are the ones who will take over air transportation in the years ahead," Ueltschi says, "and FlightSafety is working with academic institutions to help educate and mold the first generation of aviation's second century. We have already signed an agreement with Embry-Riddle Aeronautical University in Florida to provide on-campus simulator training for its students, and I'm confident that we'll expand the program to include other schools and even more training in the years ahead. FlightSafety will be a part of aviation's future."[35]

As for the future of Berkshire Hathaway, Ueltschi hasn't given it much thought. When asked if there will ever be another Warren Buffett, he says, "No, but there will never be another George Washington or Abraham Lincoln, either." He also says, "There are other people around who are smart. Everyone is replaceable somewhere along the line." Nevertheless, he believes that Buffett has "a pretty good master plan. He's smart—he's got ideas of who's going to do what. He wants to know who is going to take my place if I should get hit by a streetcar, so I'm sure he has a plan for who will replace him if he should not be around."

He believes that, with or without Buffett, Berkshire Hathaway will continue to be a good investment, and he is unconcerned about what will happen after Buffett is gone. "I don't see what the big concern is. If he dies, what the heck's going to happen? Do they think everyone else is going to die too? Warren doesn't tell me how to run FlightSafety, and he doesn't tell any of the other operating managers how to run their companies either. Once Warren's gone, sooner or later, you'll have to have someone in there, but in the meantime these companies all know how to operate."

As for his own future, Ueltschi has no immediate plans for retirement. He has, nevertheless, chosen a successor—Executive Vice President Bruce Whitman—who has worked with Ueltschi for almost four decades. Right now, he says, "I'm doing what I like to do. This isn't work for me—it's play. Warren and I have a deal. He said he'll never split the Berkshire stock. The only thing he'll do is, when I'm 100, he'll split my age and I'll be 50."

In the meantime, according to Buffett, "Al deserves a book of his own. At 84, he has not lost an ounce of intensity or energy."[36] At the same time, while Ueltschi thoroughly enjoys running the company, and the financial rewards, he is aware that there are many other things in life. "I can tell you," he says, "honest to God, that money has never been that important to me. It really hasn't. I never did this to get rich." In fact, in the late 1970s, two decades before he became a Berkshire billionaire, Ueltschi told a reporter from his native Kentucky's the *State Journal,* "Money is the reward you get that can be measured. But there are bigger things than that. You have to have a good feeling that you are doing something that is really contributing, not only to your bank account but to something else as well. I really feel that our business is making a contribution to flight safety. It's really great to do something that's making a contribution and also to be rewarded for it."[37]

One of his other contributions—and one that occupies much of his time today—is his involvement with ORBIS International. "Orbis," he explains, "is a Greek word, a word with two meanings. One meaning is 'eyes,' and the other is 'around the world.'" The nonprofit organization, which he helped found in 1977, operates a flying operating room—a converted DC-10, half of which he personally paid for—that constantly travels around the world in an ongoing effort to reduce the incidence of avoidable blindness in developing countries.

Without excellent vision, Ueltschi could not have become a pilot. Without becoming a pilot, he would not have been able to see the need for ground-based training. He has saved an undetermined amount of lives by developing FlightSafety, and he continues to save lives by bringing vision to those who need it most in developing countries. He has recognized his greatest blessing and, with his aviation connections, has developed a unique way to bring the world the ability to see.

"Forty five million people are blind today," he says, "and this figure will double in the next 20 years if we don't take action now. Nine out of 10 of the world's blind live in developing countries. According to the World Health Organization and ophthalmologists, 80 percent of this blindness could be prevented or cured because the treatments available for the prevention and cure of blindness are among the most low-cost and effective of all health-care work. It's a shame, because if you had a child that was blind and you could do something about it and didn't, you'd be sick."

Ueltschi is particularly proud of ORBIS's achievements. "We've made a tremendous impact on reducing blindness," he says. "Over 23,000 patients have been treated by the volunteer doctors who staff ORBIS's plane. But what's even more important, we have 350 of the best ophthalmologists in the world who donate their time to teach doctors in developing and underdeveloped countries. Since its inception, ORBIS has trained over 50,500 ophthalmologists, nurses, anesthetists, and biomedical engineers—training that over 9 million people suffering from blindness have benefited from."

Given this attitude, it's perhaps not surprising to hear Al Ueltschi argue that "We're all just human beings and we all do the best we can. We can make a difference by helping people. We have the greatest opportunities in the world. Sure, you want to win. We all want to win. We play hard to win. So what if you don't? It's like playing golf," a sport he plays and uses for many of his examples. "Tiger Woods doesn't always win. But that's what life is all about—it's a game. What are you going to do? I don't say, 'When I die,'" concludes the 84-year-old head of FlightSafety, "I say, 'if I die.'"

## AL UELTSCHI'S BUSINESS TENETS

★ Aim to be the leader in your field. Strive to be the benchmark against which your competitors measure their progress.

★ Success in any field can be achieved by staying disciplined.

★ Know that you're contributing back to something else, not just your bank account. Your business should be contributing to the benefit of other people.

# chapter eight

# The Innovator—
# Rich Santulli, Executive Jet

*I*n an affluent New Jersey suburb, a modern office building on main
street accommodates the headquarters of Executive Jet Aviation (EJA)
and the office of NetJets founder and chief executive, Rich Santulli. In
the hallway, rather fittingly, hangs a framed advertising poster of Warren
Buffett. The poster's headline is: "How Did One Of The Most Successful Men In The World Get That Way?"

One of the few CEOs who didn't want to see the interview questions in
advance, Santulli thinks quantitatively and logically. He lives his life without looking back. He is intellectual, entrepreneurial, and a natural born
salesman. This is someone who sizes people up fast and understands Warren Buffett and the Berkshire culture. He is exactly the type of person you
want running a corporate jet company. EJA, the fastest growing subsidiary
of Berkshire Hathaway, has doubled in size (both in revenue and employees) during the past two years.

Amid the stock market's recent irrational exuberance and the deep discount of Berkshire stock when it was trading near $45,000 per "A" share,
Santulli wanted to short some of the Internet stocks and borrow against his
existing stock to purchase more Berkshire. Warren Buffett advised against
it, saying, "You only need to get rich once."

In at least one respect, the CEO of the Woodbridge, New Jersey-based Executive Jet Aviation is an anomaly among Warren Buffett's operating managers. Unlike virtually all of his peers, Rich Santulli doesn't love the
industry he's in. He didn't even fly in an airplane until he was 21 years old.
"I am not in aviation because I love aviation," he says. "As a matter of fact,
when I started, I thought that was a big advantage for me, because so many
people were in aviation because they loved it and didn't care about the

financial side of it. They just wanted to fly airplanes and be pilots. I don't fly an airplane and I don't want to fly an airplane. I just don't care about that. What I do love," he concludes, sounding more like a typical Berkshire Hathaway manager, "is my business, my company, and my people."

Santulli's honesty—perhaps his bluntness—might be credited to his upbringing. The son of a federal government worker, he was born on August 14, 1944, and raised in a working-class neighborhood in Brooklyn, New York. He attended public school through the eighth grade, then a Catholic high school, and, after graduation, went to the Brooklyn Polytechnic Institute. In college, he majored in applied mathematics and graduated with a bachelor's degree in 1966. He continued at BPI, first as a graduate student (he earned two masters' degrees) and then as a member of the math faculty while he worked toward a PhD. Even though, as he says, "I loved teaching," the birth of his son in 1967—and the concomitant responsibilities of a family—forced him to leave academia "to get a real job."

He went to work for Shell Oil and ultimately became manager of an operations research group. "It was a good learning experience," he says. "And I probably would still be there if they hadn't announced that they were moving to Houston. I had no interest in moving. I was born in Brooklyn. My whole family lived in Brooklyn. I wasn't moving. That's when I said, 'I'd better go look for a job.'" Fortunately, he was quickly offered a job by Dr. Leslie Peck at Goldman, Sachs & Co. Peck was in the process of setting up a new group whose purpose was to start applying computer-based modeling to investment banking. Goldman Sachs was one of the first Wall Street firms to do so. At the time, though, Santulli says, "I had no idea who Goldman Sachs was. Honest to God. Didn't have a clue."

He took over the group after Dr. Peck left because of health problems, but, in 1972, he was invited by the manager of the firm's leasing operation to work in the lease financing department. "I said, 'No,'" Santulli recalls, "and when he asked 'Why?' I said, 'It's because I love using what I've learned, I love doing analysis. I'm one of the few guys in the world who can say he is really applying what he learned in college in the business world.'" At that point, his own manager said, "You know what, why don't you go up there for six months. Your group will still exist. If you don't like it, you can come back."

"So I said, 'Okay,'" Santulli remembers, "and I went up and I loved it." He ultimately not only became head of the department but also set up and became president of Goldman Sachs Leasing Corporation—at that time, the biggest leasing operation department on Wall Street.

"We were very successful," he says, "and profitable." Even so, in 1979, he tendered his resignation. "The next year was my partner year," he remembers, "and I certainly would have been a partner. And that's exactly the reason that I left. I loved the company, and I knew that if I became a partner at Goldman, it would be basically a commitment for life. And at that point in my life, I wasn't prepared for a lifelong commitment. Actually, from an ego point of view, even though I'd been so successful, I wanted to see if I could do it without Goldman's name. And the only way to find that out was to start my own business. And that is what I did."

Santulli, using his initials, started RTS Capital Services, Inc., in February 1980. The firm specialized in the same thing he had done at Goldman Sachs: leasing. In this case, it was helicopters. "I knew helicopters," he says, "and that was the good news. The better news was that I wasn't going to have any competition from the major money center or investment banks. They weren't going to bother with helicopters because they were one-, two-million-dollar deals, and too small for either. So the only competitors I had were regional banks, and they had no expertise at all in something as complicated as lease financing." Santulli's expertise paid off. By 1985, RTS Capital Services was the biggest helicopter lessor in the world.

Santulli had bought Executive Jet Aviation in September 1984, although, only a few months earlier, he'd had no intention of doing so. "I was skiing in Vail, sometime in 1983," he remembers. "Three friends and myself. And the day before we were leaving, one of my clients called and said, 'By the way, Rich, I am flying back'—he had a couple of airplanes—'Do you want a ride back to New York?' I said, 'Sure,' and the four of us took his Lear Jet. You have to understand," Santulli explains, "this was a guy trip, and it was a Sunday, and we had ratty clothes on, hadn't shaved, just didn't care. And after a couple of hours, we started to slow down, and the client says we have to stop for fuel. I didn't understand, because it was a Lear 35, and we should have been able to get to New York without stopping. I mean, why were we stopping for fuel?

"It ends up that we stop in Columbus, Ohio, and as we're landing he said, 'Rich, if you have a minute, I would like for you to stop and talk to these people at Executive Jet. I am thinking of buying the company and I would want you to finance it for me.'

"I said, 'What?' and he said, 'We have to stop for fuel anyway, I figured we would stop there.' So we got off the airplane, and a guy comes out and says, 'Hi, I am General Paul Tibbets.' And he's dressed in a suit and tie. I said, 'Holy shit! What is going on?' And the client says, 'Oh, don't worry about it.' So we walk into the boardroom and there are eight gentlemen there dressed in suits and ties, thinking that I am coming in to talk to them about buying the company. I had no idea. So I stood up, apologized, and told them exactly what had happened. I told them that I'd been snookered into this, and that I was terribly sorry that their time had been wasted. I told them the truth. I didn't want to bullshit them. I told them that I had no interest, that I didn't even know who they were. I got back on the plane and we left. But I was really pissed." Six months later, Santulli was contacted by a banker, calling on behalf of General Tibbets, who was now interested in the possibility of Santulli's buying Executive Jet. "And because I felt so badly about what had happened the last time," he remembers, "I said, 'Certainly. My pleasure.'"

Executive Jet Aviation, a pioneer in private jet charter business, had been founded in 1964 by a group of retired U.S. Air Force generals specializing in new military style and hard-to-fly Lear jets. The company's board included early business aviation enthusiasts like actor James Stewart and entertainer Arthur Godfrey. Its president was Paul W. Tibbets, Jr., the pilot who dropped one of the atomic bombs that ended World War II.[1] It was a typical aviation company built by pilots so they could continue their love affair with flying. But the company was losing money, and although Santulli decided to buy it in 1984, he was hard pressed to find a way to get it going again—until he came up with an idea. Initially, Santulli thought EJA would be a place to put planes coming off lease programs. "Now that I owned an airplane company," he remembers, "I was going to buy an airplane and have Executive Jet manage it for me. But when I looked at the numbers, taking into account how many hours I'd actually be flying, the numbers made no sense at all." The numbers told him that if he expected to fly less than 50 hours a year, it would make more sense to charter a plane when he needed one. It also became clear that buying and maintaining his own plane would be a waste of money unless he expected to fly at least 400 hours a year.

"So I got a bunch of my friends together and said, 'Okay, if we can divide the cost by four, that would be a hell of a deal!' So three friends and I had a meeting and we all agreed that this was a great deal and we would do it. Then, when we sat down, one of my friends said, 'Well, I need the airplane every Tuesday and Thursday.' And I said, 'Wait a minute. I need the airplane when I need the airplane.' And we quickly realized that four people sharing an airplane can't work. It was just impossible. It would be like four families sharing a one-bedroom summer house. So I left the meeting and said to myself, 'If there could be a way that we could take the economics of time-sharing or multiple ownership, but guarantee that when you wanted your airplane you could get it, this could be a home run.'"

Fortunately, because Executive Jet was run by military people who had maintained records of every trip they'd ever flown, Santulli had a database from which he could analyze flying patterns. After studying the records for four different years, he realized that there was a high degree of predictability in terms of geographic origin, destination (most flights are east of the Mississippi), time of day, days of the week, length of stay, seasonal use, and mechanical breakdowns. Even using his college mathematics, it took him close to half a year to work out the numbers and find a way to reconcile fractional ownership and guaranteed access.[2] When he did, in 1986, he founded the NetJets program.

The basic concept was fairly simple. For every 20 planes sold, NetJets would keep 5¼ extra planes in its corporate fleet to service all the owners. This structure would permit a 98 percent availability and profitability, and charters would cover the other 2 percent. Unlike a real estate time-share, each individual owner can demand the plane at any time, even if another owner wants it at the same time in a different part of the country. Given four hours' notice, the pickup was guaranteed. The only difference was that an owner couldn't take a friend to the airport hangar and say, "There's my jet."

An individual or a company would purchase a part interest in a particular airplane, and would pay a monthly fee that would cover maintenance, fuel, pilots, training, and catering. Buyers would also pay a certain amount for every hour they were in the air. Although Santulli knew that this was not an inexpensive proposition, he also knew that the arrangement could enable an individual to enjoy all the benefits of owning an airplane without any of the headaches involved in maintaining one. Even so, he knew that—as with all new ideas—getting started would be difficult.

"Here I was," he remembers, "starting a concept that no one believed could work, and I realized that unless we were absolutely perfect for the first 10, 15, or 20 customers, the whole deal was going to blow. I knew that when I sat down and talked with someone about buying a quarter of an airplane, they would look at me strangely and say, 'Wait a minute. I'm only going to pay for a quarter of the airplane, and I can have it anytime I want it? What happens if all of the people ask for the airplane at the same time?' And I knew I would have to be able to say, 'That is my problem. I will pick you up.' Of course," Santulli says, "I knew that most people wouldn't believe me. So, at the beginning, I would say that if you don't think it works within six months, I will give you 100 percent of your money back."

To keep that promise, and to avoid having to refund anyone's money, he hired dozens of pilots, dispatchers, and other employees, and laid out $4 million as a down payment on eight Cessnas. "But I didn't sell any of those eight," he says. "I figured I'd be able to sell an additional 25 airplanes. So I would have a fleet of 33, and I'd have more than enough back-up airplanes to satisfy any demand. Then, on days like the Sunday after Thanksgiving (NetJets' busiest day of the year), if I didn't have enough airplanes, I could go out and charter them. So that is what I did. When I looked at the numbers, I found out that it worked. The mathematics don't lie." Even so, it took some time to get the company off the ground—so to speak. "It was slow," Santulli remembers, "we knew it would be slow. But we actually sold four airplanes in the first year. In '86, '87, and '88, we sold about four airplanes a year, which is basically what I thought we would sell.

"We did well until the recession of 1989," he recalls. "Then we got murdered. From 1989 through the beginning of 1990, we didn't sell an eighth of a share. We lost a fortune, and it was all my money. I lost $35–$40 million, and, to me, that was it. I had personally guaranteed all of the debt, and we lost so much money because I kept buying airplanes. And I did that because when someone came and said they wanted to buy an eighth of an airplane, I didn't say, 'Wait a minute, I have to find seven other guys.' I had the airplane, so I'd let them start flying right away. I had to hire the pilots and the crew, so the costs were prohibitive, and since I wasn't selling anything, it was very expensive." But there was an upside to the recession as well. "During that period," Santulli says, "a lot of companies sold their airplanes to raise capital, or just to take the cost off the balance sheet. Some may have kept one or two airplanes, but some went down to zero and came to me as the alternative. I became the financial alternative that made sense. The whole mind-set changed, and we became the Chief Financial Officer's best friend."

In 1993, Executive Jet made a deal with British Aerospace to buy 25 Hawker 1000s (paying $300 million or $12 million each). It was the biggest deal ever done in general aviation at that time. "It gave us a mid-size cabin," Santulli says, "a coast-to-coast airplane, so we were now on a different level. It was a very important deal for us because now a lot of people wanted midsize. The plane we'd been using, the Citation S-2, was a three-hour airplane that could go 1,600 miles. But a lot of flight departments, or people who were accustomed to midsize airplanes, didn't want to get into the Citation because it was a small airplane. So we did the Hawker deal. We negotiated a hell of a deal with them, and I passed it along to my customers. And we went from triple-A ball to the major leagues. It really changed everyone's thinking about who we were. We had lasted through the bad times; we'd made it through. And we were going to be here forever, so people started to take notice and say to themselves, 'These guys aren't going away.'"

And they did not go away. In fact, they kept growing, increasing the size of their fleet as well as their client base. Much of the latter was—and continues to be—the result of owner referrals. Approximately 70 percent of the new clients come through referrals from existing clients. Of the 2,000 owner/clients, most are entrepreneurs, consultants, technology executives, and design teams, and many work in the financial community. Not all of these new clients are corporations. Soon-to-be or retired CEOs who are used to the luxury and convenience of corporate jet travel become share owners. Many media celebrities, including David Letterman, Arnold Schwarzenegger, Kathy Lee Gifford, and Sylvester Stallone, find it convenient to purchase parts of NetJets' airplanes. As might be expected, given their travel schedules, many professional athletes and golfers—Ben Crenshaw, Curtis Strange, Ernie Els, and Davis Love III also take part in the program.[3] Most of NetJets' target audience probably belong to a country club somewhere, so there couldn't be a better group of spokespersons to appeal to the corporate CEO. While other corporations spend millions for celebrity endorsements, NetJets has the world's best spokesmen as customers and owners: Pete Sampras, Tiger Woods, and Warren Buffett.

Among the advocates who explain the appeal of the NetJets program, Boston businessman David Mugar has perhaps been the most eloquent. A NetJets owner since 1989, the now-retired owner of WHDH in Boston says he flies about 100 hours a year and uses the plane as much for recreation as for business. "The most luxurious way to fly is all by yourself," he says. "This is as close to Air Force One as I'll ever get."[4]

Despite Mugar's eloquence, it's certain that one of the most important of the company's clients was Warren Buffett, a longtime opponent of private executive jet travel. "I first heard about the NetJets program," Buffett told his shareholders in 1998, "about four years ago from Frank Rooney, our manager at H.H. Brown. Frank had used and been delighted with the service and suggested that I meet Rich to investigate signing up for my family's use. It took Rich about 15 minutes to sell me a quarter (200 hours annually) of a Hawker 1000. Since then, my family has learned firsthand—through flying 900 hours on 300 trips—what a friendly, efficient, and safe operation EJA runs. Quite simply, they love this service. In fact, they quickly grew so enthusiastic that I did a testimonial ad for EJA long before I knew there was any possibility of our purchasing the business. I did, however, ask Rich to give me a call if he ever got interested in selling."[5]

Santulli had actually sold 25 percent of the business to Goldman Sachs in 1995, to provide capital for expansion. When Buffett heard about it, he asked why Santulli hadn't called him. "I was embarrassed," Santulli said, to which Buffett answered, "Well, listen, if ever you are going to do anything, if Goldman wants out, please call me." By 1998, the company had annual revenues estimated at close to $1 billion and, as Santulli tells the story, "Goldman kept telling me, 'Let's go public, let's go public.' I kept saying, 'No.' And finally I said, 'You know what? I will sell it to one person—Warren.'" As he later explained to the *Columbus Dispatch,* referring to the prospect of going public, "I didn't want a 28-year-old analyst telling me how to run my business. Warren Buffett is a long-term player. He's not worried about the next three months or six months."[6]

Closing the sale took less than three weeks. Executive Jet's shareholders got about half of the $725 million selling price in cash and the other half in Berkshire Hathaway stock. According to SEC documents, Santulli, the majority shareholder, received more than half of the proceeds, including cash and $250 million or 3,437 shares of Class A Berkshire stock. Both Santulli and Buffett were very pleased with the arrangement. It was a perfect business marriage because Buffett understands the stock market as fractional ownership of a business and NetJets as an extension of that concept. Because part of the deal was that he would remain at the helm, Santulli was able to tell *Forbes,* "I still think of it as my company." But Buffett was even more enthusiastic. Comparing Santulli to Fred Smith at Federal Express, he said, "Smith created a whole new business. FedEx started small and is now huge. Same thing will happen with Executive Jet."[7] He subsequently told the *Columbus Dispatch:* "Rich is a managerial artist. He could see what would be on this mural when no one else did. He's just started painting it. My job is to bring him some paint and a few brushes."[8]

That "paint" and those "brushes" have enabled Santulli's company to flourish in the years since the merger. Berkshire Hathaway's AAA credit rating has cut Executive Jet's borrowing cost substantially, which in turn has enabled the company to expand beyond the borders of the United States to open operations in Europe and the Middle East. Plans call for expansion into South America and Asia, so the service will soon be worldwide. The merger also enabled Santulli to spend $2 billion in 1999 to purchase 100 Hawker Horizon business jets from Raytheon Aircraft. It was the largest aircraft order in business-aviation history.[9] In fact, the extent to which the company has grown is staggering. At the time of the merger, the company had 900 employees in Columbus and a dozen in its corporate offices in New Jersey.[10] In 2000, it had close to 2,000 employees. In 1998, it had 1,000 clients, 132 aircraft, and flew to 88 countries. Now it has approximately 1,800 clients, 240 aircraft, and flies to 92 countries. NetJets would rank as the eighth largest domestic airline, based on an average of over 250 domestic and international flights per day.[11] By more than doubling its airplanes to 542 by 2006, EJA will be a major player in worldwide transportation.

Most telling, though, is that its revenues grew from $100 million five years ago to $900 million in 1998 and are now nearly $2 billion, making Executive Jet the fastest-growing company in the Berkshire Hathaway family. The total market that Santulli created has grown into a $10 billion industry and, according to Honeywell Industries, the fractional jet business will triple in size in the next three years.[12]

It's easy to see why EJA has been Berkshire's best investment ever, if you consider what is happening today and what will happen in the future. Sales have doubled in two years from approximately $1 billion to $2 billion. EJA's addition of 50 to 60 new aircraft every year will represent exponential growth in the initial roll-out years. Of the 12,000 corporate jets currently in use, approximately 400, or just 3 percent, have shared ownership. Eighty-five percent of all business planes are located in the United States, which will open a vast opportunity worldwide. The overall number of business planes is expected to double in the next decade. The originator—NetJets—dominates 65 percent of the fractional business. And the business has an enormous moat: all the money in the world couldn't buy you a new jet because of the backlog of orders. All new and future aircraft have already been prepurchased, predominantly by EJA. On top of that, try getting a pilot who has the average EJA experience of 6,000 hours. At its current pace, and given its worldwide market potential, EJA may grow similar to FedEx, which has a current market cap of $20 billion.

All this has occurred in spite of a tremendous increase in competition from new companies in the field. Prior to the mid-1990s, Executive Jet wasn't just the most successful aircraft fractional company; it was the *only* one. The company had virtually no competitors until 1995, when Bombardier Inc., a Montreal-based jet manufacturer, joined AMR Combs Inc., the charter affiliate of American Airlines Inc., to found the Dallas-based Business Jet Solutions. Although Santulli calls the company's Flexjet program a "high-quality competitor," he also notes that Executive Jet is two-and-a-half times larger.

The only other serious competitor to the NetJets program, among the more than 50 aircraft fractional companies that have opened their doors in the past five years, is Raytheon Travel Air, started in 1997 by one of NetJets' suppliers, Wichita-based Raytheon Aircraft. But Santulli appears to be no more concerned about Raytheon than he is about Flexjet. "It confirms the validity of our product," he told *Business Week* at the time.[13] Of course, he could afford to be magnanimous about the new kid on the block. Between 1988 and 1997, Executive Jet had expanded from 1.6 customer-owned aircraft to 132. And, during 1997, it placed orders for 129 aircraft, or 31 percent of all corporate jets ordered that year. According to Santulli, Executive Jet, with a total of $8 billion worth of aircraft now on order, is the single largest nonmilitary customer of four of the five leading corporate jet manufacturers. Besides having the deepest pockets, it has a second-to-none referral network of Goldman Sachs partners and clients, Berkshire shareholders, and Warren Buffett as its nonpaid spokesperson.

The three largest companies in the field offer fractions of aircraft at competitive prices, but NetJets continues to have several advantages. Perhaps the most important of these, besides safety, are size and support. As Warren Buffett told his shareholders when he bought Executive Jet, "Our customers gain because we have an armada of planes positioned throughout the country at all times, a blanketing that allows us to provide unmatched service."[14] In fact, because all NetJets owners can interchange and fly in the NetJets programs in the United States, Europe, and the Middle East, clients are provided with an enormous range of possibilities. Company statistics show that they take advantage of these possibilities. Nearly 40 percent of its U.S. clients fly in the NetJets Europe program, and 100 percent of the European NetJet owners make use of the U.S. program.[15] Some owners have purchased a $\frac{1}{16}$ (50-hour) share just to conveniently fly their families to, and then around, Europe for a little more than the cost of first-class travel on the Concorde. With a tax-advantageous five-year accelerated depreciation schedule and business expense deductibility available to its owners, NetJets is offering private jet transportation that is within reach of many individuals and corporations estimated at 150,000 to 200,000 potential customers.

Another advantage is that the NetJets program has a wider array of planes—and prices—for customers to choose from. The smallest share of a NetJets plane, for example, is $\frac{1}{16}$ of a Citation V Ultra, which allows buyers 50 hours' annual flying time and requires a one-time payment of about $400,000. (Note that at the end of a five-year ownership, as much as 80 percent of the $\frac{1}{16}$ investment may be returned, depending on the fair market value of the airplane. Or, an owner may choose to renew the contract without an additional capital requirement.) Monthly management fees for the Citation are an additional $5,000, and the hourly fee is about $1,300. At the other end of the spectrum, NetJets offers clients up to half of a Boeing Business Jet, which allows buyers 400 hours of flying time annually and requires an initial outlay of about $23 million, with monthly management fees of $166,000 and an hourly use fee of $4,300.[16]

Executive Jet can offer this array of aircraft because, unlike its two largest competitors, it is not a subsidiary of an aircraft manufacturer and therefore is not limited to only the aircraft the parent company makes. The NetJets program includes aircraft made by Boeing, Gulfstream, Falcon, Cessna, and Raytheon. "In effect," Buffett told Berkshire shareholders in 1998, "NetJets is like a physician who can recommend whatever medicine best fits the needs of each patient; our competitors, in contrast, are producers of a 'house' brand that they must prescribe for one and all."[17]

Another huge advantage is its $25 million state-of-the-art control center, located at the airport in Columbus, Ohio. Picture a NASA-like nerve center with 200 around-the-clock employees who are, in essence, the flight and travel department for each and every owner. Unlike the commercial airlines, every NetJets flight is unscheduled. Several departments take the initial travel request (sometimes with a four-hour notice); schedule planes, crews, meals, and maintenance by using their proprietary Intellijet software; clear airspace and customs on international flights; file flight plans; monitor current and in-flight weather with nine in-house aviation meteorologists; and arrange ground transportation and travel accommodations.

Santulli's company offers its pilots more training (22 days annually—more than double the period for commercial airline pilots); more gateway cities (27) in which to reside; the flexibility to continue flying after the airlines' mandatory retirement age; totally unscheduled trips to ten times the number of airports; and the possibility of transporting a sole passenger who may be a captain of industry or a world-class athlete.

NetJets business model is one that commercial airlines can only dream about.

Buffett doesn't only speak in glowing terms about Executive Jets' performance; he also praises its management and its potential. "It clearly is a field that's going to explode for the next decade worldwide as well as in the U.S.," he says. "NetJets clearly has the best operations and the best management and has the lead, and frankly in my opinion that lead is going to do nothing but widen over time. It's the kind of business that the leader, if it does its job, . . . just widens" its dominance over competitors. "It has that nature of critical mass. The operation with most planes in the air will be able to deliver the best service over time. So it's going to be a winner. It's going to be a big winner. And we like to hold things forever. That's our ideal holding period, and NetJets fits in perfectly with that formula."[18]

Despite Buffett's enthusiasm, Santulli displays considerable modesty when asked about the company's overall contribution to Berkshire

## Santulli's NetJet Business Model

1. The passenger owns the airplane (or a percentage of it) for five years with costs guaranteed. Clients can claim five-year accelerated depreciation if the airplane is used for business.
2. The passenger prepays (monthly) fixed maintenance costs and all usage fees.
3. No prescheduled unprofitable half-empty flights are flown. The passenger travels exactly when he or she wants to travel.
4. Owners have a greater margin of safety because of higher altitudes, more pilot training, less congested airport alternatives, brand-new jets with the latest avionics, and a personal aviation meteorologist.
5. The planes bypass the hub-and-spoke airline connection system and avoid 450,000 annual flight delays.
6. There are no tickets, ticket agents, travel agents, counter personnel, or seasonal advertising and sales.
7. There are no costly frequent-flyer programs or bumped passengers.
8. Profits come from airplane sales, monthly fees, and usage fees. Revenue is constant and not subject to seasonal changes.
9. The business is recession-proof, with increased demand for more effective use of capital during economic downturns.
10. Worldwide growth is unlimited.
11. The business is not capital-intensive once you capture a critical mass and have the financial backing of one of the world's eight AAA credit-rated companies.
12. The company creates and owns 65 percent of the corporate jet fractional market with only a 3 percent domestic corporate jet market penetration and untapped worldwide opportunities.
13. The passenger has all the benefits of ownership without any of the hassles. Being an owner gives a passenger the whole EJA flight and travel department without the costs.
14. Domestic flying hours can be traded for time on Europe and Middle East NetJets planes.

*(continued)*

15. The owner has a lifetime guarantee that EJA will buy back their share at fair market value at any time.
16. Owners can buy or trade shares on a small-cabin plane for midsize or large-cabin planes (or all three) for less than the cost of a single plane.
17. EJA controls a large portion of the supply chain of new planes and, therefore, puts it in a very competitive position.
18. Warren Buffett is the company's unpaid spokesman. (If it's good enough for the world's most famous value investor, it must be safe enough for you and your family.)
19. The company has nearly 100 percent customer retention.
20. Owners are given free unlimited air-to-ground phone use.
21. Owners receive personal attention from the transportation and travel department.
22. Deserted general-aviation terminals are used instead of crowded airline hubs. There are no lost-luggage or baggage-claim hassles. A rental car or a limo can be waiting for the owner upon arrival.

Hathaway, even though six out of seven of its board members, and several of its operating managers are NetJet customers.

"Berkshire is such a huge company," he says, "and the insurance business is overwhelming. We could never earn as much money as the insurance business. But that's not what Warren is about. If those were the only deals he did, Berkshire wouldn't be Berkshire. He buys the companies that are the market leaders in their industries, he pays good value for them, and the companies grow and produce a great return on his investment. And he's right in doing that. So if you look at all of the different companies, none of them are big enough to impact on Berkshire's financials. But when you have 25 of us, we are."

But Santulli shows no such reticence when he talks about his boss. "I like Warren," he says. "Warren had confidence in me when he bought the business. I think he is one of the greatest guys I've ever met. I wouldn't have sold my business to him otherwise. The reason I did is because of who he is. Who he is—not because he is Warren Buffett, a guy with a lot of money. It meant a lot to me that he had the confidence to say, 'I am buying it, but you are running it.' Warren is brilliant that way. He picks guys who love their businesses and lets them go on running them." In fact, when asked why other companies don't follow the Berkshire model in allowing executives to continue running their own companies, Santulli says, "Because people who buy companies usually have huge egos and think they're smarter than the people they bought the company from. One of the nicest things about being part of Berkshire," he adds, "is that if I said to Warren, 'I am going to go buy $1 billion worth of airplanes,' he would say, 'Why are you asking me? Go do it.'"

When asked if there will ever be another Warren Buffett, Santulli unhesitatingly and emphatically says, "No; impossible. One of his greatest attributes is his ability to read people. And that's an ability that you can't teach. He just knows it. He is the smartest man I have ever met, by a long shot. He's much, much smarter than me. Not even in the same league. I mean, I'm a minor-league ballplayer and he's an all-star." Santulli does, though, see some similarities between himself and Buffett. "Honesty and integrity are very, very important to both of us," he says. "Also, he doesn't want to do things that he doesn't want to do, and that's one of my problems. I don't want to do business with people I don't want to do business with, and that is the way he is too."

Although Santulli appreciates the fact that Buffett doesn't interfere in his running the business, unlike many—if not most—of Berkshire's operating managers, he speaks with his boss on a regular basis. "I speak to him almost every day," Santulli says, "four times a week, unless I am traveling or he is traveling. Sometimes there will be a specific reason for a call—he'll ask me to give someone a call, or ask me a question about something. But a lot of times, I will just call him to say, 'Okay, break time,' just to bullshit. We talk about anything. I respect his opinion on basically everything. It's really good to speak to someone like that, especially about strategic stuff. Plus," Santulli adds, "he is fun."

Looking back on his life, he says, "The most influential people in my life were my parents. I learned about hard work from my father. He really had three jobs—he worked for the federal government, then he came home and had dinner and went out and sold insurance, and on the weekends he sold real estate. So hard work was the way we were brought up. I also learned a lot from my mother. My mother was a bigger religious influence on me than my dad."

His mother's religious influence may have spilled over into his working life. "Integrity," he says, "is probably the most important quality in a person. It's so important that, when I do deals, I basically assume that I will never have to read the contract. And when I discover that I'm dealing with people with whom I *do* have to read the contract, I don't do any more business with them. I also think," he adds, "that I am a thoughtful manager. I take care of my people very well. I care about people. And I care as much about my business as anybody could possibly care about a business. I love my business, I love my people, and I love coming to work."

In fact, like most of Berkshire's operating managers, Santulli equates his success with loving the business. "You have to really care about your business," he says. "You have to love your business. You have to care about your people. You have to treat them with dignity and respect. And you have to communicate well with your people to let them know what is going on." He also believes that hiring the best people you can find is an important element. "I was always in a good position," he says, "because I was boss. A lot of managers will hire people that aren't as good as they could be because they are afraid that they are going to take their jobs. I have never been afraid that someone was going to take my job, so I've always hired good people. Then, when I know they are good, after they have worked for me, I empower them, and I delegate." At the same time, Santulli realizes the importance of looking into the future. "You must look at it from a strategic point of view and anticipate what will happen over the next 5 to 10 years. I'm not a big planner, but what I do look at all the time is what we're going to be, what the industry is going to be. We're going to lead the industry, so we have to make sure that we are doing it properly."

One way in which Executive Jet makes an effort to lead the industry is in safety. The company has not had any fatal accidents. "The only thing that would keep me awake at night is safety, and we train our people more than anybody else," he says. "We spend tens of millions of dollars more than any of our competitors to make sure that we are doing everything possible to be the safest operation in the world. Our pilot training and safety standards exceed FAA regulations, by a lot. I can't say that nothing will ever happen, because we're so large, but I can say that it won't happen because we haven't bought the right equipment. I tell every one of my customers that is the guarantee they get. . . . In private aviation," he explains, "a significant number of accidents occur because the pilots are trying to either impress the boss or the guys in the back. It happens all the time. But we have a completely different philosophy. We say, 'Prove that we can do it before we even think about doing it.' And our pilots know that they'll never be pressured into doing something they don't want to do."

When asked what he excels at, Santulli says, "My circle of competence is that I understand business very well. I understand people very well. I understand the aviation business. I don't know how to make an airplane and I don't know how to fly an airplane, but I know what customers—people—like in airplanes. I know that. And I know how to take that and turn it into something that works from an economic point of view." It is not, however, the money that's important to him. "Money isn't why I do it," he says. "I like to have it. I won't say I don't want to have it; but that was never my motivation. It's the business that motivates me. I love challenges. I love selling. I have an obligation, I think, to all of my employees. They trusted me from the beginning, they stood by me, and I have built something that I am very proud of. If I came to work and I had no challenge, then I wouldn't be here."

In fact, he is at work a great deal of the time. On a typical day, he arrives at the office before 9:00 A.M. and generally doesn't leave until 6:30 P.M. "I never really take vacations," he says, "just a few days here and there. I have a house in Florida and I go there for the week between Christmas and New Year's. Maybe once a month I'll go there on a Thursday and come back on a Sunday. But my real passion is business. And horses," he adds, "breeding and racing horses." He also spends a good deal of his time in charity work through a family foundation he set up called the RTS Family Foundation. Perhaps unconsciously following Andrew Carnegie's dictate that "He who dies rich, dies disgraced," Santulli, unlike his boss, says, "Everything that I have will be given away while I am alive, minus enough for my wife to live."

As for the future, he believes, "The future of the aviation business is very strong. General aviation is very strong because commercial aviation is only going to get worse." As for Executive Jet, Santulli says, "We have a long way to go." One way to get there may be with supersonic business jets, which would enable someone to fly, for example, from London to

Washington in four hours or less, attend a meeting, and fly back home. Today, the only nonmilitary supersonic jet is the Concorde, flying between the eastern United States and London and Paris. "I think it will happen," Santulli says. "I believe it would be successful even if it could operate only over water, but if it could fly supersonic over the U.S. and Europe too, the market would be huge. We haven't had a major technological change in general aviation for a long time. Aircraft use less fuel, they're quieter, and they have greater range, but a supersonic jet would change things dramatically. I think quite a few companies would be interested in that kind of speed."[19]

The one cloud on the horizon is the possibility that the FAA may change the way fractional airlines are regulated. Charter airlines are complaining that the less stringent regulations that fractionals are allowed to follow provide them with much greater flexibility than the charters, and, accordingly, give them an unfair competitive advantage. Fractional airlines can land at any one of about 5,500 airports in the United States. Charter airlines, like other commercial services, can only land at about 500. Clearly, if the FAA decides that fractionals like Executive Jet must operate under the same rules as the charters, fractionals would lose one of their key advantages.[20] There is also a debate over whether fractional airlines should have to operate under the same safety regulations as commercial airlines. However, the fractional airlines have an excellent safety record, and industry officials believe that the issue has less to do with safety problems than with the politics of private versus commercial aviation.[21]

When asked about Berkshire Hathaway's future, Santulli says he believes it will evolve into more of a property/casualty insurance company than a conglomerate. "The overwhelming business will be insurance," he says. "It has to be. Because you get the cost of float from the insurance, with which to buy companies. Warren basically buys companies for free, whatever the cost of float is, because he has this perpetual float." He does not, however, believe that Buffett has a master plan for the company; rather, "It is an evolving painting."

Santulli has been reported by the *Wall Street Journal* as being one of three Berkshire executives Buffett has chosen to succeed him as CEO.[22] When asked if he has a vision for the company, he defers to his boss's judgment. "When people ask me about Berkshire stock, I say that I have been around investment bankers my whole life, and I have been around these guys my whole life, and there is not one human being in the world who is smarter than Warren Buffett. There's no point in worrying about it. You've got the best guy. If he were 40 or 50 years old, I would borrow all of the money I could and buy more Berkshire stock."

He also believes that the company will operate no differently after Buffett is gone. In fact, when asked about the first thing he'd do if he were designated as Buffett's successor on the operational side, he said: "I would call all of the managers up and say, 'Okay, what did you do before with Warren? Go ahead and tell me, and that's what you can do now.' I would learn a little more about their businesses," he adds, "but then I would leave them alone."

## RICH SANTULLI'S BUSINESS TENETS

★ Offer a service that will be irresistible to customers. Executive Jet's planes are available all over the world when clients need them. The clients don't have to deal with the hassles of delays, lost luggage, or crowded airports. The company has almost 100 percent customer retention.

★ Have a plan ready for economic downturns. NetJet's profits are based on monthly and usage fees, and on airplane sales; they're not subject to seasonal changes. In fact, during recession, the company's services are more appealing because of the potential savings to clients.

★ Hire the best people and don't be afraid they're going to take over your job. After they show their abilities, empower them and delegate. You have to look long term, and hiring the best employees is one way to ensure your future success.

# Part Four

# Berkshire's CEO Family— Children and Grandchildren

# chapter nine

# The Disciple—Don Graham,
## *The Washington Post*

*T*echnically, Don Graham is not an official Buffett CEO; he doesn't
work for a wholly owned subsidiary of Berkshire. Graham does not
report to Buffett, but the two men have a close relationship and frequently
discuss important management issues.

Don Graham has known Warren Buffett, both personally and profes-
sionally, for a long period of time, so talking with Graham is an ideal way
to find out whether Buffett influences his operating company CEOs any
differently than his marketable security chief executives. For example,
does Buffett approach a wholly owned CEO any differently than a partly
owned CEO? Does he spend more time with his operating company chiefs
than with his marketable security chiefs?

Don Graham of the Washington Post offers a unique outsider/insider
perspective of Berkshire. He is, in every way, a Buffett disciple and Buffett CEO. Graham does not own stock in Berkshire personally, although
the Post's employee retirement funds have purchased a substantial amount
of Berkshire over the years. The Washington Post Company also owns
about $200 million worth of Berkshire stock.

After taking his daily subway ride to work, Graham walks past large
oil-painted portraits of his grandfather, Eugene Meyer, and his father,
Philip Graham, to get to his spacious corner office. In this office, Don
Graham was quite open about his work and his life. Surprisingly, given
his station in life, he is a regular kind of guy. He knows publishing, television, and the media, and he knows Buffett, Berkshire, the wholly owned
companies, and all the players. It is immediately obvious that, of all the
people he knows, Warren Buffett is one of his favorites. He smiles when
you mention his name. Buffett's influence on Graham's management decisions is apparent. The Post does not split its stock. The media company

*calls attention to the impact of a pension credit or expense on its income statement. Management doesn't focus on short-term earnings. The Post makes very minimal use of management stock options. Besides Don and Buffett, other board members who are part of Warren's inner circle are Dan Burke (former CEO of Cap Cities/ABC, a major Berkshire investment), Don Keough (former Coca-Cola president), and, until recently, his late mother Kay and Bill Ruane (Sequoia Fund manager, a large Berkshire shareholder, and Buffett's Columbia classmate). It's as if Buffett picked the board of directors.*

*Don Graham's company reflects Buffett's buy-and-hold investment style. As with all its operating businesses, Berkshire has never sold its ownership in the* Washington Post. *Outside of the Graham family, Berkshire is the largest shareholder and one of the oldest. Like many of Berkshire's operating companies, the* Post *is family-managed by a long-time Buffett disciple.*

One might argue that Donald E. Graham, CEO and chairman of The Washington Post Company, has a lot to live up to. After all, his grandfather, Eugene Meyer, who made a fortune in Wall Street early in the twentieth century, and who used some of that fortune to purchase the *Washington Post* in 1933, successfully guided the paper from the middle of the Great Depression through the end of the Second World War. His brilliant but troubled father, Phil Graham, who was the newspaper's publisher from 1946 to 1963, not only brought the *Post* to national prominence—partly as a result of his serving as an adviser to both John F. Kennedy and Lyndon Johnson—but also laid the foundation for the present-day company by diversifying into other media. His mother, Katharine Meyer Graham, who took over the company after his father committed suicide and was the first woman to chair a Fortune 500 company, led the organization for nearly 30 years, during which time it became one of the country's most successful media conglomerates. But Don Graham doesn't see it that way. He never worried about his parents' and grandparents' successes, nor did he ever feel that he had to prove himself. If anything, he believed that his family's history led others to have lower expectations of him. "The one good thing about being the publisher's son," he said a dozen years after becoming publisher himself, "is you can't possibly be as dumb as people think you are."[1]

It's unlikely, though, that anyone ever thought Don Graham was dumb. Born in Baltimore in 1945, the second of four children, he was a precocious child who taught himself to read by the age of three. Later, as a student at St. Albans School in Washington, D.C., Graham was not only consistently at the top of his class academically, but was also a member of the school's wrestling and tennis teams. But his real passion, which grew as he did, was journalism, and he eventually spent less time on sports and more time working on the school's newspaper, the *St. Albans News*. That passion was in full bloom when Graham started at Harvard in 1962. By the time he graduated four years later, he had been elected president of the school's daily newspaper, the *Harvard Crimson.*

His mother wanted him to join the *Post* after graduation, but Graham was drafted and sent to Vietnam. Although his family's connections might well have enabled him to avoid military service, unlike many of his generation, Graham had not opposed the United States' involvement in the war while he was in college. He accordingly felt that, having been drafted, it was his responsibility to go. He later came to believe that the war was a mistake. He spent a year as an information specialist with the 1st Cavalry Division, and returned home in 1968. When he came back to Washington, he continued to resist his mother's efforts to get him to join the *Post*. Saying that he wanted to get to know the city first, he joined the District of Columbia's police force. Kay Graham was, understandably, not pleased. Nevertheless, when Alfred Lewis, the *Post*'s police reporter, came to her and said, "Boss, we can stop this. It's dangerous out there," she said, "No, no. We mustn't do that."[2] Years later, Don Graham explained that, at the time, "Police work seemed challenging and mysterious, and the cops were desperate for people." After passing the police academy's entrance exam, he served as a policeman for about a year and a half. Then, at the age of 26, he went to work as a reporter on the metro desk of the *Washington Post*.[3]

The company Don Graham joined in 1971 was almost 100 years old. It had been founded in 1877 by Stilson Hutchins, who had come to Washington from Whitefield, New Hampshire. Over the years, it changed hands several times. In the late 1920s, Eugene Meyer, Graham's maternal grandfather, who already had a successful career as a financier and a government official, but wanted to extend his influence through the ownership of a newspaper, tried to purchase the paper.[4] Even though the *Post* was only the number-five paper in Washington at the time, when he offered its owners $5 million, he was turned down. But then the stock market crashed and the newspaper began losing money. By 1933, in the depths of the Depression, the paper was going bankrupt, and Meyer was able to buy it at auction for only $825,000.[5]

"It all started there," his grandson recalls. "That was clearly the best bargain we ever got. If you look back over our corporate history, even though we've had some pretty spectacular buys since then, they're all dwarfed by that one." Speaking of his grandfather, Graham explains that "the reason he was able to do it was actually because he was a very principled man. He had gone into the federal government right after World War I, and got a series of increasingly responsible government jobs through the 1920s. And he was one of the few people in those days who thought that if you were working for the government, you shouldn't own stock in private companies. So his whole net worth was in government bonds. Because of that, when the Depression hit, he was one of the few people who didn't lose all his money, so he could afford to buy the paper." But even after Meyer bought the *Post,* it continued to lose money—more than a million dollars a year during the next several years. Still, he was determined to make the paper a success, and he was willing to shore it up with his own money until it became one. Fortunately, as Graham explains, "He had precisely the right approach. He thought that if he made the paper better, circulation would gradually grow, and advertising would follow along. But he had no idea how long it would take. He thought he would break even in three or four years." As it turned out, the paper would actually lose money for another 21 years.

But if changes at the newspaper weren't taking place as rapidly as Meyer might have wished, other changes were taking place in his family. One of the most important of these was the marriage of his daughter, Katharine, to Philip Graham. Born in South Dakota in 1915, Graham had graduated near the top of his 1939 Harvard Law School class. He clerked for Supreme Court Justice Felix Frankfurter, and intended to return home to run for political office. Just before World War II, he met Katharine Meyer, and they were married in 1940. Eugene Meyer, like virtually everyone else who met Phil Graham, was extremely impressed with his son-in-law, and, in 1946, when Meyer was asked by President Harry S Truman to become the first president of the World Bank, he turned the reins of his company over to Graham. Two years later, Meyer transferred the company's 5,000 shares of voting stock to his daughter and son-in-law. Katharine received 1,500 and Graham received 3,500.

Over the next few years, even while the *Post* continued to lose money, Graham persuaded his father-in-law to invest millions of dollars in the paper. However, by the early 1950s, it had become clear that if the paper was to continue, it would have to combine with the city's other morning newspaper. In 1954, when Don Graham was eight years old, his father was able to arrange the *Post*'s purchase of the larger, more profitable *Times-Herald*. The deal cost the *Post* almost $10 million, but it saved the paper and enabled it to make a profit for the first time since Meyer had purchased it 21 years before. It also saved the paper in another way. Eugene Meyer was quoted as saying, at the time, "This will make the paper safe for Donny."[6] "Donny," in the meantime, wasn't particularly interested. As he told a reporter from the *Washingtonian* many years later, all he could remember of the sale was that his father came home in the middle of the day, which was out of the ordinary, and showed him the comics that the *Post* and *Times-Herald* would now be publishing. "Now *that* was exciting," the younger Graham remembered.[7]

The purchase of the *Times-Herald* was only one of the many farsighted moves Graham persuaded his father-in-law to make. At his prompting, Eugene Meyer agreed to purchase the first of several television stations in Washington, D.C., and Florida, and to acquire one of the Post Company's most important purchases—*Newsweek*—in 1961. But the company's increasing success wasn't enough to save Phil Graham from his personal demons. In 1963, having gotten a weekend off from his psychiatric clinic, he committed suicide at the family's farm in Virginia. Don Graham was 18 at the time.

Eugene Meyer had died in 1959, so, at Phil Graham's death, his widow, Don's mother, became the principal owner of The Washington Post Company. Subsequently, she received numerous offers but refused to sell it. Instead, even though she'd had no experience at running a business, she decided to take it over herself, and, in 1963, became the company's president. Despite her lack of experience, by the time Don joined the company eight years later, in 1971, she had proven herself to be an astute businessperson and had taken on the additional responsibilities of publisher of the newspaper. In that same year, Mrs. Graham decided to take the company public for $15 million. She was able to keep control within the family because, in 1947, two categories of stock had been created—Class A stock, which included full voting rights, and Class B stock, with limited voting rights. Mrs. Graham and her four children owned all the Class A stock.

In 1973, two significant events that would impact The Washington Post Company took place. Fritz Beebe, who had been the chairman of the company's board, passed away, and Katharine Graham took on his title, becoming the first woman to chair a Fortune 500 company. And, Warren Buffett began buying stock in the company. In fact, Buffett bought a considerable amount of stock in the company—about 12 percent of the Class B shares, or $10.6 million worth—making Berkshire Hathaway the largest shareholder after the Graham family. Although Mrs. Graham had met Buffett once, some years before, she still had no idea who he was. Even though ownership of the Class B stock did not bring Buffett any voting rights, his taking on such a large percentage of the company's stock made her very nervous.[8]

Anticipating Mrs. Graham's concern, Buffett wrote to tell her that he had once been a paperboy for the *Post,* and to assure her that he had no intent of trying to take over the company. But when she showed the letter to two knowledgeable friends—André Meyer of Lazard Frères, and Chicago banker Robert Abboud—they advised her to stay away from Buffett. Because Mrs. Graham was still somewhat unsure of herself, she tended to rely a great deal on her advisers. In this instance, however, she ignored their advice and, instead, wrote to Buffett to suggest that they meet. Although the meeting, which took place in Los Angeles, was a very pleasant one, Buffett could sense Graham's apprehensiveness and offered to stop buying stock in the company.[9]

Despite her nervousness, Graham invited Buffett to visit the paper when he was on the East Coast, and he took her up on her invitation. Within a year, in the fall of 1974, at the suggestion of Tom Murphy, chairman of Capital Cities, Graham also extended an invitation to Buffett to join the *Post*'s board. Buffett accepted that invitation as well, and he has been a member of the board since, except for a 10-year period when he was a major shareholder in Cap Cities/ABC (eventually, Disney). Federal laws prohibited having a board seat on more than two media companies operating in the same city. Years later, in regard to that invitation, Don

Graham (who joined the *Post*'s board the same year as Buffett) told a reporter from the *New Yorker* that "Hiring Ben [Bradlee] as her editor was the best decision my mother ever made. But getting Warren involved was an awfully close second."[10] The family's connection with Buffett has apparently had a very significant effect on Katharine Graham, Don Graham, and the company.

For Mrs. Graham, Buffett became not only a close personal friend but also a kind of personal tutor. For example, on his trips to Washington, he brought her annual reports and went over them with her line by line. As she began relying more and more on Buffett's advice, she developed a habit of responding to suggestions from the company's staff by saying, "That's interesting—let's ask Warren."[11] Some of her colleagues—who were wary of Buffett—became concerned that he was manipulating her. Her view was that he provided advice and counsel and never told her what to do. He was being enormously helpful. Her son agreed, and still agrees, with that assessment. In fact, Don Graham considers Buffett's advice and counsel to be among his major contributions as a member of the *Post*'s board. "While she was running the company," Graham says, referring to his mother, "she was at first very, very unsure of herself and very insecure in her own judgment. Even with Warren advising her, that remained true. But by telling her that her judgment was good, by being so supportive of her, Warren helped her become what she did become. And she was a fantastically successful chief executive. She took the stock from $6 to $175 in 28 years, and that outperformed 99 percent of the guys running companies in that time."

Buffett has affected the company in other ways as well. "If we had not had Warren as a director and adviser over the years," Don Graham says, "we would be much less well run as a company. We'd have had a whole different acquisition strategy, and I don't think that things would have worked out as well." Graham says that Buffett has influenced every major acquisition that he or his mother—whom he sometimes refers to as "Kay"—has made since Buffett became a board member. "There have been smaller acquisitions that I'm sure Warren would have not made," he says. "But with anything that approached the level of significance to the company, first Kay, and then I, carefully reviewed it with Warren before going ahead. Fortunately, there haven't been any instances in which he disapproved of something we really wanted to do. But he has," Graham adds, "influenced our sense of valuations. He told Kay when he thought the prices people were paying for newspapers were too high, and he held us back from overpaying for acquisitions, which we undoubtedly would have done without him. He was right. The companies that did overpay for those acquisitions were sorry about it afterward."

Another important way in which Buffett impacted the company was in urging the Grahams to buy back its stock. "In 1976," Graham says, "he told Kay to start repurchasing stock in the company. It was a wildly unconventional thing to do at the time—no companies were doing that. Fortunately, she listened to him and repurchased 25 percent of the company over the next five years, at prices averaging less than $25 a share. Now those shares are worth over $500, so that was just an inconceivable value. We also continued to do it, on and off, until we'd reduced the 20 million shares outstanding when Warren bought into the company to the 9.4 million there are outstanding today. We've made other good investments, but that use of the capital was by far the best investment our company has made."

Buffett's advice to the *Post*, to repurchase its stock, helped Berkshire's investment grow from its 12 percent ownership at that time to 18.3 percent ownership currently, without making any additional purchases. Berkshire's $10.6 million investment (for $6.14 per share) 27 years ago has grown into a valuation today of over $1 billion, representing more than an 18 percent annual rate of return. Berkshire's $9 million annual dividend from the *Post* nearly represents an annual repayment of its original purchase price.

It's worth comparing the purchase of 100 percent of a company to buying part of it. Buffett's 1977 purchase of all of the *Buffalo News* for $32.5 million has been a better investment than part ownership of the *Post*. Berkshire's *Post* investment of $10.6 million returns $9 million in dividends and $18 million in additional look-through earnings, for a total of $27 million for year 2000. The *Buffalo News* experienced additional short-term losses that pushed Buffett's net investment to $44.5 million, but it returned $52 million last year. More importantly, the *Buffalo News* has given Berkshire over $750 million in accumulated pretax earnings to make more purchases.

If Buffett's influence on Katharine Graham and The Washington Post Company could be called significant, his effect on Don Graham could fairly be described as profound. Graham recently told the *New Yorker* that when he first met Buffett, he "asked him every question I could think of" and "quickly saw that this was the smartest person I had ever met. War-ren talks so clearly that, in a way, he's very deceptive. A lot of us flatter ourselves that we are influenced by him, but we always know there are deeper layers within him that we can't see. It's like saying my chess is in-fluenced by Gary Kasparov or my basketball is influenced by Michael Jordan."[12]

There are, in fact, many ways in which Buffett's effect on Graham is apparent. One of these is Graham's adoption of Buffett's philosophy of paying for quality but skimping on frills. Among other examples of this penchant are his ban on company cars and his installation of industrial-grade carpet in the *Post*'s executive offices, as a result of which he—like his mentor—has earned a reputation for being cheap.[13]

Others would describe it as managing a business in the best interests of the owners. Like his mentor—and unlike so many other managers—he takes a long-term view of the business. "We really do not think as much about the short term," he has said. "We do not focus on quarterly results." But, he adds, "To say we're not focused on quarterly returns does not say we are not focused on running a business profitably and successfully. We have notably tough graders on our board. What we're focused on in the long term is building the value of our businesses. And that can only be measured by net income."[14]

Not at all surprising, when asked who his heroes are, Don Graham im-mediately says, "In business, Warren is really up there. You'll hear that from everybody who has been within 10 miles of the guy, including peo-ple who don't work for him anymore. That's really extraordinary. I know a lot of people who are like him to a limited degree," he says. "There are a lot of good businesspeople. There are a lot of good investors. And there are other people whom I admire greatly. But I don't know anybody else that I would put on the same plateau as Warren." To help explain why he con-siders Buffett to be so different from everyone else, Graham relates a story about an old college friend. "After we graduated he became the author of a book called the *Almanac of American Politics*. It's a compendium of polit-ical statistics, and it's a sensational reference book. What's amazing about it is that the guy writes most of it out of his head. He knows the names of ev-eryone who's ever been a congressman or senator. And he knows not only who carried Missouri in 1960, but also what the actual vote was. Not the percentage, but the number of votes cast for each candidate. When I would ask him about it, he would just say that he was using the brain cells that I used to remember the name of the second-string right guard on the Washington Redskins. That's the way Warren is about business."

Interestingly, there is another story in which, instead of Graham praising Buffett's memory, Buffett praises Graham's. As Barbara Matusow explained in a 1992 issue of the *Washingtonian:* "It's easy to underestimate Don Graham. He is so modest and unassuming that people are surprised to find that he has a steel-trap mind. Once, a group of Post Company board members was standing around kibitzing, waiting for Graham to show up, and Robert McNamara bet them nobody could name Abraham Lincoln's first vice president. Nobody could. Warren Buffett then bet $5 that Don would know the answer. 'Sure,' he said when he arrived. 'It was Hannibal Hamlin. . . . '"

"Don is incredibly smart, and his memory is off the charts," says Buffett. "If I try to remember something from my annual reports, he can quote it back. It's easier to call him than to look it up myself."[15]

Buffett has other reasons to be enthusiastic about Don Graham. The Washington Post Company is an extremely successful media organization with annual revenues of more than $2 billion and net income of more than $225 million. It's also a diversified company whose primary operations fall essentially into five categories. In broadcast television, the company owns half a dozen network-affiliated stations in Michigan, Texas, and Florida. The second is its cable operation—Cable ONE, based in Phoenix, Arizona—which serves three quarters of a million subscribers in 18 midwestern, western, and southern states. The *Post*'s magazine publishing operation, the third element of the company, includes, in addition to the regular edition of *Newsweek,* three international editions of the magazine, a teen edition, a bimonthly travel magazine, and a television production company. The fourth part of the company's operation is Kaplan, Inc., which is a leading provider of educational and career services. Last, but certainly not least, is the company's newspaper publishing operation. Although the star of this group is, of course, the *Washington Post,* the group also includes a special national weekly edition of the paper, as well as several other newspapers around the country.

The *Post* would, in fact, be a star in any company. Because of competition from other media, virtually every major daily newspaper in the country has lost circulation over the past 10 years. Daily circulation of the

*Los Angeles Times,* for example, went down 14.8 percent, and the *Philadelphia Inquirer* dropped 23.8 percent.[16] But the *Post*'s daily circulation has gone down only a little more than 4 percent in the past decade. As a result, even though Graham has been able to keep the price of the paper down to 25 cents, the paper continues to be extremely profitable. In all fairness, the paper's success is, at least in part, due to the fact that it has outlasted all but one of its morning competitors. Its last major competitor—the *Star*—went out of business in 1981, and the only remaining morning paper is the *Washington Times,* which is owned by the Reverend Sun N. Moon's Unification Church. But perhaps even more impressive than its stable circulation is the *Post*'s penetration in its market. A survey conducted in 2000 found that the *Post* reaches 46 percent of households in the Washington metropolitan area on weekdays, and 61 percent on Sundays. The *Boston Globe,* which serves a similar-size region, reaches 27 percent of its market during the week, and 40 percent on Sundays. Even the *New York Times,* which serves a much larger audience and is the newspaper to which the *Post* is most often compared, reaches only 9 percent of its market on weekdays and 13 percent on Sundays.[17]

That comparison, in fact, is something Graham has a problem with. "People do compare us to the *New York Times,*" he says, "but in some ways that's a false comparison for us. We don't compete with [the *Times*], other than journalistically." As he explained to a reporter from the *New Yorker* in 2000, "We are not a national newspaper. We are a local newspaper for a place that happens to be the capital of the United States. We're writing for the people who run the government but also for the people who clean their offices." And because of that, the paper continues to be extremely attractive to advertisers. "A lot of what makes the *Post* a good business," he told the reporter, "is that if you put an ad in to sell shirts, you'll sell a lot of shirts."[18] To maintain—and even increase—its coverage of local news, the *Post* has opened 12 bureaus in and around Washington, five around the United States, and 21 overseas. The *New York Times,* by comparison, has only 10 bureaus in its own much larger area, 11 around the country, and 26 overseas.

Managing all this, of course, is a big job, but Graham has long since demonstrated his ability to meet the challenge. After joining the *Post* as a reporter in 1971, he held several news and business positions both at the paper and at *Newsweek* before being named executive vice president and general manager of the paper in 1976. He became publisher in 1979, and succeeded his mother as chief executive officer of the parent company in 1991, when he was 45. At the time, Warren Buffett was quoted as saying that he "couldn't feel better" about the appointment, noting that it was "a total nonsurprise," and adding, "Wall Street for many years has expected that Donald Graham would be president of the company."[19] Two years later, in 1993, Mrs. Graham became chairman of the executive committee, and Don Graham was appointed chairman of the board. (As a result of the recent departure of Alan Spoon, the company's president, with whom Graham had shared his corporate executive responsibilities, Graham gave up his position as publisher of the *Post* so he could concentrate on the management of the overall operation. He replaced himself with Boisfeuillet (Bo) Jones, Jr., the paper's president and associate publisher.)

Graham is, accordingly, well accustomed to wielding power. But his management style, perhaps consciously developed to be different from his grandfather's and his parents', is very low-key. Like Buffett, he believes in letting his managers make their own decisions, and rarely gives direct commands to his staff. This low-key style even extended to the editorial page, traditionally considered to represent the voice of the publisher. As publisher, Graham made his opinions known, but in those rare cases in which they differed from those of the editorial-page editor, he usually said, "It's your call." One of the things he will not give in on, however, is what he considers unnecessary expenditures, and his ability to keep costs down has helped make the *Post* as profitable as it is. He is similarly adamant about hiring and promoting women and minorities. Employee development, in fact, is one of his greatest interests, and he has consistently promoted the company's managers from within.

Graham has a spouse and children of his own. He, his wife Mary, and their four children live in Washington, D.C. Despite their considerable wealth—Graham is estimated to be worth $200 million—the family has anything but an extravagant lifestyle. Graham takes the subway to work every day, and it's widely believed—although not true—that he buys his clothes at a discount store near his office. Rather than fly, he prefers to take the train to New York City when he visits the *Newsweek* offices. Graham rarely takes time off from work; he and his wife attend few parties, and they travel very little for pleasure.

When asked what career he might have chosen if he hadn't entered the newspaper business, Graham says, "I really don't know. When I was a kid, I wanted to be a baseball player; other than that, there is no other career I wish I'd pursued. It's a really interesting question, though; particularly because there was a long time when it wasn't at all clear to me that I was going to work at the *Post*. I think a lot of people whose families have businesses feel torn between wanting to get into them and wanting to stay the hell out. I was very torn," he says, "but I grew up in the newspaper, and I was very drawn to the business. If I had not gone to the *Post,* I would probably have gone to work on some other paper as a reporter. Newspapers are just so incredibly absorbing. When you work on a paper, you come to work every day literally not knowing what's going to happen or what the subject of conversation is going to be. It's really exciting."

Although he is no longer involved in the day-to-day operation of the newspaper, he is nevertheless excited about one of its offshoots—Washingtonpost.com, the company's Internet operation. And in this respect, he admits that he is unlike his mentor. "If you look at Warren's businesses, at Warren's investing," Graham says, "you could almost say that he's been investing to avoid the impact of the Internet. All the businesses he's invested in over the last five years—companies like Dairy Queen, Executive Jet, the jewelry companies—are among the few businesses in America in which the Internet is not going to be a huge factor." Graham recognizes, though, that the same is not true of newspapers.

In fact, he believes that "the long-run question confronting newspapers has everything to do with the evolution of the Internet and what it will mean. The *Post* is a good business today because we put out something that people really want to read. It's a quality paper that people feel is important for them to read in the morning. And while reading it, they happen across sales for clothes and cars and houses and jobs. So the *Post* causes commercial transactions to happen, almost by accident, by serendipity. Can we have ads on our Web site that cause people to go buy shirts at the Hecht Company the way ads in the *Post* do? We haven't proven yet that we can. So that's one of the questions facing the newspaper business. The other big question is about the future impact of Web news gathering. And if anybody knows the answer to that, I wish they would tell me."

Not willing or able to wait for an answer, Graham is working to develop the *Post*'s Web site to position the company for the future. Alan Spoon was involved in that development before he left the company, and he told the *Financial Times,* in 1999, that Washingtonpost.com, the online newspaper, "is becoming the national edition of the *Washington Post.*" However, as the *Financial Times* pointed out, "For a newspaper that depends so heavily on local retail advertising and classifieds, building up the web site is also crucial to catch the drift of ink-on-paper advertising on to the web."[20] Even so, while Bo Jones has noted, "There are myriad opportunities in the Internet," he has also said that "the greater Washington area will always be our focus. When the guy was brought in to run our site, I opened a map of the city and suburbs and said to him, 'This is what we are interested in.'"[21]

When asked about his vision for the *Washington Post,* Graham says, "We're not a concept-driven company. But my vision is that we'll continue to produce very high-quality newspapers and magazines and television—television news in particular—and that we'll grow the intrinsic value of the company more than most." In regard to the future of the newspaper business in general, Graham says, "Anybody in the newspaper business understands there are competitive threats to the business. But I'm a relative optimist. I think that in the last five years, newspapers have shown surprising competitive strength, particularly considering all the new competition we've got. All of our media businesses will be affected by technology. None of them is like Dairy Queen. But I think that, as a result, we have very interesting prospects in all five businesses, plus the Internet."

As far as his own future is concerned, Graham says that, at 56 (as of this writing), he has no retirement plans. "My mother worked here until she passed away at 84. We have normal retirement considerations," he says, "but we don't have any kind of mandatory policy." He is not thinking about retiring, so he is also not thinking about who might succeed him. He was treated for prostate cancer in 1997, and even though his treatment was successful, it raised the question of succession in the family business. The only member of the family's next generation currently involved with the *Post* is Katharine Weymouth Scully, who is Katharine Graham's namesake and oldest grandchild, Lally Graham Weymouth's daughter, and Don Graham's niece. It's said that people inside and outside the family have great hopes for her. Thirty-five years old as of this writing, the native New Yorker worked in the paper's legal department for two years before being appointed associate counsel and director of business affairs of Washingtonpost.com and Newsweek Interactive. The fact that Scully was given a position in the most future-oriented parts of the business may be significant, but neither she nor anyone else has made any public statements regarding any interest she might have in eventually taking over the family business.[22]

When asked if he has a vision for Berkshire Hathaway, Don Graham simply says, "It's whatever Warren wants it to be." Even so, he's willing to say that he believes Berkshire is more likely to evolve as a conglomerate than as an insurance company, although he thinks it will be "heavily weighted in insurance." At the same time, he points out, "You've seen what Warren's bought, so he's obviously quite willing to buy lots of other things besides insurance operations." When queried about who might replace Buffett as head of Berkshire Hathaway, Graham says, "I don't know and I don't care. It's up to Warren. I think that he will arrange it in the most intelligent way that he possibly can. I'm not concerned about it. The value of the company is what it is. It's true that the guy running it has made uniquely astute judgments over many years. But one of the judgments that he will make is who comes after him. I'm sure Warren will pick someone very, very good. Will the company grow as fast with someone other than Warren running it? No. Will it grow pretty fast with the people that he will select to run it? Yes. I know you've got to have something to worry about in the world," he concludes, "but that's something that would be pretty far down on my list."

## DON GRAHAM'S BUSINESS TENETS

- ★ Monitor your costs. Spend as little as possible on the extras.
- ★ Let your managers do their jobs. Don't interfere with them unless absolutely necessary.
- ★ Develop your employees. Promotion from within is important.
- ★ Strive for diversity among your employees. Hire and promote women and minorities.

# chapter ten

# The Third-Generation Family Successor—Irvin Blumkin, NFM

*P*icture five enormous Costco warehouses connected together and selling everything for your home, including furniture, appliances, floor covering, and electronics. Welcome to the Nebraska Furniture Mart—America's largest-volume home furnishings store on a single site, located in the heart of America—Omaha, Nebraska.

In his offices above the main sales floor, I met with Irv Blumkin, the 40-something CEO of this store that has become an institution. Blumkin claims he's media-shy, but he soon warmed up and provided excellent insights on the inner workings of one of America's best retail and business success stories. He guided me through the life and times of Mrs. B (see Chapter Six) and the indelible stamp she put on her home and the Blumkin family's enterprise.

Like Mrs. B (NFM's founder and Irv's grandmother), Irv is a force in the world of home furnishings retail. He's humble and hardworking like Mrs. B, but more diplomatic, like his father, Louie.

Throughout the corporate offices, visitors see quotes from Mrs. B, such as: "Tell the truth and sell cheap." Even the wastebasket lids in the corporate office feature one-word business principles: "honesty," "kindness," "attitude," and "value." On Irv's credenza is a picture of his father, one of his heroes. Framed above his desk are quotes attributed to his father ("If you've got the right price, they'll find you in a river.") and to Warren Buffett. Other than the quotes, there wasn't any indication that the NFM was part of any larger enterprise.

Irv has single-handedly brought Berkshire more business acquisitions than any other manager. He knows better than most what Warren Buffett is looking for in an acquisition candidate.

*NFM is still very much a family-run business. Irv and his brother Ron, both of whom commonly work on Sunday, run NFM with all the principles that were instilled by Mrs. B and brought NFM to the attention of Warren Buffett.*

Not many heads of multimillion-dollar companies can claim to have worked in their organizations since they were eight or nine years old, but Irv Blumkin of the Nebraska Furniture Mart, in Omaha, Nebraska, is one of them. Despite his long tenure with the Furniture Mart, however, the 48-year-old chairman and CEO has only officially been on the payroll since 1975.

Born in Omaha in 1951, he always knew that he would eventually work full-time in the family business that his grandmother, Rose Blumkin, founded in 1937. Even so, after graduating from the University of Arizona in 1974 with a business degree, Irv enrolled in the management program of a Tucson bank. He had intended to get a bit more business experience before joining the family firm, but when a tornado destroyed the store on May 6, 1975, he came home, and hasn't left since.

His father, Louis, who was president of NFM at the time, had him work on the loading docks, on the sales floor, and in administration, to show him, as the younger Blumkin puts it, "what real life was all about in retailing." Irv became chairman when his father stepped down in the mid-1980s (Louis now serves as Chairman Emeritus of the Board), and he shares the responsibility of running the store with his brother Ron, who is president and COO, and his cousin, Robert Batt, who is a vice president.

In terms of the division of labor, Irv says, "My father watches over his kids and makes sure we don't screw up too badly. My brother pretty much takes care of operations, and I take care of merchandising, marketing, and advertising." The arrangement has worked well for everyone in the family, as well as for the store.

Mrs. B—as Blumkin's grandmother was known—would certainly have been proud of her grandsons. Since 1983, when Mrs. B sold 80 percent of the Furniture Mart to Warren Buffett for $55 million, annual sales have increased more than four times—from $89 million to $365 million. Another measure of Mrs. B's grandsons' performance is that the store's sales per square foot were $443 then and are $865 now. Perhaps even more important from Buffett's perspective, although the Furniture

Mart is definitely not for sale, its current value is estimated at $548 million.* Combined with estimated accumulated pretax earnings of $272 million over the past 17 years, which includes an estimated $32 million from year 2000, the Furniture Mart has added a total estimated value of $820 million to Berkshire Hathaway—a 17.2 percent annual internal rate of return.

The store has grown in size as well. From its meager beginnings in a basement, it has grown to be the largest-volume furniture retailer in North America, with 1,500 employees and 422,000 square feet of selling space on a 77-acre campus. As might be expected, the Blumkins' store also completely dominates its market. In a 1998 survey, 69 percent of the residents in the Omaha metropolitan area named the Furniture Mart as the store in which they had spent the most on furniture in the previous 12 months. Its closest competitor had 8 percent.[1]

The Furniture Mart dominates the market to such an extent that when Dillard's, one of the most successful department store chains in the country, opened a store in Omaha, it chose not to have a furniture department. "We don't want to compete with them," chairman William Dillard said, referring to the Furniture Mart. "We think they are about the best there is."[2]

But NFM isn't only the dominant furniture store in Omaha. It's also one of the top three furniture sellers among the residents of Des Moines, Iowa, which is more than 100 miles away. It attracts a considerable number of customers from Kansas City, Missouri, which the New York Times likened to "persuading New York residents to shop in Baltimore." Local customers arrange to have the Furniture Mart ship furniture to their vacation homes in Florida and the Southwest, as well as to their relatives around the country.[3]

The company has also grown by acquisitions. In 1993, NFM bought Floors, Inc., a commercial flooring business in Lincoln, Nebraska, and, in the following year, opened a commercial appliance sales office in Des Moines.[4] In 2000, it purchased Homemakers Furniture of Des Moines, including its WoodMarc Manufacturing unit, in Winterset, Iowa.[5] In February 2001, the Blumkin family announced its first major expansion and replication: It plans to open a Nebraska Furniture Mart in Kansas City in

---

* NFM is difficult to value because it is a unique home furnishings retailer that sells at warehouse prices. Estimated valuation of $548 million is 1½ times sales, or 17 times estimated pretax earnings.

2003. Although Warren Buffett has said he would be interested in funding a Furniture Mart in another city, such as Denver or Minneapolis, he recognizes that the Blumkins make all the decisions regarding their business. "I'd love it if they'd do it," Buffett says, "but I wouldn't ask them to."[6]

Irv was already responsible for the store's merchandising and advertising when Warren Buffett bought the company nearly two decades ago. Looking back now, he thinks he understands exactly what attracted Buffett to the Mart. "He admired my grandmother and my father for many years," Blumkin says of Buffett. "He saw the business evolve into a dominant force that had a good franchise, that knew what they were doing, that continued to profit over a long period of time. It had the elements of the kinds of businesses he likes to buy."

Irv has been instrumental in the growth of Berkshire Hathaway's home furnishings group. Buffett solicited suggestions for possible acquisitions from the Blumkins when he bought the Furniture Mart, and they recommended three outstanding furniture retailers in other parts of the country. Although none of them was available for sale at the time, Buffett was able to start acting on Blumkin's suggestions years later, and eventually acquired all three.[7]

He explained how it came about in his 1995 letter to Berkshire stockholders: "Over the years, Irv had told me about the strengths of R.C. Willey, the leading home furnishings business in Utah. And he had also told Bill Child, CEO of R.C. Willey, how pleased the Blumkin family had been with its Berkshire relationship. So in early 1995, Bill mentioned to Irv that for estate tax and diversification reasons, he and the other owners of R.C. Willey might be interested in selling. From that point forward, things could not have been simpler. Bill sent me some figures, and I wrote him a letter indicating my idea of value. We quickly agreed on a number, and found our personal chemistry to be perfect. By mid-year, the merger was completed."[8]

Bill Child, in turn, seconded Irv Blumkin's recommendation that Buffett consider Star Furniture of Houston, headed by Melvyn Wolff. With two such recommendations, Buffett looked into it and decided that the company met Berkshire's criteria in that it was "understandable," possessed "excellent economics," and was "run by outstanding people." As a result, he purchased the organization for Berkshire in 1997, making it the third member of its furniture group.[9]

Buffett was so pleased with his furniture retailing acquisitions that he continued to ask Blumkin, Child, and Wolff for recommendations, and all three suggested he look into Jordan's, Eliot and Barry Tatelman's New England furniture business. Berkshire purchased the business in 1999, which enabled him to say in his Chairman's Letter that year: "Each of our furniture operations is number one in its territory. We now sell more furniture than anyone else in Massachusetts, New Hampshire, Texas, Nebraska, Utah and Idaho."[10] As a result of this latest acquisition, Berkshire Hathaway's furniture group now generates annual sales of over $1 billion.

Buffett used mostly cash to acquire his furniture holdings and, as a result, invested an estimated $600 million in businesses that are all dominating and growing with a conservative valuation of $1.5 billion.* Furniture is fashion-oriented and subject to change, but each home-furnishings acquisition has had a very wide moat around the business. The franchise value of each business may be that it consistently does well for its customers. Some have said Berkshire, starting with the Furniture Mart, has a virtual monopoly in the home furnishings markets it serves.

And what exactly was it that Blumkin—and Buffett—saw in those companies? As Blumkin tells it, "The character and the quality of the people would be number one. Second, they are all retailers who dominate their markets, who've built great businesses over long periods of time, and who still love what they do. In other words, they're people who know their businesses and are passionate about them—the best of the best."

Although Buffett has acted on more of Blumkin's suggested acquisitions than those of any other company chief in the Berkshire Hathaway family, with characteristic modesty the CEO of NFM says that after he has made a suggestion, "I let Warren make all the decisions. He looks at them and decides." Blumkin won't say exactly how many of the companies he's suggested have ultimately been purchased by Buffett, but he's willing to admit, "Our batting average is very good."

And Buffett is appropriately grateful. "There's no operation in the furniture retailing business remotely like the one assembled by Berkshire. It's fun for me and profitable for you," he told his stockholders in 1999. "W. C. Fields once said, 'It was a woman who drove me to drink, but unfortunately I never had the chance to thank her.' I don't want to make that

---

* Using the same value method of 1½ times sales or 17 times earnings.

mistake. My thanks go to Louie, Ron and Irv Blumkin for getting me started in the furniture business and for unerringly guiding me as we have assembled the group we now have."[11]

Blumkin in turn has nothing but good things to say about Berkshire Hathaway and Warren Buffett. Although Irv had input, as did the rest of the family, in the end it was Mrs. B who made the deal that merged the Nebraska Furniture Mart into Berkshire. Irv considers it to have been a "win-win deal, a great deal for all." His experience with Buffett and Berkshire since the merger has only reinforced his view that the deal was advantageous for everyone.

Just as Berkshire has been well served by the Blumkins, both from their Furniture Mart home furnishings business and their advice on other potential acquisition candidates, the Blumkins have benefited from the association with its famous parent company. Who has done better? The Blumkins were able to take $55 million out of the business in the beginning of the partnership, get an additional estimated accumulated $54 million in pretax earnings over the years, and still get ever-increasing dividends (now estimated at $6.5 million). Their remaining 20 percent business interest is now worth an estimated $110 million, and they have access to the smartest business mind available. The family has maintained control of the business, dealt with the transition of ownership and management, and solved the estate tax challenge of all successful businesses. These are remarkable returns on their investment, even by Berkshire's standards.

Like virtually all of Berkshire Hathaway's operating managers, Irv Blumkin happily says that his company operates the same way today as it did before being taken over by Buffett. "In my brother's and my father's mind, we own 100 percent of the Furniture Mart, and we act exactly like we own 100 percent. It was like nothing happened other than we got a great guy to bounce ideas off of and a perfect partner. From an operational standpoint, we've changed for the sake of changing and improving—our business has grown, we've added buildings—but in the end how we operate or what we do hasn't changed at all."

Like his grandmother and his father, he has been left alone to run the company. He says that even if Berkshire had not taken over, "As far as our business is concerned, we would be right where we are today." Nevertheless, he readily admits that "there is a full host of benefits to just being associated with Berkshire. You'd never have an opportunity to get in business with a better partner. What you see is what you get. You can go to the bank, 100 percent, on everything that Berkshire and Warren tell you, and it's a great time. Berkshire is the most perfect partner. Lets you do what you want to do and at the same time you've got access to one of the smartest minds there ever was."

Blumkin can, in fact, wax poetic on the subject of Warren Buffett. When asked for his thoughts on the best things about his boss, he said, "There are so many 'bests' to working with Warren. One of the best is that he's just a great guy who is able to take these things that sometimes seem so challenging and put them into simple terms. He is such a motivating kind of person. He is so smart. Every time we meet with him, it's just like getting to go to a class. And he is the most honorable guy you'd ever want to know. There isn't just one best—he's a great package."

He's also quick to defend Buffett against some of the most frequently heard charges against him in recent years—that he doesn't understand technology, is overly frugal, and has lost his touch. "They are all misconceptions," Blumkin says. "People who are close to him and know him, know that he's got a heart of gold. And that, as smart as he is, you can still relate to him. He's about as close to perfect as you can get. He's my hero."

When asked whether Buffett is better at allocating capital or managing people, Blumkin insists, "He is terrific at both. Of course, his primary function is allocating capital and he's done that sensationally. But he's also one of the very best managers I've ever met. He says that what he does best is capital allocation, but, as somebody who works for him, I can tell you that he's a sensational manager, as good as there is.

"He's much smarter than me," Blumkin continues. "He's much more long term, and he's been a great teacher who's taught us about patience and taking the long-term view. He's also taught us about doing right and winning. There are just *so many* lessons. We've been really lucky to have been exposed to those lessons, really lucky just being able to get to know him.

"People are motivated by different things," he says. "I think that most of the people Warren is in business with aren't doing it for the money. Generally speaking, they already have enough money. It's just the love of the game, of doing what you do, the satisfaction. And," he adds, "I do it to make Warren proud."

Even though he considers the Furniture Mart's overall contribution to Berkshire Hathaway to be small, Blumkin is—not surprisingly—very pleased to be part of the Berkshire family. He is so happy about it that he has put most of his personal investments into Berkshire, and, as already noted, helped convince Bill Child of R.C. Willey, Melvyn Wolff of Star Furniture, and the Tatelman brothers of Jordan's to join the family.

As is the case with Buffett, Blumkin has nothing but good things to say about his cohorts in the furniture group. "They are all great at different things," he says, and he thinks that diversity is one of Berkshire's greatest assets. "Mel Wolff," he says, "has a really clear vision," and is a "really smart, astute operator who knows who he is and who he isn't." Bill Child, in his opinion, is "a very aggressive, go-getter optimist who's built a sensational business through a lot of hard work." And as for Eliot and Barry Tatelman, he considers them to be the "funniest and most creative. They built the business by giving the customer a good time and good value that no other furniture retailer has been able to do. They've accomplished what we'd like to accomplish. They give the customer a sensational experience, and I admire both of them a lot."

As a result, even though Berkshire isn't a particularly close-knit family, with the addition of these three retailers—as well as Berkshire's recently acquired Homemakers and Cort Furniture—Blumkin believes that there are possibilities for synergy. Toward this end, he recently participated in a meeting of executives from the furniture group so they could get together to share ideas. One idea picked up from Jordan's was a colorful, fun, fire-engine-themed child-size pushcart. Parents can give their children a ride as they shop, and enjoy the whole home furnishings shopping experience.

"I think, over time, there is going to be some great synergy," he says. "It could be buying synergies, and could be an operational kind of synergies. There are a whole host of different possible avenues. Just the idea of being able to communicate and share information with peers who are dominant in their markets is really positive. But, in the end, we still all run our own businesses our own way, which is the beautiful thing about Berkshire."

Despite his enormous admiration for Buffett and his Berkshire Hathaway colleagues, Blumkin considers his father Louie, his mother Frances, and his aunts and uncles, Irving and Gail Veitzer and Norm and Joodi Veitzer, to have had the most influence on him and his management style. He also credits his wife Susie with being a major influence. "She's a great wife, friend, partner, and mother," he says. But he credits his father with having the greatest influence, calling him "a great teacher and coach."

He describes that management style as being "in touch and very involved," and he's clearly very people-oriented. "We think of people, our staff, as our family," he says. "We try to still run it like a family business. Fortunately, our company has grown every year so we've never had to lay people off. And because we've been so successful, we've also been able to avoid having to make other kinds of tough decisions. Of course, we try to watch our costs and continually grow, and we try to prepare our business for tough times. Occasionally we get a little overweight here and there, but for the most part we've been able to not get ourselves into a position where we really have to make those tough decisions."

When asked about the traits required to be a successful operating manager, he says, "First of all, knowing the business, and knowing what you know and what you don't know. Second is working at a circle of competence and understanding it. And third is knowing what makes the business work. Of course, these are in addition to the core value kind of things like honesty and integrity, being a low-cost operator, and trying to dominate the markets you participate in. These are the things that have made the Furniture Mart work."

At the same time, Blumkin considers the most important thing to be "satisfying customers in big volumes, and being able to do it much better" than his competition, and it's this aspect of his work he gets most excited about. In fact, he says that what keeps him up nights is trying to "figure out ways to improve and grow the business by constantly reinventing and figuring out ways to better serve the customer."

He determines how well the Furniture Mart is meeting those goals by measuring seven critical areas of the business: (1) sales, (2) margin, (3) expenses, (4) profit, (5) nonoperating profit, (6) customer survey results or customer preference studies, and (7) human resources turnover. "But, in the end," he says, "I really measure how well we satisfy the customers, because if we do that, they keep coming back and making those other things happen."

In fact, although he doesn't call it such, he sees the Furniture Mart's mission as "trying to improve people's lifestyles through selection and value." He says, "It's really about the basics: understanding your customer, taking care of your customer, practicing blocking and tackling. The kind of things that my grandmother has done, that Sam Walton has done. It's trying to take these complex businesses and getting them down to an understanding of what's really important to the customer."

Aside from not focusing on the customer, Blumkin thinks that the errors that most commonly lead to business failure are: "Becoming too big too fast, losing focus on what you do best, divesting from your core competency, and being overleveraged." He has avoided these mistakes. The Nebraska Furniture Mart has grown over the years, but not too quickly and not at the expense of moving away from the Blumkins' core competency: selling furniture, appliances, electronics, and floor coverings. In addition, the family has followed his grandmother's dictate to not take on mortgages or other debts and, instead, to pay cash for everything.

Interestingly, the mistake that Blumkin considers his greatest business failure—and his biggest personal regret—also concerns his grandmother. "Having my grandmother get mad at me and opening up her own business," he says, "was not a very good decision. It had a big impact on the family, and it confused the customers. They didn't know whether they were buying from the Furniture Mart or Mrs. B's." If he had a chance to do it again, he says, he would have "figured a way to have patience and work it out. You know," he adds, referring to himself, his brother, and his cousin, "we were aggressive young tigers who couldn't wait, who wanted everything done the way we wanted it, and right away."

Now, he says, one of his personal goals is to lighten up. Perhaps he feels the need to do so because he describes himself as "focused, passionate about my business, hardworking, dedicated, loyal, and honest. The sort of the things," he adds, "that we try to live our lives by." Although he may not continue working as late into life as his grandmother did, at age 48 he has no plans to retire. "I love my job," he says. He intends to keep doing it "as long as I am having a good time. At some time in the future I might like to take it a little easier, but I'd still like to work as long as I can and I'm able."

A typical day for Blumkin starts off at about 6:00 in the morning. He does a little exercising, gets to work early, and walks the floor. His ideal is to find the store in pristine shape for the customers, to be able to watch them pour into the store, and to see them leave satisfied. Later in the day, he attends meetings, spends time performing his buying function, and, before he goes home, tries to "get organized for the next day and figure out what I didn't get done that day so I can plan it." He typically leaves the office at around 6:30 P.M. and goes home to his wife and children, whom he considers "huge contributors to my life's successes."

He does, however, work on Sundays—every Sunday that he's in town. "We like to be close to where the action is," he says by way of explanation. "And Sunday's a good day to get a lot of things done. Not a lot of other people are working, so we can get a lot of productivity. My brother works on Sunday too, and I like it."

His grandmother would certainly have liked his working on Sundays as well. As a representative of the third generation of Blumkins to run the Nebraska Furniture Mart, Irv is a good example of what may happen at Berkshire, its parent company, when Warren Buffett retires and a second, and eventually a third, generation takes over. With less than 30 percent of businesses succeeding to a second generation and even fewer (some 13 percent) to a third generation,[12] the Blumkins have provided a long-term succession road map for concerned shareholders.

Keeping a family business alive is perhaps the toughest management job on earth. Fewer than 5 percent of all businesses ever started actually become family businesses through the appointment of a successor from the next generation. The dying family business so permeates our business culture that it has become legendary. Expressions such as "Shirtsleeves to shirtsleeves in three generations" and "Rags to riches to rags" are common. All these axioms and sayings suggest the same sequence: The first generation builds the business, the second generation "milks" or "harvests" it, and the third generation must either auction off what's left or start all over again.[13]

Keeping the family business strong, healthy, and prosperous through three family generations may be Mrs. B's greatest accomplishment. Berkshire's furniture group has solely achieved the greatest multigenerational family-management success stories. Few other business groups have had even second-generational family succession, let alone third.

As for the future, Blumkin's growth strategy is simple: "Continually to grow." While he says that he has no specific goal as far as growth is concerned, "We've grown our business for 63 years, with no down years, and what we want to do is continue that string. We are the third generation," he points out, "so we just have to make sure we don't screw it up." While admitting that he feels a lot of pressure after 63 years of success, he says, "It's only self-imposed pressure. We don't feel any pressure from Warren calling and putting pressure on us. It's just us trying to be successful all the time."

To maintain that success, Blumkin is continually looks for opportunities. "It could be acquisitions," he says, "it could be building a store somewhere else, and it could be none of the above. We just continue trying to do what we do best, and do it where we are comfortable doing it. We are painting our picture all the time. We're not sure exactly how it is going to turn out, but we continually try to improve the view."

Interestingly, when asked who will be Nebraska Furniture Mart's biggest competitors in 10 years, Blumkin doesn't cite other furniture retailers. "I think it is anybody who's looking to get a percentage of the disposable income," he says. "It's not necessarily the people in the furniture business, or electronics, or appliances. It's the travel industry, the car dealers, the clothing stores, and all the other big retailers. Those are our competitors."

As for the future of the home furnishings business in general, Blumkin only sees it getting bigger and more consolidated. "It's a tough business," he explains, "and it takes lots of capital and a tremendous amount of understanding. And there is a limited supply of people who understand the whole picture. What we need to do in the future is improve quality, improve delivery, and do a better job of understanding the customer. We also have to raise the importance of the home in people's lives."

When asked about Berkshire Hathaway's future, he says, "That is Warren's responsibility, not mine. But I have 100 percent complete confidence about his vision, even though," he admits, "I'm not sure what his vision is. I think Warren keeps his mind open to all the opportunities that are available, picks the ones that he feels most comfortable with, and works within his area and circle of competence." Not surprisingly, Blumkin thinks that Berkshire is "absolutely" a good investment. "I'm not an investment adviser," he adds, "but if I had more money, I'd be investing in Berkshire."

Despite the fact that Berkshire continues to grow larger, he's not concerned that it might become too big. "Certainly it becomes more challenging as you get bigger," he explains, "but in the end, given the way Warren has structured how the people do their businesses, I can't imagine it being an obstacle. We have our little world and we run it. We are part of a bigger world, and it's just a bunch of little pieces making up this big pie."

Perhaps as a result of this thinking, the question that is of so much concern to Berkshire Hathaway shareholders—What will happen when Warren is gone?—is of very little concern to Blumkin. He is sure that Buffett's choice to succeed himself—whether it is one individual or, as has been suggested, an operating manager and a capital allocation manager—will have been well thought out. "I don't worry about it for one second," Blumkin says. "With Warren's vision and his ability to pick people, it will be a nonissue."

Whatever happens, Buffett surely will consider the Nebraska Furniture Mart to be in as good hands as Blumkin considers Berkshire Hathaway to be. "I have been asked by a number of people," Buffett told his stockholders in 1984, "just what secrets the Blumkins bring to their business. These are not very esoteric. All members of the family: (1) apply themselves with an enthusiasm and energy that would make Ben Franklin and Horatio Alger look like dropouts; (2) define with extraordinary realism their area of special competence and act decisively on all matters within it; (3) ignore even the most enticing propositions falling outside of that area of special competence; and, (4) unfailingly behave in a high-grade manner with everyone they deal with."[14]

## IRVIN BLUMKIN'S BUSINESS TENETS

- ★ View your staff as if they were family.
- ★ Monitor your costs so you don't overspend and then have to cut back.
- ★ Work at understanding and satisfying your customers and continue to find new ways to serve them.
- ★ Know your core business and stick to it.
- ★ Avoid debt. Wherever possible, pay cash.

# chapter eleven

# The Retired Manager—
# Frank Rooney, H.H. Brown Shoe

*I*had met with Malcolm Kim Chace, a board member and one of the original family that owned and managed the Berkshire textile mills. I
wanted to understand what Buffett saw in textiles in 1962, when he first
started acquiring shares. Was that insight related to his strategy in
footwear investments? Chace, whose family watched their stock soar to a
billion dollars under Buffett's management, shared with me old annual reports and pointed out that there was a lot of value in Berkshire when Buffett first started purchasing the stock. And, in a classic Graham value
play, Buffett invested in textiles and Berkshire when the market value was
$14 million and the book value was $22 million. Textiles and Berkshire
Hathaway weren't Buffett's worst investments after all. He bought a dollar in assets for less than 64 cents, and he successfully deployed those assets into other businesses. Chace watched as Buffett increased his family's
stock from $7 per share to over $70,000 in 3½ decades.

Footwear manufacturing faced the same peril as textiles. Hundreds of
textile manufacturers closed their domestic plants and shifted production to
the Far East. So did footwear factories. Domestic footwear sales are at an
all-time high (more than 1 billion pairs annually) but profits from manufacturing are found outside the United States.

Frank Rooney, CEO of H.H. Brown, gave me a tour of his Nantucket
summer home. Situated on a bluff, with a sweeping view of the western
harbor, his home has a million-dollar view. Rooney spends eight weeks
here during the summer—one week with each of his children and their children. In the winter, he is at North Palm Beach. In the rest of the year, he
lives with his wife, Frances, in Rye, New York.

Taking a break from his daily golf game, we talked about his most unusual retirement. First, he built a business that would eventually become

*CVS drug stores. He retired but then was pressed into service when he sold his father-in-law's shoe business to Warren Buffett. Before our conversation, he called Buffett to ask, "What do I tell this guy—why you bought into the footwear business?" Buffett's reply was, "Frank, tell him I bought in because of you."*

On August 18, 1999, *The Boston Globe* reported that, a few days earlier, a fairly unusual foursome had been spotted at the very exclusive Sankaty Head Golf Club on Nantucket Island, off the Massachusetts coast. The foursome included legendary CEOs from America's largest companies: Jack Welch of General Electric; Warren Buffett of Berkshire Hathaway; Bill Gates of Microsoft, and, as the *Globe* put it, "a member of the Rooney family, which owns the Pittsburgh Steelers."[1]

He made no effort to correct the error, but the Rooney on the links that day was not a member of the family that owns the Steelers. It was Massachusetts-born Francis C. Rooney, Jr., Chairman and CEO of H.H. Brown, a Greenwich, Connecticut-based shoe manufacturing company that ranks as one of America's leading manufacturers of work shoes and boots. And what, one may ask, was the relatively unknown Rooney doing in that august company? He is a Nantucket neighbor and friend of Welch, and the company he runs is part of the Berkshire Hathaway group. He sold it to Warren Buffett in 1991.

Rooney was born in 1921, in North Brookfield, Massachusetts—the town in which H.H. Brown had been founded 40 years earlier. He received a bachelor's degree in economics from the Wharton School of the University of Pennsylvania in 1943. Upon graduation, he was commissioned an ensign in the U.S. Navy, and he served on the battleship *U.S.S. North Carolina* for the duration of the Second World War. After the war, he went into the shoe business, working first for the Florsheim Shoe Company in Chicago, and then for the Melville Shoe Corporation, which manufactured Thom McAn shoes.

He rose through the ranks, became merchandise manager and then president of the Thom McAn Division, and finally, in 1964, CEO of Melville, the parent company. As CEO, he began a program of diversification. Melville purchased companies such as Marshall's, KB Toys, This End Up Furniture, and, in 1969, the CVS chain of drugstores. When Rooney had taken over the reins, annual sales had been $180 million. By the time he retired 20 years later, that figure had increased to nearly $7 billion.

One might think that, after such an achievement, Rooney would have enjoyed retirement. After all, being able to take early retirement is a hallmark of success to a businessperson. To a professional, however, success might well mean not retiring at all. Love of what they do refuels many professionals, and Frank Rooney is, if nothing else, a professional. Six years after he left Melville Shoe (since renamed Melville Corporation), when he was invited by his father-in-law, Ray Heffernan, to step in and run H.H. Brown, he accepted the offer.

H.H. Brown had been founded in 1883 by Henry H. Brown[2] and was purchased by Heffernan, then a 29-year-old businessman, for $10,000 in 1927. Years later, one of Heffernan's daughters, Frances, married Frank Rooney, who was already in the shoe business himself. At the time, Heffernan told his new son-in-law to forget any ideas he might have about a job with H.H. Brown.[3] But by the late 1980s, even though Heffernan was still running the company at age 92, he was ailing. And recognizing that he was no longer capable of serving as CEO, he asked Rooney to take over until he was well again. But Heffernan died in 1990, and the family decided the company should be sold.

At that point, Rooney hired Goldman Sachs to make up a book on H.H. Brown, and started to look for potential customers for the business. During a golf match in Florida, a friend, John Loomis, suggested that Rooney should contact Warren Buffett, whom Rooney had once met. As Rooney tells it, he "called Warren and told him about this family business, and Warren said, 'Well, it sounds interesting. Don't send me any of that stuff from Goldman Sachs, just send me the audited numbers for the last couple of years.'" So Rooney sent Buffett the P&L and balance sheets from the preceding few years. Buffett called and asked, "How much do you want for the business?"

"I don't know." Rooney answered. "I guess we've got to test the market." Buffett suggested that Rooney should contact him once he'd decided on a figure. With sales of about $240 million and pretax earnings of about $24 million, Rooney figured the company was probably worth a couple of hundred million dollars. Some time later, Buffett called and said, "I'm coming to New York. Would you like to have lunch?"

As Rooney tells it (with a New England accent), "So my brother-in-law and I had lunch with him. And Warren said, 'If I give you the number that you're talking about, would you stop talking to anyone else?' I said, 'Yes,' and he said, 'Okay, we got a deal.' So my brother-in-law and I took a walk around the block and came back and said, 'Okay, that's it.' Warren hadn't seen a factory and he hadn't met any of the people. Why the hell did he buy a shoe company? I asked him later, and he said, 'The only reason I bought it was because of you.'"

In fact, as Buffett subsequently reported in his 1991 "Chairman's Letter to Shareholders": "Much of my enthusiasm for this purchase came from Frank's willingness to continue as CEO. Like most of our managers, he has no financial need to work but does so because he loves the game and likes to excel. Managers of this stripe cannot be 'hired' in the normal sense of the word. What we must do is provide a concert hall in which business artists of this class will wish to perform."[4]

The company Buffett acquired—along with Frank Rooney—manufactures, imports, and markets work, safety, and outdoor boots, as well as western and casual shoes. The footwear is sold, under a number of different brand names, through 22 company-operated retail outlets across the mid-Atlantic states and through such retailers as Dillard's, JCPenney, Sears, and Payless Shoe Company. H.H. Brown is the leading American producer of steel-toed safety work shoes, and competes in the middle-priced markets in which consumers are often industrial workers who are required by law to wear a certain type of shoe.[5]

For his part, Frank Rooney was no less pleased with Berkshire's takeover of the company. Although he says that the stockholders of Berkshire Hathaway got the better of the deal, Buffett did pay what Rooney thought the company was worth, and Rooney believes that H.H. Brown is considerably better off now than it would have been without Berkshire. Rooney can operate as if the business is still 100 percent family-owned. With unlimited access to capital, he can and did acquire other footwear makers to strengthen his shoe group. When asked if Buffett's company was the acquirer of choice, he readily agrees, adding that being part of the organization is "the next best thing to being in business for yourself."

Like virtually all businesses, the shoe business has changed dramatically since H.H. Brown opened its doors in North Brookfield more than a century ago. At the time, the shoe industry was entirely domestic and represented the largest employer in Massachusetts. The area around Brockton alone had more than 100 factories.[6] But cheaper labor and other lower costs overseas have led most American shoe companies to concentrate on importing rather than manufacturing their products.

During the past 10 years, the number of pairs of shoes produced in the United States has decreased from more than 234 million to less than 76 million, a drop of almost 70 percent. Of the 1,354,568,000 pairs sold in the United States in 1999, 1,305,262,000—more than 96 percent—were produced overseas, predominantly in China.[7] Fifty years ago, the industry employed 75,000 workers in Massachusetts alone; that number has now dwindled to 5,000.[8] The 25 tanneries that once operated in the United States have now been reduced to only two or three.

Faced with increasingly cheaper competition—and noting the tactic of the better known companies in the industry, such as Nike and Reebok—H.H. Brown, under Rooney's leadership, has shifted most of its manufacturing overseas. In the past few years, Brown has gone from producing 90 percent of its shoes in the United States to only 40 percent. Changing the mix of its imported and manufactured products has, of course, meant letting go a substantial number of employees. The company had approximately 3,500 people at the time of the merger with Berkshire Hathaway. It now employs only about 2,000.

Although Rooney regrets the resulting loss of American jobs, he also recognizes that this is the only way his company can continue to be a player in this increasingly competitive environment. One of the things that Warren Buffett stresses to all the companies in the Berkshire Hathaway family is the importance of having a durable competitive advantage, and what he refers to as a "big moat" (i.e., protection) around it. Rooney admits that H.H. Brown doesn't have as wide a moat as it might have—which represents a challenge—but he insists that it does have an advantage over its competitors.

"The fact is," Rooney says, "that we are a niche kind of business, and we have a unique niche. We make the specialty shoes for miners, telephone-pole climbers, and people in those kinds of jobs. It requires having a lot of short runs, and we can do short runs and still make money, which some of our competitors can't. That's also why we can't import all of our products—because we need to be fast and flexible, and be able to satisfy the customer." H.H. Brown's customers represent another unique niche for the company. Because they are largely people who are on their feet all day, and consequently consider what they put on their feet to be extremely important, they are willing to pay more for quality.

As a result, the company is growing, partly through acquisition and partly through new product development. In 1992, H.H. Brown bought the Hudson, New Hampshire-based Lowell Shoe Company,[9] a division of Morse Shoes, for $46.2 million,[10] and absorbed it into the company's existing operation, thus adding Nurse Mates, a leading line of shoes for nurses, as well as other kinds of shoes, to its product lines.[11] It also acquired Super Shoes, a chain of family shoe stores, and—in 1997—a technological company called Dicon, which makes a foam that absorbs perspiration in a shoe's insole and lining.

Brown is now involved in developing a women's shoe business and introducing several new lines, including a new brand called Börn, which has a unique hand-sewn type of construction and has been doing very well. Still, even though H.H. Brown has seen respectable growth in both sales and profits, the costs of closing factories and providing severance pay has made the company's already relatively small financial contribution to Berkshire lower than it might have been.

Nevertheless, Brown has fared considerably better than the other shoe operation Berkshire Hathaway purchased since the merger with Brown— Dexter Shoe Company—which Buffett acquired in 1993. The purchase of Dexter was similar, in many respects, to that of H.H. Brown. This time, Rooney was the matchmaker. He had known Dexter's owners—Harold Alfond and Peter Lunder—for many years, and had recommended that Buffett take a look at the company. He also told Alfond and Lunder that he thought Berkshire would provide an ideal corporate home for their company.[12] Buffett's first meeting with Alfond and Lunder took place in an airport in West Palm Beach, Florida.[13] "We went to some little restaurant based on a World War II theme," Buffett later told Forbes, "had a hamburger, and talked about shoes."[14]

Although Buffett made a cash offer on the spot, the two men told him they would prefer Berkshire Hathaway stock. Buffett rarely gives away stock, and was not enthusiastic about doing so in this instance. Nevertheless, several months later, at a time when Berkshire stock was trading at close to an all-time high, Buffett met again with the two men—this time, in Lunder's Boston apartment. Without any lawyers, accountants, or investment bankers present, the three men made the deal. In return for the Dexter Shoe Company, Alfond and Lunder received 25,203 shares of Berkshire Hathaway stock (at the time, worth approximately $420 million). This gave the two men 2 percent of Berkshire's stock, and made them the largest shareholders outside of the Buffett family.[15]

Taking over Dexter certainly seemed like a good idea at the time. The company had been founded in 1957 in Dexter, Maine, by Harold Alfond, with an outlay of $10,000. His nephew, Peter Lunder, joined the organization the following year. Thirty five years later, Dexter was a very successful operation, selling about $250 million worth of men's and women's dress, casual, and athletic shoes (particularly golf and bowling shoes). It marketed its products through 90 factory outlet stores across the country, as well as through department stores, upper-scale independent stores, and specialty retailers.[16]

But even as Buffett and Berkshire Hathaway were getting more involved in shoe manufacturing, U.S. shoe companies were in the process of changing from manufacturers/marketers to importers/marketers. H.H. Brown was able to weather the storm by closing several of its plants and shifting production overseas, but Dexter continued to insist on maintaining full employment in its four factories in Maine.[17] As a result, revenues for Berkshire's shoe business—which includes Brown, Lowell, and Dexter—began to drop in 1995, and continued dropping through the end of the decade.

What made the Dexter purchase even more of a debacle was the fact that Buffett paid for it with stock. The stock that was worth $420 million at the time of the takeover is worth nearly $2 billion today. And this for a company that has returned only $100 million in estimated pretax earnings. Using industry standards, Dexter is actually worth only $100 million, one half of its estimated annual sales, or just about 5 percent of an ever-increasing purchase price. It's no wonder that, at a meeting held on September 16, 1998, Warren Buffett found it necessary to admit that the shoe segment was "not a big winner" for Berkshire Hathaway.[18] Dexter shoes may prove to be Buffett's worst investment.

Perhaps fortunately for Frank Rooney's standing with Warren Buffett, Dexter Shoe was not the only company he suggested that Buffett should consider as a candidate for the Berkshire Hathaway family. In 1994, about a year after he'd suggested that Buffett should talk with Alfond and Lunder,

Rooney also told his boss about Rich Santulli and Executive Jet. Based in Columbus, Ohio, Executive Jet (described in detail in Chapter 8) provides individuals and companies with a variety of aviation services, most importantly through its NetJets programs in the United States, Europe, and the Middle East. These fractional aircraft ownership programs enable individuals and companies to enjoy the benefits of aircraft ownership without incurring the high cost of owning and maintaining their own aircraft.

At Rooney's suggestion, Buffett had tried the service offered by the company, and was immediately sold on its advantages. In 1998, he bought the company for $725 million, paid in equal amounts of cash and stock. The investment has definitely paid off.[19] Executive Jet's sales doubled from $1 billion in 1999 to $2 billion in 2000, and its value has skyrocketed since the acquisition. So, although Dexter Shoe has become insignificant to the overall success of Berkshire Hathaway, Executive Jet may eventually be bigger than FedEx, and may represent a considerable future share of Berkshire's sales, earnings, and net worth. Its success—and its potential—may help explain why Buffett has such positive things to say about Frank Rooney. "Frank has a low-key, relaxed style," he once told his shareholders, "but don't let that fool you. When he swings, the ball disappears far over the fence."[20]

Perhaps not surprisingly, Rooney has equally positive things to say about Warren Buffett. "He's an unusual personality," Rooney says, "like an old shoe. He is fun. He is bright. He is funny. He is enjoyable. He is crazy. . . . When he comes to visit, he makes his own breakfast, which is a ham sandwich and a Cherry Coke. It seems to me," Rooney continues, "that he only does the things that are fun for him to do. It's the people and associating with the people that he enjoys. Otherwise, he's not interested." And, as a result, Rooney adds, "It's fun to be part of Warren's inner circle."

Rooney does not, however, believe that Buffett has a master plan for Berkshire Hathaway. "I think Warren's more opportunistic than that," he says. "He obviously has a mind that looks to the future in terms of demographics and things of that nature. But, generally speaking, I don't get the impression that there is one overall master plan. I've never talked to him about it, and it may be that he wouldn't admit it. He may try to tell you he has some sort of plan. But I think if he saw a good deal for a company that was making tin cans tomorrow, he'd make the deal. And what the hell that would have to do with some long-range plan, I don't know."

On a more personal level, he credits Buffett with keeping him working. "Though 'working' means nothing to me financially," Buffett recently wrote, "I love doing it at Berkshire for some simple reasons: It gives me a sense of accomplishment, a freedom to act as I see fit, and an opportunity to interact daily with people I like and trust. Why should our managers— accomplished artists at what they do—see things differently?"[21] Rooney doesn't see it any differently at all. "He's given me purpose," he says of Buffett, "and I run H.H. Brown in order to make him proud."

Rooney has been most influenced by management guru Peter Drucker. Rooney says he met with Drucker on a quarterly basis when he was running Melville, and Drucker taught him the importance of defining one's business and concentrating on the satisfaction of the customer. He considers Drucker's *The Practice of Management* to be the best business book he has ever read. Although it was originally published in 1954, Drucker's classic dealt with all the essential questions facing business at that time, and continues to be consulted by businesspeople today. Rooney says, "It's my bible."

Rooney also says that his management style is "Keep it simple." Describing himself as "a people person," he considers decisions concerning people—hiring and firing decisions—the most difficult for him to make. The easiest, he says, are the day-to-day decisions. He believes that the most important attributes a successful operating manager needs are "integrity, honesty, and a fair amount of intelligence," and, perhaps unconsciously following Buffett's lead, that the best way to motivate his managers is to "just let them have fun." As far as skills are concerned, he believes that having the ability to delegate is essential, and not delegating is the single most common cause of business failures.

Perhaps because of the emphasis he places on these basic traits and skills, Rooney doesn't think that business and management have actually changed much over the years. "We've got all this new technology," he says, "but the people who are doing what we consider to be a good job are not necessarily doing anything different than they did 10 years ago."

Although generally self-deprecating about his own abilities, Rooney does seem to be particularly proud of one of his traits, which he believes he shares with Warren Buffett: being good with people and having the ability to accurately size them up. Like Buffett, who looks for business owners who are more interested in the business than the money, when

Rooney looks at people, he wants to know whether they have a passion about what they are doing. H.H. Brown has an unusual compensation system that both reflects and fosters that attitude among its managers. A number of key managers are paid a minimal four-figure annual salary, to which is added a percentage of the company's profits. Essentially, this places them in the position of owners rather than simply managers. The arrangement has worked well for both the managers and the company— perhaps, as Buffett has put it, because "Managers eager to bet heavily on their abilities usually have plenty of ability to bet on."[22]

The father of eight and grandfather of 26, Rooney, at age 79, describes himself as semiretired. He claims, with a laugh, that his deal with Warren Buffett allows him to work one day a week for the next 20 years—with a noncompete clause at the end of that time. When pressed, though, he admits that his agreement with Buffett isn't written; it is verbal and informal. Even so, becoming an operating manager in a Berkshire Hathaway company is like becoming a United States Supreme Court Justice: It is usually a lifetime appointment. In 34 years, no operating manager has ever left Berkshire, except as a result of death or retirement. In fact, most of Berkshire's companies are still managed by the executives who ran them before they were taken over by Buffett's company.[23]

And Rooney continues to work on a regular basis. During the spring and fall, he works five days a week, commuting from his home in Rye, New York, to the company's headquarters in Greenwich, Connecticut. Although he holds the titles of Chairman and CEO, the day-to-day operations of the company are in the hands of its COO, Jim Issler, who keeps him informed about everything he needs to know. In the summer, he stays at his home on Nantucket Island, off the Massachusetts coast, and in the winter he lives in North Palm Beach, Florida.

On those days when he goes into the office, he usually arrives between 9:00 and 9:30 A.M. and begins his day by walking around and greeting the members of the headquarters staff (between 35 and 40 employees). He then generally meets with Issler and joins him for lunch, along with between one and three of the company's key people. In the afternoon, he reads the *Wall Street Journal,* and may sit in on a meeting or two that Issler has arranged for him. Thus, despite his title, his role is really that of an adviser or consultant.

Regarding the future of the shoe business, Rooney argues: "It's always been a tough business, and it's going to be tough in the future. There will continue to be a shakeout, with fewer and fewer companies emerging out of it. But as long as people are born barefooted, there is going to be opportunity." More specifically, in regard to H.H. Brown's future, he says, "We have a strategy. We have a mission. It's not very fancy—just more blocking and more tackling, getting out there, defining the business. We talk a lot about the need to define one's business. It's not as easy as you think. Some people think it's just to make a profit, but we know that our business is one of satisfying customers. And we believe that if we stick to it, we'll be successful."

He measures his company's success against that of its closest competitor, Wolverine Worldwide. Based in Rockford, Michigan, and run by Timothy O'Donovan, Wolverine manufactures and markets a range of casual shoes, outdoor and work footwear, and slippers and moccasins, under a number of brand names, including Hush Puppies, Harley Davidson, and Coleman, among others. With approximately 5,900 employees—three times the size of H.H. Brown—Wolverine is ranked fifth in the industry. Its market value is $555 million, and it has flat annual sales of $670 million. Like Brown, it has maintained its success in large part by closing down its U.S. factories and buying most of its products from Asia.

Despite the deep cuts that have already been made in Brown's staff, Rooney says that they are only halfway through the process of making the company a leaner organization. Now manufacturing approximately 40 percent of its products in the United States, Rooney plans to cut that down to 20, or possibly 10, percent. He believes that the company can then easily become a $500 million business. And, he says, "With an acquisition here or there, we could get up to $1 billion some day."

As for the future of Berkshire Hathaway, Rooney believes that, despite its apparent recent direction, the company is more likely to evolve into something more like a conglomerate than a property casualty insurance company. "It's what Warren should do," he says. But, like everyone else, Rooney sees the designation of Warren Buffett's successor as the most important question concerning Berkshire's future. In the near term, he believes that Buffett will stay aboard and continue to make smart investments, and, for that reason, he thinks that Berkshire itself will be a good investment for the foreseeable future. Even so, he thinks that the importance of Buffett's retirement—which Buffett himself has defined as five years after he dies—has been overestimated. "As great as Warren is," he says, "I can't believe that there is only one individual who can manage a business."

Personally, Rooney feels he has no stake in the issue that is of so much concern to everyone else in the Berkshire Hathaway family. When asked if he worries about the transition from Warren to his successors, Rooney laughs. "Warren is only 70," he says. "I'm 79. So why the hell should I worry about that?"

## FRANK ROONEY'S BUSINESS TENETS

★ Management should be kept simple.
★ Let your managers share in the company profits and they'll act as if they're owners of the company.
★ Don't be afraid to delegate responsibility to your managers.
★ Encourage your managers to have fun.

# chapter twelve

# The Principled Manager—Bill Child, R.C. Willey Home Furnishings

*B*ill Child is a husband, a father, a grandfather, and a great-grandfather. His work, his family, and his faith define him.

His wife Patricia says her husband is a workaholic; he says he just loves his work. No doubt, the commitment, determination, and persistence Child has exhibited during his career were learned during his stint as an amateur boxer and runner.

Getting around Salt Lake City is easy because street addresses are determined by proximity to the Salt Lake Temple of The Church of Jesus Christ of Latter-day Saints. Bill's office and R.C. Willey's corporate address is "2301 South and 300 West," meaning that it is three blocks west and 23 blocks south of the Salt Lake Temple.

When I visited on Labor Day, Bill and his executive team were pumped. They wanted to reach their highest single-day goal: $8 million of sales of furniture, appliances, electronics, and carpet. Bill frequently checked each store's sales volume throughout the day, and kept a watchful eye on the results at his newest location, the Boise, Idaho, store.

Child is one of the most open managers I met. We were together for the entire day. During the interview, he introduced key managers, took phone calls, checked on sales numbers, listened to a customer's complaint, tested an Internet search engine, appeared on Jerry Lewis's telethon to present a check on behalf of R.C. Willey, and picked up litter in one of his parking lots.

When they observe his boundless energy and ready smile, visitors soon realize how this Buffett CEO built a business from $200,000 to $250,000,000 in 40 years and reached the pinnacle of business success by becoming partners with Warren Buffett and Berkshire Hathaway. Since the company was acquired, he has increased revenues and profits another 60 *percent and is on his way to achieving his next goal of $1 billion in annual sales. As his business has grown, so has his net worth; Berkshire's stock has tripled since he sold his business to Buffett.*

*With Bill Child, it isn't all about the money. It's about the challenge and about achieving great business success without compromising his principles. R.C. Willey was sold to Berkshire for all the logical reasons: liquidity, succession, estate taxes, and preservation of the business for his family, employees, customers, and community. This chief executive loves his business more than the money he got when he sold it to Buffett. He works harder for Berkshire shareholders than he worked for himself.*

*Bill Child's success is a genuine Horatio Alger story. It is the quintessential tale of a man from humble beginnings who has achieved great success from his hard work and high principles.*

"Many years ago," Bill Child, Chairman of R.C. Willey Home Furnishings, says, "I wanted to buy a share of Berkshire Hathaway. It was trading at $7,000 a share, which was a lot of money at the time. So I slept on it for a month or two, and finally decided to go ahead and buy a couple of shares. I called my broker and said, 'What's it trading at now?' He said, 'Well, it's a little over $10,000 a share.' So I didn't buy it. But I kept thinking about it, and six months or a year later I said, 'Well, I'd like to buy, so I guess I'll do it.' But by then it was $12,000 a share, so I didn't buy it then either. In fact, I never bought a share." Bill Child did eventually own a great many shares of Berkshire Hathaway, but not until 1995, when he sold the R.C. Willey company to Warren Buffett and traded R.C. Willey stock for Berkshire Hathaway stock. By then, each share was selling for about $25,000. As of this writing, each share is worth almost three times as much.

Born in Ogden, Utah, in 1932, William H. ("Bill") Child had just completed his first year of college when he married Rufus Call Willey's daughter, Darline. "She was a beautiful woman," he says of her, "just a choice individual." Child started working part-time for Willey in his 600-square-foot cinder-block appliance store in Syracuse, Utah. The next year, he transferred to the University of Utah, where he studied education and history, and continued working for Willey. The job didn't pay very much, but it helped to supplement the scholarship he had received. Bill and Darline lived in Salt Lake City for a year, but came home to help his father-in-law on weekends. They then moved back to Syracuse, purchased a modular home, and put it on the lot that Willey had given them, next to the store.

In 1954, when Child was in his senior year, his father-in-law became ill. Willey's son, Darrel, had decided to pursue an academic career rather than enter the family business, so, even though Child knew very little about the operation, the day he graduated from college Willey handed him the keys and said, "Here it is, take care of it, I'll be back in two or three weeks." He thought he had an ulcer but his illness was actually pancreatic cancer and he died within three months. Child had intended to be a teacher, but, he recalls, "When my father-in-law died, I felt my responsibility was to take over the one-employee business, and any thoughts I might have had for a career in something other than a retail business went out the window."[1]

When Child took over Willey's appliance business, it already had a 22-year history. Willey—called "RC" by his friends—had been working as an electrician for a number of years when, in the mid-1920s, people began asking his advice about replacing their crystal radios with the newer electric ones. In 1927, sensing an opportunity, the 27-year-old Willey began selling Atwater-Kent and Majestic radios out of a trailer, pulled by the family car, through the small towns of northern Utah. Within a few years, Willey noticed that electric refrigerators were becoming more and more popular, so, in 1932, he added Hotpoint refrigerators and electric stoves to his product line and founded his appliance company. Despite the Depression, by the late 1940s he was able to begin offering his customers additional appliances, such as vacuum cleaners, phonographs, water heaters, and Dexter twin-tub washers.

During the 1930s and 1940s, Willey sold his products door-to-door. Child explains, "A lot of people didn't realize the convenience and value of appliances. He would take a refrigerator or an electric range out to a home and talk them into letting him put it in. In some cases, he'd even do the electric wiring for them. He'd let them use it for a while, and then he would come back and say, 'Now, look, if you don't want it, I'll take it out.' But he was an excellent salesperson. He knew that once he got the product into their houses and they used it, they would never let it out. And he made a good living," Child says, "with $40,000 to $50,000 a year in sales, a one-man operation, low overhead, and 10 percent gross profit."

The Second World War brought hard times for Willey. With many of the country's industries turned toward the war effort, it was difficult for him to find any products to sell. Nevertheless, Child says, "Whatever he could get, he could sell. He actually went down to the garbage dumps and picked up old carcasses, because he could buy parts and fix them up. He would put compressors in refrigerators or units in electric ranges, and, by selling them, he could make a living." Business picked up after the war, and at the start of the Korean War three years later, it was booming. "People remembered," Child says, "there had been a real shortage of appliances during World War II, and they thought they may experience the same shortages. So, many said, 'I think we better replace our appliances.' As a result, the business improved considerably."

Success, however, came at a cost. As Child recounts the story, "RC's competitors started going to the manufacturers and saying, 'Look, you've got this guy out in a meadow who doesn't even have a retail store. He's not legitimate. How can you justify selling to this guy? How can we compete with him? He has no overhead.'" Willey didn't want a store—"What would I do with it?" he asked—but he couldn't afford to lose his suppliers, so, using cinderblocks, he built a 600-square-foot store next to his house. "He built the door quite wide," Child says, "so he could put the appliances in the crates. At first he put them all in the crates and just opened up the front. Pretty soon, he found that people liked a selection; they wanted to come and see more than the one that was on the back of his pickup. Business really increased—he went from $50,000 a year in sales to a little over $200,000 a year, and he was forced to hire one full-time employee—a repair-and-delivery man."

In 1953, a serious fire in his double-car garage burned all his appliances. The cars were not burned, but the appliances and the storage space were destroyed. He then built an 8,000-square-foot warehouse on the premises.

Child says, reflecting on his experience running the store, "My early days were a struggle. We had a good reputation, but we were not financially sound. Liabilities exceeded assets, and there was a cash deficit. So it was a struggle just to meet payroll and pay for the merchandise. The first year or two, I only drew my salary about half the time. I was supposed to get $100 a week, the same as the gentleman who was working for me, but I never took that much. I think I ended up with about $2,300 or $2,400 a year in those days. But it didn't cost me a lot to live. I worked every day except Sunday, which has always been reserved for church and family, so I never had time to spend money."

In his early business years, Child's most pressing challenge was trying to build the business as a two-man operation. "I was so busy sawing," recalled Child, "that I didn't have enough time to sharpen the saw." Within two years, though, Child was successful enough to be able to bring his brother Sheldon into the business. Even more important, he was able to expand the store from 600 to 3,000 square feet, which enabled him to begin selling furniture.

Retail selling space was limited. "The mattresses," remembers Child, "were standing up against the wall. To sell them, customers had to lean back against them to see how comfortable they were. I don't remember having any returned. Maybe customers were not as particular at that time."

Through the 1950s and 1960s, Bill and Sheldon Child worked hard to establish a reputation for offering honest deals and good values, and the business flourished. By 1964, the store in Syracuse had grown to 27,000 square feet. However, even though it drew people from as far away as Ogden and Salt Lake City (20 and 30 miles away, respectively), as the 1960s drew to a close, the Child brothers realized that the only way they could continue expanding was to open a store closer to one of those large population centers. In 1969, R.C. Willey built its second store, in Murray, Utah, 10 miles south of the center of the population of the Salt Lake Valley. The store, built on four acres of farmland, contained 20,000 square feet of selling space and cost the brothers a total of $300,000. The Murray store immediately became, and remains to this day, the highest-volume and most profitable store of the R.C. Willey chain.

Their business model, similar to the Blumkins' Nebraska Furniture Mart, evolved into offering everything for the home under one roof and giving the best value and service. They targeted the middle 80 percent of the consumer market and left the top and the bottom 10 percent to other retailers.

The brothers made another important strategic decision in 1974. They took complete control of consumer credit. R.C. Willey had offered credit in one form or another from the very beginning. When "RC" was still selling electrical appliances off the back of his pickup, he had persuaded a local bank to provide financing for his farm customers who wanted to pay for their purchases in three annual installments—one at the end of each harvest. Since then, Child had experimented with both internal and external financing for customers' accounts. By the mid-1970s, he had decided that the company should process all the credit-related paperwork itself; by then, its own creditworthiness allowed it to borrow capital and provide financing directly to its customers.

Tax incentives were available to R.C. Willey because income from a sale is not recognized until all the funds are collected. More importantly, when the prime rate shot up to 21 percent, Child's company loaned money at 18 percent and gained sales and market share because its competitors were unable or unwilling to do the same. Even today, half of R.C. Willey's profits come from its finance department—an unusual arrangement for a furniture store, and a key factor in its appeal to its eventual suitor.

Over the next 20 years, R.C. Willey continued to grow. The first two stores were expanded, and the company opened stores at other locations. By 1995, six full-service stores within the state—in West Valley, Salt Lake City, Syracuse, Murray, Orem, and West Jordan—were selling furniture, appliances, electronics, computers, and carpets. There was also a carpet outlet in Salt Lake City. The company had a staff of 1,300 people and annual sales of $257 million, and it accounted for more than 50 percent of all the furniture business in the state. Its CEO had already received offers from several companies that were interested in purchasing it. Although Child had not been looking for a buyer, he was willing to entertain the possibility of selling the company. He was not, however, enthusiastic about any of the company's suitors.

However, one day in January 1995, he found himself at a fabric industry conference with his friend Irv Blumkin, CEO of the hugely successful Nebraska Furniture Mart, which Berkshire had bought in 1983. Child tells the story: "I told Irv that I'd received offers for the company, but I really didn't like any of them because they weren't bringing in a lot of cash. One offered 40–50 percent of the sale price in cash and planned to borrow the rest of the price on the assets of the company. But then the company would be encumbered with an enormous financial obligation, and I knew that would never work. Others were willing to talk to me about stock, but I wasn't comfortable with them and their operation. So I said to Irv, 'Do you think Warren might have an interest?' He said, 'I don't know why not. You've got one of the best companies in the furniture industry.' Then he told me that he was going to have dinner with Warren and would ask him about it.

"About three days later I got a phone call from Irv, who said, 'I've talked to Warren. He's really interested in talking to you about your company, and he's going to call you.' I said, 'Great, thanks,' and hung up. Five minutes later, the phone rings. I pick up and a voice says, 'This is Warren Buffett, Bill. I just talked to Irv, and I understand you have an interest in selling your company.' I said, 'Well, I'd like to talk about it. Have you got a few minutes?' But before he answered I said, 'By the way, I'm awfully flattered that you'd call. I can't believe I'm talking to Warren Buffett. I'm very honored.' And he just said, 'I've got all the time in the world.' So we chatted for 25 or 30 minutes. I went over some of the reasons for selling, like the estate tax, succession, and future growth.

"Finally, he asked me one question: 'How much do you want for your company?' I told him that I just wanted a fair price, one that was fair to both parties. I also said that, 'We want whoever buys it to be happy two, three, or five years from now.' And when I asked him what he wanted me to do, he said, 'Send me three years' financials, send me a little history of the company, and I'll get back with you.' About four days later, I received a FedEx that said, 'Bill, you have a jewel of a company. It fits our mold perfectly. I'll have you a price in three days.' That was it. He didn't want to come out and see the store. He didn't want to check inventory.

"Sure enough, three days later comes another FedEx. I open it up, and there was a price. I called him and said, 'Warren, this looks very fair. I'll tell you what I'd like you to do. I have to talk to the family, but you've got to come out and look at the stores, look at our company.' He said, 'I don't need to do that,' and we debated for a few minutes. Finally, I said, 'Warren, I could not sell you this company without you seeing it, it just wouldn't be fair. We are proud of it and we want to show it to you.' He said, 'Well, I'm going to play golf with Bill Gates down in Palm Springs, and I can stop there on the way.'

"When he arrived," Child remembers, "we took him to every store but one, and that only because we had run out of time. One of our guys had an old van that fit about seven people, so we took him around in that. We chatted all the way, and I became very comfortable with him, as did our entire management staff. And as we were putting him back on his plane, I said,

'Well, what do you think?' And he said, 'I love the company. I'm willing to buy it if you are willing to sell it.' I said, 'You've got my vote, let me talk to the family.' I told him that it needed to be a tax-free transaction [exchange R.C. Willey stock for Berkshire stock] because if we would have to pay taxes we'd prefer not to do it. He suggested that we could work it out so it was either cash, stock, or a combination, and I said, 'You couldn't be more fair than that.'"

However, as Child explains it, "My friends, the Blumkins, told me they made a very bad mistake selling their company to Buffett for cash. They told me, no matter what, you don't take cash, and no matter what you do, don't sell your Berkshire stock. And I didn't."[2] Although Buffett normally prefers to buy companies for cash, in this case he was willing to make an exception. In June 1995, Warren Buffett got R.C. Willey Home Furnishings, and Bill Child, after all the years of watching but never buying, got a generous amount of Berkshire Hathaway stock. As a management incentive, the family was able to keep the Murray store outside the partnership and rent it back to Berkshire. "It was a very pleasant transaction," Child says. "There was just one little situation. Right at the end, we discovered that they had erred and calculated four more shares to our benefit. By then, the shares were selling for about $25,000. So we called Berkshire's vice president and treasurer, Marc Hamburg, at Berkshire the next morning, and said, 'You made a miscalculation. There are four more shares, approximately $100,000, in our favor.' He said, 'I'll talk to Warren about it and get back with you.' The next morning, he called and said, 'Don't worry about it. Warren wants you to have it.'"

Bill Child has given Warren Buffett no reason to question the wisdom of that decision, or, for that matter, the decision to purchase R.C. Willey. As a large division of Berkshire's extremely successful home furnishings group, which includes the Nebraska Furniture Mart in Omaha, Star Furniture in Houston, and Jordan's Furniture in Massachusetts, the company has continued to thrive. Child believes, in fact, that being part of that group has been a real benefit. "There's a lot of synergy," he says. "We exchange ideas. We meet together. We visit each other's stores. We are in constant communication. We don't buy together, but we do go on buying trips together to Asia. And we're thinking about the possibility of forming a buying consortium." When asked if he would like to see Berkshire acquire more home-furnishing companies, Child, a partner now in the ever-expanding circle of competence, says, "I'll leave that to Warren, but I would love it. There aren't very many out there that are really good," he says, "but there are perhaps a couple that he could acquire."

Sitting in his office in Salt Lake City, Child knows who all the successful home furnishings operators are throughout the country. Some retailers are good at merchandising and getting customers into the store. Others excel at the operational end of the business: inventory, delivery, finance, service, and follow-up. The key is to be good at both the front end and the back end, as are those few retailers that have passed the Berkshire acquisition test.

Although Child says that he doesn't do anything differently now than he did before Buffett bought the company, he is quick to point out that "Berkshire has certainly been an asset to R.C. Willey." In fact, when asked about the company's durable competitive advantages, he includes Berkshire's support along with the company's buying power, its knowledge of the industry, its connections with manufacturers, and its associates and management team. But he also feels that his company has made a contribution to Berkshire. "I think it has made a difference," he says, but adds, "I think our potential is great, and our best is yet to come."

There's no doubt that Berkshire has helped Child expand his company. In the five years between the merger in 1995 and the 2000 end-of-year report, the company grew from seven stores, 1,300 employees, and $257 million in annual sales to 11 stores, 2,000 employees, and $400 million in sales. It now sells, Child estimates, 57 to 58 percent of all the furniture, 30 to 35 percent of all the appliances, and 30 percent of all the electronics sold in Utah every year. One of the most interesting, and—as it turned out— successful aspects of that growth was the construction of the company's first store outside of Utah—in Meridian (Boise), Idaho. Bill Child was very enthusiastic about opening the store, but Warren Buffett had some doubts, largely because of a particular and somewhat unusual element of R.C. Willey's business philosophy.

As Buffett explained it to Berkshire's shareholders in his 1999 annual letter, "Bill and most of his managers are Mormons, and for this reason R.C. Willey's stores have never operated on Sunday. This is a difficult way to do business: Sunday is the favorite shopping day for many customers." It had not been an issue in Utah, where a large percentage of the population are Mormons, but Buffett was concerned about "taking a no-Sunday policy into a new territory where we would be up against entrenched rivals open seven days a week. Nevertheless," he wrote, "this was Bill's business to run. So, despite my reservations, I told him to follow both his business judgment and his religious convictions.

"Bill then insisted on a truly extraordinary proposition: He would personally buy the land and build the store—for about $9 million as it turned out—and would sell it to us at his cost if it proved to be successful. On the other hand, if sales fell short of his expectations, we could exit the business without paying Bill a cent. This outcome, of course, would leave him with a huge investment in an empty building. I told him that I appreciated his offer but felt that if Berkshire was going to get the upside it should also take the downside. Bill said nothing doing: If there was to be failure because of his religious beliefs, he wanted to take the blow personally. The store opened last August and immediately became a huge success. Bill thereupon turned the property over to us—including some extra land that had appreciated significantly—and we wrote him a check for his cost. And, Bill refused to take a dime of interest on the capital he had tied up over the two years."[3]

The Boise store, 350 miles from Willey's main warehouse, registered $50 million in sales its first year and will do $60 million this year—double the $30 million walk-away target that Child and Buffett had agreed on. It has become the largest home furnishings store in Idaho. R.C. Willey's chairman enjoys recalling the official grand opening, a month after a soft opening. As Warren Buffett cut the ribbon, he said, "When Bill wanted to build the Boise store, I didn't think it was a good idea. But as the numbers rolled in, I thought is was a great idea. It must have been my idea!"

"We have a lot of fun with this," says Child with a grin. "Every time Warren hears how well the store is doing, he says, 'Well, Bill, I'm certainly glad I didn't let you talk me out of that Boise store!'" Buffett continues to suggest that the store was such a great idea of "his" that it should be named the "Buffett" store.

This story has a postscript. Given the success of the Boise store, which achieved $1 million in sales on Labor Day alone, it occurred to Bill Child that another area ripe for an R.C. Willey outlet was Las Vegas, Nevada, which is the fastest-growing metropolitan area in America and is 425 miles from the Salt Lake City warehouse. Approximately 8,000 people move into Clark County every month, and the fastest growing community in the area is the Las Vegas suburb of Henderson. And Henderson, as it happens, is where Bill Child opened his next store. There is concern that a store that's closed on Sunday might be even less likely to succeed in the gambling mecca than in Idaho. According to Britt Beemer, an analyst and consultant who tracks the retail furniture industry, "Twenty-three percent of home furnishings sales are transacted on Sunday. That's almost a quarter of all the sales." But, he adds, "That's a national figure. It might be 35 percent in Las Vegas because of the weird hours people work."

"Opening on Sunday is like smoking and drinking," Child explains, "I don't do either and no one ever asks or offers."

Other than R.C. Willey, Chick-Fil-A, a national fast-food chain, may be the only retailer that also closes its doors on Sunday, despite being primarily located in shopping mall food courts. It lets its employees have a day to spend with their families. The third largest fast-food chain (it has nearly 1,000 locations) can follow its principles because it is privately held. Child's company can also follow its beliefs, the very ones that got R.C. Willey where it is, because although it is now publicly owned, it continues to operate, and always will, as if it were still privately owned.

In an effort to address the closed-on-Sunday issue, Child is considering the possibility of extending the Las Vegas store's hours beyond the 10:00 P.M. closing time in the Salt Lake City store.[4] This time, though, Berkshire Hathaway, rather than Bill Child, provided the cash to build the store. "I actually agreed to put up my own money," Child says, "but Warren said, 'No, I only take advantage of a guy once.'"

Not surprisingly, Child considers having a relationship with Warren Buffett to be one of the greatest benefits of being part of the Berkshire Hathaway family. "I love the association with him," Child says. "Working for him is like getting a hole-in-one, or having a dream come true. It's kind of a climax to a wonderful business career. Warren is a great hero of mine," he adds. "I love his philosophy. I love his integrity. I love the way he deals with people. Every conversation with him is uplifting, and I learn from him every time we talk." In fact, when asked if he considers Berkshire to be the acquirer of choice, he readily agrees that it is, and adds, "It's because of Warren and his management philosophy. We knew that if we sold the company to Warren we'd be able to continue to run our own business and stay closed on Sunday if we wanted to. We knew that as long as we could continue to manage the business as we had in the past and do what we had been doing, we would be very happy. Someone else would have made a lot of changes, and it probably would not have been as positive."

Child is quick to say that "Warren's a lot smarter." He adds, though, "I try to be like him in a lot of ways, and I think I am, at least in our business philosophy. But he thinks out of the box. I try to do that, but I think he can do it a lot more." He considers Buffett's greatest strengths to be "his ability to logically survey a situation, to deploy capital, and to manage and motivate people." He added: "He has a way of motivating you. He trusts you so much that you just want to perform." In fact, Child says that the things that motivate him are "the challenge, and the fact that I don't want to let Warren down, don't want to disappoint him."

Even so, when asked if he runs the company in order to make Warren proud, he says, "We think that if we continue to gain market share profitably, if we continue to be successful, he'll be proud. We want him to be proud, but I think we do it more to satisfy ourselves." One of the effects of this desire to make both Buffett and himself proud, Child says, is: "All of us have worked a little harder, felt a little more personal responsibility, and maybe felt a little more comfortable with expanding. If we'd remained a private company, I would have said, 'I just want to keep doing what I'm doing, I want to do it well, and I want to keep growing, but I don't need to stretch that much.' After all, my family and I owned the vast majority of the stock, and my brother, Sheldon [who, after the sale, left the business and answered a calling with his Church], owned the rest. But now that we're part of Berkshire, part of a public company, we have an obligation to our Berkshire shareholders."

Buffett has had some influence on him, but the two people who have had the greatest effect on his thinking have been his father and his father-in-law. "My father was a wonderful person," he says. "He had a lot of integrity, he was very honest, and he was hardworking. He was also very sharp, even though he never had much formal education. I think, though, that he probably felt kind of restricted. Farming was his life, and it was a tough business, so I think he felt limited in what he could do. I learned a lot from him, though." He learned a great deal from "RC" as well, although they were very different lessons. "RC," Child says, "was someone who enjoyed life a little bit more. He lived right up to his income, and spent freely and was generous. He enjoyed life. He enjoyed taking the family out to dinner; he enjoyed doing things for other people. I learned a lot from him, too."

Some of the lessons Child learned from his father-in-law were in the art of merchandising, flexibility, and good salesmanship. These lessons have served him well over the years, and the store's many satisfied customers still drive a long way to save money. When asked how much of his approach is art and how much is science, he says that the two are evenly matched. "I think of science," he says, "as being the numbers—the analysis—and art as being your instincts. You need them both. I like to see all the numbers," he continues, "and hope they work, but there are certain times when you just have to go with your gut feeling." In planning the new store in Las Vegas, for example, he says that he had to rely on his instincts to make a number of important decisions. "Is Las Vegas the best place to build a store?" he asked himself. "What size store should we go into Las Vegas with? How should we approach the market? Those are questions for which you'll never really have a definitive answer."

He considers the questions that arise from expansion to be the most difficult to answer. "They represent the most unknowns," he says, "and I think that if I were just starting out today I would try to think about them more, to plan our expansions better. That was one of the weaknesses we had in our earlier years. We were so darn busy selling that we didn't have time to sharpen the saw, didn't have time to step back and say, 'Okay, where do we want to go, what makes sense?' Instead, we just did it all very quickly. All of a sudden we'd find that we'd outgrown our warehouse or we'd outgrown our showroom. What do we do now? We'll expand again." He concludes, "Even though it's all worked out, I think it might have worked even better if we'd done a little more forward planning. But planning is really hard. It's hard to come up with long-range plans when everything is changing so rapidly."

There are questions, though, to which he feels there are clear and definitive answers. When asked, for example, how he would describe his business and management philosophy, he quickly says, "To conduct business in an ethical and businesslike manner. We must build trust, integrity, and value for our customers. We have to fulfill the needs of our customers. If we can't offer them a service that's worth what they pay us, then we need to make changes. We have to offer them more value in the way of service and product than what they spend with us."

Child's principles were first tested soon after he took over the fledgling appliance business. "We sold over 400 automatic washers during our early years," recalled Child, "not knowing each had a faulty mechanism that required service as soon as nine months of regular use. The manufacturer refused to recognize the defect, let alone repair it, after the warranty. But the customer purchased it from us in good faith, expecting it to last, so it put us in a dilemma right when cash was very tight. Since it was our policy to use the 'Golden Rule' and treat our customers as we would like to be treated, we sacrificed our profits for almost a year and repaired all the defective washers without charging the customers."

Forty-five years later, in 1999, a warranty company employed by R.C. Willey declared bankruptcy just days after the furniture store had released a check for an additional $180,000 for warranty service. R.C. Willey, of course, had had nothing to do with the company's bankruptcy, and was in no way responsible for backing the warranties. Even so, Child offered to pay for all current and future repairs that were to have been covered by the warranties, even though it would eventually cost $1.4 million to satisfy all the claims. "We stood behind all those warranties even though we weren't legally obligated to do so," Child said at the time. "We did it because our reputation with our customers is the most important thing our company has. Integrity must be constant, in good times as well as bad. We must be honest and trustworthy with our employees, our customers, our suppliers, and ourselves."[5]

Given these sentiments, it's not surprising that when asked what he dislikes most about his job, Child says, "Having people disappoint you through dishonesty." That appears, though, to be about the only thing he doesn't like about his job. In fact, he says that the business is his passion. "I work every day," he says, "except Sundays, of course." And although he admits that he's not an early riser and doesn't usually get to work until nine o'clock, he adds, "I usually work late, and I always take work home." He also tends to work even when he's supposed to be on vacation. "I told Warren this year," he said recently, "that I was going to take two months off, and asked him if it was all right. He said, 'Sure, that's fine. You won't be able to do it, but that's okay.' I ended up taking two weeks." One of those weeks was spent in Hawaii. "But I got very antsy," he says. "Thank heavens I had a cell phone that I could call back and forth with. It was a local call. I had 500 minutes and I used them all."

Although he has a house he seldom uses, in St. George, in southern Utah, he says that "I would really just as soon stay home. My ideal vacation would be to take a week and not do anything except all the things I'd like to do around the house." One of the things he does around the house, in his relatively small amount of spare time, is read. "I read a lot of church books," he says, "the Book of Mormon, the Bible, but I also read a lot of industry publications, like *Furniture Today, Home Furnishings,* and *High Points.*" In addition, he reads several general business and business-related publications.

Another passion is his charity work. An additional benefit from the sale of R.C. Willey was the opportunity to free up capital formerly held in the business and let the family use it to make charitable contributions. "We probably personally give more than $2 million a year, but all under the name of R.C. Willey. I don't want notoriety." He adds: "Obscurity is blessed." His favorite charities include hospitals, homeless-youth centers, and—especially—education. He and his wife are alumni of the University of Utah, and most of their children attended Brigham Young University. He donates to both of those schools as well as Weber State University and Westminster College. In fact, the couple sponsors two chairs at the University of Utah—the R.C. Willey Chair in neuroradiology and the William and Patricia Child Chair for health science.

His general outlook, Child says, "is optimistic. I always have a good outlook. I always try to look at things—even problems—as challenges and opportunities." He recognizes, though, that there are challenges he will never be able to meet. "I wish I were 20 years younger," he says, "because I have so much to do. But I'm going to run out of time before I accomplish all I'd like to accomplish. I'd love to learn a foreign language. I'd love to go back to school. I'd like to write a book. But I will never have enough time to do all I would like to do."

There is, however, at least one further challenge that he does expect to meet, perhaps within the next two or three years. As is customary, when Buffett purchased Child's company, he treated his new CEO to a round of golf at the famed Augusta National in Georgia. Child enjoyed the golf so much that he asked how he could be invited to another round of golf. Buffett promised that when R.C. Willey's annual revenues reach $1 billion, Child's reward would be more golf at the famed course, the site of the annual Masters Tournament. Accepting the challenge, Child has every intention of seeing to it that Buffett has reason to keep his promise.

To do so, Child will have to keep the company on its present course, which he fully expects to do. "I think the future of the home furnishing business is bright," he says, "although there are changes that will have to be made. The manufacturers will have to change their method of operation, because the cost of labor in the U.S. is too high for them to be able to produce certain goods. It's likely they'll have to go offshore for a lot of their products. The retailers that can't go offshore and bring in merchandise are going to be at a disadvantage. To successfully import, a retailer needs a certain size and momentum, expertise, capital, ability to buy large quantities, and an infrastructure to handle the business. That bodes well for R.C. Willey, because we have that capacity. There are definitely some great opportunities for growth, and I think we're positioned to take advantage of those opportunities."

As for his own future, the currently 69-year-old Child says, "As long as I'm healthy, and as long as I can make what I feel is a significant contribution, and as long as I can continue to learn and move forward, I want to stay involved." Child felt it was important to choose his succession team and give them plenty of opportunity to tap into his knowledge and experience. Although he has no immediate plans for retiring, he recently appointed his nephew-in-law, Scott Hymas, as CEO, and his nephew, Jeff Child, as president. This is still very much a family-managed business; Bill's son Steve is executive vice president in charge of merchandising, and serves on the board. Promoting himself to chairman, he quips, "Maybe now I'll work just 40 hours per week."

As to his other children's getting into the business, "I have a younger son that I think would be great," Child says, "but he's not sure what field to pursue. It would be an excellent opportunity for him and he has all the right qualifications." His first wife, Darline, passed away 36 years ago and left Bill a widower with four children. Remarried to wife Patricia in 1966 as the quintessential woman behind the man, she and Bill had four more children, now all grown. He admits, though, "I really haven't done a great job" in regard to teaching his children and family about the home furnishings business. "I'm not sure that I made a favorable impression on them because I work long hours," he says, and "I don't think any of them were awfully excited about the business. Steve enjoys it, but except for one daughter, Tammy, a young mother of four children, the rest of them don't really have the passion that I have."

Child discussed how he chose his successor and his insights into the process. First, he says, he "looked for someone who I thought had it all, someone who could do everything I've been doing, maybe even better than I do it, and I identified three people who seemed like likely candidates. Then I sent a letter out to all our managers that said, 'This is the role of the CEO as I see it. Who do you think is best qualified to lead our company in case I were to check out tomorrow? List the three that you feel would be the best.' And what came out of it was really amazing. All three of the names I thought would be there, were there. And it turned out that my number-one choice, but who I thought wouldn't be that strong, was actually respected by everyone."

Child realized that selecting his successor was one of his key responsibilities. "I think I had the mantle to do it," he says, although he also notes, "Warren's blessing had to come upon it. But I would hope that if I chose wisely, the business would continue to grow and improve. And I'm sure that is what Warren wants." Although he feels strongly that "the person who becomes CEO has to have the management team's support," he also believes that "once you place the mantle and the responsibility of the CEO on them, they become different people. I think Scott will rise to the occasion. That's the way I went about it. We have a great management team and I expect to be around for the next 20 years to monitor, train, teach, and counsel, to help ensure the company remains stable and has a great future."

As for the future of Berkshire Hathaway, Child believes that Warren Buffett has no set master plan but is open to all opportunities. He also believes that the company will continue to grow, whether Buffett remains at the helm or not. He is worried, though, about a successful transition from Buffett to his successor. What helps get him through that concern? "Warren's good health—I hope—insures that he is going to be around as long as I am." At the same time, when asked what Berkshire might look like after Buffett, he says, "I guess it depends a lot on the new management. I would hope it would look the same. I would hope that it would continue to perform the same way, and if whoever-it-is follows Warren's management philosophy, I think it will. Knowing Warren, I am positive he has picked his successor and a succession plan, and they will continue to follow his investment values and principles."

In the meantime, anyone who might be concerned about the future of Berkshire Hathaway, or R.C. Willey Home Furnishings, should be able to take comfort from how Bill Child responds when asked what he would want Berkshire shareholders to know about him. "I would want them to understand," he says, "that we will do our best, that we will put forth our best effort, that we are not satisfied with anything less than good performance. I'd want them to know that we do hold their trust dearly, and that we realize the responsibility we have. I'd want them to know that if we make mistakes, they'll be honest mistakes, and that we would never do anything that is not in their best interest."

## BILL CHILD'S BUSINESS TENETS

★ Integrity is sacred. Our reputation with our customers is very important. If we guarantee free service calls, then we will provide them. When a service contractor went bankrupt, R.C. Willey fulfilled all the customer-service contracts although it had no obligation to do so.

★ Provide more than what a customer expects. Added service or value is what keeps customers loyal.

★ Looking at the financials is important, but sometimes you have to go with your instincts when you're making a business decision.

# chapter thirteen

# The Partner for Life—
# Melvyn Wolff, Star Furniture

*Shortly after Melvyn Wolff sold Star Furniture to Warren Buffett, Wolff received a four-feet-high by six-feet-wide "Colossal Gram." The message read:*

*MELVYN . . . MY ENTHUSIASM FOR OUR MARRIAGE DWARFS THE SIZE OF THIS TELEGRAM. YOUR PARTNER FOR LIFE. WARREN*

*Inside his traditional second floor corner office at headquarters in Houston, Wolff was an open book. He has an intense, inquisitive, and logical mind, and when he asks you questions, you're challenged and pressed to think about your convictions. Melvyn knows his business and his competitors, and he understands Berkshire better than most people. Like three of the other four furniture retailers in the Berkshire family, he's a satisfied customer of NetJets and, like his boss, is an avid reader.*

*Much like the other Buffett CEOs, Melvyn is humble and generous. He's energetic and could easily pass for a much younger man. As expected, he's passionate about Star Furniture and Berkshire Hathaway.*

Although Melvyn Wolff, CEO of Star Furniture, doesn't relate the story himself, Warren Buffett had no reluctance about doing so. Telling his shareholders about Wolff and his sister, Shirley Wolff Toomim, and the sale of their company to Berkshire Hathaway in 1997, Buffett wrote, "When they told their associates of the sale, they also announced that Star would make large, special payments to those who had helped them succeed—and then defined that group as everyone in the business. Under the terms of our deal," Buffett noted, "it was Melvyn and Shirley's money, not ours, that funded this distribution. Charlie and I love it when we become partners with people who behave like that."[1] In fact, the payments—$1,000 to each employee for each year of service—amounted to $1.6 million. But then, Melvyn Wolff has a long history of behaving, as Buffett put it, "like that."

Born in Houston, Texas, in 1931, Wolff attended high school there before going to military school in Missouri. Planning on a career in law, he enrolled in the University of Texas in Austin, but, near the end of his first year, his father became ill. "My dad owned half of Star Furniture, with the other partner having four family members active in the business," he remembers, "and I asked him, 'Would you like me to come home and help in the business and look after your interests until you get back on your feet?' He said he didn't want to interrupt my education, but I told him that I'd come back for a year and go to night school at the University of Houston, so it wouldn't interrupt my education. That's what I did. After a while, my dad would spend an hour or two in the store every day," Wolff adds, "so he could still give us guidance and oversee what we were doing. But he never recovered to the point that he could assume a workload. And in the meantime, I kind of got the furniture business in my blood, and I never went back to the University of Texas."

By the time Wolff joined Star Furniture in 1950, the company had been in business for nearly 40 years. Louis Getz and Ike Freedman had started the business as a grocery store in downtown Houston in 1912, but soon found themselves accepting used furniture as payment for grocery bills. That first store was on the ground floor of a three-story building, the second and third floors of which were occupied, as Wolff tells it, "by a hotel of some questionable repute. My father told me that the people upstairs used to say that the downstairs of their brothel was occupied by a furniture store of questionable repute." Wolff's father, Boris, had emigrated from Russia in 1918, penniless and unable to speak English. By 1924, he had earned enough to buy an interest in the furniture store. "As best as we can tell," his son says, "he spent somewhere between $1,200 and $1,500 to get a fourth interest in the business." S.N. Hovas purchased a similar interest, so, by the mid-1920s four families were involved in the company.

By then, the store had become the anchor of "furniture row," a two-and-a-half-block area in downtown Houston where there were 11 furniture stores, all of them—like Star—selling low-priced furniture on the installment plan. The owners of Star Furniture—both new and old—used the money from Hovas and Wolff to make a down payment on the building they occupied, which enabled them to move the hotel out and take over all three floors. "It also," Wolff says, "allowed them to compete with the other guys down the street. Having a three-story building in 'furniture row' was the turning point. That put the company on a nice track." That "nice track" was, in fact, so successful that it enabled the partners to open up additional stores.

The company was hard-hit by the 1929 stock market crash and the subsequent depression. Despite the setbacks, Wolff says, "They promised their employees that they would never lay any of them off, and they never did. What they did instead was, first, freeze, and then, reduce, their salaries—including the partners' own salaries. And they assured the employees that they would all be there together or they would all go down together. Of course," Wolff adds, "if anyone left the company, they didn't replace him. They just took over the position and did more work. But they were able to make it through the Depression nicely, and, by 1935, they started going again and doing fairly well." Within five years, though, the Second World War began, bringing with it new hardships and difficult times for the company.

By 1943, it became clear that the company could not support four families. By then, Ike Freedman, one of the original owners, had long since died, so Boris Wolff and Mrs. Louis Getz bought out S.N. Hovas, who left to start his own furniture business. By the time Boris's son Melvyn joined Star in 1950, the company already had half a dozen stores, but seemed to have too many cooks. The younger Wolff remembers: "There were two families—four members from one family and three from the other—involved in the business. And there was lot of maneuvering among the partners." In 1962, Boris Wolff and Mrs. Louis Getz died within two weeks of each other, without warning or a succession plan. The five second-generation partners had to decide where to go from there.

Wolff says, "I was the youngest of that bunch, but I somehow conned the rest of the group into making me president, and I took the reins of the company. Although I didn't realize it at the time, we weren't in very good financial condition. In the previous three years, we'd had two years with a small profit and one year with a larger loss, so for the 36 months preceding that time, we had lost money. We had a lot of debt and negative net worth. To make matters worse, we had a dominant competitor . . . 20 times our size that could out-advertise Star and kept us from acquiring the furniture lines we needed. We carried our own accounts receivable, and we borrowed the money from the bank to carry it. But," he continues, "we didn't know the banker. My father was the one who dealt with him, and we had never even met him. So, about a week after my father's funeral, I put on my suit—I only had one—and a necktie, and I walked over to the bank to introduce myself to the banker. He seemed ancient to me, but he was probably the same age as I am now.

"'Mr. Greer,'" I said, "'I have come down to meet you and tell you that the money we owe you is in good hands. I have been elected president, and I wanted you to know that I am going to be your contact here. I've got the support of all the other members of the group. We're going to be able to continue to operate, and I just came down to introduce myself and give you assurance that my father's departure isn't going to change anything.' And I said, 'I don't want to do it today—I wanted this to be just a get acquainted meeting—but soon I want to come down and talk to you about an increase in our line of credit, because we really need to infuse some more money into the business.'

"And he said, 'Young man, I am happy to meet you, and it was nice of you to come down. But when you come back, we're not going to talk about increasing your line of credit. I want you to give me a plan of how you are going to liquidate the debt you have with this bank. Your outstanding loan is equal to this bank's legal limit. So I want you to come up with a plan on how to get that down.' And that was my introduction to the business world, to the *real* business world. Up until that point, I had concerned myself more with merchandising than with finance. And I didn't have quite as much spring in my step on the way back to my office as I had going over there."

Although he approached all the banks in Houston, Wolff was unable to secure another loan for his company. But then a family friend put him in touch with a banker in New York, who, much to Wolff's surprise, agreed to provide the additional money he was seeking. "But he didn't just write me a check," Wolff remembers. "He told me there were several things I needed to do. When I asked him what, he said that the first one was to get an audited financial statement by one of the big eight accounting firms. And I said, 'Mr. Baker, I can understand your wanting an audited statement, but why from a big eight accounting firm? That costs a lot of money.' And he said, 'Hell, Melvyn, for all I know, your accountant could be your brother-in-law.' I burst out laughing, and when he asked me what I was laughing at, I looked at him and said, 'My accountant *is* my brother-in-law.'"

With the infusion of additional (borrowed) funds available, Wolff developed a new business plan to change the direction of the firm. It was an aggressive plan with a high degree of risk. Too much risk, in fact, for the appetites of his partners. So Wolff developed a plan to purchase their 50 percent interest. The plan called for the main downtown store and another store to be sold. The proceeds, along with long-term notes at junk-bond interest rates, would go to the selling partners. It was an amicable transaction.

Next, Wolff rented a large warehouse/showroom facility that had been abandoned by one of Star's major competitors. Melvyn then persuaded his sister, Shirley Toomim, to give up her interior design business and join him in the furniture business. At the same time, they strategically moved away from the low-end installment business. Shirley became responsible for store design and display—"Everything related to aesthetics," according to her brother. And Melvyn became responsible for business matters and strategic planning. The plan worked and remains in place today. Wolff would later point to his close working relationship with his sister for their ultimate business success.

Under Wolff's and Toomim's leadership, the company flourished. By 1997, it had nine stores—seven in Houston and one each in Austin and Bryan—and was generating annual revenues of approximately $110 million. However, both of the siblings were in their mid-sixties. Neither had any plans for retirement, but they were concerned about the federal estate tax the business would face when one or both of them died. Wolff consequently contacted Salomon Brothers and asked for advice on whether to issue stock to the public, seek a buyer for the company, or do nothing.[2]

In the meantime, although neither Wolff nor Toomim was aware of it, Warren Buffett had been waiting in the wings. As Buffett later told Berkshire Hathaway's shareholders, "Upon our purchase of Nebraska Furniture Mart in 1983 . . . the Blumkin family told me about three outstanding furniture retailers in other parts of the country. At the time, however, none was for sale. Many years later, Irv Blumkin learned that Bill Child, CEO of R.C. Willey—one of the recommended three—might be interested in merging, and we promptly made [a deal with his company]. Furthermore," Buffett went on, "when we asked Bill about industry standouts, he came up with the remaining two names given me by the Blumkins, one of these being Star Furniture of Houston. But time went by without there being any indication that either of the two was available.

"On the Thursday before last year's annual meeting, however, Bob Denham [who was then chairman] of Salomon told me that Melvyn Wolff, the longtime controlling shareholder and CEO of Star, wanted to talk. At our invitation, Melvyn came to the meeting and spent his time in Omaha confirming his positive feelings about Berkshire. I, meanwhile, looked at Star's financials, and liked what I saw. A few days later, Melvyn and I met in New York and made a deal in a single, two-hour session. As was the case with the Blumkins and Bill Child, I had no need to check leases, work out employment contracts, etc. I knew I was dealing with a man of integrity and that's what counted."[3]

Wolff attributes Buffett's interest in his company almost exclusively to the recommendations of Blumkin and Child. "Otherwise," he says, "we would have been far too small for him to have considered. But he also had an advantage in looking at us because he was in the furniture business, understood the furniture business, didn't have to go to school to get up to speed with it, and could compare our financial statement with two other furniture companies that he already owned, to see how we stacked up. We're smaller than the other two companies," he notes, "smaller than anybody in another field that he would have picked out."

Star is smaller than other retailers because it only sells furniture to a targeted middle- to upper-income customer base. Nebraska Furniture Mart and R.C. Willey also sell appliances, electronics, and floor covering. Still, Buffett's purchase of Wolff's company demonstrates that Buffett will buy a business even if its earnings and size are smaller than targeted, if the management is right and if other advisers—especially those in the same business—approve the acquisition.

From Wolff's and Toomim's perspective, selling Star Furniture to Berkshire had several advantages. Buffett was willing—albeit reluctantly—to pay for it with stock in his company rather than cash. "The estate taxes were running 55 percent of net worth," Wolff says, "and we knew that when we died, the company would have to be sold to satisfy those estate taxes. We had spent our lifetimes building an organization of people who really depended on the firm for their income, and we wanted it to last. It wouldn't be fair for it to go away when we went away. In order to avoid that, we needed to

Tony Nicely,
GEICO Insurance

Lou Simpson,
GEICO Insurance
(photo by Michael Gamer)

Ajit Jain,
Berkshire Hathaway
Reinsurance Division
(photo by Capital Photo)

Rose Blumkin,
Nebraska Furniture Mart

Al Ueltschi,
FlightSafety International
(photo by Roger Richie)

Rich Santulli,
Executive Jet
(photo by Ed Turner)

Don Graham,
*The Washington Post*

Irv Blumkin,
Nebraska Furniture Mart

Frank Rooney,
H.H. Brown Shoe
(photo by Jay Rizzo)

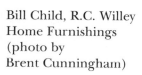

Bill Child, R.C. Willey
Home Furnishings
(photo by
Brent Cunningham)

Melvyn Wolff, Star Furniture
(photo by Alexander's of Houston)

Stan Lipsey, *The Buffalo News*
(photo by Westoff Studio)

Barry and Eliot Tatelman, Jordan's Furniture (photo by Linda Holt)

Chuck Huggins,
See's Candies
(photo by Franklin Avery)

Ralph Schey,
Scott Fetzer Companies

Susan Jacques,
Borsheim's Fine Jewelry
(photo by Regency Photo)

Jeff Comment,
Helzberg Diamonds
(photo by David Riffel)

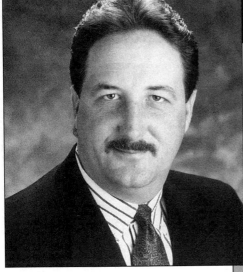

Randy Watson,
Justin Brands

Harrold Melton,
Acme Building Brands
(photo by Britt Stokes)

remove that obstacle. Selling the company for stock meant that there would no longer be any tax consequence to our death, at least not for the company, so the company would not be affected. Otherwise," he concludes, "there wouldn't have been a company anymore. It would have had to be sold, and sales like that are usually leveraged sales where the leverage buyout people make out and the company is left with huge amounts of debt." As a result, Wolff was extremely pleased with the arrangement. "Estate planning requires a lot of liquidity," he said at the time. "This deal provided that liquidity and, at the same time, let us join up with a group of people that we couldn't be happier to be a part of. We believe it's the finest family of companies ever assembled under one corporate name."[4]

In fact, Wolff had been extremely impressed with Warren Buffett even before they met. A fellow Texan, Bob Denham of Salomon Brothers, and Melvyn had developed a warm friendship. "Bob was involved in the preliminary discussions," Wolff says, "and he called and said, 'Warren would like to see three years of your financial statements. May I offer those?' I told him he could, and, about three hours later, he called again and said, 'Warren has some questions about your financial statements. May I ask you a few questions?' I said, 'Sure,' and then he said, 'In the back of your 1994 statement, your auditor has a footnote that said you recognize income from finance charge on the rule of 78, deferred finance charge recognition, and in the 1996 statement, the auditor changed the wording of that paragraph. And Warren wants to know the significance of the different wording.' And I almost fell off my chair," Wolff says. "How many people do you know that would, first, read a footnote like that, and, second, read a two-years-later statement and remember that the paragraph was written with the wording slightly changed? There wasn't actually any difference, except for the wording, but the fact that he picked that up was amazing. An incredible mind, and incredible retention."

By agreement between Wolff and Buffett, sales terms were never disclosed. If Star were purchased in an arrangement similar to NFM's and R.C. Willey's, then Buffett bought 80 to 90 percent of the whole company valued at its current annual sales. Typically, the managing family keeps 10 to 20 percent of the company as a management incentive to keep the business profitable.

As with virtually all the people who have sold their companies to Berkshire Hathaway, one of the reasons Wolff was happy to do so was Warren

Buffett's hands-off management style. "When he came down and . . . we announced this acquisition to our employees," Wolff says, "someone asked him how many people he was going to send down from Berkshire head-quarters to become part of our company. And he explained, 'I've only got 11 employees, and that includes the receptionist and secretary. So I don't have anyone to send!'"

"Executive responsibilities are exactly the same now as when he bought the company," Wolff says, "so any difference there might be in company structure has really taken place in our own minds."[5]

Wolff believes that this has been a contributing factor in the company's continued growth. "Because Warren hasn't interfered in any way in our business," he says, "our management team doesn't feel like they're work-ing for Berkshire. They think they're working for Star Furniture Com-pany. That's where their focus is. And they're not worried about how General Re is doing, or how Dairy Queen is doing, or anything else. They are devoted, day-to-day, about making this a better company." He does acknowledge, however, that there have been some changes. "We are doing some things differently," he says, "but they are the same things that we would be doing had we not sold to Berkshire. If you are not changing every day, you are not keeping up with the world." Whatever they are doing seems to be working. According to Wolff, "At the time Warren bought us in 1997, we had just cracked the $100 million mark in sales. In 2000 we did slightly less than $200 million. So we just about doubled in three years."

It took Star Furniture one family generation and 50 years to grow the business and reach $1 million in sales. It took the second generation of Wolff and Toomim some 35 years and an initial negative net worth to grow the business 100 times to over $100 million. It took just three years under the Berkshire umbrella to double sales to nearly $200 million.

Wolff does not believe, though, that becoming part of Berkshire's furni-ture group has had any significant effect on Star. "There is an exchange of information," he says. "We have a great respect for the other three com-panies—Nebraska Furniture Mart, R.C. Willey, and Jordan's—so when I do have a problem, I'm quick to pick up the phone and call one of them and say, 'How do you do thus and so?' And we share that kind of informa-tion readily. But other than that," he adds, "we've found very little syn-ergy." In fact, he says that the most significant synergy they've found has been instigated from outside rather than inside the furniture group. "There are a few factories that have come to us and said, 'If you get together and do this, we'd do that,' and that's been pretty effective. But that's about it."

He also points out, however, "Warren kind of made it clear to us that he was not looking for synergies. Most anybody other than Warren would have said, 'Okay, guys. I don't need a CFO in four companies, so you get together and decide who's the best CFO and fire the other three.' But he wouldn't even suggest that. In fact," Wolff says, "Warren says just the opposite. He says, 'I bought four freestanding, well-managed furniture companies; don't screw it up. Just keep running your companies like you do. I've got no objection to your meeting together and loving each other and so forth. But don't look for synergy for my sake.'"

Wolff is vocal about his admiration for Buffett. One of the best things about his boss, he says, is: "If Warren Buffet has enough confidence in you to acquire you, he's probably got enough confidence in you to let you go on running things. And," he adds, "he's got the money to finance whatever you want to do, as long as he agrees on its feasibility." When asked what he considers to be the best thing about working for Buffett, he simply says, "It's Warren." And when pressed for specifics, he adds, "You know that when you ask him a question, you won't get a snap answer, you'll get sound advice."

Buffett is equally pleased to be working with Melvyn Wolff, as he made clear by inviting Wolff to join him at an Alfalfa Club dinner on January 31, 1998. Usually, Warren will reward his newest operating manager with a round of golf at Augusta National with Bill Gates or Jack Welch. Wolff doesn't play golf, so Buffett treated him to dinner with the captains of business, government, the military, and the judiciary.

Being invited to such events is obviously only one of the advantages to working for Warren Buffett. For Wolff, one of the other advantages must be the similarity in their management philosophies. In discussing his plans for Star's future, for example, Wolff says that he expects growth to come from inside the company rather than through acquisitions. Although he acknowledges that Buffett has grown Berkshire in part by buying other companies, he points out, "One thing you don't transport is culture. And I don't see any companies enough like ourselves out there . . . I wouldn't want to tackle buying them and trying to convert their culture to ours. I would rather grow it internally and not have to make changes in someone else's company." This, he believes, is one of Buffett's principles as well. "I think that's why he doesn't try to change the culture when he buys."

Wolff believes that the culture he and his management team have developed at Star Furniture is an important element in the company's success. And it's an element that they take pains to maintain. "When we bring in new employees," he says from memory, "we begin our orientation by discussing our mission statement: 'Caring associates, working together, to serve our customers first by providing high perceived value in a manner that distinguishes us from all others.' And then we break that down," he adds. "'Caring associates' means we care about each other and we care about our customers. That's who we are. That's the culture of the company. 'Working together.' We don't like turf building here. We try to work together as a team. 'To serve our customers first' means we believe that our job is to serve our customers ahead of our own personal needs. 'By providing high perceived value' is about making sure that our customers believe that we have a valued product to sell. And finally, 'in a manner that distinguishes us from all others,' means that we are always looking for ways to break out of the box and not just do what we did last year or what everybody else is doing."

One of the ways Star tries to accomplish this mission, Wolff says, is by having "a horizontally integrated company. We don't manufacture our own furniture, but everything else that we do we do internally. Most companies," he explains, "farm out their delivery to an outside contractor, their service to an outside contractor, and their accounts to an outside company. But we do our own deliveries. We do our own outside service. And we carry our own credit. We also do our own advertising. So we have control over everything. We keep it all in-house, always have." As Mark Schreiber, Star's president puts it, "It is our belief that as soon as you give up the customer to someone else, you give up control over the sale and over the after-sale service. So it's an investment, and we have a good enough relationship with our manufacturers to make sure that, ultimately, the customer is taken care of." As a result, Wolff adds, "if something doesn't run perfectly, we have no one to blame but ourselves."[6]

Not surprisingly, Melvyn Wolff says his passion is his business. Somewhat more surprising, however, is how he responds when asked what career he would have pursued had he not chosen the home furnishing business. "I would have been a lawyer," he says emphatically. "No question about that. And probably not the profitable part of it—I probably would have been in criminal law or something of that nature. The thrill of the courtroom and that sort of thing would have intrigued me, not sitting in an office and pounding out real estate documents." Nevertheless, he says that the aspect of his career that he gets most excited about is merchandising. "It's always been my love," he says. "Seeing a program develop from start to finish—picking out a product and buying it properly, bringing it in and displaying it properly, setting the ad that's going to bring people in, pricing it properly so that it sells, and then seeing it sell. When all that happens, it's a kind of payday. That's the satisfying thing to me." As an addendum, though, he says, "And I like to watch the report card, the financial statement. I get turned on by good results."

When asked what specific skill has led to those good results, he says, "I am not sure that I know how to answer that. I think I am analytical. I think my competence is being analytical enough to tackle any problem, knowing when I am not qualified and need to get advice, and knowing where to go to get that advice. That's my circle of competence—not trying to be all things to all people." He finds it even more difficult to determine which is his most marked characteristic. "I think that's something you have to ask someone else about," he says. But when asked what his wife would say, he answers, "My wife Cyvia never tells me the truth about those matters. She tells me how wonderful I am and is not quick to point out my shortcomings." Perhaps not surprisingly, he describes her as "the best bargain I ever got."

Regardless of the source of Wolff's success, it's clear that, at least at this point, the significance of that success has nothing to do with personal financial gain. "I'm not working for money anymore," he says. "In fact, I have to remind myself that this isn't just my company, that I am not working to make money for myself and my family anymore. Because I'm really not. When I swapped my shares of the company for shares in Warren Buffett's company, I took on an entirely different responsibility, a responsibility to Berkshire's shareholders. I realize, though, that the contribution in profits that this company makes to Berkshire is miniscule, and someone might ask why I'm knocking myself out. But once you start being motivated by the bottom line you become self-motivated, and you can't change that." Not surprisingly, when asked how he defines success, he says, "I suppose that the report card for that is happiness. And I think I am a happy person. I think I'm satisfied. I have a wonderful relationship with a wonderful woman. I have a lot of friends. And I have had a very satisfying business career. That's my definition of success."

Unlike some—if not most—of Berkshire's other operating managers, Wolff does make the time to get away from the business and travel. "We have traveled to a lot of exotic places," he says, including two photo safaris in Africa. "But there are other places I want to see, too," he says. "We've never been to Singapore or Kuala Lumpur and that part of the world, and I'd like to do that soon." However, like the other Berkshire managers, Wolff is deeply involved in charity work. "We've set up a family foundation, and its work is divided into six areas—education, religion, health, the arts, the underprivileged, and one category called 'All other.' We have an advisory board that makes recommendations for who should get money, and how much, but we make the final decisions. We've never, though, turned down any of their recommendations. And we've set it up so when we're gone they will be the board."

Just as Wolff has prepared his family foundation for the future, he has prepared his company for the day when he will no longer be running it. Although he is currently 69 years old, Wolff says that he is not planning to retire. "My retirement plans," he says, "are governed by my health, not my desire. I intend to play some sort of active role until I am no longer able to do so. I'm Chairman of the Board now, as well as CEO, and I expect that I'll probably give up the CEO role at some point in time and be the principal agitator of other people. So that's why I don't see myself retiring." Nor does he see the company being managed in the future by another generation of Wolffs. His sister Shirley has two children that are active in the firm; one is director of education, and the other is vice president of management information systems. Neither has a desire to "run the company." "There are no other Wolffs behind me," he says. "My son was in the business for a while, but he didn't like it, and I didn't try to teach it to him. I tried to never talk business at home. I really like to leave my office and clear my head and not talk about business at home unless it involves something that affects the family."

His hope for the future of the company is that it will be "the best furniture company—although not necessarily the biggest—in whatever markets we serve," and he is now doing whatever he can to bring that about. At the same time, he is expecting major changes in the home furnishing industry. "I see a lot more consolidation coming down the road," he says. "I see it becoming more and more dependent on global sourcing, which is going to put tremendous pressure on the manufacturing capacity of American manufacturers. Importing will be a substantial part of the business, so there will be a lot of consolidating on the manufacturing side, as well as on the retail side. It's going to be the survival of the fittest," he adds. "Those who keep the door open to change and accommodate change well will survive. And those that resist change will go away."

He does not, however, expect the forthcoming consolidations to result in the development of any "category killers" in the industry. "As successful as Home Depot or Barnes & Noble have been," he says, "you can't have an operation like that in this business, because those are generic categories. I mean, there are not a lot of secrets to selling a hammer. But it takes a different mentality to sell a sofa. Every customer has a different expectation for that sofa, of what the guarantee is. 'Are you going to deliver it? Are you going to put it in my house? What time are you going to be there? How much am I going to have to pay for it? Are you going to finance it? How long will it last?' And there are a lot of other things like that. Our business is so personalized that doing it right depends on management, it depends on the team to do it. We receive our products in bulk just like they do," he concludes, "but we deliver them one at a time, and to a different customer demand on every sale. And that's what they can't do."

For similar reasons, he does not expect that selling furniture on the Internet will have a large effect on the home furnishings industry. "Those Internet companies that have tried to sell furniture on the Internet," Wolff says, "have lost hundreds of millions of dollars in the attempt, and most of them are in bankruptcy. The Internet does not lend itself to direct sales. All the things that make this a unique business are missing in that equation. Selling furniture requires individual attention to every consumer, and you can't do that on the Internet. First of all, consumers have to see the furniture in the store. They can't look at a picture on the Internet and buy a $3,000 piece of furniture. They wouldn't have any idea what it would look like. And even when they do buy it, and it comes, there are all sorts of things wrong with it. It's not right, so it goes back. Returns are staggering. We've got a whole department that deluxes the furniture and tries to get it in the right condition to go into the consumer's home. But you can't do that on the Internet. At least not now. I'm not going to tell you what's going to happen tomorrow, but today it doesn't work."

Wolff does believe, however, that other forms of technology can be important tools for the industry. "Margins are too low in the furniture business," he says, "and the only way to get them higher is to drive costs down. It's tough enough to make a profit at these levels. To win this war, you are going to have to deliver this product at the lowest possible cost. And it's going to take advanced technology to do that. And once the technology has driven down your costs, you can bring your prices down, get more market share, and grow. But if you ignore technology and continue to depend on human labor to perform the functions that could be done electronically, your costs are going to go up and you are going to lose the war. It's as simple as that." It is also, not surprisingly, a good example of Wolff's business philosophy, which he defines as: "Be open to new ideas, but don't abandon the learnings gained by experience."

As for the future of Berkshire Hathaway, although he says that he would like to see the company "continue to be a more diversified internal growth company, buying individual operating companies," he expects it to "become more and more of an insurance company." He does not believe, however, that Warren Buffett has a master plan for the company. "I think," Wolff says, "that he set out to build a property casualty company to satisfy his intended goal, which was to create the float which he could profitably invest with no cost of money. As for the future, if it takes building the company to get the money to do that, then he will build it. But if it gets to a point where it's producing more float than he can profitably invest, then he will slow down the building process."

And while he says that he considers Berkshire to be a good investment today, he does not think it's "as good as it was ten years ago." Unlike some others, though, he doesn't blame this on Warren Buffett's having lost his touch or believe that Buffett's value investment style is no longer appropriate. "I think the people who are saying that are those who are just out of business school—who think that because he's not buying technology, he doesn't understand the world. It's they who are off base, not him." It may be that Wolff's concern for the future success of Berkshire is a reflection of his concern about Buffett's eventual retirement. "I don't think there's another Warren Buffett," he says, and admits that he is worried about a successful transition from Warren to his successors. "But I've come to terms with the fact that I would be happy with my shares to have less value. They'll still probably be worth more than what I started with, even after taking a pretty good clip, a pretty good haircut. I'm prepared for that." At the same time, although he says that the stock "might initially take a dramatic hit," he also expects that "in a fairly short period of time, the calm—and the price—will largely restore themselves."

For the present, Wolff just intends to keep doing what he's been doing for the past 40 years. He admits, however, that there is one thing he would like to do differently. "I don't express appreciation," he says. "I tend to deal with problems more regularly than I reward achievement. I run my business by finding out where the problems are and attacking them. I don't spend enough time telling people how wonderful they are. And that's a shortcoming that I know I have." Perhaps in an effort to explain it to himself, though, he adds, "I don't believe that I've ever been completely satisfied with any aspect of our business. That doesn't mean that we haven't reached our goal, sometimes even exceeded it. But then I'm always saying 'What's the next goal? Where do we go from here?' We are never satisfied with where we are. It can always be better."

## MELVYN WOLFF'S BUSINESS TENETS

- ★ Develop a corporate culture. Begin new-employee orientation with a discussion of your mission.
- ★ Working together as a team is essential. Turf building by individuals won't help your business grow.
- ★ Serving your customers is more important than the needs of employees.

# chapter fourteen

# The Shoppertainers—
# Eliot and Barry Tatelman,
# Jordan's Furniture

*E*liot and Barry Tatelman do just about everything together—running Jordan's furniture store, doing television commercials, and giving this interview. They even split the President and CEO job titles.

The brothers are promotion-oriented and have media savvy. Eliot, the older one, is the organizer and the leader. Barry is the creative genius who is responsible for the commercials and the media buys. Both are entertaining, reflective, natural-born salesmen. They specialize in the soft sell and never miss an opportunity to sell or promote Jordan's. They think and act outside the box. Maybe that's why this was the only interview that was done completely outdoors. And, nothing was off the record. I interviewed the brothers during the filming of one of their trademark television commercials.

If you live in the New England area, you probably know the Red Sox' Ted Williams, the Bruins' Bobby Orr, and the Celtics' Larry Bird— perhaps the greatest baseball, hockey, and basketball players, respectively, who ever played for Boston professional sports teams. If you live in New England, you undoubtedly also know Eliot and Barry, the Tatelman brothers, who are among the most unique businessmen in all of retailing. Their face-and-name recognition is on a par with any sports hero, media star, or politician in the Hub area.

Resident Bostonians feel as though they know Eliot and Barry, the furniture merchants, because of their ever-present locally produced TV commercials. The locals can't wait for the next installment of the Eliot and Barry Show. Often, the duo will spoof whatever is currently in the news or culture. When the "Got Milk?" ad campaign was popular, they filmed and aired a "Got Furniture?" commercial.

*When the Summer Olympics were ready to begin in Australia, the Tatelmans were filming a commercial created by the brothers and their long-time director. Simulating an Olympic 100-yard dash, the brothers crouched down in their starting positions, looking as though they had every intention of competing against the other runners. To make the scene even more realis-tic, numbered signs were displayed on their chests and a mist ("perspira-tion") was sprayed on their foreheads. As the starter's gun went off, the other contestants left the starting blocks at high speed. Eliot and Barry looked at one another and decided that, instead of running, they would sit on one of their sofas.*

*Jordan's is where New England denizens go to purchase furniture. Some people simply take their children to Jordan's for the entertainment. Young and old alike are treated to beads, simulator motion rides, red-fire-engine strollers, and tokens for candy in the customer service area. The store has close-up family-parking spots for "customers with infants." In the never ending quest for customer satisfaction, the spotlights in the bedding display area automatically dim when a customer lies down on a mattress.*

*The success of a furniture retailer depends on having sufficient capital, the right location, a wide range of merchandise, good presentation, expe-rienced personnel, and effective ads. Eliot and Barry not only succeed, they also bring integrity to an industry not known for integrity.*

*Most businesspeople know instinctively to treat their customers well, but the Tatelmans go one important step further—they treat their "em-ployees like customers." They try to create raving fans among their em-ployees, their vendors, and their customers.*

Warren Buffett has called Eliot and Barry Tatelman's organization "one of the most phenomenal and unique companies I have ever seen."[1] The bright magenta parking lot outside Jordan's Furniture store in Natick, a Boston suburb, is only the beginning. Once through the revolving doors of the 120,000-square-foot store built high on a hilltop, customers find themselves standing not on a sales floor crowded with wall units, couches, and end tables but, rather, on Bourbon Street in the French Quarter of New Orleans.

Towering above are two enormous court jesters (who, as it happens, look remarkably like the Tatelman brothers). To their right is a Mississippi riverboat, the *S.S. Splash Jordan,* with a live Dixieland band playing on its deck. Directly ahead is a hotel with the Quarter's traditional wrought-iron railings, as well as a theater, a lawyer's office, an art gallery, and Madame Ophelia Pulse's House of Voodoo, each of which leads into one of the store's furniture departments. Each is also populated by state-of-the-art animatronic puppets that urge visitors to move along to the rotunda and the House of Blues. There, every hour, the lights are dimmed and customers are treated to a nine-minute multimedia show that includes a music video filmed in New Orleans and features Eliot and Barry as the Blues Brothers.[2]

These latter-day "Blues Brothers," however, are not from New Orleans. They are second-generation New Englanders who were born in Newton, Massachusetts—Eliot in 1946, and Barry in 1950. They are also the third generation of Tatelmans in the furniture business that was started by their Russian émigré grandfather, Samuel A. Tatelman, in 1918. While working as a shoemaker in Manchester, New Hampshire, Samuel Tatelman sold used furniture from the back of a truck until 1926, when he and his brother-in-law opened a store in the Boston suburb of Waltham, Massachusetts, operating under the name Gray's Furniture. Two years later, the partners broke up, and Tatelman opened his own store, called Jordan's, in Waltham. When asked why the store was given that name, Eliot Tatelman says that his grandfather put several names in a hat and "Jordan's" just happened to be the one he pulled out.

In the 1930s, Samuel's son Edward—Eliot and Barry's father—joined the company. By the 1950s, the brothers were working in the store on weekends and during the summers. "When we were kids," Eliot remembers, "there were three generations working in the Waltham store. We used to all go out to lunch together, which was fun."[3] Of course, he adds, in those days it was "a very different company. We had maybe 10 employees," he says, "but, in one respect, it was the same. Even then, it was about being good to your people, being honest to customers, and treating people fairly. That's just the way my father and grandfather were." In the early 1970s, Eliot left Boston University, where he had been a part-time student, to devote all of his time to Jordan's. In the meantime, Barry, who had graduated from B.U. in 1972, was planning to go into advertising, like their older brother, Milton. But, as Barry recalls, their father said, "Why go to work for someone else when you can work for yourself? You want to do advertising? It's yours. I'm here if you need me."[4] In 1973, with their grandfather already retired and their father thinking about retirement, the two brothers took over the store.

The brothers say that their father taught them how to run the business and how to keep it from taking over their lives. "Our father was a man without enemies and [with] very high scruples," Eliot says. "He was honest and upright and always put family before business."[5] The elder Tatelman also knew that if he wanted his sons to stay in the business, he would have to let them run it. As Eliot put it, "Our father was smart enough to let us do what we wanted to do, and we, fortunately, had the ability."[6] One of the brothers' goals was to find new ways of advertising the store. According to Barry, Milton came up with the idea that Eliot and Barry should do their own radio spots. "He was a copywriter in New York," Barry recalled, "and heard these two guys talking back and forth on the radio in an ad campaign for, I think, Barney's. He thought we should try something similar. I was game because I'd been a drama major in school, but I didn't know about Eliot. But he was game, and the three of us spent a lot of time coming up with fun scripts."[7]

Once the scripts were written, Jordan's stopped advertising in the local newspaper and used its entire advertising budget for radio spots. The commercials for water beds, in the mid-1970s, brought about what the brothers consider their big breakthrough. "The only people selling water beds were water-bed stores," and they were just selling the beds, Eliot recalled some years later. "And we said, 'We'll take the bed and match it with the rest of the bedroom set.'" So they enclosed the water-filled mattresses in wooden frames and sold them with matching dressers, night tables, and other pieces. "We were the only ones in the country doing this," Eliot says. "That put us on the map. Our business started to fly because of water beds. We had something unique, and people wanted it." Convinced they were on the right track, they ordered truckloads of bedroom sets and took out double-page ads in the *Boston Globe* to supplement the radio commercials. Their grandfather—retired and living in Florida by then—would call and say, "What are you selling, plastic bags full of water?" And, of course, that's exactly what they were selling—25 a day for $600 apiece.[8]

The spots featuring the brothers worked very well, but, as Eliot later admitted, "There was a lot of hype in the early ones. We were talking about our super-savings sale. We were yelling and screaming. And when we started saying, 'Not to be confused with [the department store] Jordan

Marsh,' well, nobody could believe that. We stood out on the radio, but the commercials gave the concept that we were a schlocky store. We started to tone it down."[9] They were selling so many water beds that now they could afford to tone down the ads a bit. Earlier, they had emphasized the low price; now, they began pointing out the benefits of sleeping on a water bed. "Everyone else was talking about price," Eliot told a reporter years later. "We came up with this 'underpricing'—one price. We've been doing it for 25 years. One price, no sales. We realized we were spending more time changing tags and more money paying for tags. And it wasn't legit. Your staff couldn't feel good about it, not if they were honest. How could it be $899 this week and $799 the next week? It didn't make sense."[10]

Because the ads were so effective on radio, the brothers decided to try them on television—but not without some concerns. They didn't know how well the ads would translate to a new medium. Potential customers would see them, as well as hear them, and they were afraid that the ads might turn them into public figures, thereby threatening their privacy. Their worries proved unfounded. The ads were equally—if not more—effective on television, and although they did make the brothers public figures, the Tatelmans have been able to maintain their privacy.[11] The ads were so successful, in fact, that, 25 years later, in 1999, Jordan's had grown from having 15 employees in one store to a payroll of 1,200 people in four stores—three in Massachusetts (in Waltham, Avon, and Natick) and one in Nashua, New Hampshire. Even more important, the company was selling more furniture per square foot than any other store in the country (an average of $1,000 when the national average was $150) and bringing in annual revenues of about $250 million.

As it turned out, Jordan's hadn't only attracted the attention of tens of thousands of customers in New England. It had also attracted the attention of a particular acquisition-minded gentleman in Omaha, Nebraska. Having already purchased three multigeneration family-owned-and-operated furniture retailers—the Blumkins' Nebraska Furniture Mart, Bill Child's R.C. Willey in Utah, and Melvyn Wolff's Star Furniture in Texas—Warren Buffett was interested in acquiring more. As usual, he asked the operating managers of the three furniture companies if there were other organizations they could recommend to him. "Their invariable answer," he told Berkshire Hathaway's shareholders in 1999, "was the Tatelman brothers of New England and their remarkable furniture business, Jordan's."[12] Although the brothers were not seeking a buyer for their company, when Irv Blumkin met his friend Barry Tatelman at an Anti-Defamation League dinner in New York and asked if he'd be interested in meeting Buffett, Tatelman said he would. "We weren't meeting him with the idea of selling," Barry says. "We just wanted to meet him."[13]

In August 1999, when Buffett was planning a trip to Boston for a Gillette board meeting, he arranged to meet the brothers. "We took him through our Natick store," Eliot said, "and he loved it."[14] In fact, Buffett was so impressed with both the store and the brothers that he asked them if they would be interested in selling him the company. They had already turned down several offers to take the company public, because they knew that doing so would mean losing control over the stores. But they also knew that Buffett's philosophy was to leave an acquired company's management in place and not interfere with its day-to-day operations. Another element made Buffett's offer attractive to them. Like many owners of family businesses, the brothers were concerned about succession. Each had two children, either in or recently graduated from college. Thus far, only one of them, Eliot's son Josh, had expressed an interest in the business. And, as Barry noted, "You want to be fair, but what is fair? What if one of the kids wants to go into the business but the other doesn't? What happens when they get married and their wives have opinions about what's fair? We started to think that if we did sell the company, we wouldn't have family problems."[15]

After mulling over the offer for about a month, the brothers advised Buffett that they were interested in discussing a sale. As Eliot explains, "We had met and spent quite a lot of time together talking, and he asked us to send him some financial figures. We still weren't convinced that we wanted to sell, but we said, 'Let's send him the figures and see what he comes back with.' Two days later, there was a Fed Ex on my desk; that was the offer. The first page was about how we have this incredible business, something he's never seen, blah, blah, blah. But he wants to be sure that we're interested in working the rest of our days to keep it going, so if we are, we should turn the page for the offer." Picking up for his brother, Barry says, "We didn't say we'd be willing to work the rest of our lives, but we did tell him that we had nothing planned in the near future, and we made a commitment to him that we would never leave him high and dry, which we wouldn't." As is often the case, Buffett didn't even ask the brothers for an audit. "Our attorneys," says Eliot, "who were big attorneys in Boston, had never seen that before." As Barry later told a reporter, "It's a new concept in business. It's called trust."[16]

Based on that mutual trust, the Tatelmans and Buffett came to an agreement, and in mid-October, the merger was announced. The exact terms of the sale were not made public, but it's estimated that Buffett paid the Tatelmans between $225 and $250 million in cash, probably leaving management with a 15-to-20 percent ownership to ensure business continuation and profitability. In any case, both parties were clearly pleased with the sale. The Tatelmans were guaranteed the opportunity to continue running their company as they saw fit. At the same time, it assured them of avoiding family squabbles in the future. There was also, of course, the advantage of working with Buffett. "Dealing with Warren and his company, and the way he does things, is exactly in line with what we want," Eliot said at the time.[17]

But the Tatelmans had yet another reason for making the deal. They know that if they had waited, they could have sold the company for more, but, as Eliot explains, "It has to do with not being greedy. Barry and I realize we can have pretty much anything we want. But it reaches a point where you ask yourself, 'How much more do I need, and for what?' We like doing what we're doing; we like the challenge and the excitement of it, but it's not so much the money anymore. We're still doing this—we're still negotiating deals, we're still running around doing everything—but the money doesn't really mean that much to us because that isn't why we did it in the first place. What the deal does is provide tremendous security for our families, and that's what's really important to us."

Almost as important to the brothers was assuaging any concerns their staff might have about the effects of the merger. They even told their employees about the sale in a typically Tatelman way. On Thursday, October 7, a few days before the sale was to be made public, Barry and Eliot visited all four of their stores dressed as characters from the Dr. Seuss books and invited all their staff members to a "green eggs and ham" breakfast at the Copley Hotel in Boston the following Sunday morning. During that breakfast, they announced the sale, and, at the same time, assured their employees that nothing would change.[18] They then made another announcement. To celebrate the merger, they were giving every member of the staff a bonus: 50 cents for every *hour* each of them had worked for the company. The average bonus came to about $1,000 for every year of employment, and one employee received close to $40,000. The gesture cost the brothers $10 million, but, as Eliot said, "We owe something to every one of them."[19]

Warren Buffett was as pleased about the deal as the Tatelmans were. "This company is a gem," he said at the time the merger was announced.[20] And when he advised Berkshire Hathaway's shareholders about it in his annual letter, he explained why he thought so. "Under the brothers' management," he wrote, "Jordan's has grown ever more dominant in its region, becoming the largest furniture retailer in New Hampshire as well as Massachusetts. The Tatelmans don't just sell furniture or manage stores. They also present customers with a dazzling entertainment experience called 'shoppertainment.' A major and unique part of the Jordan business philosophy is to recognize that the customer is the 'whole' family and if you entertain the children the parents can make purchases. A family visiting a store can have a terrific time, while concurrently viewing an extraordinary selection of merchandise. The business results," he added, "are also extraordinary." Of the brothers themselves, Buffett said, "Barry and Eliot are classy people—just like their counterparts at Berkshire's three other furniture operations." Finally, in telling the shareholders about the bonus the Tatelmans had given their staff, he noted that the money "came from the Tatelmans' own pockets, not from Berkshire's. And Barry and Eliot were thrilled," he added, "to write the checks."[21]

The Tatelmans were also delighted to become part of Berkshire's furniture group. As Barry said at the time, "We're now part of the largest furniture retail group in the country. With our other sister stores, we will probably generate $1 billion a year in business. I envision us working together on a bunch of projects."[22] Perhaps one of the reasons he expected the four companies would be able to work together was the considerable similarities among them. "We had a big meeting," Eliot says, "and they all came to our store, and brought all their senior people, so we had about 75 people. Each one of us stood up and gave a brief history of his company, and it was incredible how similar we all were—in how all the companies had started as family businesses, in how they'd grown, and in the way we all looked at our businesses. You could see it. And then," he continues, "we went around the room and everyone said who they worked for, what department they were in, and how long they'd been with the company. And it was 20 years, 15 years, 25 years, 12 years. You don't see that today.

Everybody's changing jobs. But here was a group of people who had been with the same companies for years. It was phenomenal."

Being part of the group has also provided some practical benefits to the Tatelman brothers. "We've been in our own cocoon for years," Barry says, "and one thing we found interesting is that there's more than one way to skin a cat. You always think the way you do something is the best or the right way, but when we sat down and discussed how we all did things, we found out that even though other people might do things differently it can still be very successful. The people in all the other furniture companies really have it together. It was a mind-opening experience." The brothers believe that another practical benefit could be the establishment of a buying consortium by the group, although none has been established as yet. "All the manufacturers know we're part of Berkshire," says Barry, "and that Star, RC, and Nebraska are too. So when we come in, if we're all buying a specific line, there's a lot more clout there. But we still run very independently of each other—most of our merchandise is a lot different from Nebraska's, which is a lot different from Star's and RC's." He also notes, "We all have a lot of buying power individually. Our feeling is we don't want to beat up on the manufacturers. We get the best possible deal that we can, and we get delivery, and things like that, that are very important to us, but we know the manufacturers have to survive."

The Tatelmans have been able to establish a certain amount of synergy by physically bringing the managers of the four furniture companies together. "We were the last one to come on board," Eliot says, "and the other stores hadn't been doing anything as a group. They'd never even gotten together for a meeting. When we came in, we felt there was a good reason to do it, that there were some things that we could help each other with, so we set it up. At first it was very strange because we've always tried to protect everything we do and keep it to ourselves. But we opened up to everyone else, and eventually it started to build until everybody was working together. Now everybody's trusting each other and it's great. But it's not only that we trust each other," Eliot adds. "We all really like each other. So it's working."

Warren Buffett makes no effort to foster synergy among any of the Berkshire Hathaway companies, but he apparently has no objection to members of "the family" making such efforts. In fact, as the Tatelmans had heard, and have now learned themselves, their boss has no interest in telling them how to run their business. "The beautiful part about Warren," says Eliot, "is that when we joined forces with him, absolutely nothing changed. We called him the day after we got the check—we both got on the phone—and we said, 'Okay, Warren, you're up. What do you want from us? Do you want us to call you every day? Do you want us to call you once a week? Do you want us to call you once a month? What do you want us to do?' And his answer was, 'What do you want? You want to call me every day, call me every day. If you don't want to call, me, don't call me. It's, like, just keep doing what you've been doing.' "

"I think a lot of people talk about Warren," Barry says, "as being this great businessman, which of course he is. But I think Warren's greatest asset is the way he analyzes people, the way he sizes up people. He can tell, when he meets people, what they're really like. I think he likes to be involved with people that he likes and trusts, and he is a great judge of character. I'm not saying that because he picked us, but because he's picked a lot of great people over the years." Eliot adds, "He's a great motivator, and a very down-to-earth guy. He has the ability to put everyone at ease and make you feel special. And that's a great ability in management, to make each person who's working for you feel great, special, and important. He does that to each of us, and that's one of his great abilities."

"Another great thing about Warren," Barry says, "is that no one's afraid of him. We really love the guy. He's become a friend, almost like a father figure, and everyone feels that way. When you hear that Warren's on the phone, you don't think, 'Oh my God, he's checking on us.' It's more like, 'Oh great, it's Warren.' And he always says something funny, you always get a laugh, you always have a good time. It's really just like having a friend. And you can call him as often or as little as you want and he's always got an answer for you." Eliot adds: "He's a smart friend. He knows about everything. I just called him a few weeks ago on something we were working on, and I couldn't believe how much he knew about it. Here I am calling him out of the blue to discuss this thing with him, about the numbers and everything else, and he says, 'Don't they just lease it? They won't sell it to you?' And I said, 'Warren, is there anything you don't know?' "

"I really respect Warren," Barry says, "not because he's made billions of dollars. Some people look upon that as success, but I don't because there's a lot of billionaires out there who are very unhappy. Warren lives his life the way he wants to live it. It's very basic and it's very simple. He keeps everything very simple. Money doesn't rule him at all. He still drives the same car he's been driving for six years, and he still lives in the same house he's lived in for years. But he enjoys getting up to go to work every day; he enjoys the people he works with. He'd be a success even if he had just enough money to survive, to pay the bills; because he enjoys what he does every day. To me, that's true success."

As much as the brothers admire Buffett's management style, though, they tend to do things in a somewhat more complex—although equally positive—way. For example, one evening in January 1999, each of their company's 1,200 employees arrived home to find something unusual in the mail: a package containing a fleece jacket, attached to which was a button that read "J-Team! May 10, 1999?" The "J-Team" is what the Tatelmans call their staff. When the employees got to work the next day, they found "May 10?" posters on the walls of the stores. At that point, of course, as Eliot Tatelman later explained, "The rumors start—we're going public; a ground breaking for a new store. What does it do?" he asked. "It gets them talking." Several weeks later, employees came to work and found fortune cookies on their desks. But instead of a fortune, each cookie contained a slip of paper reading "May 10?" And a month after that, the staff began receiving one piece of a jigsaw puzzle with each weekly paycheck. After three weeks, they were able to read the message: "Attention J-Team!! Listen for Eliot & Barry on KISS 108 FM with 'Matty in the Morning' on Thursday, February 25th, during the 9:00 hour to find out more about May 10th, 1999! Don't Miss It!"[23]

That morning, of course, a large number of staff members tuned in to Matty Siegel's radio show, one of the most popular in Boston. And when the host asked the Tatelman brothers what was going to happen on May 10, they told him. On May 10, they said, all four of their furniture stores would be closed. And, starting at 6:30 in the morning, the first of four jets would leave Logan Airport to take all 1,200 of Jordan's staff members for a day's outing—in Bermuda. "It's our way of saying 'Thank You' to a great group of employees," said Eliot. "They are definitely worth it."[24] During the day they spent on the island, the staff were treated to food, live bands, games, shopping, and water sports. The last plane returned to Boston by 8:00 that evening. The outing cost the company $750,000, but the Tatelman brothers thought it was worth it. "It's making the employees feel important," Eliot said, "and they are. I'm not selling furniture right now. I'm not greeting people at the door. I'm not sweeping the driveway. Without them, I'm nothing."[25] He recognized that the trip was something out of the ordinary, but, as he told a reporter at the time, "If you do normal things, you only get normal things back. If you do something special, you get something special back."[26] Among employers who think that way, it should come as no surprise that when Eliot subsequently asked a new salesman how he liked working in the store, the man said, "Why are all your employees smiling?"[27]

The Tatelmans know that happy employees make happy customers. In fact, they say they treat their employees like customers. "Our feeling is," Eliot begins, "if you can't make raving fans out of your employees," and his brother finishes, "how do you expect your employees to make raving fans of the customers?" Eliot believes, "If our employees feel good about what they're doing, and they feel compensated properly, and they feel appreciated, then they're going to have smiles on their faces. Now you come in to shop, what's going to happen? They're passing that on to the consumer."

They maintain as much personal contact with their employees as possible. For example, Ed Wise, a salesman in the Natick store, recently told a reporter: "I came back to work after my wife had a baby, and Eliot says to me, 'How's your son?' Then he says, 'You named him Joshua, right?'"[28]

Another way they try to keep their employees happy is by keeping them involved. "Everything we do is a team approach," says Barry, "and we don't have any reserved parking spaces for the executives or any of that stuff. We're all part of the same team. Nobody is better than anybody else; we all deserve the same respect. It doesn't matter if you're sweeping the floor or if you're the head of a store." Eliot adds, "We make everybody realize that if somebody isn't performing, eventually they're going to stop store earnings. If the guy sweeping the parking lot stopped sweeping, eventually there would be so much dirt that nobody would be able to get in the front door. So everybody's important here and everybody's equal."

At the same time, the brothers closely monitor the shopping experience. Someone from the store contacts every customer after every sale to ask about each aspect of the buying experience. They ask, for example, how helpful the salesperson was, and whether the delivery person removed all the packing material before leaving. But the brothers are also concerned about how much fun their employees are having, and how much fun they are. Referring to the company's practice of having managers scrutinize each salesperson's "daily report card," Eliot says, "It's not just how much you write, it's how good you are with our customers and how much fun you are. If you're the number-one writer and you're not getting a good daily report card, if you don't wow the shopper, then you're costing us business in the future. I need every person who comes here to recommend us to other people. That's our secret." Almost as an aside, though, he adds, "It's no secret. It's common sense."[29]

"Our goal," Eliot says, "is to overwhelm the customers to the point we own them, to make a raving fan of every consumer. The more we do that, the more we own them as a customer, and that is something you can't buy. If people feel comfortable buying from us—knowing that we service, knowing it's fun, knowing they're treated with respect, knowing that it's an honest place—that makes it very hard for our competitors. Our reputation is more important than anything, and that's why we work so hard at it, and why we will do whatever it takes and whatever it costs us to keep that reputation." Among the things the Tatelmans will do to maintain that reputation are: Give out free milk and cookies to their customers; provide live music, movies, and a robotic show; give out umbrellas when it rains; and provide free in-home consultation services to determine customers' needs. "It's the little things that count," says Barry.[30]

As Eliot puts it, "It's all about thinking out of the box," to which his brother adds, "Doing the unusual. Let's say there are four gas stations on four corners at an intersection. One of the stations knows his customers by name. He also knows who reads the sports pages and he gives them a free copy of the sports section. He also gives out free coffee and homemade cookies." Now Eliot steps in again and asks, "Now which station would you go to? Of course you'd pick the one with the cookies and coffee. This is the kind of thinking we try to do at Jordan's. People get too much into routines," he explains. "More people need to work on breaking the mold. Thinking in different ways—which isn't always easy."[31] The brothers' ultimate goal, as Barry puts it, is for people "to have a good time and buy some furniture too. We have tried to create an environment where those two ideas are not mutually exclusive."[32]

"We market by personality," Eliot says, "we market by entertainment, and we market by giving good values." In other words, he says, "We market by emotions." He explains, "When you buy furniture at our store and you come to pick it up, the first thing we do is, we greet you and we wash the windows in the car. Then we ask if you'd like something to eat. You can get out of your car while we're putting the chair in your trunk and tying it up for you, and there's a little refreshment stand with hot dogs and cold drinks. I've seen people standing there and go, 'Wow, I just bought a damn chair, and they're washing my windows, and I'm eating a hot dog.' And then we'll call them up afterward and ask if everything was all right, and they say, 'I can't believe the hot dogs when I picked up the furniture.' Here they just came out of a beautiful store, they saw a great show, the salesperson was wonderful, and they got great values, but what impressed them was the hot dog. That's emotions."

However, although the brothers may market by emotions, they never let their emotions get in the way of managing the company. Drawing on their individual strengths, they have divided up the responsibilities of running the company. Eliot, who is the company's president, oversees all of its administrative and operational functions. Barry, whose title is CEO, concentrates on marketing and public relations, or what he refers to as "the fun part." Doing it this way, according to Barry, is what makes it work. "By ourselves, we are useless," he says. "Together, we get the job done. We think alike. When he says something that is completely off the wall, it's exactly what I've been thinking. And we agree on almost everything. It's always been that way." One of the things they've always agreed on is that Eliot can always have the last word, an arrangement with which Barry is quite happy. In fact, he admits that he'd "screw everything up royally if I was running the company."[33]

The brothers have neighboring offices and share a secretary. But they have very different personalities, and that difference is reflected in their offices in the Avon store. Eliot's office is all business. The only suggestions of anything whimsical are his collection of kaleidoscopes and a toy motorcycle that represents his full-size Harley Davidson. Barry's office provides numerous examples of his sense of fun, including a "Simpsons" chess set on his desk, cardboard cutouts of the Beatles, and pictures of Dick Van Dyke and members of the "Mary Tyler Moore Show." One wall is devoted to his family; there are pictures of Susan, his wife; his son and daughter; and Charlie, the family dog—plus a photograph of the summer house he and his wife built on Martha's Vineyard in 1997. Although he does not have a picture of it in his office, Eliot also has a second home, on Lake

Winnipesauke in New Hampshire. Eliot's wife, June, is a schoolteacher, and he has two sons who are the same ages as his brother's children.[34]

Despite the fact that her husband and his brother sold their company for nearly a quarter of a billion dollars just a few years ago, June Tatelman continues to work at the Ephraim Curtis Middle School in Sudbury, Massachusetts, where she teaches wellness classes to seventh and eighth graders. She and her husband also run, and fund, a very special camp every summer—a camp for about 75 HIV-infected children between the ages of five and 16 years. They started the camp in 1999, and it's very much a family effort. Their sons, Josh and Michael, serve as camp counselors, and a variety of cousins and friends join the Tatelmans each summer for the week that the camp is in operation. Because of the stigma that is still attached to the AIDS virus, the Tatelmans reveal neither the name of the camp nor its location. It does, though, have very special significance to them. As June Tatelman told a reporter in 1999, "[Although] everyone says 'It's amazing what you give to the kids . . . ,' what's amazing is what I get from them. It's something we look forward to all year."[35]

The camp has significance to the Tatelmans for other reasons as well. As Eliot explains it, "It started because we lost our older brother to the AIDS virus, and it just brought us to the idea of a camp. Barry and I both love kids, and the kids we're dealing with at this camp were born into the world, through no fault of their own, with mothers who are crack addicts, fathers who are in jail, and sometimes with no fathers at all. All we're trying to do is give them a week of fun." And giving something—particularly of yourself—is, he believes, what's really important. "Giving money is one thing," Eliot says, "but giving time is something else. Writing out a check isn't nearly as important as giving your time and energy. Why do these people who are so wealthy write out a check for a million dollars? What difference does it make to them? Is it changing their lifestyle? Are they not going to buy something because they're doing this? They still own six houses and a yacht and everything else. It doesn't affect their lifestyle. It's very nice they're doing it, but they're not giving up anything when they do it. When you give up time—you give up a week or you give up a month or you give up a day to do something—*that's* it. You've given up something."

The Tatelmans give of themselves outside of work in other ways as well. For example, as Barry explains, "Every week we go to a different high school and talk to the kids about thinking outside of the box and doing things a little differently. We like to talk to kids and get them excited. We got a letter the other day from some kid who saw us three years ago, and because he saw us, and heard what we were saying about thinking and doing things differently, he invented a wooden computer and he's doing really well with it." Eliot adds, "The kids who are going off to college listen to us because they want to be successful. We try and take advantage of that, get them thinking outside the box. Get them to ask themselves what they could do. And this guy came up with the idea that an executive would rather not have a big plastic box on his or her desk, so he puts a computer inside a wooden case that's really beautiful, and then he gives us credit for it. He says, 'You're the ones that motivated me to come up with this,' and that's really gratifying."

Planting seeds like these—seeds that will grow in the future—is very important to the Tatelmans, and that applies to the future of their business as well. And yet, there is at least one important area in which they have not yet begun planting seeds—technology. "Everyone thinks we're crazy," Barry says, "but we haven't done anything on the Internet yet. We're going to, but we're waiting for the dust to settle." His brother agrees: "I think the Internet is going to be an important part of our industry and our business," Eliot says, "but not the way it started out. Up until now, the focus has been on making sales, and I think it's clear that it doesn't work. The cost of handling and servicing our particular product is too high to be able to do it globally and do it efficiently, and the return rate on our product is huge. People get it in a room and it doesn't fit, it's the wrong color, it's this, it's that. We run into that all the time, even when people come into the store, sit on it, feel it, and touch it. They get it home and they don't like it. So now you've got people not even feeling it and touching it, just looking at a picture, and they get it in and say, 'Oh, I didn't know it was going to be this tall . . . it's covering my window . . . come and take it out.' But," Eliot continues, "we will be able to use the Internet for many other things—like letting people check on when their order's coming in, or check on where the delivery truck is if they're waiting at home."

They are, nevertheless, aware of the need to adapt and change. "If you look at the furniture business," says Eliot, "and you go back and look in the Yellow Pages from all over the country from, say, 10 years ago, you'll see how many stores there were that don't exist anymore. It's a very difficult business. It requires a big real estate investment because of big stores. It requires advertising. It requires marketing, and merchandising, and fashion, and big labor. And putting all these factors together is hard to do, and that's why there've been so many failures. If you look at the successful companies, you see the ones that have weathered all that. And it's those companies, the ones that were smart enough to weather all of that and become successful, that know what they're doing."

When asked about who their biggest current—and future—competitors might be, Eliot says, "Our biggest competitor right now is probably not in the furniture business, it's companies that produce all kinds of consumer products. Cars, computers, other products that in some respects can be more exciting. We're dealing with a consumer product," he continues, "so they go buy an expensive house and then have no money left for furniture. Or they go buy that big-screen TV, the digital TV; they want a laser disc player. All these other products can be more exciting than a new sofa, and that's probably our biggest competition right now, fighting against that. Trying to make the product exciting. And that's not going to change in the future."

Neither Eliot nor Barry seems to be very concerned about the future of Berkshire Hathaway. Of the much-debated issue of Warren Buffett's successor or successors, Barry says, "He's so smart that I can't imagine that he has not planned for his succession. For some reason, he doesn't want to let everybody know, and it must be a good reason." And Eliot adds, "You've got to trust the man." Nor are the brothers concerned about whether Berkshire or Jordan's will operate any differently after Buffett is gone. "I only know one way to run the business," says Eliot, "and if that's a problem with whoever is running Berkshire Hathaway, I'm gone. If all of a sudden I've got to change and do things that don't make sense to me, I won't do it."

As for the company's future, when it's pointed out to the brothers that Jordan's is already the largest furniture retailer in Massachusetts and New Hampshire, Eliot says, "It doesn't matter. We want to be the best, not the largest. That's the most important thing. We're not trying to own the world. I think the challenge for us is to do things in a different way than other people, and see smiling faces on our employees and smiling faces on our customers." In fact, Eliot says that's the way he measures the company's success—"with smiles. And," he adds, "if that's your motivation rather than just the bottom line, then the bottom line comes anyway. It really does."

## THE TATELMANS' BUSINESS TENETS

★ Treat your employees as if they were your customers. An employee who loves his or her job will pass on that feeling to the customers.

★ Aim to meet all your customers' concerns. Good service and quality merchandise are important, but let your customers also have fun. By providing music, food, umbrellas when it's raining, and other services, we know our customers will keep coming back.

★ Be creative; don't limit your employees to performing specific duties. Involve all your employees in team projects. People almost always work better when they're part of a larger group effort.

★ In a family-run business, emotions cause hurt relationships. Recognize your strengths and skills and those of your siblings. Then divide up the responsibilities of running the business.

# Part Five

# Berkshire's CEO Successors— The Professional Managers

# chapter fifteen

# The Turnaround Manager—
# Stan Lipsey, *The Buffalo News*

*S*tan Lipsey's newspapers were among the first businesses to be acquired by Berkshire. This made Lipsey the Buffett CEO with the most sen-iority and a true company insider. Lipsey, a native of Omaha and a long-time friend of Buffett, was an officer (vice president) in Berkshire Hathaway before the GenRe acquisition. Lipsey was there when Berkshire had just $50 million in assets and $5 million in annual earnings. During the past 30 years, he has watched as his boss added a digit, every decade, to Berkshire's assets, book value, earnings, and stock price, and to his own personal worth.

Lipsey has made more money as an investor in Berkshire Hathaway stock than as a Buffett CEO, but had he not first sold the Sun newspapers to Berkshire he might never have become a shareholder.

Warren Buffett has always chosen to purchase companies with manage-ment already in place, and to pursue the principle of managing his wholly owned subsidiaries just like his partly owned businesses. The Buffalo News is an exception on both counts. Going against his long-held acquisition philosophies—don't buy a business that needs fixing, leaving management alone, interceding only if asked or if the business is in trouble—Buffett has made Stanford Lipsey and the Buffalo News examples of how Berkshire can provide management and turn a business around.

Sandwiched between the Buffalo hockey arena and the new baseball stadium is the Buffalo News building, where Stan Lipsey has his office. The business and the building it is in look just as they did when Berk-shire acquired them in 1977 for $32.5 million. Like the city of Buffalo, they haven't changed on the exterior. But just about everything else—the product, the owner, the competition, the sales volume—has changed.

Stan Lipsey, the publisher of the Buffalo News, is an old friend and business associate of Warren Buffett. Along with Warren's wife Susie and another Buffett CEO, Chuck Huggins, Lipsey loves jazz. The man simply known as "Stan" to parking lot attendants, security guards, and employees of the Buffalo News is the kind of guest a host or hostess wants at a dinner party. He is youthful, friendly, good-humored, and an engaging conversationalist.

Stan could well be the mayor of Buffalo; he's that dedicated to his adopted hometown. He speaks and cares about it like a proud founding father. He personally sponsors the city's annual jazz fests with his annual Berkshire owner-designated charitable contribution.

Inside his office, two historic front pages of the Buffalo News are framed behind his desk. The headlines are: "President McKinley Shot," and "Man Walks on the Moon." In another frame is the Omaha Sun's front-page article and the Pulitzer Prize-winning investigative news story on Boys Town, which is located in Omaha but became famous via Hollywood. In the center of the wall is a framed copy of his Columbia School of Journalism's Pulitzer Prize, which resembles a college diploma.

Stan Lipsey is proof that, when necessary, Berkshire can indeed supply management after an acquisition. Warren Buffett doesn't like to acquire companies without management in place, but Stan has been a very successful draft choice. After five early years of losses, Stan's company has earned over $750 million (and counting) in pretax earnings.

In the spring of 1990, Tim Medley, president of an investment counseling/financial planning company based in Jackson, Mississippi, journeyed to Omaha, Nebraska, to attend Berkshire Hathaway's annual shareholder's meeting. The night before the meeting, at a party held at Borsheim's Jewelers, one of Berkshire's companies, he met and converged with a slight, fair-haired man named Stan. Later in the evening, he told some other shareholders, "While you all were over talking to those bigwigs, I was talking to some regular fellow named Stan, who said he was with the *Buffalo News*." Medley had the impression that "Stan" was with the newspaper's circulation department, partly because he had offered to drop off some copies of the newspaper at Medley's hotel room the next day. He was then told that he had been talking to Stanford Lipsey, a Pulitzer Prize winner and the newspaper's publisher. And he did find two copies of the *Buffalo*

*News* outside his hotel room door the next morning, delivered, as promised, by the publisher.[1]

Lipsey has been the publisher of the *Buffalo News* for almost two decades, but when asked to describe himself, he doesn't talk about his responsibilities as a businessman running a multimillion-dollar operation. Rather, he says, "I'm a newspaperman. That is my religion. That is what I am devoted to." To him, that means a great deal. Newspapers, he believes, "are a vital institution in society, an institution which in many respects is on the same plane, and can exert the same amount of force, as religion." Given such evangelical fervor, it might be assumed that Lipsey had been raised in a newspaper family. Not so. When Lipsey was born, in 1927, his father was running a wholesale meat and poultry company in Omaha.

Stan Lipsey grew up in Omaha and graduated from high school in 1945. He majored in economics at the University of Michigan but also got his first taste of journalism there, as a photographer for the school's daily newspaper and as the photography editor for its yearbook. Before he graduated in 1948, his father, who was planning to retire to California, asked the 20-year-old if he wanted to take over the family business in Omaha. "But," as Lipsey says, "the bane of my existence was that I didn't know what I wanted to do," and he declined the offer. His father was, however, willing to back him in any kind of business he might want to start, and the younger Lipsey followed him to Los Angeles. But after two years on the West Coast he still couldn't decide on a career path. He returned to Omaha and took a job with a weekly newspaper—the *Sun*. "My rationale for taking the job," he explains, "was that since I didn't know what I wanted to do, if I went to work for a small paper I would learn about all kinds of businesses and then be able to decide which one to go into." It turned out that he loved newspapers.

He worked only briefly for the newspaper before his Air Force Reserve unit was called to active duty during the Korean War. While assigned to Offutt Air Force Base, in Fort Crook, Nebraska, he became editor of the base newspaper for Strategic Air Command Headquarters. He had found his niche. After the war, he returned to the paper and moved up from photographer to reporter, to editor, and eventually to publisher and majority owner. In 1965, Warren Buffett, also a native of Omaha, approached him about selling the newspaper. Lipsey wasn't interested in selling the paper at that time, but, four years later, the idea of selling had grown on him. "I didn't know Warren that well then," he says. He was seriously considering another offer—one of many that the *Sun* received. "But I checked him out, and he had the right stuff. Besides having the ability to buy, he understood newspapers, and I felt I was putting the *Sun* in good hands. While I liked Warren the minute I met him, I certainly didn't guess how significant a relationship it would be."

Buffett's experience with newspapers went back to his teen years in Washington, D.C. His father, Howard, was a member of the House of Representatives, and Warren had a newspaper delivery route in the capital while he was in high school. On that job, he personally earned the $10,000 nest egg that would later become Berkshire Hathaway. While he was attending the University of Nebraska, he was country circulation manager for the *Lincoln Journal*.[2] His friend, Carol J. Loomis, senior editor of *Fortune* magazine and editor of Warren's famed annual letter to shareholders, once observed, that "if he had not been an investor, he might well have picked journalism."[3] Now he wanted to own a newspaper, and buying the *Sun* from Stan Lipsey would provide him with that opportunity.

Lipsey, to this day, considers selling his newspaper to Buffett, "the best decision I ever made." Not only did he receive cash for the company, Warren agreed to take him into his partnership. Even more important, he says, he got "Warren Buffett as a friend and how he manages his managers." "You probably can think of hundreds of people," he says, "who own their businesses, or executives who have been running businesses, and when their companies are sold they're eventually cast off for one reason or another. That's just not going to happen with Warren. He doesn't want to have to provide management, and there are businesses he would have bought but didn't because the management wasn't right." Lipsey stayed on as publisher of the *Sun,* and the relationship was very successful. In 1972, the paper won a Pulitzer Prize for investigative journalism for a financial exposé of Boys Town—the first time that a weekly had won the prestigious award in that category.

"Warren has always loved papers," Lipsey says, "and he understands media—not only as a business but also as something that has significant value in society. Many people focus on it as a business—and I'm not saying that Warren doesn't do that—but he also sees more than just that aspect of it. He's got more of what it takes than most owners in the United States."

As a result of his interest in—and understanding of—the industry, Buffett had purchased a substantial number of shares in several other newspaper and publishing operations, including The Washington Post Company, Gannett, and Time, Inc. He was, nevertheless, always looking for new possibilities. When he heard, in 1976, that the *Buffalo Evening News* was for sale, his interest was piqued.

Founded in 1880, the *Evening News* was a conservative Republican newspaper. For many years, it had been owned by the Butler family. Kate Robinson Butler (Mrs. Edward H. Butler, Jr.) had run it until her death in 1974. Henry Z. Urban, who had been with the paper since 1953, had been appointed publisher and president after Butler's death, but, by 1976, Butler's estate was seeking a buyer. Vincent Manno, a newspaper broker working with the estate, offered the paper to both the *Washington Post* and the *Chicago Tribune* for $40 million, and both seriously considered it. Afternoon newspapers like the *Evening News* were disappearing, but the paper had a good reputation and was supported by Buffalo's largely blue-collar population.

There were, however, several drawbacks that potential buyers had to take into account. First, the paper didn't publish a Sunday edition—the one advertisers are most interested in and the one that brings in the most revenue. Second, Buffalo itself—a cold, old, rusting industrial town—was considered a negative location. Finally, the paper's employees were represented by 13 separate unions, all of which had contracts that were extremely favorable for their members, who were, consequently, among the best-paid newspaper people in the country. For a business that had earned only $1.7 million the previous year, $40 million was a lot of money. As a result, neither the *Post* nor the *Tribune* made an offer.[4]

Manno subsequently lowered the price to $35 million, but still had no takers. Then he got a phone call from Warren Buffett, who had learned of the paper's availability in his role as a director of The Washington Post Company. Buffett viewed the situation somewhat differently. He saw that the paper was firmly established in the community, and that its daily circulation was twice that of its morning competitor, the *Buffalo Courier-Express*. He also saw that the paper's daily editions were purchased by a higher percentage of local households than those in any other major cities. He knew that Buffalo had a particularly stable population, and he believed that the paper was capable of earning more than its current income.[5] Finally, as Lipsey says, "Warren always wanted to own a major newspaper."

After a brief negotiation at Manno's house in Weston, Connecticut, one Saturday afternoon in January 1977, Warren Buffett bought the *Buffalo Evening News* for $32.5 million. It was the largest purchase Buffett had made up to that time. (The paper was actually purchased by Blue Chip Stamps, which was controlled by Berkshire Hathaway at the time, and which has since been merged into the larger company.) Buffett knew that there was work to be done, and as soon as he took over the paper, he began instituting changes. One of the first changes was to name Murray B. Light, the paper's managing editor, as its editor, and to instruct Light to begin designing a Sunday edition to compete with the *Courier-Express*'s Sunday paper. It was rumored that the *Evening News* had never published a Sunday edition because of an agreement between the Butler family and the Connors family, which owned the *Courier-Express*. At the time Buffett bought the *Evening News,* the *Courier-Express* was barely making any money, and its Sunday edition was the only thing keeping it alive. The *Evening News'* daily circulation was 268,000; its rival's was 123,000. But the Sunday edition of the *Courier-Express* had a circulation of 270,000.[6]

The owners of the *Courier-Express,* apparently realizing that if the rival paper began publishing a Sunday edition, their main source of income would suffer, decided to take action. In November 1977, two weeks before the first Sunday edition of the *Evening News* was scheduled to be published, the *Courier-Express* brought suit for violation of the Sherman Anti–Trust Act. The suit alleged that the *Evening News* was using unfair business practices by offering subscribers seven papers for the price of six during a brief promotional period, and by planning to charge only 30 cents for the Sunday edition (the Sunday *Courier-Express* sold for 50 cents), the purpose of which was to force its competitor out of business. Under the law, though, the *Courier-Express* had to prove not only that Buffett was using unfair business practices, but also that he was also trying to establish a monopoly.

A hearing on the suit started on November 4, 1977, in the federal courthouse in Buffalo, before Judge Charles L. Brieant, Jr., and lasted for five days. Although Buffett took the stand himself, and provided a spirited defense of both his actions and his intent, the judge issued an injunction that restricted the *Evening News'* plans to publish a Sunday edition, pending a trial. "There are only two newspapers now," the judge wrote in his opinion. "If the [*Evening News'*] plan works as I find it is intended to work, there will be but one left." The injunction allowed the paper to begin publication on Sundays, but placed severe limitations on its ability to promote and market the new edition. Needless to say, the *Courier-Express* splashed the news of the injunction across its own front page, which only added to the bad publicity Buffett and Co. had already gotten for their efforts.[7]

The two papers then began an all-out war. Both were very aware that, in the end, only one of them would survive. Warren Buffett decided that he needed some help, so he called on his friend, Stan Lipsey. "Warren asked me about moving to Buffalo," Lipsey says, "and I told him that I really didn't want to go. But then he said, 'How about going up one week a month; it will just run better with you up there,' and I said I'd do it." Acting as a consultant to Henry Z. Urban, the publisher who had been appointed by the executors of the Butler estate, Lipsey went to work strengthening the Sunday edition, but, given the restrictions imposed by Judge Brieant's injunction, it was an uphill battle. Throughout 1978, the *Courier-Express* Sunday edition outsold the *Evening News* by more than 100,000 copies each week. By the end of the year, Buffett's company had lost $2.9 million.

In April 1979, two years after Buffett had bought the newspaper, the U.S. Court of Appeals in New York reversed Judge Brieant's injunction, arguing: "All that the record supports is a finding that Mr. Buffett intended to do as well as he could with the *News* and was not lying awake thinking what the effect of its competition on the *Courier* would be. This is what the antitrust laws aim to promote, not to discourage."[8] The court's decision put an end to the litigation, but not to the paper's problems. Two months later, the *Courier-Express* was sold to the Cowles family's Minneapolis Star & Tribune Company, which meant that the war would continue. In 1979, the losses for the *Evening News* amounted to $4.6 million.

Early in 1980, Stan went to see Warren at his home (they met there as often as at his office).

"I had decided that it was time for me to make a change. And, if I was going to leave the Sun Newspapers after 30 years, I also thought about leaving Omaha. In my mind, it was either Buffalo or San Francisco. Many would think that decision would be easy, but I had gotten hooked on the battle between the *News* and the *Courier-Express,* and in traveling there over two years, I found Buffalo to be an area with a lot of assets and very nice people.

"While in my mind Warren was the boss, our relationship was one of being good friends and partners. I really wanted his opinion as a friend. While I knew Warren wanted me to go to Buffalo in the worst way, he never pushed it. Ultimately, I decided I'd be happier in Buffalo, and I am. No small part of it is the continuing relationship with Warren, as well as being a part of the mission and the importance of newspapers in our society.

"So I moved to Buffalo," Lipsey recalls, "and was doing what we needed to do to make the Sunday paper successful, to make sure that the *Evening News* survived. The editorial part of the paper was always good, but there were other aspects that weren't as good as they needed to be. And I was running into internal obstacles that were getting in my way. Warren solved that quickly; he made me Vice Chairman and Chief Operating Officer of the *News* in the January of 1981." By early 1982, the *News* Sunday edition still trailed the *Courier-Express* but now only by 70,000 copies—and gaining. The *News* was still losing money, even if at a smaller rate, but the *Courier-Express* had been losing twice as much—as much as $3 million a year—and, ultimately, its owners decided that they'd had enough, and announced they would close.

Before it closed, the *Courier-Express* was put up for sale. The only buyer was Rupert Murdoch, a fierce competitor by any standard. Stan and Murray flew to Washington to strategize with Warren, who was attending a *Washington Post* board meeting.

If the *Courier-Express* closed, they had to be prepared, within a few days, to start an entirely new morning edition, which involved news content, production, and delivery. Simultaneously, they had to figure out how to slash all costs, including payroll, by one-third, to meet the lean promotional product that Rupert Murdoch would produce.

As soon as the *Courier-Express* closed, the *Buffalo Evening News* changed its name to the *Buffalo News* and started publishing a morning edition. Within six months of its competitor's demise, the Sunday edition of the *News* had a weekly circulation of 360,000, more than its rival had ever had. Within a year, Henry Z. Urban retired as publisher, and Stan Lipsey took over the position. The war with the *Courier-Express* had cost Berkshire an additional $12 million, for a total investment of $44.5 million, but now that the *News* was the only game in town, profits began to soar. In 1983, the paper's first year without competition, it earned $19 million; by the end of the 1980s, it was earning more than $45 million a year. Within seven years, the *Buffalo News* had earned back the purchase price plus the additional losses, and has been profitable ever since.

When the *Courier-Express* closed, Stan and Warren had a long conversation about advertising rates. To meet the *Courier-Express* pricing (classified ads were free), *News* rates had been marked down to a noneconomic level. Warren's philosophy on circulation was to raise rates very slightly, but annually—a far cry from the policy of most papers.

However, a sharp increase in advertising rates was now necessary. It was agreed that an increase was justified by the paper's high penetration and close-in circulation, which gave advertisers a superb medium—perhaps the best in the nation—for reaching their customers.

In the discussion, Buffett and Lipsey agreed that it was better to raise advertising rates sharply, one time, instead of having a series of fairly high increases. This rate increase contributed substantially to the future *News* profits.

"Warren gave me this wonderful opportunity in Buffalo," Lipsey says. "He wanted me to come up here much more than I did, but the fact of the matter is, I have always believed that one must personally continue growing, and I have always tried to do that. Coming to Buffalo gave me a major arena in which to operate. A big paper. A big city. A big challenge. A city with a lot of problems. I feel like I have been able to do many rewarding things up here."

One of those things has been to make substantial changes not only in the newspaper's financial standing but also in the newspaper itself. Lipsey doesn't insert himself into the daily operation of the newsroom, but he does make suggestions to the editor. For example, the paper now focuses much more on local news than it ever did in the past. According to Gerald I. Goldberg, the editorial page editor, it once took "a very big local story to get on page one. Now, it takes a good national story to break onto page one."[9] Another change that has taken place is in the size of the paper's "news hole"—the percentage of the paper that's filled with news, as opposed to advertising. Prior to Buffett's takeover, the news hole was approximately 35 percent, or about average for the industry. Buffett felt that a larger news hole—at least 50 percent—would benefit the paper. As he explained in his 1989 "Chairman's Letter to Shareholders": ". . . a high percentage news hole, by itself, reduces profits significantly. A large and intelligently-utilized news hole, however, attracts a wide spectrum of readers and thereby boosts penetration. High penetration, in turn, makes a newspaper particularly valuable to retailers since it allows them to talk to the entire community. . . ."[10]

The penetration achieved by the *News* is nothing less than extraordinary. Its daily editions reach 56 percent of Buffalo-area households, and its Sunday edition reaches 75 percent, the highest penetration in the top 50 U.S. markets. Even though circulation declined somewhat in the waning years of the twentieth century (at least in part because of Buffalo's decreasing population), the *News* has continued to be a serious profit maker. It has a 32.8 percent operating margin, the highest of any publicly owned newspaper in the country and the most profitable (measured as a percentage of sales) of all the Berkshire companies, by a wide margin.[11] In 2000, the newspaper earned pretax profits of $52 million.

Even more amazing is that the paper is now earning $52 million a year on just $30 million in assets. By comparison, the *New York Times* and Berkshire's partly owned the *Washington Post* earn just 10 percent on their assets, against an industry norm of 6 percent. This is due in large part to Lipsey's hands-on management and his attention to what he and Warren would regard as unnecessary expenses. In addition, the *Buffalo News* has given Berkshire three quarters of a billion dollars in pretax earnings to purchase more businesses, which is the virtuous circle and the secret of the Berkshire capital allocation machine. The *Buffalo News* has netted nearly an 18 percent annual rate of return in 23 years of ownership, even including the heavy losses during its first six years as part of the Buffett empire.

Despite its financial success—or perhaps because of it—the newspaper has also run into criticism from several sources. For example, it has been criticized for not providing sufficient coverage of Buffalo's black residents, who represent approximately a third of the city's population. And, although former editor Murray Light insists that the paper provides significant and appropriate coverage of the black community, the paper had only had eight full-time black editorial staff members out of a total of 187.

Another criticism has been leveled by the people who work at the paper. It is seriously understaffed. A study conducted a few years ago by the Buffalo Newspaper Guild found that, of nine newspapers with comparable circulation and markets, the size of the *News* staff was almost a third lower than the average for the group. Although Light does not deny that the staff is smaller than those of comparable papers, he says, "That's a challenge I like," adding that "When reporters need time on a story or a series, they get it." Some reporters confirm this statement, but others insist that, as a result of the smaller staff, the paper does not do enough in-depth reporting.[12]

The current editor, Margaret Sullivan—chosen by Lipsey in 1999 after a full national search—has made diversifying the staff and strengthening the aggressive reporting of local news her priorities. The editorial staff now includes nearly 12 percent minorities, or 24 of a total of 201 full- and part-time employees.

"It's extremely important to reflect the community we cover in the makeup of our own staff," she said. She appointed the first African-American member of newsroom management in the paper's history, and has created a new editorial column written by a black woman.

The paper's reporting has won its share of journalism awards, including the prestigious George Polk Award (second only to the Pulitzer Prize) in 1996. In 2001, the *Buffalo News* practically swept the New York State Publishers Awards, competing successfully against the *New York Times* and Long Island's *Newsday*. The paper also boasts the formidable talents of political cartoonist Tom Toles, a Pulitzer Prize winner.

The editor and publisher share the aim of making the *Buffalo News* recognized as "the best regional newspaper in America," Sullivan said.

About Lipsey, Sullivan notes: "Stan has a thorough understanding of the journalism part of this business, as well as the business side. He's always accessible, and extremely smart and well-informed."

Other criticisms have arisen out of the newspaper's status as a monopoly. For example, it's difficult to maintain any drive to "beat the competition" when there are no competitors. Even the former editor admits that, although he did his best "to keep the competitive spirit going in the newsroom, . . . it kind of slowly but surely disappeared."[13] Warren Buffett is aware of the problems that can result from being the only game in town. As long ago as 1984, he told Berkshire Hathaway's shareholders that "The economics of a dominant newspaper are excellent, among the very best in the business world. "Owners, naturally, would like to believe that their wonderful profitability is achieved only because they unfailingly turn out a wonderful product. That comfortable theory wilts before an uncomfortable fact. While first-class newspapers make excellent profits, the profits of third-rate papers are as good or better—as long as either class of paper is dominant in its community. . . . Once dominant," he wrote, "the newspaper itself, not the marketplace, determines just how good or how bad the paper will be. Good or bad, it will prosper."[14]

(Warren's 1984 opinion has changed dramatically. His comments at the 2000 Berkshire Hathaway annual meeting were quite negative toward newspapers because of the Internet's threat.)

No one has ever suggested that Warren Buffett was unhappy with either the financial or the editorial aspects of the *Buffalo News,* but if he was, and was looking for someone to blame for it, it wouldn't be Stan Lipsey. Buffett and Lipsey have been friends for many years, and Buffett has only had positive things to say about Stan. For example, when Lipsey took over as publisher of the *News,* Buffett told his shareholders: "Stan . . . has worked for Berkshire Hathaway since 1969. He has been personally involved in all nuts-and-bolts aspects of the newspaper business from editorial to circulation. We couldn't do better."[15]

Lipsey and his team are so in touch with the *Buffalo News* operation that they don't do something that almost every other business has to do: They don't budget.

"Each of my department heads has a great deal of autonomy. They run their department, and we communicate well. If you ask the average newspaper publisher how much time they spend budgeting, it is enormous . . . and sometimes, it's not productive. We save all of that time and put it to good use," Lipsey said.

Two years later, Buffett wrote that "Stan has been with us 17 years, and his unusual business talents have become more evident with every additional level of responsibility he has tackled."[16] In 1989, he told shareholders: "I believe Stan's managerial skills deliver at least five extra percentage points in profit margin compared to the earnings that would be achieved by an average manager given the same circumstances. That is an amazing performance, and one that could only be produced by a talented manager who knows—and cares—about every nut and bolt of the business. . . . Stan and I have worked together for over 20 years, through some bad times as well as good, and I could not ask for a better partner."[17]

Lipsey has equally—or even more—positive things to say about his boss. The best things, he says, about working with Buffett are that "he is totally moral and honest, that you know when he is talking to you he is thinking

about you, and that he is so accessible." The last, he says, "is terribly important. The fact that I can call him, as a friend, with a business problem or
a personal problem—that's a joy." At the same time, as Lipsey says, "He is
the boss. Years ago, when Warren bought the *Sun,* he asked me what
would happen if we had a disagreement on a given issue. And I said, 'Well,
I would try my darndest to convince you to my way. And if I couldn't, you
are the boss.' And he was perfectly satisfied with that. But it's never come
up. We've been working together for more than 30 years and we've never
had a disagreement. In fact," he adds, "the biggest compliment that I've
ever had was when Warren said to me, 'Stan, you and I would make the
same mistakes.'"

When asked about the differences between himself and his boss, Lipsey
says, "You can't put Warren and me in the same sentence. Warren is so
much smarter than I am. That's number one. He just thinks better than I
do, and his breadth and retention of information is extraordinary." One
aspect of Buffett's personality that Lipsey finds particularly remarkable is
that "he can take a complex situation and make it simple. I have sent a
number of people who have had business problems to Warren. They've
traveled to Omaha; they've come back, and said, 'He just made it so simple.' They had been tussling with it—with attorneys, with accountants,
with banks. Then they flew to Omaha, and in a few minutes they knew
exactly what they had to do. So they came back sort of in awe, with their
eyes a little glazed, because he made it so simple."

Given that the first thing Lipsey says in praise of his boss is that he is
moral and honest, it's not surprising that when asked what ingredients he
feels make a good operating manager, the first thing he says is, "Integrity."
He adds: "Focus, continued learning, thinking strategically, communicating, knowing how to hire well, having your finger on the pulse of where
you think things are going to be in the near future, and having a superb
peer group that you can counsel with. Warren is 50 percent of my peer
group, and even though there are others I can talk to, the fact that I can
pick up the phone and talk to him is invaluable." Lipsey also evokes his
boss's name when discussing how a manager should treat his or her associates. "I think you treat them like you want to be treated," he says. "That's
what Warren has done. You go out of your way for your key people, and
think hard and creatively about how you can keep an individual happy. But
you also have to have certain fundamental rules, and to be up front about

them. Even though you will be challenged—as I have been here—you have to stick to the rules because you know there are certain things that won't work out well. And if it comes down to where you can't do something, you have to just say so."

He does not, however, place high values on being first. "I always like to see the other guy break paths," he explains, "and if I can come in late, I will. I tell my people that sometimes the smartest decision you can make is to do nothing. I don't like being a pioneer, and I won't be one unless I see an opportunity where the first guy is going to benefit, and I watch that very closely. I am particularly watching it on the Web, but the Web changes so quickly that you have to do your homework and then make good judgment calls." As Lipsey points out himself, his paper's stance in regard to the Internet is "a perfect example of not wanting to be the first guy in."

"I had to work hard to learn the Internet. In fact," he quips, "I'm still working at learning newspapers." Buffalo.com, the paper's Web site, did not go online until September 1999, but now it has four times the viewers of its next competitor. "When I felt that we could no longer stay out of positioning ourselves on the Internet," Lipsey says, "we did a lot of studying, and reading, and talking. Then I told Warren Colville, now our President, I wanted him to get the site up, and I sent him to Boston, Kansas City, and Portland, Maine—newspaper portals that made sense to me—to see what they were doing. After that, we made our decisions on how we were going to operate. I figure we saved a fortune not being the first guy in. On top of which," he adds, "doing that enabled us to avoid making a disastrous mistake in structure that could have burdened us for a long time. Buffalo.com is still a very small operation. There are only seven full-time staff members, so most of the work is jobbed out."

Lipsey claims generally that he is unwilling to be a pioneer, yet he says that the aspect of his work that most excites him is "taking an initiative. I think that initiating something—conceiving it, and executing it well—is more important than just getting good numbers." In fact, when discussing his successes, he talks about them in terms of having initiated things. "I think my success is measured in what I have been able to do with the *Buffalo News,* and what I have done in Buffalo. If you are the publisher of a paper," he says, "you have to champion your community. Our problems are seriously economic—jobs—so you look and see what your assets are.

Well, I looked around and I saw a city with extraordinarily fine period architecture. So one of the things we're doing is restoring one of Frank Lloyd Wright's premier homes—the only six-building prairie-style home he was commissioned to do. When we're through, we will be able to attract architectural tourists, who spend much more than the average visitor." Although he is clearly proud of this accomplishment, he was reluctant to admit that Governor George Pataki gave him an award to recognize his efforts on behalf of the city's architectural heritage. (The previous year's recipient was Laurance Rockefeller.) It's the only award he's been willing to accept since he became publisher of the *News*.

Outside of his work, Lipsey's primary interest is photography. "I love it—particularly when things aren't going well, because when I am shooting pictures, I am totally occupied. It's like Warren and bridge," he explains. "Photography occupies my mind the same way bridge does his. So I know how much he values it."

He also says, "I do a number of participant sports, all badly," and he admits to being "a big jazz buff. In fact, I take the contribution that Warren allows each stockholder and use it to put on seven free jazz concerts every year at the art gallery in Buffalo," an activity he began nearly two decades ago. "I have a lot of interests," he adds, "but between this job and the reading I have to do, and like to do, I don't have much time for other things."

One thing he recently had time for was the purchase of a home in Palm Springs, California. "Buffalo is overcast all winter," he says, "so to get out in the sunshine is really wonderful. I travel back and forth between Buffalo and California all winter. I'm out there a lot, but I have a complete office set up, and it's amazing how easy it is to communicate, between the phone, Federal Express, the Internet, and the fax machine. I have a wonderful secretary of 15 years, Barbara Urbanczyk. I told Warren that I'd learned how to use a fax machine, and he said, 'Well, that's more than I can do.'" The fact that he recently set up an office in his winter home suggests that Lipsey—73 years old as of this writing—is not giving much thought to retirement. "I'll know when it is time for me to do something about it," he says, "but I don't see it now." He has, nevertheless, selected a successor, even though he will not identify the individual except to say that he has "the right instincts . . . I know him extraordinarily well [and] . . . he has been at this company for many, many years."

He has every intention of continuing to run the *Buffalo News* for the foreseeable future, although he is aware that, given the new technologies, the future is in question. "There's no question that there's a threat," he says. "When you talk to newspaper people, the first thing they talk about is declining circulation. Much of that is societal. There are people who can't function without their daily newspaper, but there are also millions of people who have no need for a newspaper at all—and, for that matter, don't feel that they have to watch television news or anything else. They just function without it. In our society today, in many cases, the man and the woman both work, and time-famine makes just getting through life a problem. That doesn't leave room for a lot of other things." However, as he points out, "Surveys show that television—not newspapers—is losing more viewers to the Internet."

On the plus side, "One of the things that we are fortunate about . . . ," he says, "is that people live and stay in Buffalo. It's hard to get people to come here, but once they do, they love it. And they don't leave. Those are good consumers of newspapers. It's a good paper," he says of the *News*. "It has always been a good editorial product, but part of the high reader-ship reflects on the makeup of the community, the fact that people still live in the same homes, the same areas. They have more of an interest in Buffalo. Someone who used to work at the paper once told me that he was born three blocks from where he lived and had never been more than three blocks away. I am not saying that that is true of everybody, but that is the kind of area we are in."

To whatever extent Lipsey is concerned about the future of the *Buffalo News,* he is certainly less concerned about the future of Berkshire Hathaway. "I don't know that Warren has a specific master plan," he says, "but I think that, in the back of his mind, he has a matrix that sets the course, the parameters, on what he will and will not do. I don't think there is any company that he would not consider, and I think that doing that is really his joy." Nor is Lipsey particularly concerned about an effective transition from Buffett to his successor, or about the future of the company after Buffett is gone. "I know that Warren has provided for the transition," he notes, "and no one could do it better. I also think that people are probably overestimating a crisis at Warren's retirement. There's no question about his uniqueness, about his record or his performance, but I think Berkshire certainly will survive. I trust Warren, and I know he has thought through who is going to do what. It's a solid company," he concludes, "and I'm not worried about it."

Stan smiles at the very thought that his paper, along with all the other daily newspapers across the nation, will one day have to add another column to its stock-activity pages when Berkshire's share price reaches the $100,000-per-share mark.

## STAN LIPSEY'S BUSINESS TENETS

★ Don't rush to adopt new technology, but when you're ready to start something, do your homework and help people get the necessary training.
★ Go out of your way to help your managers.
★ It's okay to have rules; just make sure you tell your employees what they are, and stick to them.
★ Trust your managers and give them autonomy. My managers run their departments so effectively that we don't have to set budgets.

# chapter sixteen

# The Loyalist—
# Chuck Huggins, See's Candies

*See's Candies is particularly interesting because of both the business and the operating manager. Mr. Huggins, which is how his staff addresses him, has always been an employee. He was not part of the founding family and didn't participate directly in the ownership of the company. Therefore, he could well serve as a model of what Berkshire management will be like 50 years from today.*

*Now 10 years past the typical corporate retirement age, Chuck Huggins shows no sign of slowing down.\* I caught him during a labor strike at his South San Francisco plant, before he left on his honeymoon, just after his second marriage.*

*Well known in the world of candy commerce, Mr. Huggins is also a talented jazz singer and drummer. He is hip enough to sing "scat," the unique form of singing sounds instead of words, made famous by Louis Armstrong.*

*See's Candies is often described by Warren Buffett as the perfect business. It was one of the first wholly owned businesses purchased by Berkshire and was the first investment for which vice chairman Charlie Munger influenced Buffett to pay a premium for quality. It was the first multigenerational family-owned business to be added to the Berkshire family of businesses. It was also the first Berkshire-owned consumer franchise business with a built-in ability to raise prices from 50 cents a pound during the 1929 stock market crash to $12 per pound today. Without the See's Candies purchase, there may not have been a major investment in*

---

\* Huggins is the only living Buffett CEO I interviewed by phone rather than in person. Chuck Huggins, the longest serving professional chief executive, now with over 50 years of service, reviewed my 200-plus questions in advance and determined which ones he wanted to answer.

*Coca-Cola nearly 20 years later. With superior management, sustainable competitive advantages, scarcity of close substitutes, ability to raise prices without losing customers, high profits, low capital investment, and extraordinary returns on capital, it's the perfect business for any student of business, management, and investment. In many ways, See's Candies was and still is a family-managed operation.*

*See's Candies fulfills all the criteria Buffett looks for. The business is profitable and has no debt. It has a solid franchise brand name and is a multigenerational family business that maintains uncompromising business values. A long-term management team is in place, and the company is able to grow without any additional influx of capital. Critical to See's Candies' success has been the management by Chuck Huggins.*

Charles N. Huggins, president and chief executive officer of See's Candies, a South San Francisco-based company, doesn't mind being told he has made a mistake. As the longtime head of the firm, Huggins asks store managers, from time to time, to suggest which (if any) of the company's 100 types of chocolates are the least popular. These unpopular varieties are then discontinued to make room for new confections in the company's stores. In the late 1980s, the store managers voted almost unanimously to oust a green product called Marshmints. Being the kind of CEO who believes that the people who deal with customers every day know best, Huggins ordered Marshmints dropped from the list of the company's offerings.

Almost immediately, complaints started coming in. During the first six weeks after the labor-intensive handmade candy was dropped, Huggins received 500 letters letting him know, in no uncertain terms, that he had made a mistake. Although the candy was not selling well by See's standards and Huggins was therefore reluctant to reinstate it, it was clear that the Marshmints following was unusually devoted, and Huggins wanted to keep those loyal customers. Believing that "You should treat a complaint as an opportunity," Huggins searched for—and found—a way to take advantage of the opportunity. Everyone who had written a complaint letter received a gift certificate and was invited to join the newly formed Marshmints Club. The members would receive a newsletter, membership card, and a lapel pin, and could special-order their favorite chocolate. By the mid-1990s, the club's membership had grown to 16,000.[1]

Although those thousands of chocolate lovers may have been surprised by Chuck Huggins's innovative response to their complaints, those who know him identify him with exactly that type of tactic. The Marshmints Club typifies the leadership and creativity that Chuck Huggins has exhibited in his various capacities at See's Candies for more than 50 years. It could be, in fact, that the ability—and desire—to create something is in Huggins' blood. Ancestors of both of his parents were among the pioneers who helped create the new community of Portland, Oregon, in the early 1880s. Huggins's parents subsequently moved to Vancouver, British Columbia, where he was born in 1925. He lived in Canada for part of his childhood, until his family returned to the United States in 1935.

After serving as a paratrooper in the Second World War, Huggins married Marian Carr (who preferred being called "Mime") in Dayton, Ohio, in 1947. They moved to the campus of Kenyon College, in Gambier, Ohio, where he majored in English. When he graduated in 1949, the couple moved to the San Francisco area, and Huggins took a job as a salesman. "But I didn't like that," he recalls, "so, starting in late 1950, I made some inquiries through the dean of men, Dick Balch, at Stanford University, about placement in some local company. See's Candies was one of the companies on Stanford's placement list, and I was interviewed, and hired, by Laurance See, who was then the CEO."

See's Candies was already a venerable California institution. Founded by a Canadian, Charles A. See, and his widowed mother, Mary, the company began operating out of a small bungalow in Pasadena in 1921. (That bungalow, incidentally, is now a state historic landmark.) Producing candy from 50 of Mrs. See's recipes, they attracted customers by developing an "old-time" and "home-made" reputation for quality and consistency. Pictures of Mary See and a cottage in the woods were printed on their boxes, to reinforce the theme.[2] Within a year of opening the first store, two additional stores were opened in Los Angeles, and the company continued to flourish through the 1920s. The venture was so successful that the Sees were able to stay in business during the Great Depression partly because of their ability to maintain operations even while they cut prices and reduced volume to maintain their products' quality. By 1935, Charles's son Laurance was involved in the business, and the Sees decided to expand their operation to northern California. Their first San Francisco store was established on

Polk Street in 1938. By 1949, when Charles See died, and Laurance took over as CEO, the company had 78 stores and more than 2,000 employees.[3]

Chuck Huggins remembers that when Laurance See hired him in 1951, he reported to Ed Peck, the general manager in San Francisco, and "did a little of everything." Huggins says, "Ed was dissatisfied with the packaging operation and he asked me if I would be willing to run it. I told him that I'd been an English major in college, and I didn't know that I was very well equipped to run that kind of operation. I mean, I knew what a package was, but that was about it. Also, I'd heard that he had a reputation for looking over your shoulder and not allowing the people who reported to him too much latitude or creativity.

"So I said, 'I'll be willing to do it on one condition. This may sound outrageous coming from a new employee, but I'll do it only if you leave me alone and let me do the job. You can check the product, the results, the statistics, and all of that, as long as you don't bother me. Just trust me to do it.' And he agreed. So I went to talk to the packaging supervisor, Anna Rizzo," Huggins continues, "and, after listening to her, and making some of my own judgments, I was able to come up with some ideas for how things could be improved and controlled and disciplined. We put those ideas into practice and they worked. Of course that pleased Ed Peck, who touted it to Laurance See, who was also very pleased. And that's how I came to Laurance's attention. And the See family began to look upon me as sort of a member of the family, and I gradually received promotions and expanding responsibilities."

Under the leadership of Mary See's grandsons—Laurance See and his younger brother, Charles B. ("Harry") See—the company continued to thrive through the 1950s and 1960s, at least in part because of some very astute real estate planning. One strategy the brothers used, whenever possible, was to locate their stores on the shady side of downtown avenues, on the assumption that, when it's hot, people are more likely to walk on that side of the street. More importantly, they recognized the potential of malls. When developers started creating them in the 1950s, See's established early relationships to ensure that See's would have prime locations for its stores.[4] To this day, most of the company's outlets are located in malls.

In 1969, Laurance died, at the age of 57. Two years later, Harry, who had become CEO after his brother's death, decided he was no longer interested in running the company. With no one in the family to take over, after being owned and operated by the Sees for 50 years, the organization was put up for sale. Several parties expressed interest in purchasing the company, and Chuck Huggins, who was then the firm's executive vice president, was asked by Harry See to act as a liaison between the company and its potential buyers. In that capacity, he first met Warren Buffett.

"I was called to a meeting in a hotel room in Los Angeles," he says, "just after Thanksgiving of 1971, and I walked into the room and there was Harry See, and there was Warren and Charlie [Munger] and Rick Guerin [Munger's friend and partner, and an early Berkshire investor]. I had no idea who Warren was, much less Charlie or Rick, and I don't think Harry did either. And they were talking about buying the company, and it eventually came to the point where Warren said, 'Well, Harry, we are going to make an offer to you for See's, but first we have to know who is going to run the company, because we don't do that.' And Harry looked around the room, and I was the only guy there from See's, and so he said, 'Well, Chuck is.'" Laughing, Huggins notes, "I think he just wanted to sell the company," but then admits that "he may have given some thought to his answer. So I was knighted, you might say. And then Warren said, 'Well, okay then, before we go any further, we want to meet with Chuck,' and we agreed that we'd meet again the next day.

"Harry didn't really give me any instructions about what I was supposed to do or say, so what I did was just tell them all the bad things I could think of that they'd learn about sooner or later if they did buy the company. I figured they wouldn't be preparing to make Harry an offer if they didn't think there were some good things, so it would be best to reveal the others. We spent about three hours together, and that's the way I conducted myself. Warren would ask a question, I'd start to give him an answer, and then Charlie would interrupt and ask me a question on a completely different subject. And Rick would just roll his eyeballs, while making an occasional observation.

"But what really impressed me," Huggins says, "was that Warren's line of questioning was so astute. At that point I didn't know anything about him, and I didn't know what he'd done in business. I think he and Charlie explained that they had this little investment company, but that didn't mean anything to me, and I really wasn't sure what they were up to. But they got right down to brass tacks, both Warren and Charlie, and they asked me things about the company that you wouldn't know to ask unless you were inside a manufacturing and retail sales business. That did two things. First, it made me very comfortable. Second, it made me feel that these guys were real geniuses. They were obviously as different as they could be, but they are very brainy, very astute, and they sure asked the right questions. I had a lot of respect for both of them—and Rick as well.

"To be honest," Huggins adds, "the thought did cross my mind that they might just be interested in buying the company so they could turn around and sell it to someone else. But I didn't have enough details, nor did I know about their record regarding resales, to make any kind of judgment. I figured I was a pawn in whatever they were doing anyway, so I just kind of dismissed it from my mind. But what did give me a clue as to their motives," he says, "was what they told me they wanted me to do. They said that they wanted the ethics of the See family kept in place. And they said, 'Keep doing what you are doing. Make sure that the brand name is sacrosanct, and that you do everything you possibly can to enhance it, along with the service and the other things. We want you to run the business. You've been with it all this time, and you know what's good, and we just want you to try and make it better, to broaden your horizons.' And that led me to believe that they were in it for the long run. I liked them, I trusted their motives, and I just decided that I'd buy into it with all my power and do the best I could."

The best Chuck Huggins could do has been very good indeed. Buffett paid $25 million for See's Candies in 1972—six times earnings and three times its book value. Under Huggins's stewardship, the company now earns, pretax, $75 million a year—three times its purchase price.[5] Sales have grown from $31 million in 1972 to $306 million in 1999. Furthermore, over the years, See's has earned Berkshire Hathaway pretax profits of $900 million, enough to buy both R.C. Willey Home Furnishings and Executive Jet (Berkshire's fastest growing division). If See's were valued today, similar to publicly traded Tootsie Roll® (NYSE symbol: TR) at five times sales and 30 times earnings, it would have a conservative estimated market value of $1.5 billion. This represents nearly an 18 percent annual return on investment. See's Candies has returned over $900 million in pretax earnings over the past 28 years on an initial capital base of $7 million, and has required additional retained earnings for capital investment of only $71 million. Huggins's candy operation is returning 100 percent each year on its capital. Almost unbelievably, Huggins achieved these results without setting foot in Omaha, the site of Berkshire's meager headquarters, for more than 20 years after the purchase of See's Candies.

Recently, Buffett wrote this about Chuck Huggins and his candy division's profits: "When he [Huggins] took charge of See's at age 46, the company's pretax profit [$4.6], expressed in millions, was about 10 percent of his age. Today, he's 74, and the ratio has increased to 100 percent [$74 million]. Having discovered this mathematical relationship—let's call it Huggins's Law—Charlie and I now become giddy at the mere thought of Chuck's birthday."[6]

Like most businesses, See's Candies has had some ups and downs. Candy sales are affected by the economy, as well as by other events, such as the Persian Gulf War in 1990, which decreased traffic in the malls, where most of See's stores are located. In addition, efforts to expand the business into Colorado, Missouri, and Texas in the late 1980s—80 percent of the company's stores are located in California—were considerably less successful than had been hoped, and See's quickly pulled out of those markets. In the early 1990s, even though the company was earning considerable profits, See's chose to close a dozen of its 218 stores because those profits had begun to drop.

Like all traditional storefront candy companies, See's business is very seasonal—an impulse purchase—except at Christmas, Valentine's, Easter, Mother's Day, and Father's Day when See's is a destination purchase. The company does almost half of its annual business, which represents 90 percent of the company's profits, during November and December. The end-of-the-year holiday sales are crucial, as Warren Buffett explained to Berkshire Hathaway's shareholders in his 1984 "Chairman's Letter to Shareholders": "We also earn significant sums in the Easter and Valentine's Day periods, but pretty much tread water the rest of the year."[7] The variations in sales over the course of the year require variations in staffing, and the number of employees goes from approximately 2,000 during most of the year to 6,700 during the peak sales period.

See's now has 200 company-owned stores in 11 states, licensees in airports, and See's-managed "holiday gift centers" throughout the east coast and the Midwest. The company sells more than 30 million pounds of chocolate every year. Nevertheless, like all CEOs, Chuck Huggins worries about competition. When the company was started in the 1920s, and even through the 1950s, it had numerous competitors—Barton's, Fannie May,

Russell Stover, and Fannie Farmer, among others—but most have long since gone out of business or out of store sales. Even so, Huggins is extremely conscious of the fact that the company still faces considerable competition. "I consider our biggest current—and future—competitor to be Godiva," he says. "They are opening more stores, and they have exposure in both domestic and foreign markets. There are now over 150 locations in the United States alone where Godiva is sold, mostly department stores, and they've done a terrific job of positioning themselves. Most people think they're made in Europe," he notes, "even though they're really made by the Pepperidge Farm division of Campbell Soup Company in Reading, Pennsylvania." Huggins believes See's insistence on maintaining quality, old-fashioned service, and good prices—See's Candies priced half as much per pound as Godiva's—has enabled the company to not only survive but to flourish.[8]

Being part of Berkshire Hathaway is one reason the company is thriving, but Huggins is aware that, despite the company's continued success, it has become an increasingly smaller part of Berkshire's total operation over the years. "In relation to the whole Berkshire organization," he says, "Warren and Charlie have done so many things to add to it [Berkshire] over the last 30 years, and changed the nature of the business so much, that you'd have to say we are just small potatoes." Small potatoes or not, when asked if he feels he is treated in any special way because he is one of Berkshire's operating managers, his answer is a resounding "Yes."

"That special way," he says, " is having direct access to Warren. That means that I can call him, and if he is there, he answers the phone. And if he's not there and I leave a message, within an hour at the most the phone will ring, and it will be Warren. He's always available, and that's really remarkable. So I don't feel that I'm his employee, or a provider of things that he wants his company to do, but that I am also his friend and confidant. Right from the beginning, and ever since, he has treated me as a partner and an equal." Nor, Huggins says, has any of the other fundamentals changed in the years they have worked together. "But what has changed," he says, "is the world. And it's on the question of whether or not we're keeping up with changing opportunities and technology that Warren's been invaluable. He looks at the successes and mistakes of all these companies that he deals with directly, as well as those where his contact is not direct, and he's always willing to share whatever lessons there are to be learned."

Huggins adds, "He never forgets anything. I could call him right now and say, 'Do you remember the teamster union problem we had in 1977 in San Francisco, and what we did about it?' And he'll recite it to me, just like that. He won't look anything up. He won't have me send him anything. I can say, 'It worked, but now it's back again, with a twist. And here is the twist. And here is what I think we ought to do.' And then I'll tell him what I think we ought to do, and then say, 'What do you think?' And he won't say, 'Do this.' He never orders me to do anything. He'll give me an example, or he'll say, 'Have you thought of this?' Or 'How about trying this?' And, then he'll say, 'Well, what do you think?' And I'll say, 'Sounds good. We'll try it and I'll let you know.' And that's the way it goes. It's a blessing," he concludes, "and a rare treat."

Not surprisingly, Buffett speaks extremely highly of the head of See's Candies as well. In 1983, for example, after Huggins had been running the company for more than a decade, Buffett told Berkshire's stockholders that he had the utmost confidence in the candy company's ability to continue growing. "This confidence arises out of our long experience with the managerial talents of Chuck Huggins. We put Chuck in charge the day we took over, and his record has been simply extraordinary. . . . "[9] The following year, he wrote: "The success of See's reflects the combination of an exceptional product and an exceptional manager, Chuck Huggins."[10] And the year after that, he said, "At See's we have Chuck Huggins, the man we put in charge the day we bought the business. Selecting him remains one of our best business decisions."[11]

Offering greater insight into the investment process and management tenets of Chuck Huggins, Buffett wrote, "See's has a one-of-a-kind product 'personality' produced by a combination of its candy's delicious taste and moderate price, the company's total control of the distribution process, and the exceptional service provided by store employees. Chuck rightfully measures his success by the satisfaction of our customers, and his attitude permeates the organization. Few major retailing companies have been able to sustain such a customer-oriented spirit, and we owe Chuck a great deal for keeping it alive and well at See's."[12]

In 1988, Buffett could not have expressed his fondness more directly. "Charlie and I put Chuck Huggins in charge of See's about five minutes after we bought the company. Upon reviewing his record, you may wonder what took us so long."[13]

And in terms of CEO compensation, in an era of ridiculous management stock option grants and multipage employment contracts negotiated by lawyers, Buffett and Huggins set another precedent. "When the purchase was made, we shook hands with Chuck on a compensation arrangement—conceived in about five minutes and never reduced to a written contract—that remains unchanged to this day."[14] (Those words were written 20 years after buying See's.)

In the 1990s, an era focused on technology investments, See's became another example of the importance of a consumer franchise and a "lack" of business change. The See's investment led Buffett and Co. to consider major investments in Coca-Cola and Gillette. The secret to investment success is a durable competitive advantage based on a consumer franchise. The motivation that causes a consumer to buy and consume chocolate was the same 50 years ago and will be the same 50 years from now.

Two management tenets that Huggins insisted on early to ensure See's survived when other retail candy stores failed:

1. Concentrate the efforts of all employees in all departments to attain ever-increasing excellence in customer services and product quality.
2. Never compromise quality ingredients or quality service over profits.

Huggins credits Buffett with being a major influence on his management style. "I kind of made up my management approach as I went along," he says, "but with help. I learned from the way the people I reported to handled themselves, as well as from how my peers handled themselves. But I learned more from Warren, and from his example, than from anyone else." He believes that wanting to learn, being curious, and constantly searching for knowledge are among the essential characteristics of a successful manager, along with discipline, creativity, and patience. He also considers the ability to solve problems (which is how Sharon Osberg, Buffett's bridge partner, and two-time world champion, described the essence of the card game) to be extraordinarily important. "I firmly believe," he says, "that managers spend most of their time solving problems. That's what I do. And I think every problem has a solution of some kind. It may not occur to you exactly at the time you're dealing with the problem, but eventually, by trial and error, or just by luck, you'll find a solution to any problem."

One problem the company rarely runs into is finding staff members. In keeping with See's history as a family business, and in contrast to many other businesses, employment of family members is not only allowed, it is actually encouraged. Family recommendations have been an excellent source of employee talent. All four of Huggins's now-grown children at one time or another have worked for See's, and one son, two daughters, and a daughter-in-law still do. The company's vice president of marketing, Dick Van Doren, notes that although many operations are unionized, "Nepotism is rampant." His own wife, daughter, and son have worked at See's.[15] But nepotism is not reserved only for senior managers. There are families in which three generations have been employed by the candy company, and many employees—most of whom are women—have been with the firm for more than 20 years. In fact, Huggins says, many women have worked for the company on and off for most of their lives. They work part-time while they're in school, full-time until they have children, part-time again once the children start school, and full-time once more when the children are grown (and often hired into managerial positions). "And when they are in their 60s or 70s," he says, "they often step down but continue as seasonal clerks" during the holidays.[16] The seasonal nature of the fall-and-winter indoor candy manufacturing and packing business, and its rotation with the outdoor spring-and-summer California harvest season, has worked well for See's, and, in turn, Mexican and Hispanic migrant workers have found stable seasonal employment.

Having "lifers" working for the company helps toward maintaining continuity and culture plus an emphasis on the importance of quality and customer satisfaction. "We stand for longevity," Huggins says, "something that doesn't really change; and, in this day and age, that counts for a hell of a lot."[17] When asked to explain See's business, he says, "It's about the customers. It's about making sure the customer is pleased, whatever it may take, no matter how outrageous. Pleasing them is the most important thing we can do, and is absolutely vital to our success. We try to make the best product we possibly can, but sometimes we make mistakes. And there are certain things that we do inadvertently, or because we're not watching things carefully enough, where we dissatisfy the customer. And when that happens, we always admit that we blew it, and ask what we can do to make it right. And then we stand on our heads until we get that done."

Getting it done—whatever "it" may be—is of the utmost importance to Huggins, and he admits that it often requires taking work home with him. "I do a lot of my brain work at home," he says. "And if I want to think hard about some problem I'm trying to solve, or some strategy I'm trying to come up with, I have a practice of thinking about it just before I go to sleep. And then, by some freak of nature, quite often I'll wake up at two or three o'clock in the morning and my brain will say, 'Eureka! Here's your answer.' So I'll write it down and then go back to sleep."

He insists, however, that solving business-related problems takes up only a small percentage of his time outside of the office. One of his other principal interests, he says, is jazz. "I'm a musician, a drummer, and I also sing all of those old jazz songs. I've had a jazz band for 33 years," he says, "a long time. My great friend, Tom Ford, who passed away recently, was a pianist. He and I kind of cooked up the idea, and called ourselves 'T. Ford and the Model A's.' But then we decided that Tom would get a big head over that, so we cut out the 'T. Ford' part and took to calling ourselves just 'The Model A's.'" The band, which is made up of CEOs of several companies in the San Francisco area, now plays at political events and for charities. Any payments it receives are donated to local music schools and/or to organizations helping disadvantaged children. Not surprising, given his interest in the genre, Huggins likes to have a traditional jazz band perform at new store openings. Some years ago, he commissioned the Jim Cullum Jazz Band to compose and record music for a See's advertising campaign.

His outside interests are not confined to jazz. "I'm also interested in the opera," he says, "in the symphony, in art, in lots of creative things. The Bay area is great for all kinds of culture. I also love the mountains, I like to fish, and I like to play tennis." His wife Marian died in 1995. He has four grown, married children and nine grandchildren, all of whom, he says, share many of his interests. He notes, too, that his new bride, Donna Ewald, whom he'd known for about three years before they were married in October 2000, also "likes to do the same kinds of things." Referring to his recent remarriage, Huggins adds: "I think this is something that's going to be good for me. I am not built to be a single man."

Nor, apparently, does he consider himself built for retirement. At the age of 76, he is not Berkshire Hathaway's oldest operating manager, but he is its longest serving employee. Nevertheless, he has no plans to step down from his job in the foreseeable future. "I enjoy what I'm doing," he says.

"This job is marvelous, challenging, and varied. It's what I'd call 'serious fun.' And it's just so special that, as long as Warren and Charlie will tolerate me, and I don't lose my grip or good health, I'd like to be around." He makes a point of the fact that his boss has neither any interest in retiring himself nor any expectation that any of his operating managers will necessarily retire. "When Mrs. B was 90 years old," Huggins says, referring to Rose Blumkin, the CEO of the Nebraska Furniture Mart who died in 1998, "Warren said that the mandatory retirement age for his managers would be whatever age she reached when she retired. And he renewed that pledge every year, until she was 104. And I took that seriously."

He is also serious about his belief that "forced retirement for executives at age 65 is probably a disadvantage to a corporate administration. I'm a member of the Bohemian Club," he says, referring to an exclusive San Francisco men's club with a membership list that includes most—if not all—of the important business leaders in America, "and I have a lot of elderly friends. And I know a lot of guys in their nineties who were captains of industry or did interesting things in life, and who are probably just as able to think creative thoughts as they ever were. Of course, you do have to take into account the pressures of the job. When you get older you can only do so much. But I think the intelligence, the experience, and the brainpower that a lot of older people have can be a really valuable asset to any corporation. That's one of the great things about Warren," he adds, "the fact that he understands that. That's so remarkable and so unusual."

Confident in his knowledge that he will not be forced to retire, Huggins continues to plan for See's Candies' future. He notes that the company intends to maintain its commitment to quality and customer service, but he also says, "Of course, we'll still poke at everything we do, because we believe there is no such thing as perfection and we believe we can always do better."[18] One of the ways he believes See's can do better is through selling its products on the Internet. He prizes innovation but he was slow to take advantage of the possibilities offered by the new technology. According to Dave Harvey, a See's executive, Warren Buffett, rather than Chuck Huggins, pressed the issue. "Buffett called Huggins," says Harvey, "and told him to get on the Internet."[19] The company did not set up its Web site until July 1998, but it still managed to sell 31,000 pounds. In 1999, the first full year of Net operation, sales from that source amounted to 174,000 pounds of candy, representing revenues of $2.1 million and 13 percent of all mail-order sales. In 2000, nearly $4 million was sold via See's Web site (23 percent of all mail-order sales). Huggins now believes that Internet sales may represent a sizable revenue stream in the future, because it offers the customer greater worldwide accessibility and order simplification.

Even as Chuck Huggins looks toward the future, See's Candies continues to practice the philosophy that has sustained it for more than three-quarters of a century. The company has a simple three-word motto: "Quality Without Compromise." Inside each box of the company's products, customers still find, for more than 50 years, the following message:

> For over 80 years, we have worked hard to maintain the tradition of quality which literally millions of faithful See's candy eaters have come to expect, year after year.
>
> Our philosophy is quite simple: Be absolutely persistent in all attitudes regarding quality—buy only the best ingredients obtainable—offer the most delicious and interesting assortments of candies available in the United States—own and operate all See's sparkling white shops, while providing the highest level of customer service.
>
> This may seem old-fashioned, if not unusual, in this day and age—but it works. At the same time we fully believe that we can always do a better job at what we try to do—ultimately making people happy!

## CHUCK HUGGINS'S BUSINESS TENETS

- ★ Nepotism isn't a bad thing. My children have worked for the company, as have several generations of other employees, from every employee category through management. Having people work for the company for 20 and 30 years is good.
- ★ Managers spend most of their time solving problems. They need to make the time to figure out solutions, whether at work or when they get home.
- ★ Mandatory retirement is not a policy I endorse. As long as someone is healthy and interested in working, he or she should stay on the job. The intelligence and experience of older people can be a tremendous asset.
- ★ Pleasing the customer, no matter how ridiculous the issue, is important. When customers can count on something being the same over an extended period of time, they're going to keep coming back to you.

# chapter seventeen

# The Professional—Ralph Schey, Scott Fetzer Companies

*I*t's hard to believe, but little known Scott Fetzer has been a better in-vestment than the most heralded of Berkshire's investments, Coca-Cola. Ralph Schey's diversified companies (which include Kirby Vacuum and World Book Encyclopedia) may prove, more than any other invest-ment, the value of buying all of a wholly owned business rather than part of a publicly traded company.

Scott Fetzer, purchased for a net cost of $230 million 15 years ago, has produced pretax earnings of over $1 billion, which, coincidentally, repre-sents most of Berkshire's net investment in Coke. This means that Scott Fetzer's earnings could have purchased Coca-Cola stock and made Berk-shire its largest shareholder. Furthermore, Scott Fetzer's estimated value (20 times annual earnings) has increased almost 15 times to $3 billion. Most importantly, unlike Coca-Cola, the Scott Fetzer companies now generate approximately $150 million in annual pretax earnings, which is redistributed into other wholly owned businesses. Scott Fetzer does this with only $300 million in capital, representing a 50 percent annual re-turn on capital.

By comparison, Coca-Cola has grown from an investment of $1 billion 10 years ago to a market value of $9 billion today, a handsome 24 percent annual rate of return. Coke gives Berkshire "look through" earnings (you can look at them but you can't get at them) of $160 million. To tap the increase in market value and the real earning power of Coca-Cola, share-owners would have to sell the company and pay off the taxes. Scott Fet-zer is the superior investment because 100 percent of its pretax earnings are available for the owners to allocate in a way that will maximize the overall shareholder value. It should be noted that along with the $160 million of Coke's allocated earnings, Berkshire has access to an additional

*$136 million in annual dividends. Buffett's ownership and board seat give him substantial influence, but that perk doesn't compare to his 100 percent control of Scott Fetzer. The $150 million annual return on $230 million invested is better than the $300 million return (with dividend access to just 45 percent) on $1.3 billion invested. Scott Fetzer is returning 65 percent on Berkshire's investment. Coca-Cola is returning a respectable 23 percent.*

*Scott Fetzer headquarters is in an industrial park in Westlake, a suburb of Cleveland, Ohio. Displayed in a room on the premises are products from the company's 22 different manufacturing firms, which are staffed by 7,500 employees. The majority of profits come from Kirby Vacuums, World Book Encyclopedias, and Campbell Hausfeld (air compressors).*

*Ken Smelsberger, President and Chief Operating Officer, talked enthusiastically about what each business manufactured, where it was, and where it was going. Ken walked around the room as if it was a display of his grandchildren. Little did I know I had just met the next Buffett CEO and the successor to Ralph Schey.*

*Ralph Schey and I spent more than three hours discussing his companies and his approach to management. Shortly after that interview, he retired. But Mr. Schey's principles and his experiences as operating manager reinforce the picture of the types of companies and managers Warren Buffett selects.*

*During my interview with Ralph, I was struck by the similarities among the Buffett CEOs. I immediately thought of Al Ueltschi of Flight-Safety. He had never met Ralph, but the two men had much in common. Both are well past the traditional retirement age (Schey is 76 and Ueltschi is 84); both saw the merits of business aviation long before Buffett did; both invest heavily in safety; both consider themselves in the education business; both have a global perspective; both have defined succession plans; both have more energy than men half their age; and both are chairmen of world-renowned health organizations (Schey at The Cleveland Clinic and Ueltschi at Orbis International).*

It's very unusual for a Berkshire Hathaway operating manager to retire. Yet, as the century began, that's exactly what Ralph Schey did—even though he was *only* 76 years old. As Warren Buffett explained in his "Chairman's Letter to Shareholders" for the year 2000: "In 1985, we purchased Scott Fetzer, acquiring not only a fine business but the services of Ralph Schey, a truly outstanding CEO, as well. Ralph was then 61. Most companies, focused on the calendar rather than ability, would have benefited from Ralph's talents for only a few years. At Berkshire, in contrast, Ralph ran Scott Fetzer for 15 years until his retirement. . . . Under his leadership, the company distributed $1.03 billion to Berkshire against our net purchase price of $230 million. We used these funds, in turn, to purchase other businesses. All told, Ralph's contributions to Berkshire's present value extend well into the billions of dollars. As a manager, Ralph belongs in Berkshire's Hall of Fame," Buffett concluded, and, although he didn't say so, the managers already inducted into that "Hall of Fame" constitute an extraordinarily elite group.[1]

Ralph Schey's journey began in Brooklyn, Ohio, where he was born on July 24, 1924. His mother was from Hungary and his father from Austria. He started his entrepreneurial career at an early age, going door-to-door among his neighbors to sell magazines and potato chips, among other things. "I always had a lot of things going," he remembers, "whether it was collecting bottles and turning 'em in for cash or cutting someone's lawn."[2]

He graduated from West Tech High School in Cleveland in June 1942 and was inducted into the army in March 1943. This led to what he now considers one of the most fortunate—and important—events of his life. "I went down to the railroad station where they 'ran' you through the recruiting process," he says, "and I was in the line that said 'Infantry.' But I'd always thought that I would like to be an engineer, so I asked one of the recruiters standing there, 'Where would I go to try to be an engineer?' He thought that was pretty funny, but he told me which line to stand in, and as a result I was actually able to get into the Army Corps of Engineers. And, I was assigned to the 249th Combat Engineering Battalion, commanded by Colonel John K. Addison. The colonel taught me more about people, about motivating people, and how to understand people, than anyone I had ever known. That is," he adds, "anybody except my mother. She was great at it."

"We sailed to England in a convoy of more than 300 ships," recalled Schey. "Fortunately we never met a German submarine." He shipped out for France in 1944, just before D-Day, and, that winter, was present at the Battle of the Bulge. Shortly after that, as he remembers it, "The colonel came to me one morning and said, 'I want you to read this army regulation thing,' and it was all about the GI Bill. 'You have got to get an education,' he said. 'There are going to be floods of people going to school, and I want you to apply for college right now.' I said, 'I don't even know what to study,' and he said, 'Study engineering.' But I told him that I liked journalism and wanted to study how to be a professional writer, so he said, 'Well, then you want to go to Columbia.' So I applied to Columbia, and I was accepted. And one of the things they wanted to know was when I could start, and I asked the colonel what I should tell them. And he said, 'This war is over. Put down September.'"

Although the colonel was right—the war in Europe ended in May 1945—Schey wasn't able to return to the United States until December, so he missed the fall term at Columbia. Not wanting to wait another nine months to start school, he contacted the university to ask where he could study journalism in the interim. He was referred to Ohio University in Athens, Ohio, where he enrolled in February 1946. "But when I got there," Schey says, "I met a professor who said, 'You don't want to study journalism. Why don't you study engineering?' And when I found out how much money journalists earn, I decided being an engineer wasn't a bad idea." Graduating from the university with an engineering degree, and realizing that he wanted to pursue a career in business, he attended Harvard Business School. In June 1950, he left there with a master's degree in business administration.

But before he left, there was another chance meeting. In retrospect, Schey considers it one of the most important events of his life. "I was walking across the campus," he remembers, "and I met a Professor Georges Doriot, a French-born military man who is considered the father of venture capital and founder of the first publicly traded venture capital firm, American Research and Development. He asked me where I'd decided to work once school was over, and I told him I was going to Ford Motor Company. 'You are going to *what?*' he said, and I repeated it. And he said, 'Are you crazy? You go to all the trouble to get the education you have and you are going to work for Ford Motor Company? Come up to my office right now.' So I went up to his office and he said, 'This is crazy. You should be running a business.' I told him I didn't have any money to buy a business, and he said, 'Then find a distributorship or a franchise.' I told him that I didn't know how to go about doing it, and he said, 'Well, I will help you.'

"So I thought about it and came up with two possible kinds of franchises," Schey says. "Beer and coal. In those days, the early 1950s, coal was still being delivered to people's homes and much of it was franchised. But television was just coming on, and I felt that there was going to be a lot of advertising, so I picked beer. I wrote to six breweries and I got five job offers." Returning to Cleveland, he took a trainee job with Leisy Brewing on the basis of the company's promise that he would be made a distributor within a year. But Schey wasn't happy with the job, and after 10 months he left the company because he found out that they wanted him in sales for five years before being made a distributor. "What I didn't realize at the time," he says, "was that guys were paying under the table to get distributorships. I wasn't doing that."[3] He worked at General Motors for six months but then was offered, and accepted, an engineering position at Clevite Corporation. He flourished at the company, received numerous promotions, and was still there 17 years later when, as its executive vice president, he was appointed by the company's board to find a buyer for it.

The company was sold in 1968 to Gould Instrument Systems (a manufacturer of a wide range of electronic instruments). Schey's severance package, not typical at the time, included $500,000 in cash plus a five-year consulting contract at $100,000 a year. Over the years he had purchased, through options, a substantial amount of stock in Cleveland Graphite Bronze, later known as Clevite, and selling it enabled him to get started as a venture capitalist. Although, as he admits, "I made a couple of flubs before I bought the right thing," he eventually bought a company called Ardac, which he thought had a lot of potential.[4] But the company didn't grow as fast as he had anticipated, and in 1974 he contacted Scott & Fetzer (the company eventually dropped the ampersand) to see if they would be interested in purchasing it. One day, as he remembers, while he was in the process of discussing it with Scott Fetzer, "The chairman, Niles Hammink, called and said, 'I would like to have lunch with you.' So I went to lunch and he said, 'You know, I want to retire, and I don't have anyone I am confident in to promote to COO. I have been looking at your background, and I would like you to consider taking over as president and COO.'"

At the time Schey joined the firm, Scott Fetzer had been in business for almost 60 years. In 1906 inventor James A. Kirby developed an early cleaner that used water. But it wasn't until after the First World War, when Kirby joined with Scott & Fetzer, a machine shop in Cleveland, that the vacuum cleaner really began to take off. Working together, they produced a machine called the Vacuette, a manually operated carpet cleaner, and sold a million units in the first five years. In 1925, the company introduced an equally successful electric model. By the mid-1950s, it was selling about 200,000 vacuum cleaners a year—considerably more than any of its competitors. Flush with cash, in 1964, the company started buying other companies. By the mid-1970s, when Schey became president, Scott & Fetzer had acquired more than 30.[5]

But the purchases had been made with no strategy in place to develop a synergistic approach to multiple markets. As a result, the company's divisions were in a wide variety of industries, and consequently had no clear-cut identity. "Everybody's first question," Schey says, "was, 'What's a Scott & Fetzer?'" To alleviate the confusion, Schey began to streamline operations by selling off some companies and combining others. One of his most important purchases was the acquisition of World Book, Inc., producers of the World Book Encyclopedia, from Field Enterprises in 1978. With a business model similar to Kirby Vacuum, World Book was a natural fit into an organization that specialized in direct selling of a consumer product door-to-door.

Scott Fetzer thrived under Schey's direction, but its success also attracted the attention of corporate raiders. In April 1984, Schey and several other corporate officers tried to take the company private through a leveraged buyout. They offered $331 million in cash, or $50 a share, just five dollars over the then-current market price. But two weeks later, Wall Street arbitrageur Ivan Boesky, who was subsequently sent to prison for insider trading, upped the offer to $60 a share, or $400 million. Schey and the company's other officers withdrew their bid, but the company's board rejected Boesky's proposal, as well as a later offer.[6] But the sharks could smell the blood in the water. Over the next 18 months, several other companies made efforts to take over Scott Fetzer, as did Schey and his executive group through an ESOP (employee stock ownership plan).

"We ruled out a lot of different companies that we didn't like," Schey remembers. "Why in the hell should I help those bastards buy it? So we didn't have any big companies that were after us, because we had too many different pieces, too many appendages. A few suitors wanted to buy parts of the company, but nobody with enough money came in and said, 'I will buy the whole thing.' Even Boesky and Michael Milken [another of the company's suitors who also went to prison] had that problem. They didn't know what to do with all those pieces. They were sort of baffled and overwhelmed by them. I felt an obligation to our employees to see that they were all treated about as equally as possible. I didn't want any one group of employees—people in companies that were small but very important to us—to suddenly find themselves out in a marketplace where nobody wanted them."

At that point, Warren Buffett stepped in. Buffett had been interested in the company for a long time. By October 1985, he owned about 5 percent of the stock. Sensing an opportunity, although he had never met Schey, on October 10, he wrote him a letter that said: "We own 250,000 shares. We have always liked your company. We don't do unfriendly deals. If you want to pursue a merger call me."[7] As Schey recalls, "I didn't know about Warren. Everything that I found out about him I did after he made his first inquiry. I was away at a Harvard reunion when the letter arrived, and when I came back on Monday morning my secretary gave me this letter and said, 'This came in Friday afternoon. I think you better call right away.'" So I called, and Warren said, 'When can we meet for dinner?' I said, 'As soon as you want,' and he said, 'How about tomorrow night in Chicago?' This was Monday, so we met on Tuesday night. Wednesday he came to look at the company, Thursday we completed the deal, and Friday he announced it to the public." In less than a week, Berkshire Hathaway had bought Scott Fetzer for a price of $60.77 per share, or $315 million.

Not surprisingly, Buffett was very pleased with the deal. He told his stockholders: "The company has sales of about $700 million derived from 16 businesses, many leaders in their fields. Return on invested capital is good to excellent for most of these businesses." He was also able to tell them that "World Book, Inc.—accounting for about 40 percent of Scott Fetzer's sales and a bit more of its income—is by far the company's largest operation. It also is by far the leader in its industry, selling more than twice as many encyclopedia sets annually as its nearest competitor. In fact, it sells more sets in the United States than its four biggest competitors combined." But perhaps best of all, he noted, "The Scott Fetzer acquisition, plus major growth in our insurance business, should push [Berkshire's] revenues above $2 billion in 1986, more than double those of 1985."[8]

Interestingly, Buffett also used the Scott Fetzer deal to explain to Berkshire's stockholders the kind of company—and acquisition—he was interested in. "Scott Fetzer is a prototype," he wrote, "understandable, large, well-managed, a good earner. The Scott Fetzer purchase illustrates our somewhat haphazard approach to acquisitions. We have no master strategy, no corporate planners delivering us insights about socioeconomic trends, and no staff to investigate a multitude of ideas presented by promoters and intermediaries. Instead, we simply hope that something sensible comes along—and, when it does, we act. . . . "[9]

Buffett then went on to describe the six acquisition criteria that are still published annually in his famed letter to shareholders: large purchases, consistent earnings, little debt, ongoing management, simple businesses, and an offering price.

"We will not engage in unfriendly takeovers," Buffett noted. "We can promise complete confidentiality and a very fast answer—customarily, within five minutes—as to whether we're interested. We prefer to buy for cash, but will consider issuance of stock when we receive as much in intrinsic business value as we give. . . . We invite potential sellers to check us out by contacting people with whom we have done business in the past. For the right business—and the right people—we can provide a good home. On the other hand, we frequently get approached about acquisitions that don't come close to meeting our tests: new ventures, turnarounds, auction-like sales, and the ever-popular (among brokers) I'm-sure-something-will-work-out-if-you-people-get-to-know-each-other.' None of these attracts us in the least."[10]

Whatever Buffett's reasons for wanting to buy Scott Fetzer, Ralph Schey was very pleased with the sale. "One of the most important reasons we decided to go with Berkshire," he says, "was that it increased the probability of our coming through the financial and legal battles whole, as one company rather than three or four. But in making the decision, the number-one factor was how it would affect our shareholders, how they would fare best. And that is what made this the final decision because that was the easiest one for us to look at. There was no question that they came off better with the Berkshire deal than they would with us staying public and independent."

Initially concerned about his new boss's long-held disdain for corporate jets, Schey gingerly approached Buffett with Scott Fetzer's policy to fly customers in its own aircraft. Keeping to his character, Warren said, "Keep the jet and run all of your businesses just like you ran them before the merger." Absolutely no changes were made to the existing Scott Fetzer businesses or management, and the entire business (and its jet) was preserved.

Since the merger, Schey says, he has recognized several additional advantages to being part of the Berkshire family. One of them, he says, is that "We spend more time on the business. I would guess that when we were a public company, of the roughly 200 working days a year, we probably spent at least 50 of them outside of the company, talking to public relations people, investor relations people, investment people, and others like that. We don't do that anymore, so we have more time to concentrate on growing the business." Although he had hoped, at the time of the merger, that "taking away that burden would give us a lot of time to diversify our business, we haven't really done that. But it did enable us to focus on earning more money, and we do earn more money today, out of the same businesses, than we did when we were independent."

He also believes that being part of Buffett's company provides Scott Fetzer with "an opportunity to take something and make it as unique as you want to make it without having to fight to get the money to do it. I don't ask Warren to put any money into the businesses," he says emphatically, "or to take money from other businesses and put it into Scott Fetzer. I just want to be able to take the money that Scott Fetzer is generating and invest it in anything that we want to. As a public company, we couldn't do that because every investment we wanted to make was scrutinized. You never get that at Berkshire."

Finally, he says that the merger with Berkshire has "caused us slowly, very slowly, to raise our own horizons of what kinds of businesses we think we can be in. Originally we were thinking that we could only grow into the businesses we were already in, but now we're starting to realize that we may be able to grow in other directions as well. One of the things I've looked at is for us to expand vertically rather than just horizontally. Rather than just making product and selling it to dealers who take it and resell it, we ought to develop a distribution system that would coincide with our production system."

Even without moving into other businesses, Scott Fetzer has been extremely successful. With 7,500 employees in 22 different divisions, the company, which would rank in the top 500 companies in its own right, now reports revenues of approximately $1 billion a year and earnings of approximately $150 million a year. About 80 percent of the company's profits comes from three areas: (1) Kirby, the largest and most important business, along with wholly owned companies of Scott Fetzer that service Kirby, (2) World Book Encyclopedia, and (3) Campbell Hausfeld.

The World Book intrigued Buffett and Munger the most, before the acquisition. First published in 1917 by the Hanson–Bellows Company in Chicago, the World Book was purchased by Marshall Field III to be the flagship of a new company that eventually became Field Enterprises Educational Corporation, and was sold again, in 1978, to Scott Fetzer. Twelve million sets of the World Book are in use worldwide, and four of every 10 homes in the United States and Canada own a set. The traditional hardcover-book edition of the World Book continues to be sold to schools and libraries but few are sold door-to-door. Beginning in 1994, it became available on compact disk, and it is now online, having recently announced an alliance with AOL Time Warner. The Internet has dramatically affected World Book sales, which are down from 40 percent of Scott Fetzer's total sales in 1990 to just 7 percent today. During the same time period, annual profits have slid from $35 million to $17 million.

Another major component of the business is Scott Fetzer Manufacturing and its major subsidiary, Campbell Hausfeld, which produces powered equipment such as air compressors, winches, air tools, generators, painting systems, pressure washers, and welders. The original company, founded in 1836, is one of the oldest companies in Ohio. Campbell Manufacturing made a corn planter and other farm equipment. Later, Joseph Hausfeld started a company and manufactured an air compressor called Pressure King. In the 1940 merger, Campbell became Campbell Hausfeld. In 1971, Campbell Hausfeld became part of Scott Fetzer. Today, Campbell Hausfeld's six product lines generate approximately one-third of the company's revenues and profits. This division's emerging challenge is to handle the pressure from major retailers like Home Depot and Wal-Mart to self-brand and commoditize all of their products, including air compressors.

The biggest revenue and profit producer for Scott Fetzer is Kirby vacuum cleaners. About 500,000 Kirbys are sold all over the world each year; approximately a third of sales are outside the United States. They're not recommended for anything other than home use, but they are such powerful vacuums that they are often used for commercial purposes. Scott Fetzer sells the vacuum cleaners to about 835 factory distributors, who, in turn, sell the vacuum cleaners door-to-door. In the late 1990s, the distributors' door-to-door sales system generated some controversy, an event quite out of the ordinary for a Berkshire company.

In the fall of 1999, in a front-page article in the *Wall Street Journal,* it was reported that some individuals had accused Kirby of high-pressure sales tactics that took advantage of elderly people and low-income consumers. According to the *Omaha World-Herald,* after the *Journal* article was published, Ralph Schey contacted Warren Buffett to seek his advice. But, according to Schey, "He only said what he has said to me many times before: 'Be very careful that customers are treated fairly.'" Even so, Schey was sorry about any embarrassment the story might have caused his boss. "Warren has such an impeccable reputation," he told the *World-Herald.* "The *Journal* article kind of said, 'Here's Warren Buffett. He's Mr. Clean, and he's involved in a dirty business.' But the truth is," Schey insisted, "This isn't a dirty business." Kirby's selling methods today are the same ones used in the 1930s and its complaint ratio is insignificant. The *World-Herald* also reported that Buffett receives about 100 letters a year from disgruntled Berkshire Hathaway company consumers, and only about 1 percent come from Kirby customers.[11]

Schey needn't have worried about how his boss would react to the Kirby vacuum cleaner story. Buffett had never had anything but positive comments to make about his managerial performance. His enthusiasm for Schey was evident in the first "Chairman's Letter to Shareholders" that he wrote after Berkshire acquired Scott Fetzer in 1985. "An equal attraction at Scott Fetzer," Buffett said, "is Ralph Schey, its CEO for nine years. . . . Ralph's operating and capital-allocation record is superb, and we are delighted to be associated with him."[12] And a year later, in discussing Scott Fetzer and Schey, he told shareholders: "A year's experience has added to my enthusiasm for both. Ralph is a superb businessman and a straight shooter. He also brings exceptional versatility and energy to his job: despite the wide array of businesses that he manages, he is on top of the operations, opportunities and problems of each. And, like our other managers, Ralph is a real pleasure to work with. Our good fortune continues," he concluded.[13]

Eight years later, he expanded somewhat on why he was so positive about Schey's abilities. "The reasons for Ralph's success," he told shareholders, "are not complicated. Ben Graham taught me 45 years ago that in investing it is not necessary to do extraordinary things to get extraordinary results. In later life, I have been surprised to find that this statement holds true in business management as well. What a manager must do is handle the basics well and not get diverted. That's precisely Ralph's formula. He establishes the right goals and never forgets what he set out to do. On the personal side, Ralph is a joy to work with. He's forthright about problems and is self-confident without being self-important."[14] And, as already noted, in assessing Schey's contribution on his retirement, Buffett said, "As a manager, Ralph belongs in Berkshire's Hall of Fame."[15]

Not surprisingly, Ralph Schey speaks with equal admiration of his boss. "What I admire about him most," Schey says, "is his ability to grasp a problem as quickly as he does and have some idea of how to solve it. He's also a great guy to be around. He is very inspirational, although in a quiet sort of way. I also like the fact that he creates a sense of equality, even though there may not be equality, either in intellectual capacity or financial resources. But he gives you the idea and the feeling of equality." Like many of Berkshire's other operating managers, he says that when he first met Buffett there were two things that surprised him. "First," Schey says, "that he was as approachable and amicable as he is. And, second, that he understood as much as he did about our business."

But Schey finds Buffett's management style to be the most praiseworthy. "We talk maybe every other week," Schey explains, "so I keep him informed. He gives good advice, but he doesn't say, 'You have got to do it my way.' And I don't say to him in general, 'Can I do this or can I do that?' because he doesn't expect you to do that. That's the greatest strength he has— giving you a lot of freedom to run the businesses the way you want. And that way, you can't pass the responsibility back to him. If he says, 'You do what you are going to do,' and it doesn't work out, there is only one guy that you can look at, and that's yourself. There aren't many people around like that." And by treating his managers that way, Schey says, "he creates the image of ownership without having it, and that's hard to do. I look at my job as though this was my company, as if I was the majority shareholder and I can do what I want to do with it. That way, I won't take risks greater than I am personally willing to take. On the other hand, I am constantly trying to press so that we can do better than we're doing today."

Schey also says that Buffett has had an influence on him since Scott Fetzer became part of Berkshire. "He's had an impact on my own thinking in relation to things that we ought to look at, particularly the relationships we have with our retail customers. I've spent a lot more time on the retail customer side of our business as a result of Warren than I did before. I have taken the position that I'm the CEO but also that, as an investor, I've got a stake in the customer, too. So if our relationships with our customers aren't good, we are going to suffer. And Warren thinks that way—there's no question about it—and that's a unique philosophy."

As far as his own management style is concerned, Schey places a great deal of emphasis on communication as a tool. "I spent a lot of time trying to learn how to communicate," he says, "and one of the things I realized was that when I communicated with people I tended to be authoritative. 'Why didn't you do this? Why was that wrong?' And I realized that it would be better to use a more subjective, more restrained way of communication, as opposed to a blatant, objective, commanding, kind of telling rather than asking. If you communicate that way you'll be much more helpful to people, so they can be more independent. That's how you inspire people to think for themselves." In fact, Schey says that he measures his success by "the people who I've inspired to do something that makes them successful. And when somebody recognizes what I did to mentor them, to get them to do something that they may not have done, and they come back and say, 'I appreciate it,' I feel very good about that."

Not surprisingly, Schey is a great believer in entrepreneurialism. As he wrote in *Cleveland Enterprise* a decade ago, "What drives an entrepreneur" is "to be in control of his destiny, and to do something better than anyone else can do it. . . . The entrepreneurial opportunity is more than just making money and creating user satisfaction with [a] superior product of superior value. Opportunity is manifested in changing people's lives and making them aware of challenges and goals that they had not previously envisioned."[16] And when asked, accordingly, if he were to start another company, what kind of company it would be, he says, "One that would invest in businesses that were run by entrepreneurs and entrepreneurial managers, companies that could be divided up into smaller pieces. I think the issue of ownership is the most critical thing that you can give to someone. I just see a huge difference between people who own a business, even if it is a small business, and professional managers in big companies."

As for the future of his own big company, Schey says, "I would like to see us diversify in some of the categories we're already in, like education. I think it would be good if we could move over and become more than just an information source, if we could get more involved in the process of how people get educated. Things like helping kids learn to read more effectively, or learn math faster. I think the new interactive technologies are going to provide a lot of new opportunities for ways to teach kids. In the past you always had a teacher standing in front of a class of 30 kids—all with different abilities, different interests, and different skills—and trying to get through to them. But you can't do it. It's got to be customized. And I think there will be a lot of opportunities there."

But how does one discern where those opportunities are? "We are focused on markets," Schey says, "and therefore we are constantly trying to appraise what the next market phase is going to be. We're not looking at the one we are in now as an end in itself. We're looking for that next market opportunity, and trying to figure out how to get into it early on." Again using Scott Fetzer's educational business as an example, he says, "Take the World Book. We know that education is going to have to be improved, but we have to figure out if that's going to be accomplished by changing the delivery system, such as through some electronic means, or by changing the content of the material that's being used. But one way or the other, there are going to be changes, and we want to do the best we can to figure out what those changes are going to be."

One such change, Schey knows, will be brought about by new technologies. Although he believes that technology will have relatively little effect on Kirby, and somewhat more on Campbell Hausfeld, he recognizes that because it is changing the face of information gathering and dissemination, technology will continue to have a profound effect on the World Book. When asked, for example, who the World Book's biggest competitor is likely to be 10 years from now, Schey says, "I don't know who it will be, but it won't be a company that's in the encyclopedia business today. This field is going through a dual revolution, one of how you put the news together and digest it, and the other of how you regurgitate it so that people can understand it. World Book does that better than anybody else, but I think that we're going to find more people who will try to compete with that. And one thing I do know," he concludes, "is that it's going to be people who are in the electronics business."

The future of World Book and Scott Fetzer's companies is now the responsibility of longtime employee (28 years) and newly appointed CEO Ken Smelsberger, who is 64 years old. This well-defined and implemented succession plan is an example of Schey's professionalism and leadership, and possibly how other Berkshire subsidiaries will handle future management transitions. Smelsberger was brought up through the ranks as manufacturing manager, vice president of operations, division president, corporate group vice president, senior vice president of finance and administration, and president and chief operating officer. Few CEOs have done a more thorough job of grooming their replacement than Ralph Schey. According to Ralph, there isn't anyone who is more qualified to run Scott Fetzer today. This is a reflection of Schey's picking the right person, exposing him to all the right areas of the business, permitting him to succeed or fail, and then stepping out of his way at the appropriate time.

As for the future of Berkshire Hathaway, Schey says: "I am hopeful that it gets grouped together in such a way that if it ever has to be disassembled, it can be disassembled without tearing the company apart. I've had discussions with Warren about it, and I would appear to be on the other side of the fence, but I think that once he's gone, no one is going to be able to run it the way he does. I know the shareholders have some concerns," he says, "and I think they should, because no matter who he names to take over the company, none of them are going to be Warren Buffett. He's a very unique guy, so you just don't find many like him. There are not many guys who are comfortable operating the way he does, or who can affect people the way he does. He makes you want to do well, partly for yourself, but also because you know it will make him proud, and you want to make him proud. And that's a very rare thing."

## RALPH SCHEY'S BUSINESS TENETS

- ★ The way you communicate with your employees is crucial. You should talk with them and hear their concerns rather than simply being a manager who tells them what to do. You want to inspire them so they want to accomplish something.
- ★ Entrepreneurial spirit is powerful. Even in large companies, you should let managers have some degree of ownership so, like entrepreneurs, they can develop and grow their parts of the business.
- ★ Look to technology to help grow and diversify. So many occasions can arise from these advancements that we can't even predict what they are. We have to be open and look for these opportunities.

# chapter eighteen

# The Appointed One—
# Susan Jacques, Borsheim's Fine Jewelry

*Susan Jacques, the only woman among the current Buffett CEOs, has three full-time careers: CEO of Borsheim's Fine Jewelry, wife, and mother of two young children. Like Rose Blumkin, Susan is foreign-born (Zimbabwe) and didn't attend college. Susan came with the business, but unlike any of the other Berkshire Hathaway CEOs, she was promoted from within by Warren Buffett. She is the first nonfamily chief executive of Borsheim's.*

*We sat in her second-floor conference room, which overlooks the mall that is the site of the annual Berkshire shareholder reception. She has the grace and charm of a political leader, is quick minded, but is always a salesperson. Warren was right when he said, "Hold on to your wallet"; after being charmed by Susan Jacques, all of your future jewelry purchases will be from Borsheim's.*

In his 1997 "Chairman's Letter to Shareholders," Warren Buffett wrote: "As a manager," Susan Jacques, president and chief executive officer of Borsheim's Fine Jewelry, was "everything that an owner hopes for."[1] She represents an anomaly among the company's CEOs. She is the only female currently running a Berkshire operation (the only other woman was the late Rose Blumkin of the Nebraska Furniture Mart), and she is the youngest now and was only age 34 when she became president. In addition, she is one of only three current operating chiefs and nonfamily members to have been appointed to their positions by Warren Buffett himself. (The other appointees are Stan Lipsey, publisher of the *Buffalo News,* and Brad Kinstler, CEO of Fechheimer's.) Jacques manages the smallest Berkshire operating company, as measured by annual sales. Unlike virtually all the other Berkshire CEOs, she was neither wealthy before her company became part of Berkshire, nor—since she never owned any part of the company—did she become wealthy as a result of the sale. She is proof that the Berkshire succession model works.

Jacques is an anomaly, not only among Berkshire's managers but in her own industry as well. In a business dominated largely by middle-aged Jewish men, she says, "One of the jokes I made when I first got my position was that I had three strikes against me: I was young. I was a woman. And I was a *goy,* a non-Jew." Jacques does not feel that these strikes have hindered her. "I think people are taken for their abilities," she says. Given Buffett's glowing praise and the continued success of the Omaha-based jewelry concern, her abilities are considerable.

Born in Africa in 1959 in what was then called Rhodesia—now Zimbabwe—Jacques was the second of three daughters born to English and Australian parents who ran their own timber business. Like many little girls, she had a penchant for jewelry. On Friday afternoons, when she and her sisters received their weekly allowance, Jacques remembers, "We'd go to the store, and they used to sell those inexpensive little rings—the 5-cent, 10-cent rings. Every Friday I bought a ring. Even back then, I loved jewelry. . . ."[2] When she graduated from high school, she was unsure of what she wanted to do. "I didn't know what I would study at college," she says, "so I didn't want to go. My mother said if I wasn't going to go, then I should at least take a secretarial course, because I could always fall back on a secretarial position. I took a year-long secretarial course, and the first position I got was as a junior secretary at Scottish Jewelers," the largest jewelry company in the British colony. But the colony of Rhodesia was in the throes of its transition to the independent nation of Zimbabwe, and, soon after she started working, her parents sent their three daughters to England for a year.

When Susan returned, she was offered two positions at Scottish Jewelers—another secretarial job or a position in marketing. "I decided to go into marketing and do something a little different," she says, "but I very quickly realized I didn't know much about what I was doing, and if I was going to get into the industry, I'd have to get a jewelry education." Some of her associates at Scottish Jewelers had taken correspondence courses from the Gemological Institute of America (GIA), in Santa Monica, California, and Jacques decided to come to the United States and take the institute's six-month course. When she earned her diploma from the GIA in 1980, she intended to return home to Africa. Instead, she began working at the U.S. Gemological Services gemstone-grading laboratory, and, at the same time, studying to become a Fellow of the Gemmological* Society of Great Britain. In 1982, Jacques passed with distinction and won an award as the most outstanding student worldwide. Later that year, one of her friends and fellow students at the Institute, Alan Friedman, who happened to be a member of the family that owned and operated Borsheim's Jewelry, in Omaha, Nebraska, recruited her to join the company.

Founded in Omaha by Louis Borsheim in 1870, and run by the Borsheim family for three quarters of a century, the company was purchased by Louis Friedman and his wife Rebecca in 1947. (Rebecca Friedman was the younger sister of Rose Blumkin, founder of the Nebraska Furniture Mart, a Berkshire Hathaway company. Blumkin did not recommend the Friedmans' business to Warren Buffett. He discovered it on his own.) Louis's son, Isadore ("Ike"), joined Borsheim's in 1948, and began its transformation from a small family-owned business to one of the leading jewelry concerns in the world. Ike bought the firm from his father in 1973. By the time Jacques joined the company as a sales associate, in September 1982, it was being run by Ike, his son Alan, and his son-in-law, Marvin Cohn.

"Ike Friedman was a remarkable character," Jacques says. "A computer mind . . . ; knew people by their jewelry, knew people by their previous purchases, knew exactly what everybody had. Incredible negotiator, an incredible buyer, an incredible salesman."[3] As she tells it, working for him was a learning experience from the beginning. "My very first day on the sales floor," she says, "I went up to Ike and said, 'You know, I've never done any sales before, and I'd like to maybe take the first week and watch everybody and get some experience and learn how things are done.' But he said, 'Well, I think I am going to need you out there, and, in fact, there is a customer coming in the door right now. Would you please go wait on him?' So I waited on this gentleman, and I had absolutely no training, no introduction, nothing. I sold him a pin for $295 out of the case, and I wrote it up, and I charged it, and I gift-wrapped it, and I handed it to him, and he left. And then Ike came over and said, 'Well, did he buy something?' I told him he had, and he said, 'You didn't come and get a price.' I said, 'I didn't know I had to come and get a price,' and he said, 'Oh yes;

---

*Jacques notes that "Gemmological" is the British spelling of the word.

you never sell it for what it says in the case. You have to come and get a price from me.' So that poor man was probably the only customer who ever paid retail at Borsheim's at the time."

When Jacques joined the company, Borsheim's had already become a landmark in downtown Omaha; it had 7,500 square feet of operating space, and 35 employees. Four years later, in 1986, the operation expanded into a 27,000-square-foot space at the Regency Court, a small, enclosed, suburban mall off Omaha's Dodge Street. In the same year, Susan Jacques was promoted to Jewelry Merchandise Manager and Buyer, a considerably more demanding position. Initially, she enjoyed the increased responsibility, but within a few years, having grown tired of the long hours, she began considering a teaching job she'd been offered at the Gemological Institute in California. The family, however, wanted her to stay and was willing to make concessions about her working conditions. And, she had another reason to stay in Omaha. During the Christmas sales season, in 1987, the store hired a man named Gene Dunn. One of 10 children of a prominent Omaha couple, he had enjoyed several careers and was in the process of buying a cabinetry and casework company when he met Susan. "His joke is that he had to give up a budding career in gemology to ask me out, because I wouldn't date him if he worked here," Jacques says.[4] She stayed in Omaha and married Gene Dunn in 1990.

Meanwhile, there had been changes at Borsheim's. During the 1988 Christmas season, Warren Buffett had come into the store looking for a ring. Having shopped there many times before, he was well known to both the staff and the management, and while he was looking, Donald Yale, one of Ike Friedman's sons-in law, called out, "Don't sell Warren the ring, sell him the store!"[5] Early in the new year, Buffett called and asked if the Friedman family might indeed be interested in selling. "I think there were a few things that attracted Warren to Borsheim's," Jacques says. "One was the fact that the jewelry business is a happy business. You're dealing with happy people; you're helping people commemorate special occasions. More of it, though, was the fact that we were a successful business. We had a tremendous reputation, and I think that was appealing to Warren. But probably the most important reason Warren was interested," Jacques continues, "was Ike Friedman. Ike was a dynamo—I mean, he really was. He's a legend in our industry, and, even now, every time I see people who knew Ike and had experiences with Ike, they tell me stories about him. Part of what Warren was purchasing was definitely the persona of Ike. There is no question about that."

Ike Friedman *was* interested in selling, so, in February 1989, a meeting was set up with Friedman, Donald Yale, and Warren Buffett. "The substantive part of the talk," Yale says, "was 10 minutes. He asked us five questions and Ike had a price." The five questions Buffett asked were: "What are sales? What are gross profits? What are expenses? What's in inventory? Are you willing to stay on?" Friedman was able to answer the first four without even looking at his books, and his answer to the fifth was affirmative. "The three of us later met at Buffett's office," Yale remembers, "and Ike and Warren shook hands on the sale." After the agreement was reached, Yale recalls, "Buffett said, 'Now forget that it happened, and just keep doing what you were doing.' There was no discussion of future growth and absolutely no discussion of changing our way of making decisions, planning expansion, or bringing in additional profits. He made it very clear that he was not in this as a quick-return deal." Warren Buffett wrote a check for 80 percent of Borsheim's, and family members retained the other 20 percent. The purchase price was not disclosed. Borsheim's thus became the first jewelry concern to be a part of Berkshire Hathaway. It would not, however, be the last.

The Friedmans and Buffett were very pleased with the acquisition. Like a casino owner who places a high-end jewelry location at the entrance and the exit of the gambling floor, Berkshire now had a way of capturing the disposable dollars of its hometown shareholders and their out-of-town partners during the Omaha annual meeting weekend, the city's second largest event. Although Borsheim's will never be sold and is small, it has been a great strategic investment, and probably earned its purchase price within a few years.

Buffett told Berkshire's stockholders, in his 1989 "Chairman's Letter to Shareholders": "In its first year with Berkshire, Borsheim's met all expectations. Sales rose significantly and are now considerably better than twice what they were four years ago when the company moved to its present location. . . . Ike Friedman, Borsheim's managing genius—and I mean that— has only one speed: fast-forward." Warming to his subject, Buffett went on to say: "Ike Friedman is not only a superb businessman and a great showman but also a man of integrity. We bought the business without an audit, and all of our surprises have been on the plus side. 'If you don't know jewelry, know your jeweler' makes sense whether you are buying the whole business or a tiny diamond."[6]

As an additional explanation for why he liked Friedman so much, Buffett offered his stockholders a story: "Every two years," he said, "I'm part of an informal group that gathers to have fun and explore a few subjects. Last September, meeting at Bishop's Lodge in Santa Fe, we asked Ike, his wife Roz, and his son Alan to come by and educate us on jewels and the jewelry business. Ike decided to dazzle the group, so he brought from Omaha about $20 million of particularly fancy merchandise. I was somewhat apprehensive—Bishop's Lodge is no Fort Knox—and I mentioned my concern to Ike at our opening party the evening before his presentation. Ike took me aside. 'See that safe?' he said. 'This afternoon we changed the combination and now even the hotel management doesn't know what it is.' I breathed easier. Ike went on: 'See those two big fellows with guns on their hips? They'll be guarding the safe all night.' I now was ready to rejoin the party. But Ike leaned closer: 'And besides, Warren,' he confided, 'the jewels aren't in the safe' "[7]

Whimsical though he may have been, Friedman was also a tough-minded businessman. Over the next two years, Borsheim's continued to thrive. Then, in September 1991, without having made any succession plans, Friedman passed away. As Jacques explains, "When Warren Buffett purchased Borsheim's, he was buying Ike Friedman. And then Ike was tragically struck with lung cancer two years later, which was never in the plan. I'm sure that when Warren bought the company he thought Ike was going to be there for the next 20 years, so there wasn't any need to seek a successor or anything like that." To further complicate things, Alan Friedman, who might have become president after his father's death, left to open his own business, first in Omaha and then in Beverly Hills, California, and Ike's son-in-law, Donald Yale, became president. All of these changes left the senior vice president's position open, and Susan Jacques was promoted into the job.

Although she was, again, pleased to be entrusted with additional responsibilities at the store, the birth of her first child 14 months later presented her with new concerns—and with the dilemma of wanting to be with her child while still pursuing her career. With her husband's help, she made the decision to return to work. "Gene wouldn't hear of me quitting," she told a reporter several years later. "He is the backbone of my success. He's very, very supportive of women in business, and succeeding, and is very gracious with his support." She was able to balance her work and her personal life and became a role model for other women on the staff. "We have a lot of young women in our management team," she says, "and family is a very important focus. We feel that if you have a very, very good home life and a good family life and devote the necessary time to it, . . . you'll be more productive at work, as long as you've made the decision to work. There's some guilt that goes with it, but, fortunately, I've learned to realize I would not be a good stay-at-home mom."[8]

By the beginning of 1994, her boss, Donald Yale, was having difficulty striking the same kind of balance. His wife, Janis, had cancer and, as Yale put it at the time, "I have family responsibilities and business responsibilities, and it got to the point I couldn't do both. My family responsibilities are my priority," he said, and he felt it necessary to resign as president of Borsheim's. "This is my decision solely," he noted. "Warren was very understanding and supportive of my decision."[9] However understanding and supportive Buffett may have been, he again had to choose someone to run the jewelry company. As part of his effort to do that, or so Susan Jacques thought at the time, Buffett began inviting the company's executives to meetings in his office.

"Shortly after Donald had given notice," she recalls, "Warren called me at about 10 o'clock one morning, and said something like, 'Is there any chance you can come down to the office this afternoon to meet with me?' Of course, we all knew that Donald was leaving, and I assumed Warren was meeting with all of the executives on the team. I thought he probably just wanted an update on how things were going, so I told him that I'd be happy to go down and see him. But then I realized that I wasn't wearing one of my favorite suits. And, you know, I wanted to look very professional if I was going to have a meeting with Warren."

At the time, she and her husband were living on a farm that was about a half hour's drive from the store, but they also had a small apartment just around the corner from her office. "So I called up my husband," she recalls, "and I said, 'Warren's asked me to go down to his office and I have to go home and change. But, Gene,' I said, 'my shoes are at the farm and my suit is at the apartment.' So he said, 'You go get the suit and I'll run to the farm and get the shoes for you.' So Gene is speeding along the Interstate to get my shoes and he gets pulled over by a cop. And he says to the cop, 'You are never going to believe this, but my wife has an appointment with Warren Buffett this afternoon and I've got to go get her shoes.' And the cop said, 'That's a good one, I haven't heard that one today,' and he let Gene off with a warning."

After dressing appropriately, Jacques went to her meeting with Buffett. Soon after they began talking, she discovered that he hadn't just called her in for an update—he wanted her to take over as president of the company. "I was flabbergasted," she says. "I was truly taken completely off guard. I said to him, 'I'll give it a try. But if I don't do very well at it, will you let me go back to doing what I do now?' And he said, 'Sometimes that gets a little difficult, Susan, but we can certainly try.' And he did. He gave me a tremendous opportunity, and, fortunately, it's worked out." But that's not quite the end of the story. "When it was announced that I had become president," she adds, "we got a nice phone call congratulating us from the cop who had stopped Gene on the Interstate. I guess he was happy to discover that there really had been a meeting."

Since becoming president in January 1994, Jacques has striven to maintain Borsheim's traditions. Like Ike Friedman, she is a visible, constant presence on the sales floor. She keeps an accessible office on the main floor, and continues to practice Friedman's philosophy of taking care of the customer. Doing so has, in turn, enabled the company's sales and profits to continue to grow exponentially and to feed additional expansions and increases in staff. In 1997, Borsheim's CEO was inducted into the National Jeweler Hall of Fame—the third female recipient of this award.

When Jacques joined the company in 1982, it had 7,500 square feet of sales space and 35 employees. By 2000, the sales space had grown to 20,000 square feet, and the employees numbered 375. Since she became president, sales have doubled, and Borsheim's is now second only to the Tiffany store in New York ($130 million) in terms of merchandise sold from a single location. She admits, though, that all these changes have come at a cost. "We occasionally hear negative comments from customers that it is not the same as it used to be," she says. "We've tried to maintain a family culture. A tremendous number of us, even those on the executive team, worked closely with the Friedman family prior to the acquisition. But it's not the same as when the patriarch of the business is the owner, and the business represents the family's sole livelihood. It has to play out differently when you are part of a larger organization. Even though we try to run it very much with Ike's philosophy, some of the corporate side of the business has had to change."

She is nevertheless convinced that the acquisition by Berkshire has been a real benefit to her company. She believes that "Borsheim's still would have been very successful and would have continued to be a leader in the industry," even if it hadn't become part of Berkshire, but she acknowledges that "the Berkshire affiliation has helped us to grow our customer base tremendously." One contributing factor has been the company's participation in Berkshire's stockholders' meeting in Omaha every May. Although the store is normally closed on Sundays, it stays open for stockholders during the annual meeting (the weekend before Mother's Day), and some 15,000 loyal Berkshire stockholders become Borsheim customers. Only the store's Christmas sales outdo this three-day weekend of the year.

At the annual shareholders' meeting, Jacques has had the opportunity to meet other Berkshire operating managers (she sold See's Candies' CEO, Chuck Huggins, his wedding bands). She feels that more communication among all of them would be beneficial. Borsheim's Omaha neighbors, the Blumkins, have already been very helpful. "We do rely on them and have conversed on numerous occasions about everything from commission pay for sales associates, to human resource issues, to marketing, because they are a retailer in our same environment. But," she adds, "we would like to—and are planning to—get more conversations and brainstorming sessions going with some of the other companies." As an example, she cites Executive Jet, the Woodbridge, New Jersey-based company that sells shares of jet planes to corporations, entrepreneurs, superstar athletes, celebrities, and wealthy individuals. "It would probably be a benefit to us to get together with them," she says, "because we cater to some of the same clients."

She believes, however, that the greatest potential for synergy exists among Berkshire's three jewelry concerns: Borsheim's, Kansas City-based Helzberg Diamonds, and Seattle-based Ben Bridge Jewelers. "There are many, many possibilities," she says. "There are synergies for buying, credit card processing, and extension of credit. There are also inventory and inventory management, compensation, and appraisals, shop repairs, and industry-related issues. I think there is a tremendous amount that we could do together, and I hope we can make better use of *all* the talent we have to make each of our businesses stronger."

In some respects, the members of the jewelry group are competitors—Helzberg's, for example, has four stores in Omaha—but Jacques believes that there is sufficient trust among them to make working together in some ways possible. "Before Helzberg's was acquired by Berkshire," she admits, "we did have a different feeling toward them. We definitely saw them as competitors. But I think we truly have a different philosophy now that they're part of the company. I mean, I'll tell customers that if they don't want to buy from me, then they should buy from Helzberg's. I'm not about to give them sales and they're not about to give me sales, but I will certainly recommend a sister company before I'd recommend anybody else. At least they'll be buying from another Berkshire company."

Working for Warren Buffett, Jacques says, is "a tremendous honor. I mean, he is a very, very special man. He's compassionate, he's warm, and he's probably one of the most brilliant people I've ever met. But he never speaks over you; he never speaks above your head. He is extremely savvy about each and every thing he does. He's also a great person to work for. He's always very available. Any time there's something I need to speak with him about, he is always readily available."

When asked the difference between her boss and herself, with her British accent and quick wit she responds, "Warren likes to buy and I love to sell."

Because Berkshire is "the acquirer of choice, particularly in our industry," she is occasionally contacted by colleagues who are interested in the possibility of selling their operations to Buffett. Although she insists, "I always send them off to Warren, because acquisition is not part of what I do," she admits that she has, on occasion, "consulted and confided with Warren on things that have come about." She also believes that there are other potential Berkshire family members in the jewelry industry. "There are," she says, "a tremendous number of jewelry operators, family businesses somewhat similar to, perhaps, Ben Bridge's, who have multiple family members involved in the business and who have concerns about what will happen when the patriarch or the matriarch passes away. It's a tremendous honor to be able to say Warren Buffett picked your business, and that's something of which we're very proud."

Given that sentiment, it's not surprising that Jacques says Buffett is the individual who has had the greatest impact on her professional life. "When you work for somebody," she says, "he will always have some influence on you, and I think Warren has influenced me in a positive manner with respect to really caring about what I do. He's also influenced me in regard to believing in myself, having self-confidence, and always doing what I think is right. He always says, 'Conduct yourself in a manner that you would never be ashamed to read about on the front page of tomorrow's paper,' and I keep that foremost in my mind in everything I do. I think that's a terrific way to live your life—to always be honest with yourself, to be honest with everybody around you, and to admit your mistakes." In fact, she considers honesty, integrity, and trustworthiness to be "elements that are critical in our business. If those elements are lacking in a business," she says, "you won't be in business very long."

Another element she considers critical to business success is the ability to get along with people. "I tend to get along with most everybody," she says. "I think that if you can deal with people, and listen to their side of things, and work through issues, you're more likely to have their respect, and that gives you a much better chance of being successful." At the same time, she is quick to acknowledge the contribution of the other members of her team. "I surround myself with people that have talent in areas that I am not as talented. We have a great team here—a very young team—that I think has done very, very well." Finally, she thinks the ability to focus is an important element. "It's essential," she says, "that you never lose sight of what it is you do on a daily basis, and that you never stop trying to improve that, to make it a better experience for your customers."

Describing Borsheim's current status, she says, "We actually have three separate businesses. We sell jewelry, we sell watches, and we sell gifts. They are three distinctly different businesses. About 80 percent of our business is jewelry, and the other two are about 10 percent each. But our overall philosophy is exactly the same in each of them, and that is: trying to completely satisfy our customers. I'm a real stickler on making sure that customers are taken care of when they walk in the door. We like people to get acknowledged, on numerous occasions, to make sure that everybody gets waited on, and everybody gets acknowledged very rapidly. It drives some customers nuts, because some of them just like to look around and don't like being constantly bugged by an associate. But the last thing I ever want is a customer not being taken care of. If you stop taking care of the customer, you don't have a business."

Consistent practice of that philosophy has provided the company with an excellent reputation, which Jacques considers to be one of Borsheim's important competitive advantages. There are, however, several others. Among them, she believes, is "the fact that we have a tremendous amount of expertise. We have 15 graduate gemologists on staff, for example, and most stores are lucky if they have one. We also do almost everything in-house. We have our own bench shop, we do our own repairs, and we warehouse our gift products here in one location."

The store's location itself is another advantage. "Being in Omaha," she says, "affords us the ability to keep our operating expenses as low as we can possibly keep them." The result, as Warren Buffett explained it some years ago to Berkshire's stockholders, is: "Our operating costs . . . run about 18 percent of sales compared to 40 percent or so at the typical competitor. . . . Just as Wal-Mart, with its 15 percent operating costs, sells at prices that high-cost competitors can't touch, and thereby constantly increases its market share, so does Borsheim's. What works with diapers works with diamonds. Our low prices," he went on, "create huge volume that in turn allows us to carry an extraordinarily broad inventory of goods, running ten or more times the size of that at the typical fine-jewelry store."[10] The company typically has approximately 100,000 items available for sale at any given time. Jacques summarizes it all as: "The most incredible selection at the very best price by the most professional associates with the most exemplary customer service."

Interestingly, despite her obvious devotion to Borsheim's, when asked what her passion is, Jacques unhesitatingly says, "My family. And my job. But my family always comes first, because I believe my family will be with me 'til the bitter end. I also believe I'm going to be at Borsheim's for a very long time, but I'm not quite sure whether it will be to my dying day." She admits, "When I leave here and go home, I really try to close the door. I don't take my work home with me, because I can't. I've got a whole other life when I get home. It's not fair to my family to take it all with me. So, on my drive home, I go from one part of my life into the next part." She admits that balancing those two parts of her life has not always been easy. "The greatest challenge," she has said, "has been the juggling of my personal life as a supportive wife, and mother of two, with the daily commitment to Borsheim's growth and success. I really feel that my choice to be a working mother was the best decision for me. At times, it is difficult when my commitments necessitate traveling, such as when on a jewelry buying trip or when attending various association board meetings that take time away from home and family."[11]

Other than presenting her with the need to resolve this conflict, she does not feel that being a woman has had an effect on her career. "I've never been," she says, "one of those who truly believes that women are treated that differently. I think there was something of an age issue when I became president of the company, because I was only 34 at the time, but I don't know that my sex was really an issue." In fact, she believes that "some of the opportunities that have come my way have come *because* I am a woman. So I feel very, very fortunate to be a woman, because it's opened doors for me. But," she adds, "it wasn't as if I necessarily made the changes. The changes were definitely coming down the road. I was in the right place at the right time. It just so happened I was in the first wave."

In 1999, the Women's Jewelry Association awarded Jacques its prestigious Annual Award for Excellence in Retail. She recognizes that the number of women executives in the jewelry business has increased substantially over the past few years, and, with just two women currently leading Fortune 500 companies, she is aware that there is still much room for improvement. "I think it's very encouraging for young women to see that the jewelry business is no longer the very male-dominated business it used to be," she says. "And I think that my having gone through the ranks of this organization and been named CEO gives a lot of hope to a lot of people. As I tell my staff all the time, I'm not here forever. In fact," she adds, "I suppose one of the greatest things I can hear is when one of the gift-wrap girls tells me that she hopes to have my job one day. I think that's great. So is when I've given a speech at a jeweler's conference and a young woman comes up to me and says, 'You are such an inspiration. You've really excited me.' That kind of thing really makes me feel good." In the meantime, Jacques has done her share in moving women into executive positions. Of the seven executive managers at Borsheim's, two are men and the other five are women—a good indication of what the future may hold for the entire industry.

Jacques believes in giving back to the industry and community that have been so good to her. She currently serves as a Governor of the Gemological Institute of America, Secretary of the Jewelers of America Board, and a member of the Jewelers Vigilance Committee Board. Locally, she serves on the boards of the Omaha Chamber of Commerce, Creighton University, and the American Lung Association, and is a member of the University of Nebraska Medical Center Advisory Council. She has been a member of the Nebraska Chapter of Young Presidents Organization since 1995.

Jacques is convinced that, because it fills a particular need, the industry's future looks extremely bright. "Of course, we sell jewelry," she says, "but we're really in the love-and-romance business. The jewelry is just a token to commemorate very, very special occasions in people's lives. When a young man comes in to buy an engagement ring, it's not the diamond and the metal mounting that he's buying. He's buying the symbol of his love for a woman who he cherishes, and with whom he wishes to spend the rest of his life. So this is a business that deals with happy occasions, and people will never stop having happy occasions. Of course," she admits, "our business is very affected by disposable income. In good times it's extremely strong, and it's less strong during recessions or other quiet times. But even then, it's never dead. People don't miss the occasion because they don't have as much money; they just spend less. So I think the jewelry business is very strong, and we have some great opportunities ahead of us."

Jacques also sees a rosy future for Borsheim's itself. "Our sales have grown exponentially over the last several years," she says, "because we've focused on our core business—providing excellent service, wonderful prices, and great selection. And because of that, a tremendous amount of our business comes from word of mouth. And that's the best. The best business we could possibly get is from somebody who's had a fabulous experience and recommends us to their family and friends. And I think that as long as we continue to do that, we'll continue to grow." Jacques expects that growth will be internal, rather than as a result of acquiring other stores or opening additional branches. "Our single store location, and the ability to maintain our expense ratio," she says, "are among our greatest strengths. And we couldn't replicate or duplicate that. The last thing we'd want to do is open a 4,000–5,000-square-foot store somewhere that would be just the same as the majority of our competitors out there. Our size—and selection—are what differentiate us from everyone else."

Nor does she expect sales on the Internet to become a large part of the company's business. "It's hard to sell love and romance through the click of a mouse," she says. "I don't know of too many young women who would be thrilled to receive an engagement ring that someone clicked and bought for her. There is a huge emotion to that purchase, and it just can't be replicated with a computer." At the same time, Jacques says, Borsheim's is taking advantage of the new technology. "I think it affords us an ability to market to a much broader audience than we've ever been able to in the past. And I think that as the Internet becomes more of an everyday tool for a lot of people, and as more households acquire computers and more people become comfortable with them, it will probably become an excellent medium of communications for us, and that will, ultimately, lead to greater sales. Our addition, in late 2000, of Borsheim's bridal registry on-line has significantly increased our Web-based sales and increased our exposure to existing and new customers."

She recognizes that the Internet will present the company with additional competition, but she believes: "Our biggest competitors will ultimately be some of the larger chains, and the companies that, like us, have a physical presence and a click presence. I don't think that, in the long run, the pure clicks are going to succeed. They can't sustain the margins. And with the marketing dollars they are looking to expend, they're losing money. I don't think they can sustain that for long. I also don't think that the investment money that was available to these upstart companies a year or two years ago will continue to be available. Investment bankers expect some return. They don't expect to just constantly be flushing it away."

As for her own future, Jacques says that she expects to stay with the company for the foreseeable future, and that retirement plans are "a long way off." "Truly," she says, "I've got a lot of working years ahead of me." At Warren Buffett's request, however, she has designated a possible successor. "But," she adds, "when you're my age, it's very hard to groom somebody to take over for you because of the likelihood that you'll be here for another 20 years. You know, nobody wants to sit second fiddle for 20 years."

In the same way that she paints a rosy picture of the jewelry industry and Borsheim's place in it, she is extremely optimistic about the future of Berkshire Hathaway. When asked how the company will look after Buffett is gone, she unhesitatingly says, "Extremely successful. He is guaranteeing that. He is working hard to guarantee that. I think he doesn't want it to be any different after he's gone. I think he wants the growth to continue, and I think that will happen, because he's been remarkably astute in choosing the people he believes are going to be able to do that. I'm sure," she adds, "that he's given tremendous thought to this, and to what these people require, to make sure that the transition goes as smoothly as it can. I truly don't worry about it at all."

But then, Susan Jacques is not the type of person who worries excessively. In fact, she believes that her most admirable trait is her optimism. "I think a positive attitude is contagious," she says, "and I act that way at home as well as at work, because a smile costs nothing and a cheery hello means the world. I think that your attitude, and the attitude of the people around you, make a big difference in your life. If somebody grumbles at you, you're going to react a lot differently than if somebody is happy and cheery. And if you grumble at someone else, they'll react a lot differently than if you are happy and cheery. I think having a positive attitude is important, and I work really hard at it."

## SUSAN JACQUES'S BUSINESS TENETS

- ★ Admit your mistakes.
- ★ Be honest, trustworthy, and have high integrity.
- ★ Try to get along with everyone. Having a positive attitude affects the people around you.
- ★ Assemble a great team to work with.
- ★ Keep your focus. I'm always thinking of how to keep our customers completely happy.

# chapter nineteen

# The Gem of a Retail Merchant—
# Jeff Comment, Helzberg Diamonds

*H*elzberg Diamonds' corporate offices—in a converted JCPenney building—are located in an old downtown area right across the Missouri River in North Kansas City, Missouri. As befits a retailer, there's a jewelry store adjacent to the corporate offices.

People immediately feel comfortable around Jeff Comment. As might be expected, he's passionate about his business but he's equally enthusiastic about his faith, his family, sailing, sports cars, and cigars. This Buffett CEO revealed a few management secrets. First, selling merchandise to consumers on the Internet for more than $300 has proven difficult, and this widens the moat around Berkshire's retail businesses. Second, each individual business has a well-defined succession plan. Just as the Berkshire owners' designated charitable contribution program helps shareholders think about charity, gift giving, and their own estate, the annual exercise of naming, writing down, and mailing to Berkshire the choice for the CEO's successor helps the chief executive think about the business's future management structure. Buffett asks each of his subsidiary managers to mail him annually, or every few years, their confidential choice for a successor. Buffett also performs this management task. He has left a document to be opened at his death. It begins, "Yesterday I died and it is my recommendation that [name] succeed me as CEO of Berkshire Hathaway."

Third, Comment noted that almost every Buffett CEO has a well-defined community involvement and charity program. Fourth, it is difficult to duplicate and capture the passion a founder has for his or her business. Fifth, to compete against Helzberg and the other Berkshire companies, a business needs a strong infrastructure, which requires talent, time, and capital. Helzberg Diamonds has a durable competitive advantage and is very profitable. However, Comment is one Buffett CEO who admits that *he made some mistakes after his company was purchased by Berkshire. Fortunately, he was able to restore the business and it is currently one of the leading jewelry retailers and has the highest per-store sales average.*

Jeffrey W. Comment, chairman and chief executive officer of Helzberg Diamonds of North Kansas City, Missouri, likes to tell how he got to his position. He had been the president and chief operating officer of the company until Barnett C. Helzberg, Jr., who was the chairman, chief executive officer, and principal owner, sold it to Warren Buffett in 1995. "Barnett wanted to retire," Comment says, "and I'd agreed to stay on to run the company. So after the sale went through, I said to Warren, 'Oh, by the way, we haven't talked about what I should call myself.' And Warren said, 'You can call yourself anything you want, as long as it's appropriate for what you're doing.' So I gave myself the title of chairman and chief executive officer. And now, when people ask me if we have a president, I say, 'No, the last one wasn't very good, so we haven't replaced him.'"

Regardless of the title, Jeff Comment insists, "I'm really a salesman. The company can call me chairman and CEO, Warren can call me chairman and CEO, but what I really am is a salesman. I really love to sell. And that's my role in this company—to make sure we're doing everything we can to sell more diamonds." Given his intense devotion to selling, it's not surprising that Comment always knew that's what he wanted to do. Born in Fort Wayne, Indiana, in 1943, he earned a bachelor's degree in marketing from Indiana University in 1966, and, as he remembers, "got my first job out of college with Ford Motor Company. I was a district sales rep, the person between the company and the dealerships. But I didn't do very well at that," he says, "because it wasn't a sales type of job. It was just going back and forth between the company and the dealerships. And I knew that I really wanted to get into something where I could use my passion for selling."

As it turned out, the job with Ford was the last one Comment would ever have that wasn't, in one way or another, involved with selling. "I decided to pursue retailing," he says, "and I went to Florida and went to work for a department store—Maas Brothers in Tampa. They wanted me to go through their executive training program, but they couldn't put me in the class because I was too late. So they said, 'We'll put you on the sales floor for six months, and when the class comes around, we'll put you into it.' So I sold men's accessories for my first Christmas. I was committed to selling more neckties that Christmas than anybody in the company, and I *did* sell more neckties than anybody in the company. I knew after that experience that retailing was the right place for me." The job with Maas Brothers led to others, with greater levels of responsibility, at Burdines and Jordan Marsh in Miami, in 1971 and 1974, respectively. In 1979, he joined John Wanamaker in Philadelphia as a senior vice president, and was subsequently promoted to executive vice president in 1983 and president and COO in 1984. In 1988, Barnett Helzberg, Jr., recruited him to take over as president of the Helzberg family's jewelry business, and Comment moved to Kansas City.

Founded by Barnett's grandfather, Morris Helzberg, in Kansas City, Kansas, in 1915, Helzberg Diamonds was truly a family business. "In the first year, Morris's landlord offered to spend $500 fixing up the store front if he could raise the rent from $25 to $29 a month," his grandson later explained. "After much deliberation, the family decided to accept the offer. From the outset, the concerns of a small store belonged to the family. Serious matters, such as the $4 raise in rent, were debated and discussed for hours. The voice of each family member counted." Morris's youngest son, Barnett, succeeded his father as head of the business in 1945, and his son, Barnett, Jr., in turn succeeded him in 1963.[1]

By 1988, when Jeff Comment became president, the Helzberg business had grown from its original 12-foot-wide store into 70 stores throughout the Midwest, and under Helzberg's and Comment's leadership, it grew larger every year. By 1994, Helzberg Diamonds had 134 stores in 23 states, and annual sales of $282 million. But by that time, at the age of 60, Barnett Helzberg had begun to develop some concerns about all of his assets being placed in one basket, even if it was his own family's basket. Also, he was becoming more interested in his numerous nonprofit community projects. He began considering several options, including selling the company, or taking it public, and he began working with Morgan Stanley to develop a prospectus on his business. He no longer wanted the responsibility of running the company on a day-to-day basis, but he was intent on making sure that whatever he did would not adversely affect the company's staff, its culture, or its philosophy of focusing on customer service. In addition, he wanted to be sure that the company would remain intact in Kansas City, and that it would be able to continue growing in the foreseeable future.[2]

He was still trying to find a solution to his problem that spring, when he had to travel to New York City for some business meetings. At that point, Warren Buffett came into the picture. As Buffett later told the story to his shareholders, "In May 1994, a week or so after the [Berkshire] Annual Meeting, I was crossing the street at 58th and Fifth Avenue in New York, when a woman called out my name. I listened as she told me she'd been to, and had enjoyed, the Annual Meeting. A few seconds later, a man who'd heard the woman stop me did so as well. He turned out to be Barnett Helzberg, Jr., who owned four shares of Berkshire and had also been at our meeting. In our few minutes of conversation, Barnett said he had a business we might be interested in. When people say that, it usually turns out they have a lemonade stand—with potential, of course, to quickly grow into the next Microsoft. So I simply asked Barnett to send me particulars. That, I thought to myself, will be the end of that."[3] But it was not the end of it. Curiously, even though Helzberg was interested in selling the company, and had himself initiated the conversation, he was reluctant to send Buffett the information he'd asked for. As he subsequently remembered, "I'm the kind of guy who likes to get someone's Social Security number before I tell them the time. But finally, I said to myself, 'You idiot, send him the stuff.' "[4]

After reviewing the material, Buffett told Helzberg he was interested. "When Mr. Buffett first wrote me back," Helzberg subsequently said, "he said we're a great deal like Berkshire Hathaway. To me, that's the ultimate compliment."[5] Buffett also invited Helzberg to Omaha for a meeting, and, as Comment remembers it, "Barnett and I flew up on a Monday morning, and we brought all the Morgan Stanley material that we had prepared. But Warren said, 'I'm not interested in the books. I'm not interested in working with Morgan Stanley.' Then he turned to Barnett and said, 'Why do you want to sell it?' Barnett talked for 10 or 15 minutes, and Warren said, 'Okay, you're ready to get out and do some other things in life.' Then he looked over at me and said, 'Tell me about the business and why I should buy it.' I said something kind of corny like, 'Do you want the short version or the long version?' I was trying to be sensitive to his time. But he looked at Barnett and said, 'Well, I am sure that he is going to want a lot of money for the business, so you better give me the long version.' So I talked for about an hour and a half, and answered a dozen questions that he had. When I was finished, he looked at Barnett again and said, 'I'll give you a call in a couple of days and tell you what it's worth.' It was that simple."

Buffett did call Helzberg within a few days. As Helzberg later recalled, "Basically the way to negotiate with Warren Buffett—you don't negotiate. He tells you the deal and that's the deal."[6] All Helzberg was interested in was a stock trade—he didn't want any cash for the business, and eventually he and Buffett were able to agree on a price (which was never made public). They also agreed that Jeff Comment would take over the responsibilities of running it, an arrangement with which Buffett was extremely pleased.

As he subsequently told Berkshire's shareholders, "It took us a while to get together on price, but there was never any question in my mind that, first, Helzberg's was the kind of business that we wanted to own, and, second, Jeff was our kind of manager. In fact, we would not have bought the business if Jeff had not been there to run it. Buying a retailer without good management is like buying the Eiffel Tower without an elevator." He added: "Though he was certainly under no obligation to do so, Barnett shared a meaningful part of his proceeds from the sale with a large number of his associates. When someone behaves that generously, you know you are going to be treated right as a buyer."[7]

Helzberg was equally happy with the arrangement. "Warren Buffett was our dream from day one, a ridiculous dream," he said.[8] "I am extremely pleased with the fact that we have been able to take a three-generation business and allow it to continue its growth and prosperity under the respected umbrella of Berkshire Hathaway. I believe this ownership change is a win for the associates of Helzberg's Diamond Shops, a win for the investors of Berkshire Hathaway, a win for our family, and, most importantly, a win for the customers of our fine company."[9] For his part, Jeff Comment was, and continues to be, equally pleased that the company was sold to Berkshire.

The sale has had almost no impact on the company. Comment says, "The only change that really took place happened the day after we were purchased. Warren called me up and said, 'Guess what you get to do today.' And I said, 'What's that?' And he said, 'Start breaking all your banking relationships, because from now on I'm your bank.' I was very professional about it, but a couple of times I was snickering—for all those years that [the banks] didn't want to give me what I wanted. But other than our bank relationships, Berkshire Hathaway hasn't asked me to do anything that's really changed the business. There have been some strategic redirections, but that would have happened in the normal course of events anyway. And they were all triggered by us, not by Berkshire. Nothing else has been changed."

Even if Buffett were the kind of chairman who was inclined to meddle in the companies' various businesses, he has had very little reason to do so with Helzberg Diamonds. There was only one instance in which he might have been tempted to get involved. "We had a fairly good year in '95," Comment says, "and that was the year he bought us. And then the first full year after he bought us, we went into the toilet. We had a serious downturn in 1996, for a whole bunch of reasons. We overexpanded. We outran our people. Zales came out of bankruptcy with a clean balance sheet so it was a viable competitor again. Signet dumped a whole bunch of money in Sterling [another competitor]. And," he adds, "I fell asleep.

"So I called Warren and gave him the December numbers, and a forecast for the year, and it wasn't good. He said, 'Well, what do you want to do?' And I said, 'I need 30 days'—that's about all I thought I'd get—'and I would like to come to Omaha and tell you what we're going to do.' So I went and talked to him—that's the only trip [after being acquired] I've ever taken to Omaha to see Warren Buffett—and I told him that we were going to make some changes in the company's infrastructure, as well as some other changes. I wasn't there looking for his approval, just to tell him what we were doing. He wanted to know the projection for 1997, and he wanted to know when the business would be back to being the business that he had bought. I told him we would stabilize it in '97 and have a significant turnaround in '98. We stabilized it in '97, and we had a significant turnaround in '98. Since then, we've just kept going, with our 2000 performance the best in 86 years."

The company has been increasing the number of its stores every year. Helzberg Diamonds now has 236 stores in 38 states, and is the fifth largest jewelry chain in the country. "But," Comment says, "the most exciting thing about Helzberg Diamonds is our store average. We have the highest store average in the industry—close to $2.2 million. A lot of our competitors are between $1 million and $1.5 million. Some of them are getting up to around $1.5 million, but we're still way ahead of everybody else."

Helzberg's secrets for such a huge store average are: selecting premium locations, being on the "A" list of premium shopping-mall developers, spending more money up front, and building first-class store upgrades, trained-in-store personnel, merchandise assortments, and a strong branding component.

Putting all of those components together, Helzberg's annual sales in 2001 should exceed $500 million with estimated annual pretax profits of $50 million. This represents more than a 40 percent growth in sales since Berkshire acquired Helzberg.

The vast majority of the Helzberg stores are located in malls, but approximately 20 percent of them are stand-alone stores or, as Comment calls them, "free standers."

Comment believes that much of the company's success can be credited to the fact that Helzberg Diamonds was one of the first in the jewelry business to perceive of itself in a different and nontraditional way, and to act accordingly. "The jewelry industry was kind of enamored with the product, with jewelry," he says, "and . . . didn't really understand retailing. They didn't understand that a jewelry store shouldn't be seen as a jewelry store but, instead, as a retail business that sells jewelry. There's a big difference. And now we're really retailers. That doesn't mean that we don't understand the product. What it means is that we understand that the retailing principles of how to deliver a product are every bit as important as the product itself."

The first such principle, Comment says, concerns the ambiance of the store. "You have to design your store," he says, "so the customer can come in and feel comfortable in it. We build the best-looking stores in the fine jewelry category. Nobody builds a better-looking mall store than we do. The second thing," he continues, "is assortment planning. You have to buy an assortment that will guarantee that you are covering your categories, your price points, and you have to display it in such a way that when customers look at the showcase, they see something that's attractive, something they want to pick up and buy. Our niche used to be middle, and you can still buy a $99 piece of fine jewelry in our stores, but today our niche is middle with a nice swath of upper middle. We know our customers and are true to them.

"The third thing is that you have to make sure that your people are geared toward service. We have a very focused associate team—people who want to take care of the customer, who've got a passion for what they do. They conduct themselves better, and have more product knowledge, than most of our competitors. In fact," he says, "our cornerstone is our incredible team of people. Anybody can build a beautiful store. Anybody can buy the product. Anybody can copy our catalogue or our radio ads. But you just can't copy people. It's taken years and years and years for us to build a group of loyal people." Comment concludes, "You have to understand exactly what your branding and your marketing should look like, so that it ties the ambiance of the store, the assortment, and the service components together. That kind of thinking didn't exist in the jewelry category. It existed in some other specialty retailing—The Gap and The Limited were doing a pretty job of it years ago. But fine jewelry people weren't. That's what kick-started us. We started doing some of it way before the rest of the pack, and that's how we got a head start. We built a lot of market share, in the '90s, that we've been able to maintain."

Perhaps not surprisingly, when asked to catalogue his accomplishments since joining Helzberg, Comment first says, "[Seeing that] the business has become much more of a retailer than a jewelry store. We've changed the focus, and I am very proud of that." He considers his second greatest accomplishment to be "that the professionalism of our associates has improved dramatically. When I started, we had about 70 stores and about 800 associates. Now we have 236 stores and 3,000 associates. But even though the business has tripled in size, the associates are still passionate about it. We haven't lost that." The third most important accomplishment, he says, is: "I am proud to give to Berkshire Hathaway investors the kind of return they are getting from us. We're a very, very profitable business—in the top 10 percent in the jewelry category, at least as far as our pretax profit rate is concerned."

The company's excellent performance has no doubt enhanced the good relationship that Jeff Comment shares with his boss. That relationship, however, began somewhat differently from Buffett's relationships with his other operating managers, because Comment was an employee rather than an owner of Helzberg Diamonds. As a rule, Buffett buys companies from their owner/managers, with the understanding that those individuals will stay on to run the companies. In this instance, however, the owner was not actually running the company—Jeff Comment was, and was expected to continue to do so after the merger.

Although the acquisition scenario was therefore somewhat different, Buffett knew about it in advance, and, apparently, neither he nor Comment ever had a problem with it. "Barnett was such an honest guy," Comment says, "that he acknowledged what was going on both publicly in the company and with the people he was trying to sell the business to. And, of course, he shared it with Warren. He would say things like, 'I'm the majority owner, but Jeff's the guy that runs it, and has been running it. And he knows the business better than anybody. Everybody in the company looks to him for leadership today, they don't look to me anymore. I mean, my name is still on the door, and it always will be. But Jeff's the guy in charge.'

"There was such honesty in that," Comment says, "it probably helped Warren's trust level with me. I mean here was a guy like Barnett who had entrusted a guy like me with most of his net worth. That said volumes to Warren. I think he knew that getting me would be as good as getting the owner who sold him the company. Even so, he did ask me if I wanted to run the company, and when he did, I said, 'I love this business. I love the people in it. I am dedicated to it, and I want it to be everything it can be. I think being a subsidiary of Berkshire would be a terrific deal for the business, and I would enjoy working for you.' "

Like the other CEOs, Comment has found that he does indeed enjoy working for Buffett. When asked how it feels to be part of his boss's inner circle, he says, "Secure. It's not a false sense of security. It's the kind of security that you can go out and be everything you can be for your company, your associates, and your investors, and you don't have to worry about the political stuff. That's pretty tough to do in a big organization. I try to emulate the sense of security I feel with Warren here as well." Comment adds, "Warren and I are two very, very different people, but we really trust one another, and we have a high degree of respect for one another. I think all his managers are like that. But there is a lot of trust. People on the outside don't understand that chemistry. That chemistry is what's missing in a lot of businesses today. They're functional, they're tactically correct, but, boy, you lose the passion, and you lose that love of the business. That doesn't happen here.

"In his own way," Comment says, "and he would probably bristle at this, I think Warren is a genius. Sometimes people exhibit genius in a cold, mechanical, computerlike way. But Warren is an incredibly cordial, warm, personable person. Two years ago, because a lot of our store managers had never met him, I invited him down to one of our leadership conferences, invited him for supper. He doesn't do this very often. But we called it 'A Night with Warren.' We had about 250 people. We had a little stage, a little card table with a cover over it, a couple of Cherry Cokes and a microphone on the card table, and one crummy old wooden chair behind it. I mean, it looked like we had just gone broke. Warren sat down at the table, and he started off with a couple of one-liners, a couple of jokes, and then he sat back and said, 'Ask me anything you want, anything that you've ever thought that you would want to ask me.'

"Now, you know," Comment continues, "Warren never gives investment advice. But there was this one store manager who's divorced, 30 years old, with two children, and she said, 'Here's where I am, this is what I'm doing, what would you suggest?' And he said, 'I don't do that, except for you.' He talked about diversification, about being a little more aggressive when you're 30, but being a little bit more conservative when you're 40 or 50. He talked about the stock market. He said, 'Don't be scared of the ups and down. Don't buy and sell. Don't get trapped in that stuff. Don't look at the newspaper every day. Don't get spooked.' He talked for 10 minutes. When he was finished, he said, 'And that's free, and that's just for you.' But it was just like a dad talking to his daughter, except it was in front of 250 people. It was priceless. And two hours later, I finally had to get up and close the thing down because I could see that he was getting tired. But our store managers just loved him. That is the Warren Buffett people don't know," Comment concludes.

As far as his own relationship with Buffett is concerned, Comment is exceedingly modest. Although Buffett is known for expanding his circle of competence by asking his operating managers to recommend other companies in their industries that might be appropriate members of the Berkshire family, and has recently purchased Ben Bridge Jewelers, based in Seattle, Comment insists that he doesn't deserve any credit for the deal. "I would never in a million years take credit for the Ben Bridge deal," he says vehemently. "I'll let all the guys at Ben Bridge take credit for that." He will admit, however, that "Warren used me as a resource. He and I had a couple of conversations," Comment says, "and every time we got off the phone, I'd hang up and say, 'Boy, I really feel good, I gave Warren Buffett some advice.' Warren didn't ask me for a recommendation, but, very early on, I told him that Ben Bridge was a business full of people with great character. They had a nice niche in the marketplace. Sometime later, we were at the Berkshire shareholder meeting and he pulled me aside and put his arm around me and said something like, 'I want you to know that we closed the deal on Bridge, and I will be announcing it within a week or so.'"

Comment is clearly reluctant to claim any influence over Warren Buffett, but he readily admits that Buffett has influenced him. He doesn't credit his boss with helping him to develop his management style, beliefs, or philosophy; he says that Buffett "has reinforced them. I think that one of the reasons he bought Helzberg Diamonds was that there was a great chemistry between the two of us. He and I have like minds on many philosophical issues, and we have an appreciation for each other, as well as respect. And because of that, I think he's reinforced a lot of the basic values that I have." When asked about those who did influence the way he conducts business, he mentions, first, his mother. "She was probably one of the biggest influences in my life," he says. "She's got the salesmanship in her. And she was a buyer and a salesperson, and she's got a lot of personality and charisma."

Comment describes the management style these individuals helped him develop as "leading by setting the direction of the business. That's number one," he says. "Making sure that we are true to our mission. I think any good CEO has to do that. You can't delegate that. But once you've done that," he adds, "you have to put a team of people around you who are tactically competent to carry out the strategy, and then give them the opportunity to do it. Sometimes," he admits, "I think I get a little too far from some of those tactical things. But I've got seven wonderful vice presidents who are very tactically equipped to do their jobs, and who do a superior job. And, because I leave them alone and let them do their jobs, they have the fulfillment of running their aspects of the business." One thing he does keep a close eye on, though, is the numbers. "I know where the business is," he says. "I know the stores that are rocket ships. I know the stores that are really struggling. I know the merchandise categories having problems. I know, for the most part, why those stores or categories are struggling. I also usually have a pretty good sense of what has to be done to fix them."

When asked about what he considers the most important elements in the makeup of a successful operating manager, he says, "The very first— and it's always been this way, although it's especially true in today's world—is character. I would write character and underscore it and underscore it and underscore it. And that's exactly the way Warren feels. He tells his managers that 'We can lose a sale, we can lose a deal, but we can't ever afford to lose our character and integrity.' And he's right on the money. And I've got to be the point person for that in this business. I've got to be the role model for character in everything I do." The second most important element, he says, is to have "a passion for the mission. To understand the mission and help the company choreograph the mission. I have an incredible passion for our mission, and I want everyone around to think, 'I am going to have to put on my sneakers to keep up with Jeff, because he has such a passion for what we're doing.' And finally," he says, "you have to continue to push yourself to make sure that you're personally equipped to do what you've got to do to make the company successful. And that could mean a lot of things. For me, right now, that means getting a little more involved in technology, to learn more about it so we can make better use of the technology that's available."

There are areas, of course, in which he feels he already has the competence he needs to do his job. "I have good instincts," he says, "I have a good instinct for where this business belongs in the niche of specialty retailing. That's something that has probably been acquired over 30 years, but you also have a natural instinct for it. We've had opportunities to do things with this business that I looked at and said, 'No, I'm not going to go there.' For example, we had an international expansion opportunity. A group from Japan approached us to open 50 Helzberg stores in five years. I declined the offer and then one of our competitors did go there and got hurt."

In addition, he says, "I am entrepreneurial. I'm always willing to allow the company to do different things. But, at the same time, I make sure that we stay extremely focused and never forget who our customers are and how we're creating a brand out there to be associated with them." In the end, though, he feels that his greatest competence is the ability to "put a group of people together, and lead them, and let them feel like they're running their shows. I can get far enough above it," he says, "so that I know when we are getting off track, and I can bring my plane down to 10,000 feet. But the people who work for me like me to be at 40,000 feet, and I like to be at 40,000 feet. And it really works well. But," he adds, "you have to have the right group around you to be able to do that."

Being a leader is not, however, just something Comment does at Helzberg Diamonds. He is also a leader in his community and is deeply involved in numerous community organizations, including the Greater Kansas City Chamber of Commerce, the Civic Council of Greater Kansas City, Heart of America, United Way, and the William Jewell College, among others. "I love them all," he says, "and they all do good work, and they are all good for the city." But he says that the organization closest to his heart is Santa's

Gifts, a philanthropic program he founded in 1995. Santa's Gifts sends Santa Clauses to visit pediatric hospitals for the two weeks before Christmas every year, and gives each child an "I Am Loved Bear," which is Helzberg Diamonds' company mascot. Comment himself dons a Santa suit and visits children all around the country—in 2000, he visited nine pediatric hospitals in Dallas, Chicago, Philadelphia, and Kansas City. There were over 40 Santas in the program worldwide, and they gave bears to about 15,000 children, along with Polaroid pictures of themselves with Santa. For the past two years, General Electric and FedEx have been major partners. "Everyone wins with these types of programs," says Comment. "They are good for your company, your consumers, your associates, and your trade partners. And they touch the lives of the participants in any number of ways."[10]

Comment's experience in the program also led him to write and self-publish a book titled *Jonathan Through Santa's Eyes*. The book was inspired, he says, by an 11-year-old named Jonathan, whom Comment visited in Lutheran General Hospital in Chicago in 1997. "Jonathan was dying of AIDS," Comment recalls, "and the nurse told me that he probably had only a month to live. She wasn't even sure he wanted to visit with Santa. But I went into his room. And his eyes lit up and he sat up in his wheelchair. At first," Comment says, there were a number of people in his room—his mother, a nurse, a child life person, a public relations person, and a cameraman. Jonathan could no longer talk—his vocal chords were gone—but as I talked to him, he made noises and motioned with his hands. One by one, the people who were in the room broke down and had to leave until, after about 15 minutes, it was just Jonathan and me. We had a wonderful time. And even though he couldn't talk, in his own way he was able to say to Santa, 'I am glad you came, you really made my day.' It was an incredibly moving experience," Comment adds. "He was a real inspiration to me."

Both the publication of the book—proceeds are donated to the Elizabeth Glaser Pediatric AIDS Foundation—and Comment's involvement in the Santa's Gifts program are a reflection of his faith. "I'm a Christian," he says, "and although I don't talk about my Christian faith a lot in the business, I would hope that it really is a light and a beacon of the person I want to be." His faith was also the impetus for an earlier book Comment wrote and self-published, *Mission in the Marketplace*. "I was in transition at the time," he remembers. "I was the president of John Wanamaker in Philadelphia, and we were folding it into Woodward and Lothrop in Washington.

And I was tearing apart a lot of the things that I had spent eight or nine years building in Philadelphia, and it was difficult. But my faith made it easier. And the book, which grew out of that experience, was an effort to convey how you can live your faith and still be a successful businessperson, how it will actually help you be a better businessperson." One aspect of that faith, as he expressed it to a reporter for the *Kansas City Star* in 1997, was the importance of integrity. "One of the primary principles of the Old Testament and the New Testament," he said, "is character in treating and dealing with people in a very honest fashion. This doesn't mean you're soft, but a leader with conviction and character. If you run a business with conviction and character, you will get a lot further than the cutthroat guys."[11]

He did not always feel that way. "When I was back in my mid-twenties," Comment says, "I was rough-and-tumble, drank too much, and was kind of a crazy young man. And one day I went into a Methodist church and filled out one of those little cards. Don't ask me why. I wasn't very interested in anybody calling on me. The pastor of the church was an old Navy chaplain, and he was a man's man kind of guy. And at eleven o'clock one Thursday night, somebody knocked on my door. I was drinking a beer and smoking a cigar, and it turned out to be the pastor of the church. For about six months, the guy came by almost every Thursday night and had a beer with me. He became my best friend, and the inspiration for me to find my faith as a Christian. And when I did, it changed the whole direction of my life. I started changing my value systems and I began to think about how I was living my life. And that," he continues, "is when I met my wife Martha, who had a very similar value system. If it hadn't been for the chaplain, Martha wouldn't have given me the time of day, because she sure wouldn't have been interested in the old Jeff." Not surprisingly, he considers finding his faith and finding his wife to be two of the highlights of his life.

He says that his wife has had the greatest impact on his personal life. "She's my greatest critic," he says, "and of course, the love of my life. We've been married 30 years, and a lot of who I am today, she has helped mold. She has truly been a partner." Among the many things they share are their two adult children—Ryan and Kristen. But Comment has numerous other interests as well, including collecting antique sports cars and sailing. In 1999, he had an opportunity to fulfill one of his almost-lifelong dreams. "The CEO of Citizen Watches called me," he told a reporter for the *Kansas City Star,* "and said: 'I understand you love sailing.' He said in kind of a kidding way: 'Have you ever been on an America's Cup boat?' I said, 'No, that's a little out of my class.'" Out of his class or not, Comment was subsequently offered—and accepted—the seventeenth-man spot in the first trial-heat race on Dennis Conner's boat, which was being sponsored in part by Citizen Watches.[12] Such an opportunity is, as Comment is quick to point out, something out of the ordinary, and not something he expects to happen on a regular basis.

At age 57, he has no interest in retiring and every intention of staying with Helzberg Diamonds. Although he has received job offers from several companies, he says, "I have no interest in working anyplace else, for three reasons. One, I feel a real obligation and responsibility to Berkshire Hathaway. Berkshire Hathaway and Warren made a significant investment in this business when they bought it. And I was primary in selling the business to Berkshire Hathaway, so I feel obligated to Berkshire Hathaway. Second, I feel a real sense of responsibility and obligation to the 3,000 people working for us. I don't treat that lightly. Every decision I make can affect their livelihood. And they have entrusted me with the business. That may sound a little old-fashioned, but to me that's pretty important. And, finally, I'm just really having a lot of fun and I feel like I'm making a contribution. So, when somebody calls me and says, 'Hey, how would you like to go to work for ABC company. It's a $5-billion company and you can get in the big leagues,'" I tell them, 'Hey, I am in the big leagues.'"

As far as the future of his "big league" company is concerned, Comment says that he is hoping to continue the same kind of growth the company has experienced in the recent past. He has no intention, however, of doing it through major acquisitions. "I've looked at acquisitions," he says, "and looked at acquisitions, and looked at acquisitions, and I think that it would just be the worst thing in the world for us. We might be able to do a little 20-store deal," he explains, "but, for us, with our culture of service, and service being one of the biggest contributors to our high store average, going out and acquiring a 100-store chain would bring us to our knees." Citing the company's current per-store average of close to $2.2 million, he says, "We have a real goal of getting to $2.5 million per store. While we are doing that, we would like to think that we could open up 10 percent more stores every year. That means we are going to continue on a track of opening 20 or 25 stores a year and continue to grow sales per store. Every one of those new stores is going to be a little gem. It is going to be a perfect store in a perfect mall. It's our store. Our look. Our product. Our people. That's the way we do it."

He does not expect the Internet to play a significant role in his business. "We have a wonderful Web site that we're very proud of, and it educates the customer about the company, the jewelry products, and then absolutely pushes the customer to our stores. We've got an Internet store, but I'd go broke if I had to live off the sales of the Internet store. We're finding 95 percent of the people who visit our Web site want to go to the button that tells them where the nearest store is. By and large, it's really difficult to close a sale over $300 on the Internet. Our average ticket on the Internet is much less than what it is in our stores. People like to look at the diamond. If they are going to spend $1,000 or $2,000 on a diamond, they want to see what it looks like, because every diamond is different. We think the Web site is a part of the branding strategy, and we're getting more and more hits per day, but we're not going to try to do a lot of business on the Internet per se."

Comment does, however, think that the outlook for America's $43-billion retail jewelry business[13] is very good. "The [Baby] Boomers are coming of age," he says. "There's a lot of money moving around, a lot of wealth. And as more and more of that wealth starts maturing, and people get tired of just seeing their money sitting in mutual funds, there is going to be a lot of jewelry bought both in America and worldwide. I think the jewelry industry is on the front end of a wonderful, wonderful 10 years." Nor does Comment seem to be particularly concerned about competition. "I expect that our biggest competitors will continue to be the national retailers," he says, "but we will continue to differentiate ourselves. Trying to catch us will make us stronger."

As for the future of Berkshire Hathaway, Comment says, "Personally, I think there will be a day when Warren will have to put some infrastructure together. I mean, it will still be minute compared to the infrastructure of most companies, but he's got such a large group now that I think putting something together will make some sense. And," he adds, "if there was a little infrastructure at Berkshire Hathaway, and I didn't get to talk to Warren every week, it wouldn't be the end of the world. As much as I enjoy him, I want what's good for our associates and Berkshire Hathaway investors. One way or another, it will have to change. You just can't go forever and not have something change.

"People ask if I'm worried about when Warren Buffett retires. I'm not worried. There is so much brainpower in the operating managers that Warren Buffett has, and I'm sure he's done the work that's needed to make sure that this company is in good hands after he retires or dies. It's the old trust thing. I trust him. We've talked about succession planning, but he doesn't tell me what the infrastructure is going to look like, who the key individuals are going to be. He doesn't get into the intricate details, but he's just too savvy not to have that in place." Nor is Comment worried about a lot of changes taking place after Buffett is gone. "I don't think it's going to look a lot different," he says. "I don't see Berkshire changing radically. I just don't. There may be two or three people running Berkshire, rather than just Warren, but if the people in those key positions are committed to the way Berkshire operates, I think the company will do just fine. I think the managers of the businesses of Berkshire Hathaway will continue to run their businesses in a very similar way."

One thing that Jeff Comment clearly is concerned about is his legacy. "I don't have any wild goal to be the champion jeweler of the world," he says. "What I do want is to leave a legacy that people would want to emulate, a legacy that I would be proud of, that my kids would be proud of, and that my wife would be proud of." As he told a meeting of the Jeweler's Charity Fund in 2000, "Life for me is about the word 'Legacy.' I often tell my kids that the key to life is: 'What did you accomplish to make this world a better place?' As you take a look at what kind of a legacy you want to leave in your life, it does come back to making sure your priorities are right. For myself: it's faith, then it's family, and then it's how I treat all of those people who have been brought into my life over time."[14]

## JEFF COMMENT'S BUSINESS TENETS

- ★ Be a role model for your employees and your customers.
- ★ Be passionate about your business.
- ★ Stick to your core strengths and your business will flourish. We emphasize great service, comfortable stores, and an array of products that we know cover our customers' needs.

# The Newcomers—Randy Watson, Justin Brands; and Harrold Melton, Acme Building Brands

*T*hey *are newcomers to the Berkshire family of businesses, but Justin Boots and Acme Brick have been in business for a long time, and each firm has all the characteristics of a classic Buffett investment.*

*It is fitting that Berkshire, a conglomerate that is technologically shy, would buy the premier western boot brand and would invest in a brick company. While everyone else was chasing Internet and clicks-and-mortar deals, Buffett and Berkshire were closing this boots-and-bricks merger.*

*Berkshire's previous investments in the shoe business have been disappointing, but Justin Brands seems likely to do better.*

*John Justin was too ill to give an interview, so John Roach, the current chairman of the board, who is a longtime board member and friend, agreed to talk about John Justin, Justin Industries, Acme Brick, Justin Boots, Warren Buffett, and Berkshire Hathaway. Roach had a unique vantage point. As former chairman and CEO of Radio Shack, he was a participant, on both sides of the table, in hundreds of mergers, acquisitions, and partnership and business deals.*

*Roach is a tall Texan, a southern gentleman, and the quintessential CEO. If Hollywood were casting a handsome Texas business chief or politician, John Roach would be an easy selection.*

*Along came Harrold Melton, chief executive of Acme Brick. And then came Randy Watson, CEO of Justin Brands, so I ended up with a three-way interview. They were also the first CEOs I'd met who were attired in Justin black cowboy boots.*

Justin Industries, based in Fort Worth, Texas, is unusual in that it consists of two groups of entirely different companies. Essentially, their only connection is that they are part of the same corporate entity. The oldest company in each of the groups has been in business for more than 100 years. The older of the two, Justin Boot, was founded in 1879 by Herman J. Justin in Spanish Fort, Texas, and the younger, Acme Brick, was founded in 1891 by George E. Bennett in Fort Worth. They were brought together in 1968, when First Worth Corporation, which then owned Acme Brick, bought Justin Boots from John S. Justin, Jr., the grandson of the boot company's founder. Justin became chairman of First Worth in 1969, renamed it Justin Industries in 1972, and spent the next 25 years building it up by purchasing additional companies and adding them to the groups.

But by April 1999, Justin was 82 and in ill health. After being in the family business for 61 years, he felt the time had come to give up his day-to-day involvement. In anticipation of selling the company, Justin had developed a plan to make some changes. On his retirement, the corporation's board appointed one of its members, John Roach, to act as a nonexecutive chairman and oversee the final implementation of the plan. Roach, currently 62 years old, had been the chairman and CEO of Tandy Corporation—now Radio Shack Corporation—and had just given up the latter position when Justin's board asked for his help. Experienced in corporate reorganizations and a veteran of hundreds of mergers and acquisitions, Roach was the right man at the right time for Justin Industries. "John did an excellent job of growing the businesses over the years," Roach says of Justin, "and was certainly a gentleman of great integrity, great stature, and great pride in his companies. He was really an icon in the western world. He felt that the plan we were implementing was a good one, but he also felt that he probably didn't have the energy, at that age, to be able to execute it. The heart of the plan," Roach explains, "was to gather the various companies of Justin Industries into two companies, one in footwear and one in building materials, so they could be made entirely separate operations." As part of that effort, during the summer of 1999, the corporation's board named Randy Watson, who had been with Justin Boot since 1993, as CEO of the newly named Justin Brands, and Harrold E. Melton, who started with Acme Brick in 1958, as CEO of the newly named Acme Building Brands.

"We made good progress on the plan," Roach says. "We were able to integrate the various companies into the two groups and to get their managements functioning. We also devised different growth strategies for each of them, because we knew that if they were going out on their own, they would both have to be in a strong growth mode. Both of the companies had nice increases in sales and earnings. By the late spring of 2000, a little over a year later," Roach remembers, "we had interest from several people who wanted to buy either the footwear operation or the building materials one, but no one who was interested in both. Then one day the phone rang, and it was Warren Buffett."

As Buffett later explained to Berkshire Hathaway's shareholders, "On May 4th, I received a fax from Mark Jones, a stranger to me, proposing that Berkshire join a group to acquire an unnamed company. I faxed him back, explaining that with rare exceptions we don't invest with others, but would happily pay him a commission if he sent details and we later made a purchase. He replied that the 'mystery company' was Justin."[1] At that point, Buffett contacted John Roach. "Warren had clearly studied the businesses," Roach says, "and he expressed a strong interest in both of them. I kept waiting for him to tell me exactly how he wanted to proceed, but he didn't make any suggestions. So finally I said, 'Warren, how do we want to go forward? Do you want to send in some accountants to review the books? Do you want to have factory tours and review the operations?' And he said, 'John, you know Berkshire Hathaway's headquarters operates with only 12.8 employees [one employee works four days per week], and I don't have anybody to send to do a review of the books, or to visit the plants either. If anybody's going to come, I'm going to have to come myself.' I said, 'Great,' and we made arrangements for him to visit.

"We were still talking to other people at the time," Roach says, "and the day that Warren came to see us, one of them had their accountants poring through Justin's books in the corporate offices. So John Justin and I met Warren at my office"—which was not at the Justin Industries' headquarters but in the Tandy building in downtown Fort Worth—"and he encouraged John to tell him the real history of the business, how it evolved through his family, and how it came together. Of course, John loved being able to tell the story. And when he was finished, Warren started talking about Berkshire Hathaway, and after maybe three quarters of an hour, it was clear that John was very impressed with Warren. Then John (Justin) left and the management team of the companies came in and made a relatively short presentation. Warren had said he'd studied the numbers and didn't want to get into a lot of detail on financial history. What he really wanted to know about was the companies' competitive advantages, positioning, and market shares, and who their competitors were.

"Of course," Roach says, "he also wanted to get a sense of the people who would be running the business. We spent the whole day together, and all that time he was doing two things: he was gaining information so he could understand the business better, and he was gently selling Berkshire Hathaway. At the end of the day, we talked about how much the businesses might be worth, and discussed some possible price ranges. Quite frankly," Roach admits, "while the price ranges were very interesting, and pretty much where we ended up, I was delaying him to give these other people who had an interest in the business time to get to a point where they could make an offer too. We were going to have a regularly scheduled board meeting a few weeks later, so I told all of the people who had an interest that we needed to have their proposals in by the day of the meeting. Naturally, even though I gave Warren, and everyone else, a couple of days to get it in, he had it in within a couple of hours. He sent it by fax, and then he called and asked if we'd gotten it. I said we had, and he said, 'I haven't shown it to my attorney yet, but this is what the deal is.' I considered that a big plus, because sometimes attorneys have a way of prolonging and complicating deals.

"We'd also invited everyone who was interested in buying the company to make presentations at the board meeting. Warren wasn't able to come so he sent his outside attorney, Bob Denham, from Berkshire's Los Angeles-based law firm, Munger, Tolles, and Olson. Bob made a little presentation, and, at about five o'clock in the afternoon, we told him that we would like to work toward a definitive contract with him. We also told him that there were about half a dozen points we'd like to have included in the deal, and he said he could get ahold of Warren in about 20 minutes. Sure enough, about 20 minutes later, Warren arrived at a hotel somewhere and Bob got him on the phone. He went over the points we'd raised, and Warren said, 'Sure, that's great. That's the way we should have planned to do it in the first place.' The definitive contract was put together in a couple of days, and we announced the deal less than a week later."

Both sides were, not surprisingly, very satisfied with the arrangement. When the merger was announced, John Roach said, "John Justin and I are extremely pleased that one of America's most admired companies is acquiring Justin Industries. Warren Buffett's and Berkshire's business philosophy and practice will provide current management the opportunity to build on our strong market presence and on our corporate traditions. We believe this acquisition is great for our shareholders, our customers, our employees, and our communities." Buffett, in turn, said, "Berkshire has over 60,000 [now over 100,000] employees, but only 13 people work in our 4,000-square-foot home office. We not only encourage extraordinary autonomy in our operating businesses, we depend on it. Justin will fit this pattern perfectly. It is an absolutely first-class business run by first-class people. The managers who have produced Justin's outstanding results will continue to run operations from Fort Worth just as they have in the past."[2] Despite this clear statement of intent, a reporter subsequently asked Buffett if he would be going to Fort Worth to check on and/or run the businesses. Buffett's response was "No. The management that's there is supposed to do that. If John (Justin) wants to invite me down to have a steak, I'll come down and have a steak, but I'm going to let the managements run the businesses."

John Justin celebrated the closing of the sale by giving Buffett a pair of ostrich-skin cowboy boots.[3] Having guided his business into the hands of someone who would preserve it, John Justin died seven months later.

When asked whether he thought Buffett bought Justin Industries for the boots or the bricks, John Roach says, "I guess there's a certain amount of romance to the boot business and its ties to the Old West. But the value in the company is really in the brick and building material business. It's not very glamorous, but it's the big cash producer overall. Warren paid $22 a share for the business"—for a total of approximately $600 million—"but, out of that, probably $18 [approximately $500 million] should be attributed to the building materials business and the other $4 [approximately $100 million] to the footwear business. I think, though," Roach adds, "that the real reason Warren was interested in Justin was that we had a strong, competitive position, strong market share in each of our businesses, old and well-established trademarks that were highly recognized, and management teams that he was comfortable with. I think he recognized that, in Justin Industries, he was dealing with people with a very high level of integrity, which isn't the case in every business situation. Plus, a lot of our people had been here for a very long time and had a lot of experience, and Warren wanted to utilize that tenure and that experience."

Roach was, in fact, extremely impressed with Buffett overall. "It's very clear," he says, "that the managers of the companies he's acquired over the years have tended to stay with him because he gives them free rein. You just don't know of many acquisitions where management continues to have free rein, and where the acquirer doesn't have some grand scheme for how to improve the business, even though in most cases they don't know much about it. Warren knows he's bought a good business, and he's going to let the people in charge continue to run it the way they have been. He did," Roach notes, "come to collect that steak, and while he was here, he spent about an hour with the management of each of the two companies. He made it very clear to each of them that they were an independent operation, and that it was up to them to do their planning and execution, and to continue to strengthen their competitive advantage in the market. Overall," he says, "it's been the least contentious negotiation and transition that I've ever seen. But that's because Warren is in a different league than everyone else. He's unique among the people I've dealt with, and I've had the opportunity to deal with some of the best-known executives in this country. He definitely marches to the tune of a different drummer."

Given his positive appraisal of Buffett, it's not surprising that Roach has equally positive things to say about Berkshire Hathaway and its future. "Berkshire is clearly a value-driven company that has a wonderful perspective," he says. "It's a different perspective, but a wonderful one, on building value over the long term, as opposed to being driven by quarterly earnings. I don't think there's any question but that a long term, value-driven philosophy has got to be very worthwhile. It's proven to be in the past for Berkshire in many ways. The fact is that when you get down to it, value is value, and, in the final analysis, having great brands, great market share, and great cash flow has got to be a winning strategy."

Other than the already planned separation of Justin's two businesses into freestanding units within Berkshire Hathaway, almost no changes have taken place since the merger. One of the few changes was the retirement of two corporate executives—J.T. Dickenson, president and chief executive officer of Justin Industries, and Richard Savitz, senior vice president and chief financial officer—whose positions were eliminated as a result of the two groups' separation. Other than that, Roach says, "More than Berkshire Hathaway telling or asking us how to proceed, it was us asking Berkshire Hathaway how they wanted to proceed. And the most common answer was 'Do it however you think best.'" As planned, John Roach stayed on for a time after the merger to help in the transition. And when he left a few months later as Justin Industries was dissolved, the management of the two operations was placed entirely in the hands of Randy Watson at Justin Brands and Harrold Melton at Acme Building Brands.

The company Watson took control of in the spring of 2000 had been founded in 1879, when Herman J. ("Joe") Justin, a leather craftsman from Lafayette, Indiana, began custom-making boots for trail hands in Spanish Fort, Texas. Few stores carried high-quality boots at the time, and, in his first year, Justin managed to sell 120 pairs at $8.50 apiece. He also developed a measuring kit that could be sent to customers to use on their own feet, which enabled him to begin building a mail-order business. As satisfied customers passed Justin's name on to others, his business grew. Ten years later, he moved his operation to Nocona, Texas, where he continued to develop what ultimately became a family business as his wife and most of his seven children joined the company. In 1908, when the two oldest children, John and Earl, became partners, the name of the company was changed to H. J. Justin and Sons.[4]

"Joe" Justin died in 1918. In 1924, the company was incorporated. John, Earl, and their younger brother Avis were made members of the board of directors, and all of Joe's children received shares in the corporation. A year later, in need of more space and a larger labor pool to expand the company, H. J. Justin and Sons moved to Fort Worth, 95 miles away. But one of Joe's children, the boys' sister Enid, didn't want to move. She stayed in Nocona and founded the Nocona Boot Company. Enid's company eventually became one of Justin's major competitors. Despite the competition, between the end of World War I and the beginning of World War II, manufacturing tripled, due in part to the popularity of cowboy movies in the 1920s and the resulting enthusiasm for western culture. Even the Depression had little effect on sales. The company was, in fact, so successful that John, who was running it by then, decided to expand its product line to include field and laced boots.[5]

But John's expansion proved to be unprofitable, and, by 1949, the company was in some difficulty. John's son, 32-year-old John, Jr., thought he knew how to turn the company around. He bought out his Uncle Avis's share of stock, which made him the majority stockholder, and took control from his father. As head of Justin, John Jr. quickly modernized the factory and developed the company's first management system. He also implemented marketing and advertising techniques that enabled the company to expand sales beyond the Southwest and into the entire country. Justin Boots became so well established that it was known by its motto: "Standard of the West."[6]

In 1968, John Jr. sold the company for stock in First Worth Corporation, the parent company of Acme Brick, then headed by D.O. Tomlin, with the understanding that he would continue to run what had always been his family's business. The sale made Justin the largest shareholder in First Worth, but he agreed that Tomlin would continue to serve as the company's president and chief executive officer. Initially, he was extremely pleased with the deal, but Justin quickly became disillusioned with his new partners, for a variety of reasons. Within a year, he was threatening to sue to nullify the merger agreement. But rather than get involved in what he knew would be a long, drawn-out, and expensive lawsuit, Justin told First Worth's board that if he were appointed to replace Tomlin as president and CEO, he would drop the suit. "I laid it on the line," Justin subsequently said. "Most of the members of the board knew I was right. They were worried about the way things were going. So they fired Tomlin and named me to replace him."[7]

Three years later, in 1972, Justin renamed the corporation Justin Industries. Over the next two and a half decades, he proceeded to build both the footwear and the building materials operations. He bought Nocona Boots from his Aunt Enid in 1981, and, in 1985, he purchased the Chippewa Shoe Company of Wisconsin. He also directed the company's expansion into belts, hats, and biker boots; oversaw the licensing of Justin Jeans; and, in 1990, acquired the Tony Lama Company, an El Paso, Texas-based boot manufacturer.[8] By the time he sold the company to Warren Buffett 10 years later, Justin Boots had a 35 percent share of the overall $450 million U.S. market for western boots, and close to a 75 percent share of the market at current price points.

By that time, 41-year-old Randy Watson, who was about to take complete charge of Justin Brands, had been with the organization for five years, having joined it in 1993. Although Watson owned no part of the company and was not involved in negotiations for its sale, his agreement to continue running the operation was one of the elements that made it attractive to Buffett. And Watson was as pleased with Buffett as the head of Berkshire was with him. "When we heard that the company was going to be sold," Watson says, "there was, naturally, some anxiety within the entire corporation and a concern that, after 120 years, there wasn't going to be some major changes. But to have a businessman like Mr. Buffett purchase Justin is the ultimate compliment to John Justin and the company he built. He understood our business; he understood the brands, and the importance of the history and heritage of the company. With a family-owned company that has been around as long as we have, there was the potential for this sale to have a negative impact within the Western industry. With Berkshire Hathaway buying us, that has not happened—there is no downside."

One of the things that particularly pleased Watson was that "Mr. Buffett came in and talked about autonomy. 'I've got 4,000 square feet in Omaha,' he said. 'I've got 12½ employees. And we don't have room for your 950. You're going to stay in Fort Worth and run your business. You can use me as little or as much as you'd like.'" In addition, Watson says, "I'm excited about the capital that's now available for us to do the things we deem necessary to widen the moat." In addition to Justin, Berkshire owns H.H. Brown and Dexter Shoe Company. "With the acquisition of Justin, Berkshire gains more market share in the footwear business," says Watson. "I think we bring a lot to the table with 120 years of history and heritage, strong brand awareness, and significant brand equity to his line of footwear companies. I've seen footwear up, and down, and flat, and I'm convinced there will be a day when all these footwear companies will be making a big impact on his cash flow."

In Justin's case, gaining market share is difficult because it already owns so much of a fairly limited market, and is accordingly its own biggest competitor. "The Western retail base isn't growing," Watson says, "so rather than try to reinvent the wheel and pour money into creating a new brand, we're taking existing brands and entering into new price points. And so far," he adds, "it's been successful, and we're gaining shelf space." They have also launched Justin Original work boots. "We've gotten into the workplace by capitalizing on the strength of the Justin brand," he says. "We've taken the quality, the history, and the heritage of a brand that people have grown to trust, and we put it into steel toes, and nonsteel toes, and other kinds of work boots, and it's worked really well."

As far as Justin's future is concerned, Watson says, "I think we need to stay focused on the size of the western market and the fact that we sell a lifestyle and an attitude. If the western market shows a sudden growth or remains the same or declines, we'll continue to work on a way to grow and gain market share through new channels of distribution and new price points and providing the product the consumer demands." When asked if he'd like to see Berkshire purchase other footwear operations, Watson says, "I think a diverse representation of footwear lines would be great, but whether he does or not is really irrelevant. We're part of a company and a strategy in which we feel very comfortable."

As for his own future, the 43-year-old Watson says, "I've been in the western industry since 1980—20 years—and I plan to stay in it. It's something that gets in your blood. It's the fascination with the Old West and how it still represents a way of life where a handshake was your word, and the American dream of 'Go West, young man.' It has a mystique, a unique atmosphere, that's different from any other business. Our customers are very special to me."

The western industry atmosphere that pervades Justin Boots is certainly very different from the atmosphere of Acme Brick, its former sister company. That difference largely explains why the complete separation of the two companies since the merger with Berkshire Hathaway has had virtually no effect on how either operates. According to Harrold Melton, CEO of the company that's now called Acme Building Brands, "There never were any synergies between Randy's division and mine. Randy and I see each other at social events and that's about it, because we essentially have totally different businesses. We don't have the same kinds of products, we don't have the same channels of distribution, and we don't have any of the same customers." In fact, even before the merger, Justin Industries was, in that respect, very much like Berkshire Hathaway, which may be one of the reasons that Berkshire's chairman took such an interest in it.

Like Justin Brands, Acme Building Brands is actually an amalgam of several different companies in the building materials business—Acme Brick, Featherlite, American Tile Supply, Texas Quarries, and Glass Block Grid System. Acme Brick, the oldest part of the operation, was founded in

1891, in Fort Worth, by George E. Bennett. Born in 1852 in Springfield, Ohio, Bennett left home at 16 and headed west. He worked first for a wholesaler named James McCord in St. Joseph, Missouri, and then, in 1874, started his own business in Butler, Missouri. But there was a depression in the mid-1870s; the business folded, and Bennett moved on to Texas. He took a job in Dallas as a salesman for the McCormick Reaper and Harvester Company, and was quickly promoted to the position of state sales manager. In 1884, he left McCormick to become general manager of the Tomkins Implement Company in Dallas. At the same time, he opened up another merchandising business of his own.[9]

Bennett, an ambitious young man, was always on the lookout for new opportunities. In the late nineteenth century, the brick industry in Texas was still in its infancy, but the demand for brick was increasing dramatically. Aware of this trend, and interested in getting into the business, Bennett began searching for appropriate sites for a factory. In 1890, he found a site at Rock Creek, in Parker County, that contained clay that was suitable for brick making. He proceeded to buy the land and build his first factory. A year later, the Acme Pressed Brick Company was chartered. As Bennett had anticipated, the demand for brick was so great that as soon as Acme opened its doors, it had more orders than it could fill, and, over the next 20 years, the company continued to expand and grow. In 1907, George Bennett died. His 20-year-old son, Walter F. Bennett, succeeded him as president. The younger Bennett, however, inherited not only his father's company but its problems. In the year George Bennett died, a financial panic led to declining sales, which, in turn, led to layoffs and strikes by the workers. The situation deteriorated to a point where George's son closed up shop and began seeking buyers for the company. But then an enormous fire in Midland, Texas, destroyed almost the entire city, created a huge demand for building materials, and enabled Bennett to get his company up and running again.[10]

Acme Brick continued to be a successful operation, but the use of bricks started to decline by the 1920s as builders began using other materials, particularly steel and concrete. This trend continued through the 1950s, when the extensive use of glass, particularly in office buildings, took away even more of the brickmakers' market. By the 1960s, builders were using an even wider array of materials: concrete, asbestos cement, aluminum, steel, plastic, and adobe. Over the years, the vast majority of brick manufacturers were either absorbed by other companies or simply went out of business. When Acme had been chartered in 1891, there were 5,000 brick plants in the United States, producing 10 billion bricks per year. By 1968, there were only about 450 companies, and they were producing only 9 billion bricks per year.[11]

To counter this trend, under the leadership of its then-president, D.O. Tomlin, Acme Brick began purchasing building materials companies outside of the brick industry. These purchases included three Texas-based companies—Nolan Browne Company, of Dallas, a concrete block company; McDonald Brothers Cast Stone Company of Fort Worth; and ACF Precast Products of Lubbock—as well as the Concrete Casting Corporation of Little Rock, Arkansas. The addition of these companies meant the organization was no longer just making bricks, so it was considered advisable for Acme Brick to change its name. It was subsequently renamed First Worth Corporation.[12] First Worth's continuing interest in growing by acquisition led it to purchase Justin Boot Company in 1968. As noted above, in the following year, John Justin, Jr., took D.O. Tomlin's place as president and CEO of First Worth, and, in 1972, renamed the corporation Justin Industries. Justin continued to expand both operations. By the time he sold them to Warren Buffett in the spring of 1999, they had revenues of more than $500 million a year—about three quarters of which came from the building materials operation—and annual earnings of more than $28 million.

When Harrold Melton took over as president and CEO of what then became known as Acme Building Brands, he took the lion's share of Justin Industries' business, and the part that, by all accounts, was of the greatest interest to Warren Buffett. "My impression," Melton says, "is that historically, over a long period of time, the brick business has been the most profitable part of Justin Industries, but we have great brands on both the footwear and building materials sides of the business. I think that Warren Buffett got a great value on the footwear side of the business, relative to the total deal. On the building materials side, he probably paid a very reasonable price for the company on the basis of that business's earnings record. He may have liked the brick business for what we've accomplished when compared with other building materials companies," he says, noting that Acme has more than a 50 percent market share in its six-state regional area—the region with the highest brick usage in the country.

If Buffett was pleased at the prospect of taking control of Acme, Melton was equally pleased at the prospect of working for Buffett. "When I first learned about Warren Buffett's visit," he says, "it wasn't a matter of his being ready to make an acquisition. It was more one of his just coming to talk with us. And, frankly, I thought it was pretty neat that a man of his stature, with his business acumen, and with his approach to investing, would come to look at our business based upon what he knew about it. I have friends who wish that Warren Buffett would come talk with them, who wish that they were running their businesses so well that he would be interested in their companies. I thought that was quite a compliment to the business that we've put together—a compliment to me and to all of our employees, present and past."

Nor was Melton disappointed when he actually had the opportunity to meet Buffett. "I've spent a lot of my life working with accountants and financial people, in our business as well as in others," says the former finance professor, "and I thought Warren would be a tad more like the typical numbers person. I'm not casting any stones. I'm just saying that numbers people sometimes have a 'reserved' personality. But he's not like that at all. He's very personable, very down to earth, and extremely easy to visit with. He's also a logical thinker who grasps a business almost immediately. I think that basic businesses are really easy for him, because when he and I talk about the unique aspects of our business, how we've reached this point, and what we plan to do in the future, he immediately understands where we've been, what we are, and where we're going. And that's pretty unusual. In fact," he adds, "my feeling is that even if this company had remained for sale for the next 10 years, we couldn't have made a better choice than Warren Buffett. His attitude toward companies, his attitude toward people, and his business philosophy essentially coincide with Acme Building Brands' and with our management team's. Without question, we are all happier with Warren Buffett than we would have been with any other buyer."

When asked if he would welcome a meeting of Berkshire Hathaway's operating managers, he says, "I would love to do that, to meet the other people. That would be fun for me because I don't know anyone in the Berkshire organization other than Warren Buffett and Marc Hamburg (Berkshire's vice president and treasurer). That would be great." But such a meeting doesn't only appeal to him for personal reasons. He also feels that, from a business standpoint, there might be real benefits to having discussions with managers from the other divisions. "I have never had a single conversation in my life, with a reasonably intelligent person, in which I didn't learn something useful, either in my personal life or in my business life. So I think the opportunity to meet and spend time with a group of people who are a part of Berkshire Hathaway, people who were basically selected by Warren Buffett, would certainly be helpful to me. I don't know that they would get very much from me, but I think I could learn a lot, both personally and about running the business."

It is obvious, though, that Melton already knows a good deal about running his business. "Acme Brick," he says, "is the best-known [brick] brand in the United States, by all the studies I've ever seen. And in our major brick markets in the Southwest, Acme has 75 percent name recognition among new home buyers. Not among builders, but among consumers. The next best brand recognition might be 15 percent, so there's just no comparison." This enormous name recognition, Melton says, is largely a result of advertising. "We began an advertising and publicity campaign in the mid-1970s," he says, "and it's still going on today. So we've had a strong program in place for a long time." Recently, Acme Brick used Warren Buffett to tote its brand on a special advertising cover of *Sports Illustrated* with the following quote, "Brick could have been my best investment ever."

Acme Brick's chief executive notes, though, that there is another factor as well. "By plan and by design," he says, "Acme Brick Company sells about 95 percent of our production directly to the person who actually pays for the product, who actually uses the product. Nationwide, that percentage would probably be 35 percent or so. Over the years," he says, "we've put together our own distribution system, so we have our own locations and our own people—40 locations throughout the six-state area, through which we sell direct to the person who uses the product."

As for *how* he runs his business, Melton says he believes an operating manager must do three things in order to be successful. "The most important," he says, "is to have a business philosophy within which honesty and integrity control all the decisions that you make. Whether it's a decision about personnel, a decision about a customer problem, or any other kind of decision, you have to be sure that all decisions are made on the basis of honesty and integrity. Second," he says, "you have to be sure that employees know each day that we are all working together to create a better company and to add value to the company. You have to be sure that they feel that they're a part of that—maybe the most important part—so that they take ownership in the business in the same way that you take ownership in the business. And the third important thing is that you need to have controls in place so that you have a feel for how the business is doing on an ongoing basis. You must have a good management information system, one that continuously provides data that will enable you to understand just how well that business is doing."

As for how he determines whether his efforts have been successful, Melton says, "I guess that I measure success in a couple of ways. First, we have stable employment in our company. I think that is because we've built a family environment, even though we have 2,800 people. We really care about our people. They know me, I know them. I know a lot of their children and spouses. Another measure," he says, "is that we operate the most profitable multiplant brick business in the United States. What that means to me is that the philosophy that we've had in place in dealing with our employees and our customers, and the strategy that we've had in place in establishing Acme as a brand, have worked. We have taken the dollars to the bottom line."

When asked about the future of that bottom line, Melton says, "The brick industry nationwide has grown somewhat over the last 10 years. There had been a decline in the use of bricks—builders were using other materials—but there's been a resurgence over the last decade or so. Through our national association, we now have a number of promotional units called "brick councils" set up all around the country, and, for the first time in the history of the brick business, we're doing advertising and publicity to promote the use of bricks. And it's working. So I think that the brick industry will continue to grow so long as we in the industry aggressively advertise our products."

As for his own future, Melton says that, at age 64, he has no plans to retire. "When I first met with Warren Buffett," he says, "that was one of the questions he asked, and I told him that I would stay in place until he's comfortable with a replacement for me. So I don't have any retirement plans now. I'm just moving forward. But even if I did leave," he notes, "I don't think anything would change very much at Acme, because everyone in the company has the same philosophy that I have. It's embedded in the company. We've conditioned the people in the field to understand the Acme philosophy. We've attempted to teach them, to help them, and to lift them, and we all work together." Nor is he concerned that his departure might bring about changes from outside, because, as he says, "Our philosophy of how to run a business basically coincides with what I believe Warren Buffett's philosophy is."

As for what might happen when Buffett leaves, Melton says, "I know nothing about his succession plans, but given his logical mind and the brilliance that he's shown over the years, I have confidence that he has carefully drafted his succession plan, and that his plan will be good for his business as well as for all of the operating companies. I'm not worried at all."

## HARROLD MELTON'S BUSINESS TENETS

- ★ Honesty and integrity should govern all your business decisions.
- ★ All your employees should have the shared goal of working to add value and create a better company.
- ★ Have a good management information system, and other controls, so you can continually monitor your company's fiscal performance.

# ★ *Part Six* ★

# Conclusion

# chapter twenty-one

# Buffett CEO Comparisons

Confidence, courage, drive, creativity, and the ability to balance risk and reward. Study any successful group of managers and you will undoubtedly discover these shared traits. It's only natural to wonder just what the Buffett CEOs have in common and how they are different.

Since the members of this unique group don't know one another and have never gotten together on a formal basis, they make an excellent control study group. On the surface, the four things Buffett CEOs have in common are: (1) being selected by the same person with the same criteria; (2) doing everything the same after being acquired that they did before; (3) having no synergy or requirement to work with another Berkshire business or industry; and (4) not experiencing any effort to get the Buffett CEOs together.

Here are some other affinities:

1. *Autonomous.* Each CEO is expected to manage his or her enterprise as if it were not part of a larger organization. The chief executive can report in as often or as little as each prefers. Outside of a simple monthly financial report, there are no required reports, meetings, or phone calls, and no need to consolidate job functions or eliminate redundant staff. Each CEO is completely detached and has little concern, outside his or her own division, regarding what the other managers are doing. No time is spent on the ongoing valuation of the enterprise, earnings forecasts, or media relations.

2. *Organizational Structure.* The companies are completely horizontal, with no infrastructure and bureaucracy. They are structured for self-sufficiency, less outside interference, and quick decisions. They have worldwide business connections and resources, an expanded circle of competence, and access to abundant capital.

3. *Developed Independently.* The CEOs were not shaped or influenced by Berkshire. Each individual and organization became desirable before Buffett acquired the companies.

4. *Importance of Mentors.* Most of the CEOs were fortunate to have a strong parental influence and a powerful mentor. None achieved his or her leadership role without one.

5. *Love of Work.* The CEOs love their jobs and the organizations they developed and continue to manage. None would ever consider leaving and becoming a competitor. The founders and entrepreneurs, like Mrs. Blumkin, expect to die still doing what they love to do. This is one of the real secrets of the extraordinary success of Berkshire—one that will help secure its future.

6. *Long-Term Orientation.* Berkshire has attracted long-term shareholders and Buffett has developed a unique team of managers who expect to continue with their operational roles as long as they are healthy. Berkshire has the benefit of home and family orientation and multigenerational family management and family ownership.

7. *Values.* Every Buffett CEO has a strong set of values and is driven by deeply held convictions, principles, and unyielding integrity. While their success may be measured by money, they value their relationship with their boss, their business achievements, and their associates. Each believes in doing first-class business in a first-class way.

8. *Humility.* Despite reaching the pinnacle of business and financial success, each CEO is humble, modest, and self-deprecating. (Most didn't think readers would be interested in their story.)

9. *Skepticism Toward Wall Street.* The CEOs whose corporations were publicly traded before merging with Berkshire expressed disdain for the short-term emphasis of analysts, earnings forecasts, whisper numbers, media relations, legal requirements, and so on. All say they would rather focus on getting the job done. Berkshire management and shareholders, with a long-term view and attitude, give them the opportunity to ignore external distractions so they can focus entirely on the betterment of their enterprise.

10. *Fair Price.* The CEOs wanted a *fair* price for their business, not the best price. Many could have gotten a higher price from a different buyer of the stock market but preferred Buffett's unique

style and long list of satisfied sellers. An owner/manager's willingness to sell at a fair price is one of the unwritten criteria that need to be satisfied. Berkshire has no interest in the assets, customer base, natural monopoly, employees, net worth, or dominant market share, without management. If an owner intent on selling for top dollar cares more about his wallet than preserving the institution he has built, on such managers Berkshire takes a pass. If the seller cannot justify a premium price, it may become too uncomfortable for him or her to stay. Other aspects of the acquisition— independence, business continuation and preservation, employee protection, customer retention, access to capital, a boss who is admired and respected, cash, simple and quick (and compatible) business philosophies—are preferable. Many CEOs report that selling to Berkshire and having Buffett become their boss is the best thing that has ever happened to them.

11. *View of Business.* Buffett CEOs seem to view Berkshire as just another stage in the life cycle of their independent business. None thinks of his or her business or job differently, after selling the company. Each has spent years building it up and views the business as more of a mission to fulfill than as work to do.

12. *Sleep Factor.* All the CEOs sleep with few worries. They don't worry about external pressures or the threat of their business being sold. There is no micro management from headquarters and no internal politics. The CEOs can keep their independent wealth and have time for self-determined charity work.

13. *Years Building Business.* The ideal CEO to acquire is the one who has spent his life building a business. Better still is a family business with a third generation managing a simple nontech business that has extraordinary market share. Each CEO constantly invested in the improvement of his or her enterprise.

14. *Focus on Operations.* Executing good blocking and tackling is a more important focus of each CEO than even the financial aspects of the enterprise. Some CEOs work without a budget. Others are focused on growth and expansion; they keep their eye on operations rather than on short-term earnings. All focus on the internal rather than the parent company, other subsidiaries, the stock market, the economy, or other businesses.

15. *Succession.* Each CEO has a well-defined plan and a designated successor. One manager took an anonymous poll of his management team to ensure acceptance of his chosen successor. Two turned over their CEO roles within a few months after being interviewed for this book. Each year or so Buffett sends a letter to his CEOs asking them to update their named successor. The Buffett CEOs then send a confidential response to Buffett (at his office or his home) with their recommendation.

16. *Owner Managers.* They eat their own cooking. Each CEO and most of their managers are also Berkshire shareholders. They attend the annual shareholders' meeting at their own expense. They make decisions in the best interest of shareholders. Most of the management team has 90 percent or more of their net worth in Berkshire stock. The majority have a personal financial interest in their division, and their compensation is directly related to how well their business performs. Each CEO's compensation is not related to how well other subsidiaries are doing or to the performance of the parent company. Most are not comfortable giving others investment advice.

17. *Charity and Corporate Citizenship.* Every Buffett CEO has at least one charity to which he or she donates both time and money. Most of the charities are local, health, children and education related. Each business, particularly the retailers, is a responsible corporate citizen and believes in community involvement.

18. *Management Style.* Buffett CEOs are hands-on, friendly, flexible, and practical. Although several CEOs have MBAs from prestigious business schools, none uses a typical MBA management approach. Most view managing as more of an art than a science. They lead by inspiration and example. Fellow workers are associates and are treated with respect.

19. *Country Club Set.* Most of the Berkshire operating managers are white, male, college-educated, 64 years old, and long-term managers. Most belong to a country club and play golf. They were not selected because of their affinity to golf or country clubs or prestigious business school degrees; they just happen to have this profile.

20. *Special Compensation.* Most of the new managers who enjoy golf have gotten a unique reward and management perk after joining the Berkshire team—a round of golf at Augusta National with

Warren Buffett and fellow operating managers. As a special reward, several reported being treated to a round of golf with Bill
Gates and several of his Microsoft managers. Many have had the
pleasure of playing golf with other captains of industry, including
Jack Welch (GE) and Tom Murphy (ABC Capital Cities). For
those who don't enjoy golf, Buffett extends an invitation to an
annual dinner gathering of government leaders and captains of industry in Washington, D.C. Guests include the President of the
United States.

21. *Office.* Small and functional. Many CEOs answer their own
    phone if their secretaries are away from their desks. Their desktops
    are cluttered with multiple projects, stacks of papers, and reading
    material, although one manager had a very tidy desktop with pa-
    pers neatly stacked and paper clipped. One manager had a stapler in
    the middle of his desk, stacks of papers everywhere, and only three
    small Berkshire advertisements are on the wall.

22. *Strengths.* History of earnings, simple business, reputation, in-
    tegrity, access to capital, management depth and succession, and ac-
    cess to Warren Buffett.

23. *Geographic Reach.* Primarily domestic, but evolving into more of
    a global enterprise.

24. *Home-Grown.* All have grown up with the business. Some had
    no choice as a member of a family business. Except for Stan
    Lipsey, no one has been brought in from the outside to fix the
    business or to solve problems.

25. *Excess Capital.* Each CEO must meet the test of using his or her
    earnings to increase the overall long-term profits of the business or
    to send the excess to headquarters to be reallocated. Likewise, if a
    CEO needs to borrow internally, he or she must meet the same ex-
    acting financial standards and pay an internal rate of interest on
    borrowed capital.

26. *Motivation.* All the CEOs were motivated before they became
    Buffett CEOs, and their business achievements are self-determined.
    Each CEO has high job expectations and doesn't want to disap-
    point the boss, employees, customers, suppliers, or shareholders.
    Motivation is no longer a pursuit of financial freedom. It is now
    based on personal achievement, job satisfaction, the challenge, the

fun, the accomplishment, the involvement, the boss, and the definition of self.

27. *Retirement.* The Berkshire view is untraditional and full of common sense. Why would a manager who is having so much fun retire? Many CEOs reported that Buffett has given them a purpose to keep working. "If it wasn't for Warren," said Frank Rooney, "I would have retired long ago. He keeps me going." For the typical Buffett CEO, retirement would be work. Berkshire may be the only large enterprise that talks acquired managers out of retirement or persuades those who are already retired to start managing again. No one is encouraged to retire. In fact, the opposite is true at Berkshire. Every manager is asked to stay on board as long as he or she is having fun. Retirement at Berkshire has been defined by Mrs. Blumkin (also known as Mrs. B), the founder of Nebraska Furniture Mart, who finally "retired" at the age of 104, having worked until her last few days. Only the Berkshire model encourages and facilitates managers to work well past the traditional age of retirement.

28. *Business Improvements.* These are incremental and more of an evolution than a revolution. Improvements in management, methods, technology, systems, marketing, production, engineering, distribution, and every other area affecting a business enterprise are constantly evolving. A manager with an ownership perspective and business dedication will recognize each major change as it occurs.

29. *Quality.* At Berkshire, quality is without compromise at all levels— management, ingredients, ethics, suppliers, customers, and employee relations.

30. *Synergy.* This word, found in every other acquisition and merger, is nonexistent at Berkshire. The thought of combining forces to make a stronger whole by building a larger headquarters staff, making employees redundant, and imposing headquarters mandates on each division for the betterment of all is foreign to Berkshire and runs contrary to its culture. There have never been, and probably will never be, any employee layoffs as a result of a Berkshire acquisition.

31. *Technology.* The Internet and technology are accepted and embraced where they are important but nonacceptance has ruled where they are not important. The Tatelman brothers, at Jordan's

Furniture, merely put an "Under Construction" sign on the company's Web site, and they have no intention of developing it until it proves feasible. Stan Lipsey of the *Buffalo News* waited until others developed the site and then bought www.buffalo.com. Still others like Chuck Huggins, waited until Buffett strongly suggested that See's Candies should develop a Web site. As a direct-response consumer-oriented insurance company, GEICO has and will continue with substantial investments in the Internet.

32. *Admiration.* Each CEO believes that, in Buffett, he or she has the best boss possible, and admires him. Most attend the annual meeting at their own expense and sit in the audience without a special badge. All report in, once a month or more. All like to have an excuse to call him. All seek his counsel. All treat him like a partner.

33. *Bakers, Not Butchers.* As other CEOs gain reputations for slashing staff and salaries, and restructuring failing enterprises, Buffett's operating managers have been net hirers. Each year, Berkshire grows; the number of employees now exceeds 100,000. The original Berkshire textile business closed, and the U.S. shoe manufacturing industry struggles with cheaper foreign production, but outside of these industries, there has never been a major layoff or restructuring of a wholly owned Berkshire business.

34. *Boundless Energy.* Another secret of Berkshire managers is their energy level. It's easy to have high enthusiasm when you are doing what you have been born to do and working with people whom you like and trust. Few will outwork this tireless self-selected group.

35. *Politics.* Most of the CEOs hold the business and management view of politics—the less government interference, the better. Most are willing to help those who help themselves. The majority thought the estate tax is too high. Contrary to their boss, the majority are Republican. A few thought that after you take care of your family, you should help others and give away your wealth during your lifetime.

36. *Biggest Extravagance.* One of the benefits of being part of the Berkshire family is the access to corporate jet travel. Just about all the board members and the majority of Buffett managers have purchased (at their own expense) an ownership interest in NetJets, allowing them to travel in the ultimate luxury. Few traveled by private jet before Berkshire assumed ownership of the enterprise,

and the proceeds from the sale made the fractional jet possible. Berkshire may be the only large business that doesn't supply a corporate jet fleet to its managers (another benefit to having a small headquarters office).

37. *Active Readers.* Buffett and company prove that leaders are readers. Most list reading as the activity that consumes the largest percentage of their typical day. Each CEO was naturally inquisitive.

38. *Berkshire after Buffett.* Although a few think it will be Berkshire's toughest time, most trust that Warren will do the right thing, as he has always done. Everyone believes he has given careful thought to succession. The issue of succession is more defined at Berkshire than at any other company. After Buffett's retirement (which he defines as five years after his death), every manager would continue to manage his or her business the same way as before. Management evaluation and compensation will stay the same. Ownership interests in partly owned and wholly owned businesses will continue. Everyone reported that they would continue to run their business as they have always done.

39. *Outside Consultants.* There is no need for outside counsel when each manager has available a world-class and experienced business consultant just a phone call away. Major decisions are discussed during short telephone calls—sometimes, just a few minutes in length, no matter what dollar value is involved.

40. *Physical Fitness and Health.* All of the CEOs are amazingly trim and fit. Most seem to be just wired with a fast rate of metabolism. Most drink lots of water. Most get some form of exercise: walking, morning treadmill, taking the stairs instead of the elevator, occasional golf. All appear younger than their age.

41. *Durable Competitive Advantage.* All CEOs would give back anywhere between $100 million and $1 billion and more, if it was offered to them to compete against their own operating businesses. Even with the knowhow, the contacts, and the capital, to a person they respect the infrastructure and the Berkshire reputation too much to ever compete against it.

42. *No Management Contract.* Without ever losing one manager to a competitor, no Buffett CEO is under contract. Anyone can leave and compete against Berkshire, but no one has. The only contract is

an offer and acceptance to purchase the business. Each manager's word is given; he or she will to stay on and act in the best interest of the business.

43. *Family*. Berkshire is about family, family businesses, family management, family shareholders, and home. The ideal business has third- and fourth-generation ownership and management. The Buffett Foundation will ensure family control and influence for many generations. Many managers report selling their business to Berkshire for family reasons. Few other large enterprises understand the needs and desires of family businesses more than Berkshire.

44. *Expanding Circle of Competence*. With each new acquisition, Berkshire gets an ever-expanding circle of competence. Every new and existing chief executive becomes a resource base for advice on the next acquisition within his or her industry or line of business. Each manager becomes part of the referral network for additional CEOs, and develops a discerning eye for those managers they would most like to add to the Berkshire family.

45. *Due Diligence*. From the outside it appears that Warren Buffett doesn't perform due diligence before an acquisition. Typically, an acquirer will read the investment banker's report, send in a team of accountants and consultants, and, at a minimum, perform an inventory audit. Berkshire does none of the above. Instead, Buffett, with 50 years of experience, knows what he is seeking, can recognize it, and makes a decision within minutes. He then studies the last three years' balance sheets and profit and loss statements. Then he makes a fair offer.

46. *Expanding Margin of Safety*. Ben Graham taught Buffett that every investment should have a margin of safety. With each new CEO, Berkshire increases its margin of safety for the same reasons it expands its circle of competence. Adding an existing retail jewelry store chain to an existing business adds to Buffett's margin of safety because he knows that business and the current CEO can advise properly.

47. *Honor*. To have a business selected to be part of Berkshire's family of companies has been the highest honor of those acquired. To be selected to run a Berkshire subsidiary is also an honor. Several managers reported that it's a further honor to the management and

employees to run their business in such a way as to be acquired by the foremost investment expert and capitalist.

48. *Unique Culture*. The culture of Berkshire is one of a kind. Every Buffett CEO reports that they don't feel like they have a boss. The very concept of buying a business and leaving it in the same hands as present management is very unusual. There is no real corporate headquarters. There is no organizational chart and there are no corporate or divisional vice presidents. The Berkshire model is not for everyone, but it does attract a certain business owner/founder. It attracts the best of the best.

49. *Nonpublished Acquisition Criteria*. Buffett will purchase a business if the numbers are attractive—in other words, if it fits the value investment model. However, he won't purchase a business if he doesn't get approval from his current operating managers. Berkshire's best single source of acquisition candidates is its current managers, and its best single source of a potential management team's reputation is its current managers.

50. *Reference Base*. With each new acquisition comes a new person to add to the reference base for those considering selling their business. All you have to do is pick up the phone (many of the operating managers answer their own phone, and one has gone as far as putting his home phone on his business card so customers can call him any time) and call a current operating manager for a reference.

51. *Quick Deal*. In less than the time it takes to sell a typical home, Berkshire has the decisiveness, the money, and the expertise to buy most businesses in an unlimited industry classification. Most of the businesses were acquired within days, if not hours, in a very simple manner.

52. *Maintains Status Quo*. Berkshire likes to acquire businesses that are simple and easy to understand. All operating managers report that there is absolutely nothing they do after selling to Berkshire that they did not do before, except get rid of some of the external headaches like meeting with the press or analysts, and managing quarterly instead of long term. They even don't have to think about allocating excess capital. Instead, they send it to Omaha to be redeployed in the best possible use.

53. *Acquirer of Choice.* When considering a buyer, most sellers consider who has the cash and which is the best organization to take over the business. If the seller doesn't care who buys the business, then Buffett isn't interested. Berkshire prefers to purchase operating owners over financial owners.

54. *Better with Experience.* With each new acquisition, Berkshire gets better. Just as McDonald's can model its most successful franchisee, Berkshire can model its future acquisitions after its most successful past purchases.

55. *Ignore Market Price.* The subsidiaries that make up Berkshire don't concern themselves with the market price of Berkshire; they concern themselves with the day-to-day business operations. Eventually, the market price will properly reflect the underlying changes in book and intrinsic value, and both will properly reflect the collective individual earnings of each operating business.

56. *Competitive Secrets.* While no manager willingly explains secrets to help the competition, some did let a few ideas slip. But the Berkshire culture is so unique, it is difficult for competitors to compete, even with full knowledge of the Berkshire game plan, gained right from the locker room.

57. *Excellent Communicators.* All the CEOs are extremely articulate and were able to express themselves. All can hold their own during a public debate or media interview, but they are so focused on their individual businesses that doing that type of thing would only take away from their passion and goals.

58. *Business with Honor.* To a person, all of the operating managers are attracted to Berkshire because of this long-held underlying belief.

59. *Fewer and Better Decisions.* While individual investors are out making more and worse decisions, the Berkshire investment model is the opposite of the market.

60. *Competitive.* Each Buffett CEO is intensely competitive. All want to win—and win big!

# Buffett CEO Evaluation and Compensation

After the careful selection of his operating managers, the chief executive must motivate, evaluate, and compensate. The opening chapters of this book explored how Buffett selects his CEOs. The middle chapters featured the managers' discussing how Buffett manages and motivates them. This chapter will examine the unique Berkshire methods of evaluation and compensation.

Buffett wrote to his shareholders in 1988 to explain the difference between Buffett CEOs and typical CEOs.

"Their performance, which we have observed at close range, contrasts vividly with that of many CEOs, which we have fortunately observed from a safe distance. Sometimes these CEOs clearly do not belong in their jobs; their positions, nevertheless, are usually secure. The supreme irony of business management is that it is far easier for an inadequate CEO to keep his job than it is for an inadequate subordinate.

"If a secretary, say, is hired for a job that requires typing ability of at least 80 words a minute and turns out to be capable of only 50 words a minute, she will lose her job in no time. There is a logical standard for this job; performance is easily measured; and if you can't make the grade, you're out. Similarly, if new salespeople fail to generate sufficient business quickly enough, they will be let go. Excuses will not be accepted as a substitute for orders.

"However, a CEO who doesn't perform is frequently carried indefinitely. One reason is that performance standards for his job seldom exist. When they do, they are often fuzzy or they may be waived or explained away, even when the performance shortfalls are major and repeated. At too many companies, the boss shoots the arrow of managerial performance and then hastily paints the bull's-eye around the spot where it lands.

"Another important, but seldom recognized, distinction between the boss and the foot soldier is that the CEO has no immediate superior whose performance is itself getting measured. The sales manager who retains a bunch of lemons in his salesforce will soon be in hot water himself. It is in his immediate self-interest to promptly weed out his hiring mistakes. Otherwise, he himself may be weeded out. An office manager who has hired inept secretaries faces the same imperative.

"But the CEO's boss is a Board of Directors that seldom measures itself and is infrequently held to account for substandard corporate performance. If the Board makes a mistake in hiring, and perpetuates that mistake, so what? Even if the company is taken over because of the mistake, the deal will probably bestow substantial benefits on the outgoing Board members. (The bigger they are, the softer they fall.)

"Finally, relations between the Board and the CEO are expected to be congenial. At board meetings, criticism of the CEO's performance is often viewed as the social equivalent of belching. No such inhibitions restrain the office manager from critically evaluating the substandard typist.

"These points should not be interpreted as a blanket condemnation of CEOs or Boards of Directors: Most are able and hard-working, and a number are truly outstanding. But the management failings that Charlie and I have seen make us thankful that we are linked with the managers of our three permanent holdings. They love their businesses, they think like owners, and they exude integrity and ability."[1]

Berkshire's method of manager evaluation first starts with the selection process. By making the right selection, Buffett gets the results he desires. He chooses managers who love their business and have the highest standards of ethics. This remains true after the acquisition.

None of the operating managers has selected or influenced the Berkshire board of directors, so the board remains an objective evaluator of the business, thus properly representing the larger shareholder group.

Berkshire's operating manager evaluation is quite simple. The business and its chief executive set a benchmark of performance before the purchase. It becomes the standard by which the CEO is measured and evaluated. Evaluation then is self-administered.

Buffett also uses another manager evaluation tool: his annual report and letter to shareholders. In it, he frequently commends outstanding managerial effort. The report is read by the vast worldwide financial community and other Buffett CEO peers, so being mentioned in it has become a real feather in the cap of highlighted operating managers.

Each manager is recognized in a custom company video at the beginning of Berkshire's annual meeting, so 15,000 owners applaud the efforts of the Buffett CEOs. In 2000, after his retirement, Ralph Schey was acknowledged and announced into the Berkshire manager hall of fame. No other public company gathers as many owners and managers together in one place for this annual pat on the back.

## STOCK OPTION COMPENSATION

Management stock options have become an important part of compensation, particularly at some technology-related companies, but Berkshire Hathaway simply doesn't have stock options. They may be introduced by the board of directors at some future date, to compensate Buffett successors who are in charge of the whole enterprise, but it is safe to say that stock options will never be offered to the operating managers.

The chart on page 350 explains the difference between an Option CEO, typically found at most large public companies, and an Owner CEO developed by Berkshire.

You can see that the "owner CEO" method is the best way to align the interests of the long-term shareholder with those of the manager.

Not surprisingly, even when Buffett purchases a company that uses management stock options, Berkshire brings the practice out of the closet, recognizes it as an expense, and replaces it with an equivalent cash compensation program.

"Indeed, their [management stock options] reported costs (but not their true ones) will *rise* after they are bought by Berkshire if the acquiree has been granting options as part of its compensation packages," stated Warren Buffett in his "Annual Letter to Shareholders." "In these cases, 'earnings' of the acquiree have been overstated because they have followed the standard—but, in our view, dead wrong—accounting practice of ignoring the cost to a business of issuing options. When Berkshire acquires an option-issuing company, we promptly substitute a cash compensation plan having an economic value equivalent to that of the previous option plan. The acquiree's true compensation cost is thereby brought out of the closet and charged, as it should be, against earnings."[2]

| Option CEO | Owner CEO |
| --- | --- |
| Earnings may be overstated, and management stock option costs never show up on the earnings statement or balance sheet. | Earnings are properly reported, including the full cost of the CEO's compensation. |
| Typically sells all or most of his stock to pay taxes due on the stock's appreciated value at the time he exercises his options. | Pays taxes up front and is able to benefit from long-term tax-free compounding. |
| Option CEOs cannot lose money on their options. Worst case is: they do not make money. | Owner CEOs share the same downside as other owners. |
| Option CEOs can reprice their options to benefit from volatility in the share price. | Owner CEOs are like every other shareholder: they must stay with the original cost of their shares. |
| Can influence the timing and amount of options issued to take advantage of stock price volatility. | Owner CEOs make no attempt to manage the business to influence short term stock price movements. |
| Option CEOs prefer stock buybacks to cash dividends, regardless of the valuations. | Owner CEOs tend to act in the best interest of all shareholders because their interests are aligned. |
| Option CEOs lose their motivation once the stock options are exercised. This encourages manager turnover. | Owner CEOs are increasingly motivated. As the value of their stock increases, they are less likely to leave. |
| Fast wealth without risk, and not necessarily dependent on the underlying value of the enterprise. Makes money if stock prices rise. | Slow wealth with risk, and totally dependent on the underlying value of the enterprise. Makes money if book value increases. |
| Option CEO has the corporate treasury buy his or her stock. | Owner CEOs buy their shares with their own money. |
| Very concerned about short-term stock market movements, and tempted to influence the media and analysts for favorable forecasts. | No outside interest; only an internal focus on how his or her business is doing over the long haul. |

*Note:* Buffett owner CEOs are not just owners of Berkshire; many remain minority owners of their actual business.

# BUFFETT CEO COMPENSATION

It is no surprise that Berkshire does not issue management stock options, and most managers are owners of Berkshire stock. This arrangement is typically worked out in a matter of minutes, without a contract, or noncompete clause, and it lasts for the life of the manager. They are all employees at will.

"At Berkshire," wrote Buffett, "we try to be as logical about compensation as about capital allocation. For example, we compensate Ralph Schey based upon the results of Scott Fetzer rather than those of Berkshire. What could make more sense, since he's responsible for one operation but not the other? A cash bonus or a stock option tied to the fortunes of Berkshire would provide totally capricious rewards to Ralph. He could, for example, be hitting home runs at Scott Fetzer while Charlie and I rang up mistakes at Berkshire, thereby negating his efforts many times over. Conversely, why should option profits or bonuses be heaped upon Ralph if good things are occurring in other parts of Berkshire but Scott Fetzer is lagging?

"In setting compensation, we like to hold out the promise of large carrots, but make sure their delivery is tied directly to results in the area that a manager controls. When capital invested in an operation is significant, we also both charge managers a high rate for incremental capital they employ and credit them at an equally high rate for capital they release.

"The product of this money's-not-free approach is definitely visible at Scott Fetzer. If Ralph can employ incremental funds at good returns, it pays him to do so: His bonus increases when earnings on additional capital exceed a meaningful hurdle charge. But our bonus calculation is symmetrical: If incremental investment yields substandard returns, the shortfall is costly to Ralph as well as to Berkshire. The consequence of this two-way arrangement is that it pays Ralph—and pays him well—to send to Omaha any cash he can't advantageously use in his business.

"It has become fashionable at public companies to describe almost every compensation plan as aligning the interests of management with those of shareholders. In our book, alignment means being a partner in both directions, not just on the upside. Many 'alignment' plans flunk this basic test, being artful forms of 'heads I win, tails you lose.'

"A common form of misalignment occurs in the typical stock option arrangement, which does not periodically increase the option price to compensate for the fact that retained earnings are building up the wealth of the company. Indeed, the combination of a ten-year option, a low dividend payout, and compound interest can provide lush gains to a manager who has done no more than tread water in his job. A cynic might even note that when payments to owners are held down, the profit to the option-holding manager increases. I have yet to see this vital point spelled out in a proxy statement asking shareholders to approve an option plan.

"I can't resist mentioning that our compensation arrangement with Ralph Schey was worked out in about five minutes, immediately upon our purchase of Scott Fetzer and without the 'help' of lawyers or compensation consultants. This arrangement embodies a few very simple ideas—not the kind of terms favored by consultants who cannot easily send a large bill unless they have established that you have a large problem (and one, of course, that requires an annual review). Our agreement with Ralph has never been changed. It made sense to him and to me in 1986, and it makes sense now. Our compensation arrangements with the managers of all our other units are similarly simple, though the terms of each agreement vary to fit the economic characteristics of the business at issue, the existence in some cases of partial ownership of the unit by managers, etc.

"In all instances, we pursue rationality. Arrangements that pay off in capricious ways, unrelated to a manager's personal accomplishments, may well be welcomed by certain managers. Who, after all, refuses a free lottery ticket? But such arrangements are wasteful to the company and cause the manager to lose focus on what should be his real areas of concern. Additionally, irrational behavior at the parent may well encourage imitative behavior at subsidiaries.

"At Berkshire, only Charlie and I have the managerial responsibility for the entire business. Therefore, we are the only parties who should logically be compensated on the basis of what the enterprise does as a whole. Even so, that is not a compensation arrangement we desire. We have carefully designed both the company and our jobs so that we do things we enjoy with people we like. Equally important, we are forced to do very few boring or unpleasant tasks. We are the beneficiaries as well of the abundant array of material and psychic perks that flow to the heads of corporations. Under such idyllic conditions, we don't expect shareholders to ante up loads of compensation for which we have no possible need.

"Indeed, if we were not paid at all, Charlie and I would be delighted with the cushy jobs we hold. At bottom, we subscribe to Ronald Reagan's creed: 'It's probably true that hard work never killed anyone, but I figure why take the chance.' "[3]

# chapter twenty-three

# Buffett CEO Opportunity

*I*t's hard to imagine the future of Berkshire with its $100 billion public market valuation.

The key to Berkshire's future is its past and present business model. While it is primarily a property and casualty insurance company, it is much more. No other private or public company has as many diverse sizes and types of companies under one corporate ownership. Berkshire has more companies representing more SIC (standard industrial codes) categories than any other enterprise. (See Appendix Three.)

More significantly, Berkshire does not come close to antitrust concerns in any of its sprawling enterprises. Buffett's empire owns a very small percentage of each business category that it represents.

This means more opportunity for Berkshire and more for each Buffett CEO. Because it has never restricted and will never restrict itself to the types of business that it will acquire, the opportunities for Berkshire's expansion are limitless.

More than 3,000 domestic and non-U.S. companies are listed on the New York Stock Exchange (NYSE), and their total market capitalization exceeds $17 trillion. Even with an overwhelming $100-billion market cap, Berkshire represents just 0.6 percent of the NYSE. With even a greater opportunity, the Buffett CEOs collectively represent a mere 0.2 percent of the worldwide public markets. But since their reach is also to private enterprises, Berkshire has managed to capture a mere 0.1 percent of the total world capital markets. This means that Berkshire has a future opportunity of 99.9 percent of the world's capital.

Just as Berkshire's capital is constantly growing, so does the world's capital. The basic principle of capitalism is survival of the fittest, and the world's best capital allocators end up with more of the capital.

Here is a list of each Buffett CEO's opportunity: Blumkin, Child, Wolff, and Tatelman own the majority of furniture sales in Nebraska, Utah,

Idaho, Texas, Massachusetts, and New Hampshire, but, all together, the furniture merchants represent just 2 percent of the $37 billion U.S. furniture market. In their home state, Blumkin and Child represent a large percentage of sales of appliances, electronics, and floor covering, but an insignificant percentage nationwide. With each new store, any of these four Buffett CEOs has the potential to add another $60 million in revenue. Blumkin is replicating Nebraska Furniture Mart in Kansas City and will potentially double its sales within a year. Child opened a store in Las Vegas and has several more major markets within a day's drive from Salt Lake City. The Tatelmans will soon expand to the North Shore of Massachusetts and have more opportunity throughout New England. Wolff has more opportunity just within his home state of Texas.

Comment and Jacques's division represents a mere 1½ percent of the $43 billion annual U.S. retail jewelry market. Each new Helzberg store Comment opens generates $2.2 million in additional revenue. Borsheim's low-cost location, capital base, affluent customers, site of the annual pilgrimage of 15,000 loyal and affluent customers/owners, brand awareness, and the economics of the Internet will all help it continue to grow exponentially.

Nicely and Simpson's GEICO represents just 5 percent of the $135 billion annual domestic auto insurance market. The combination of the Internet, a superior proven business model, a huge advertising budget, and access to vast capital will help GEICO capture more business than any other competitor. Simpson has more opportunities to invest in the public markets because more companies are within his market capitalization criteria. In addition, he is not limited to the U.S. capital markets.

Jain sells just a tiny fraction, or 2 percent, of the $289-billion U.S. property and casualty reinsurance market, and less than 1 percent of the $2.13-trillion worldwide insurance (nonlife) market. Berkshire's GenRe division, America's largest reinsurer, has staff and an office presence in every significant worldwide reinsurance market.

Ueltschi's company trains approximately 10 percent of all licensed pilots in the United States. FlightSafety provides training to the majority of small regional airline and corporate professional pilots who fly for a living, and a small percentage of airline, military, instructional, and private pilots. FlightSafety is the largest manufacturer of flight simulators in the United States, but it produces just 20 percent of the worldwide market. Barriers to entry are high; the average cost of a simulator is $15 million. Less military pilot training, a growing base of air travelers, federal laws requiring both retirement at age 60 for airline pilots and annual commercial pilot training, and a doubling of the private jet business all bode well for FlightSafety's future. Its largest customer is a sister company.

Santulli created and owns 60 percent of the fractional corporate jet market, but, currently, a mere 3 percent of all corporate jets have shared ownership. The winner in his business is the one who controls the supply chain of new aircraft, and NetJets controls one-third of all future corporate jets yet to be manufactured. Santulli's division has 480 jets on order and options on another 150 planes. 155,000 wealthy individuals and corporations worldwide are potential fractional owners. Currently, just 2,000 owners are NetJets customers, which means a 97 percent market opportunity. With an incredible business model and a huge "first one in" advantage, NetJets has the potential to be to the private jet transportation business as FedEx is to the overnight package delivery business. The payoff on this investment will be enormous.

Lipsey owns the newspaper business in Buffalo. Little future growth and maybe less revenue and profit are predicted, due to declining readership, the Internet, and other competing forms of media. Berkshire's newspaper division can acquire other daily newspapers if they become available at attractive prices and come with outstanding management. Alternatively, it could expand into other media categories in Buffalo or outside that market.

Huggins captured the majority of the California boxed chocolate and candy store market but still has very little sales outside California. It is not likely that anything in the future will replace chocolate. Annual chocolate consumption in the United States alone is nearly one pound per month per person! California alone represents 35 million pounds of chocolate consumed per month, and See's captured a mere 7 percent of those sales. See's is reaching a mere one percent of the 3.4 billion pounds of chocolate consumed each year in the United States. Although tests in Japan and Texas have proven that boxed chocolate does not travel well, freshly stocked stands in airports around the United States and seasonal stands in shopping malls have proven successful. Figuring out how to capture more sales outside California and the United States is an enormous opportunity and the Internet will help See's expansion.

Schey, and now Smelsberger, own 85 percent of the printed school and library encyclopedia domestic market, 5 percent of the North American upright vacuum opportunity, and 29 percent of the small consumer and commercial air compressor market in North America. Personal computers and CD-ROMs have hurt the in-home printed encyclopedia business, but there is still an enormous opportunity for all in-home educational products. World Book's challenge is to capture the $15 billion educational product market with not only encyclopedic products but others like "Tudor Link" (a peer tutoring system) and "Earning for Learning" (a plan to use a school's influence to sell into homes). Kirby vacuum cleaners continue to sell worldwide with the same business model that has been successful for 70 years. Small air compressor manufacturers are under pressure to commoditize their industry and produce private label brands for Home Depot, Lowe's, and Wal-Mart, but the worldwide opportunity for small portable power tools and accessories is a huge opportunity for Scott Fetzer. As important are another 19 seedling-size companies of Scott Fetzer that are being tasked to grow into giant oaks to become the pride of Buffett and Berkshire.

Watson's division owns the majority (35 percent) of the $450 western boot business. Western wear sales will gain if another "Urban Cowboy" craze or fickle western fashion shift happens.

Melton produces 1 billion bricks (11 percent) out of 9 billion manufactured in the United States each year. Nothing is more permanent than brick and, to many people, nothing is as important as the investment in their home. Brick has always been around and will continue to be the building material of choice, particularly in the south and southwest. With a capital-rich parent company, Acme is likely to acquire more building material manufacturers. Berkshire continues to add insulation, roofing, and carpet manufacturers to its wholly owned businesses.

Rooney manufactures a very small percent of the 1.2 billion pairs of shoes sold each year in the United States. As he says, "As long as people are born barefoot there will be a need for footwear manufacturers." Shifting more of its production overseas, H.H. Brown will lower its costs and increase its profits.

With over $40 billion in annual sales, Berkshire represents a mere 0.4 percent of the United States Gross Domestic Product, or just 0.2 percent of the worldwide annual purchasing power. Even more dramatic, 99.8 percent of worldwide annual sales represent the Buffett CEOs' opportunity.

# chapter twenty-four

# Berkshire Post Buffett

One day in the not so distant future, Berkshire Hathaway will pass the leadership baton from its present chief executive to the next. To some, this event will be one of the most defining moments in American capitalism.

What will Berkshire look like after Buffett? What criteria will be used to select an operational CEO? What is the future of Berkshire Hathaway? Questions like these can only be answered with certainty by Warren Buffett, but research and analysis of the past offer some likely scenarios.

Maybe only a handful of board members know for sure who will be the next Berkshire CEO and operational head of this emerging business empire. He or she is named in a succession letter contained in an envelope in Warren Buffett's desk. The letter is to be opened upon his death.

A letter suggesting their own successor is mandatory for all the Buffett CEOs. Here is the actual annual memo sent to the Buffett CEOs, requesting a successor:

Memos

To: Berkshire Hathaway Managers ("The All-Stars")
From: Warren Buffett
Date: August 2, 2000

It's been two years since my last memo setting forth the few rules we have and also asking your input on the succession situation at your operation. We've had more than half a dozen acquisitions in the intervening period so for some of you this will be new.

Here are a couple of things to keep in mind:

1. We can afford to lose money—even a lot of money. We cannot afford to lose reputation—even a shred of reputation. Let's be sure that

everything we do in business can be reported on the front page of a national newspaper in an article written by an unfriendly but intelligent reporter. In many areas, including acquisitions, Berkshire's results have benefited from its reputation, and we don't want to do anything that in any way can tarnish it.

2. All of you do a first-class job in running your operations with your own individual styles. We are going to keep it that way. You can talk to me about what is going on as little or as much as you wish with only one caveat: If there is any significant bad news, let me know early.

3. The only items about which you need to check with me are any changes in post-retirement benefits and any unusually large capital expenditure. I encourage you to look for "tuck-in" acquisitions. Several of our businesses have successfully completed such tuck-ins and they almost invariably added to our intrinsic value.

4. We are trying to widen at all times the moat that protects our businesses from invading hordes. Therefore, look at the business you run as if it were the only asset of your family, one that must be operated for the next 50 years and can never be sold. Search for all ways—in distribution, manufacturing, branding, acquisitions, etc.—to build a sustainable long-term competitive advantage.

5. If you run into any owners or managers of large businesses—with good economics and management—that might be prospects for a merger with Berkshire, be sure to send them along to me. A couple of our managers have been most helpful in this respect; most recently, Ron Ferguson, in facilitating my introduction to Bob Berry at U.S. Liability.

6. One group, *don't* send to me: people who are looking for a speaker at any kind of function—trade meetings, college graduations, forums, etc. Please say no to all such invitations without checking with me.

7. Finally, I would like you to send me a letter (at [my] home if you wish) updating your recommendation as to who should take over tomorrow if you became incapacitated tonight. Please summarize the strengths and weaknesses of your primary candidate as well as those of any possible alternatives. Most of you have participated in this exercise in the past and others have offered your ideas verbally. However, it's useful to me to get a periodic update, and now that we have added more operations, I need to have your thoughts in writing rather than to try to carry them around in my memory. Anything you send me will be confidential. Of course, there are a few operations that are run by two or more of you—such as the Blumkins, the

Tatelmans and the Bridges, etc.—and in these cases, just forget about this item.

Thanks for your help on all of this.

This memo speaks to the culture of Berkshire and the importance of management in everything it does. Succession is well defined at every level within Buffett's company, including his own spot.

Buffett has named Lou Simpson as his investment CEO backup, so the focus is on determining an operational heir. Buffett's job will be split into a triumvirate: chairman of the board, CEO of capital allocation, and CEO of operations. Buffett's oldest son, Howard, is most likely to succeed as chairman and will keep the business "in the family." Preserving the culture his dad created and maintaining a home for multigenerational businesses will be his primary goals. Selecting, evaluating, motivating, and compensating the co-CEOs will also be vital to the future of Berkshire Hathaway.

One way to determine how the successor to Buffett will be selected is to analyze how he selected Simpson as the CEO in charge of capital operations. Simpson is a long-term employee with over 20 years of service. He is one of a handful of money managers who is very successful in his chosen profession. Simpson's style and belief system are similar to Buffett's. Simpson is admired by and in close contact with Buffett. Berkshire's board is familiar with Simpson; he has a well-documented record for comparison and scrutiny. Simpson is independently wealthy, enjoys his work for the fun of it, is loyal, and has no plans to retire any time soon.

Using these criteria, Buffett's operational CEO will be a long-term employee, a very successful executive, and a hands-off manager. In addition, he is probably in touch with Buffett frequently, if not daily; is familiar to Berkshire's board; has an extraordinary operational record; is independently wealthy but keeps working for the fun of it, and has no plans for retirement. Only one current manager fulfills the criteria on this list.

Shareholders know for sure that the operational successor will not be Simpson because he has been selected for the capital allocation side of the business. Also, the cost of managing Berkshire will rise. When the CEO duties are split into three portions, the candidates are unlikely to work for the current salary of $100,000, or $33,333 each. But as the management costs rise, the job will probably demand less from Buffett's successors. Most jobs become easier when they are split into smaller parts. As long as there is respect among the chairman, the capital CEO, and the operational CEO, their separate responsibilities will be full of challenges but should be rewarding and fun. Having three managers step into the shoes of a legend is a better design for success than trying to find one individual who has all the predecessor's unique characteristics. In some ways, this parallels having a manager, a pitching coach, and a batting coach because the trio produces a better managed baseball team.

Here are some of the variables that may define the selection of Buffett's operational successor:

1. *Insider Status.* The successor to Buffett will be an insider who is already working as an operating manager. Berkshire is so unique that an outsider without a complete understanding of its culture would have a difficult time gaining the respect necessary to serve as CEO. Furthermore, it isn't Berkshire's or Buffett's style to bring anyone in from the outside. This factor eliminates Don Graham and the other five million CEOs who do not work for a Berkshire subsidiary.

2. *Age.* The operational successor has to be young enough to qualify, probably 10 years Buffett's junior, or not yet 60 years old. This criterion alone strikes out nearly half of the Buffett CEOs because they are not young enough and there's not enough difference in their ages: Ueltschi (84), Child (69), Wolff (69), Lipsey (73), Huggins (76), Schey (76), Rooney (79), and Melton (64).

3. *An Understanding of the Culture.* To successfully lead it into the future, the CEO must understand the culture of the enterprise. Any attempt to destroy or alter the Berkshire method of operation will lead to manager defections and will dramatically hurt the overall intrinsic value of the enterprise. That is why a Buffett will always be represented on the board and is likely to be chairman of the board for a long time. This is also another reason why a non-family successor and professional manager like Jacques, Comment, and Watson would be ruled out. Founding family managers and entrepreneurs are more likely to respect someone who intimately understands a laissez-faire management style. Any attempt to manage the autonomous managers with an MBA cookie-cutter

approach would destroy what has already been built and would drive the owner/managers to early retirement or to start another competing business.

4. *Small Headquarters.* Buffett's successor will naturally gravitate toward a small staff of key people and will prove himself as a macro manager. Only one manager—Santulli—qualifies as having a small headquarters staff and a large operational center in another city.

5. *Years of Service.* It would be preferable if the operational successor has at least 10 years' experience running a wholly owned subsidiary. It would be even better if he had founded the business or had grown up with it as part of a family business. This eliminates some of the newest nonfamily professional CEOs, like Watson.

6. *Independently Wealthy and a Substantial Shareholder.* Like Buffett, the best successor would be one working for the betterment of the overall enterprise—only doing those things that add shareholder value and add to his own personal wealth as a result. Any large owner-manager would make owner-friendly decisions and manage in the best interest of the shareholders. This group includes Santulli, the Blumkins, and the Tatelmans.

7. *Manager and Board Member Familiarity.* The managers don't know one another well, so an ideal successor/manager would be someone who knows and does business with all the managers and board members. Being based in Omaha is obviously helpful because most managers and all the board members make a yearly pilgrimage to the annual meeting. Shareholders, managers, and board members eventually do business with the wholly owned Omaha retailers and may arrive by NetJets. This group would include Jacques, the Blumkins, and Santulli. In this category, Santulli has an advantage. Just about every successful Buffett CEO does business with NetJets.

8. *Intelligence.* To succeed Warren Buffett, superior intelligence is an obvious requirement. Special knowledge of property and casualty insurance and numbers will also be very helpful. Several managers hold advanced business degrees from prestigious universities, but two Buffett CEOs are well known for their math smarts—Jain and Santulli. As a former college mathematics professor with an advanced degree in math, Santulli may have a slight edge.

9. *Single Most Profitable Manager.* Looking strictly at who currently brings in the most profits, the successor would be Jain.

10. *Manager of the Most People.* Managing one out of every five of Berkshire's employees is Nicely, although Bob Shaw of Shaw Industries manages the most (but is not profiled).

11. *Management Model.* GEICO's current management structure is the very model that Berkshire will follow, post Buffett. One CEO manages capital (Simpson) and a second manages operations (Nicely).

12. *Developed an Organization.* The best successor would have built a worldwide subsidiary, Berkshire's largest subsidiary, and an organization—all from scratch. Only one qualifying Buffett CEO—Santulli—has done so.

13. *Wall Street Contacts.* Having work history on Wall Street, and having a business that services the most successful investors would be helpful for future Berkshire deals. As a former Goldman Sachs executive, with a New Jersey location and a business service that caters to the most successful Wall Street types, the manager of choice would be Santulli. Also, while other companies are spending millions to gain endorsements, Santulli's division has the luxury of having the world's best endorsers as paying customers.

14. *Daily Contact with Buffett.* On-the-job training includes daily phone conversations with Buffett. Only two managers report speaking to him every day—Jain and Santulli.

15. *Media-Wise.* Handling the press, speaking without notes—or without benefit of knowing the questions in advance—are skills valued by Buffett and Munger, who sit before the public for six hours every year to answer unscripted questions and spend another two-and-a-half hours taking hard-hitting questions from the media. Any Buffett CEO who has refused an interview will not be a successor because experience with handling a never-ending journalistic inquisitiveness is a critical job responsibility. The edge goes to Santulli and the Tatelmans, the only CEOs who employ an in-house public relations manager and actively seek media coverage.

16. *Innovator.* Buffett's successor should clearly be very innovative. The only qualifying manager who created his industry from scratch is Santulli.

17. *Global Perspective.* Berkshire is an American company with American-based businesses, but its future will indeed be global. The manager with the most global business experience is Rich Santulli.

18. *Four Leadership Skills.* Berkshire's chief executive must have four outstanding skills: communication, motivation, manager evaluation, and compensation. Both Nicely and Santulli are strong in all four areas. Santulli has the natural charm and influence of a leader.

19. *Large Assets.* Experience with (billion-dollar) assets and revenue would best position Buffett's operational successor. Jain, Nicely, and Santulli all qualify.

20. *Largest Potential Subsidiary.* NetJets will one day be as large as FedEx and Berkshire's largest wholly owned company. Therefore, Santulli would be a natural successor.

21. *Confidence of the Managers and Board Members.* It would be most important for Buffett's successor to have the confidence and the respect of those he has to manage and those who have to appoint him. Just about every manager would qualify, but the most natural is Santulli.

22. *Experience Dealing with Owners.* The one division that deals with owners regularly is NetJets. Santulli's employees call their customers "owners" because they indeed own the jets. His experience in exclusively dealing with "owners" will aid this executive if he does take over for Buffett. Dealing with the board of directors is dealing with a representative ownership group. Having the confidence of the majority of shareholders who want their CEO to act in their best interest is a vital characteristic of any successor.

23. *Up for the Challenge.* Only one of the managers interviewed rose to the challenge of being a potential backup on the operational side of the business. Rich Santulli had a plan for what he would do if he were the one recommended by Buffett and asked by the board of directors. His plan is to call all the managers and ask them what they have been doing under the Buffett administration. After they have told him, he would ask them to continue doing the same thing—just like Buffett does after each acquisition.

By defining all the criteria that Buffett has probably considered, and everything the Berkshire board may consider in the future, the most likely candidate is NetJets founder Rich Santulli.

Why hasn't Buffett publicly named him? Probably for several reasons:

★ Buffett is having the time of his life growing and expanding Berkshire Hathaway.

★ Buffett plans to manage Berkshire as long as he is in good health and of sound mind.

★ Naming a successor is premature with a life expectancy of 15 more years. When recruiting new Buffett COOs, its comforting to them to know who they are reporting to.

★ Many things can happen between now and the actual time that Buffett's successor takes over.

Berkshire has transformed itself, in recent years, into a collection of wholly owned companies and a significant property and casualty insurance company. Berkshire may shift in another direction and a different candidate could end up being better suited. Lastly, although not likely, Rich Santulli may choose to retire or may simply be too old to assume the demands and duties, or may not have an interest when the time comes.

Bottom line, Buffett will recommend and Berkshire's board will choose a successor who will best maintain the Buffett culture.

And how will Buffett's successor be measured? Warren Buffett said his successor should be judged after 10 to 15 years by his standard and record of never losing a CEO.

## THE FUTURE OF BERKSHIRE HATHAWAY

Many shareholders wonder what Berkshire Hathaway will look like in the future. It was founded in 1889 as a textile manufacturer. Over the past 35 years, Warren Buffett has transformed it into one of the largest and most diversified public companies. It has become the most significant domestic company not included in the S&P 500 index. Berkshire is the most watched acquirer of both public companies and privately held subsidiaries. Buffett and Company have created more personal wealth for more individuals than any other mutual fund, investment company, partnership, hedge fund, private company, or publicly traded company. This has been done without the benefit of an infrastructure. Berkshire simply manages its companies like it manages its stock portfolio: Buy both the company and the managers, and let them continue to operate as they always have. Don't expect synergy among subsidiaries. Plan to keep them forever.

How will that philosophy change after Buffett? The deeply rooted Berkshire management culture will continue long into the future. Berkshire has been built to stand the test of time and the passing of its chief architect.

A comparison with GE may be useful. General Electric, founded by Thomas Edison, has emerged as a powerhouse under the leadership of Jack Welch. Welch's plan for GE was to concentrate its business into 12 categories with the intention of being either number one or number two or getting out of that business segment. GE, to fuel most of its growth, makes some 100 acquisitions each year, *without* wanting to keep current management. GE, like most other acquirers, looks for synergy between companies. In fact, GE's recent antitrust problems in Europe probably arose because it is focused on being the leader in 12 industries.

Also, Jack Welch took over management of GE at the age of 45 and had enough time (20 years) to influence the culture. Buffett, on the other hand, took over Berkshire at the age of 34 and wasn't replaced at the typical American retirement age of 65. He, therefore, has had one of the longest tenures of any other major CEO—37 years and still counting.

To imitate GE, or to restructure Berkshire as a large conglomerate with an infrastructure, a large headquarters, and layers of vice presidents, would destroy what Buffett has artfully created. Even to model it after AIG, America's largest insurance company, would stifle what Berkshire is all about.

Because it has a totally different business model, Berkshire doesn't have a long-term strategic plan. It will simply grow and expand as opportunities present themselves. Growth at Berkshire has come by focusing on increasing book value of the businesses it already owns, not by growth by acquisition. Berkshire will always be comfortable buying parts of a business or a whole business, depending on where the greatest value is for shareholders. It stays stock-market-proof by purchasing more wholly owned than partly owned businesses. Berkshire has not had a strategic plan, nor will it have one. Except for textiles and shoes, Berkshire has never participated in an acquisition that wasn't also an excellent value. Berkshire has always preferred declining bear markets and will always perform better with a pessimistic economy. Berkshire will expand its ever-growing collection of earnings-rich, value-priced, and superior-managed businesses as each one presents itself.

Although Berkshire has focused its efforts on U.S.-based businesses, it is likely to be a global powerhouse in the future—acquiring international enterprises that fit the same acquisition criteria. It is not likely to pay a dividend as long as it can allocate capital for a better use than rewarding individual shareholders.

Berkshire post Buffett will mean that ownership of a third of the company will shift from Warren Buffett and his wife, Susan, to the Buffett Foundation. The life expectancy of a 71-year-old male is 15.3 years, for a 69-year-old female its 16.8 years, but combined its 20.7 more years (it should be noted that for some reason Nebraskans and wealthy individuals have longer life expectancies).

So the future of Berkshire will be the eventual funding of the Buffett Foundation. With a current value of $35 billion over the next 21 years it will grow (at 10 percent) to an estimated value of $260 billion. Then by current law, 5 percent of the foundation or approximately $13 billion per year of Berkshire stock will be sold or transferred. Distributions may be made from annual growth of the stock or a dividend (if paid) without invading the foundation's principal. Although a substantial dollar amount, if the annual 5 percent distribution is from the sale of stock it would only involve 1 percent of the company's total stock each year. Also, under current law, a foundation cannot control more than 20 percent of a business. So the Buffett Foundation can meet this future requirement by converting a portion of its "A" shares to "B" shares and give up voting control.

In the future, more businesses will choose to associate themselves with Berkshire because of its management autonomy, cash assets, and long-term owner orientation and loyalty. As long as there are owner/managers who care about the long-term survival of their enterprises for the sake of their families, employees, customers, and suppliers, there will be a need for a parent company like Berkshire.

As long as there is an estate tax, particularly on large estates, there will be buyers for entrepreneurs seeking to protect the future of their business.

Companies seeking to lower their costs to attract and keep capital may choose to become a subsidiary of Berkshire. A merger may save, according to Ralph Schey, 50 days per year spent on external capital matters and redirect the CEO's time to internal business development.

As long as there is capitalism based on merit, capital will flow from the least profitable to the most profitable. The golden rule will always apply: The company with the most gold will set the rules. Business deals will go to the capital allocator at Berkshire.

As long as there is a meritocracy of capitalism, the poorly managed enterprises will give way to the ones with superior management. Business in competitive industries will continue to be determined by survival of the fittest. Berkshire's corporate structure will continue to attract and keep outstanding managers.

Will there be such a dynamic and one-of-a-kind annual meeting, post Buffett? With the owner mentality that Berkshire has attracted, and with a group of owners like Buffett who intend to own their stock until their death, the annual meeting will attract owners who want to gather with like-minded investors. Much like an Amway convention, Berkshire shareholders will always support the businesses they own. With Buffett gone, the owners will still prefer to gather annually, improve their businesses, and purchase products and services among themselves.

Berkshire will survive long past Buffett because of its structure, growth opportunities, principles, managers, and, most importantly, its long-term shareholders. Any business can survive, grow, and prosper with the managers and shareholders that Buffett has been able to attract.

# Buffett CEO Interview List

February 7, 2000    Lou Simpson, GEICO President and CEO of
capital operations
Rancho Santa Fe, California

April 13, 2000    Al Ueltschi, FlightSafety International, Founder,
President and CEO
Flushing, New York

August 3, 2000    Tony Nicely, GEICO President and CEO of
Insurance Operations
Washington, D.C.

August 5, 2000    Ralph Schey, Scott Fetzer, President and CEO
Westlake, Ohio

August 8, 2000    Stan Lipsey, *The Buffalo News,* Publisher and
President
Buffalo, New York

August 9, 2000    Tony Nicely, GEICO President and CEO of
Insurance Operations
Washington, DC
Telephone interview

August 14, 2000    Ajit Jain, Berkshire Hathaway Reinsurance Group,
President
Stamford, Connecticut

August 16, 2000    Malcolm "Kim" Chace, Berkshire Hathaway Board
Member
Providence, Rhode Island

August 17, 2000    Eliot and Barry Tatelman, President and CEO,
Jordan's Furniture
Natick, Massachusetts
On location of commercial filming—Weston,
Massachusetts

| August 18, 2000 | Frank Rooney, H.H. Brown Shoe Co., Chairman and CEO<br>Nantucket, Massachusetts |
| --- | --- |
| August 25, 2000 | Susan Jacques, Borsheim's, President and CEO<br>Omaha, Nebraska |
| August 27, 2000 | Irv Blumkin, Nebraska Furniture Mart, Chairman and CEO<br>Omaha, Nebraska |
| September 4, 2000 | Bill Child, R.C. Willey Home Furnishings, President and CEO<br>Salt Lake City, Utah |
| September 6, 2000 | John Roach, Chairman, Justin Industries<br>Harrold Melton, President and CEO, Acme Brick<br>Randy Watson, President and CEO, Justin Brands<br>Fort Worth, Texas |
| September 7, 2000 | Melvyn Wolff, President and CEO, Star Furniture<br>Houston, Texas |
| September 8, 2000 | Jeff Comment, Chairman and CEO, Helzberg Diamonds<br>North Kansas City, Missouri |
| September 21, 2000 | Jeff Comment, Chairman and CEO, Helzberg Diamonds<br>North Kansas City, Missouri<br>Telephone interview |
| September 21, 2000 | Chuck Huggins, President and CEO, See's Candies<br>South San Francisco, California<br>Telephone interview |
| October 17, 2000 | Don Graham, Chairman and CEO, *The Washington Post*<br>Washington, D.C. |
| October 18, 2000 | Richard Santulli, President and CEO, Executive Jet<br>Woodbridge, New Jersey |

This list does not include numerous follow-up telephone interviews, e-mails, and written correspondence with all the Buffett CEOs.

# Buffett CEO Family Tree

| Business Name | Buffett CEO | Web Site |
|---|---|---|
| Berkshire Hathaway Inc.<br>3555 Farnam St., Ste. 1440,<br>Omaha, NE 68131-3302<br>Phone: 402-346-1400 | Warren Buffett | www.berkshirehathaway.com |
| Acme Brick<br>American Tile Supply,<br>Featherlite,<br>Glass Block Grid<br>System,<br>Texas Quarries | Harrold Melton | www.acmebuildingbrands.com |
| Ben Bridge Jewelers | Ed and Jon Bridge | www.benbridge.com |
| Benjamin Moore | Yvan Dúpuy | www.benjaminmoore.com |
| BH Homestate Insurance<br>Brookwood,<br>Continental Divide,<br>Cornhusker,<br>Cypress,<br>Gateway Underwriters,<br>Oak River,<br>Redwood | Rod Eldred | www.bh-hc.com |
| Berkshire Reinsurance<br>Division (see National<br>Indemnity) | Ajit Jain | www.brkdirect.com |
| Blue Chip Stamps<br>  Wesco Financial<br>    Precision Steel<br>    Wesco Financial<br>      Insurance<br>    Kansas Bankers Surety<br>    Cort Furniture<br>    MS Property | <br>Charlie Munger<br>Terry Piper<br>Don Wurster<br><br>Donald Towle<br>Paul Arnold<br>Robert Bird | <br><br>www.precisionsteel.com<br><br><br><br>www.cort1.com |
| Borsheim's Fine Jewelry | Susan Jacques | www.borsheims.com |
| *Buffalo News* | Stan Lipsey | www.buffnews.com |
| Central States Indemnity | John Kizer | www.csi-omaha.com |
| Dexter Shoe<br>  Pan Am Shoe | Peter Lunder | www.dextershoe.com |

| Business Name | Buffett CEO | Web Site |
| --- | --- | --- |
| Executive Jet<br>  Executive Jet Management,<br>  Executive Jet Sales,<br>  NetJets,<br>  NetJets Europe,<br>  NetJets Middle East | Richard Santulli | www.netjets.com |
| Fechheimer Brothers<br>  All Bilt,<br>  Nick Bloom,<br>  Bricker-Mincolla,<br>  Command,<br>  Eagle,<br>  Farrior's,<br>  Fechheimer Band,<br>  Flying Cross,<br>  Griffey,<br>  Harris,<br>  Harrison,<br>  Kale,<br>  Kay,<br>  Martin,<br>  McCain,<br>  Metro,<br>  Nationwide,<br>  Pima,<br>  Robert's,<br>  Silver State,<br>  Simon's,<br>  West Virginia,<br>  Zuckerberg's | Brad Kinstler | www.fechheimer.com |
| FlightSafety International<br>  FlightSafety Boeing,<br>  MarineSafety,<br>  Instructional Systems,<br>  Simulation Systems,<br>  Visual Simulation,<br>  FlightSafety Services,<br>  Learning Centers,<br>  Training Academies | Al Ueltschi | www.flightsafety.com |
| GEICO<br>  GEICO Casualty,<br>  GEICO Financial Services,<br>  GEICO Indemnity,<br>  GEICO General,<br>  Insurance Counselors, Inc.,<br>  International Insurance<br>    Underwriters,<br>  Safe Driver Motor Club | Tony Nicely | www.geico.com |

| Business Name | Buffett CEO | Web Site |
| --- | --- | --- |
| GEICO Capital | Lou Simpson | |
| General RE<br>  General Cologne RE,<br>  Faraday,<br>  General Cologne Life RE,<br>  GenRe Securities,<br>  General Star, Genesis,<br>  Herbert Clough,<br>  New England Asset Mgmt.,<br>  US Aviation Underwriters | Ron Ferguson | www.genre.com |
| Helzberg Diamonds | Jeff Comment | www.helzberg.com |
| H.H. Brown Shoe<br>  Carolina Shoe,<br>  Cove Shoe,<br>  Double H Boot,<br>  Isabela Shoe,<br>  Super Shoe Stores,<br>  Lowell Shoe | Frank Rooney | www.hhbrown.com<br><br><br><br><br>www.comfort2u.com |
| International Dairy Queen<br>  Dairy Queen,<br>  Orange Julius,<br>  Karmelkorn Shoppes | Chuck Mooty | www.dairyqueen.com |
| Johns Manville Corp. | Jerry Henry | www.jm.com |
| Jordan's Furniture | Eliot and Barry Tatelman | www.jordansfurniture.com |
| Justin Brands<br>  Chippewa Boot<br>  Nocona Boot<br>  Tony Lama Boot | Randy Watson | www.justinboots.com<br>www.chippewaboots.com<br>www.nocona.com<br>www.tonylama.com |
| MidAmerica Energy<br>  Northern Electric & Gas<br>  CalEnergy | David Sokol | www.midamerican.com<br>www.northern-electric.co.uk<br>www.calenergy.com |
| MiTek | Gene Toombs | www.mitekinc.com |
| National Indemnity Group<br>  Columbia Insurance<br>    Company,<br>  Berkshire Hathaway Life<br>    Insurance Company of<br>    Nebraska,<br>  National Fire & Marine<br>    Insurance Company,<br>  National Indemnity Company,<br>  National Indemnity Company<br>    of Mid-America,<br>  National Indemnity Company<br>    of the South, | Don Wurster/Ajit Jain | www.nationalindemnity.com |

| Business Name | Buffett CEO | Web Site |
| --- | --- | --- |
| National Liability & Fire Insurance Company, Wesco-Financial Insurance Company, Northern States Agency, Inc., Pacific Gateway Insurance Agency, Ringwalt & Liesche Co. | | |
| Nebraska Furniture Mart Floors Inc., Homemakers Furniture | Irv and Ron Blumkin | www.nfm.com |
| R.C. Willey Home Furnishings | Bill Child | www.rcwilley.com |
| Scott Fetzer Companies | Ken Smelsberger | |
| Adalet | | www.adalet.com |
| Campbell Hausfeld | | www.chpower.com |
| Carefree of Colorado | | www.digidot.com/carefree |
| Cleveland Wood Products | | www.cwp-sfz.com |
| Douglas/Quikut (Ginsu) | | www.quikut.com |
| France | | www.franceformer.com |
| Halex | | www.halexco.com |
| Kingston | | www.kingstontimer.com |
| Kirby Vacuum | | www.kirby.com |
| Meriam Instrument | | www.meriam.com |
| Northland | | www.northlandmotor.com |
| Powerwinch | | |
| Scot Laboratories | | www.scotlabs.com |
| Scottcare | | www.scottcare.com |
| Stahl | | www.stahl.cc |
| United Consumer Financial Service | | |
| Wayne Combustion | | www.waynecombustion.com |
| Wayne Water Systems | | www.waynepumps.com |
| Western Enterprises | | www.westernenterprises.com |
| Western Plastics | | www.wplastics.com |
| World Book Encyclopedia | | www.worldbook.com |
| See's Candies | Chuck Huggins | www.sees.com |
| Shaw Industries | Bob Shaw | www.shawinc.com |
| Star Furniture | Melvyn Wolff | www.starfurniture.com |
| United States Liability | Tom Nerney | www.usli.com |

# Buffett CEO SIC Codes

Often, large companies are involved in related businesses. However, the range of companies owned by Berkshire Hathaway is enormous. The Buffett CEOs manage 125 categories of business. They are listed here in the order of their Standard Industrial Code (SIC).

## SIC Code and Business Description

| | |
|------|--------------------------------|
| 1752 | floor laying |
| 2023 | ice cream mix |
| 2024 | ice cream manufacturer |
| 2026 | manf dairy queen mix |
| 2064 | candy manufacturing |
| 2273 | carpet manufacturer |
| 2311 | men's and boys' uniforms |
| 2321 | uniform shirts |
| 2326 | service uniforms |
| 2331 | shirts |
| 2337 | police uniforms |
| 2339 | women's and juniors' uniforms |
| 2389 | band uniforms |
| 2711 | daily newspaper |
| 2731 | book publishing and printing |
| 2741 | database publishers |
| 2841 | manf of soaps and specialty cleaners |
| 2842 | manf of polish |
| 2851 | paint |

3086   shoe insulation and cushioning

3089   manf of rv accessories

3089   molded plastic

3142   manf of house slippers

3143   men's footwear manufacturer

3144   women's footwear manufacturer

3149   athletic shoe manufacturer

3251   brick manufacturer

3312   processor of specialty metals

3316   steel warehousing

3363   aluminum die-casting

3364   nonaluminum die-casting

3421   cutlery

3429   clamps and couplings

3433   manf furnace burners

3451   machine tool attachments

3469   manf truck bodies

3494   manf compressed gas fittings and regulators

3496   gauges

3499   fabricated metal products

3531   boat winches and windlasses

3536   hoists

3545   precision measuring devices

3546   power-driven hand tools

3548   welding eqpt

3561   pumps

3563   air and gas compressors

3589   service industry machinery

3612   sign ballasts and transformers

3621   manf fractional horsepower motors

3629    electrical industrial apparatus

3635    household vacuum cleaner manufacturer

3644    manf fitting and junction boxes

3678    electronic connectors

3699    flight simulator manufacturer

3712    aircraft sales

3713    manf of truck bodies

3715    truck trailers

3822    automatic controls

3823    measurement devices

3841    medical eqpt

3842    shoe prosthetic inserts

3914    silverware

3949    sports eqpt

3991    jewelry, precious metal

4213    building materials transport

4226    warehousing

4522    aviation charter

4581    aircraft maintenance

4729    travel management

4911    energy production and distribution

5032    brick, stone, and construction materials

5033    insulation

5051    steel service center

5063    construction materials

5074    plumbing and heating eqpt

5087    firefighting eqpt

5088    aircraft parts

5094    precious metals

5113    paper products wholesaler

| 5136 | wholesale uniforms |
|------|--------------------|
| 5143 | dairy products |
| 5145 | confectionery |
| 5149 | disposable plastic wholesaler |
| 5441 | candy, nut, and confectionery stores |
| 5632 | handbags |
| 5661 | shoe stores |
| 5699 | retail uniforms |
| 5712 | furniture stores |
| 5713 | floor covering stores |
| 5722 | household appliance stores |
| 5731 | consumer electronic stores |
| 5734 | computer stores |
| 5812 | ice cream stores |
| 5944 | jewelry stores |
| 5946 | camera stores |
| 5947 | retail silverware and gifts |
| 5961 | catalog and mail order |
| 5963 | direct sales of encyclopedias |
| 5999 | police supply stores |
| 6036 | savings and loan |
| 6099 | foreign currency exchange |
| 6141 | consumer finance companies |
| 6153 | short-term business credit |
| 6211 | registered investment advisor, and broker/dealer |
| 6231 | security and commodity exchanges |
| 6282 | investment advice |
| 6311 | auto, life, fire, marine and casualty insurance/reinsurance |
| 6321 | accident insurance carriers |
| 6331 | fire, marine, and casualty insurance |

| 6351 | fidelity insurance |
|------|--------------------|
| 6399 | aviation insurance |
| 6411 | insurance agents |
| 6512 | nonresidential building operators |
| 6519 | lessors of real property |
| 6531 | real estate agents and managers |
| 6719 | investment holding company |
| 6794 | licensing and franchise sales |
| 6799 | commodity contract trading company |
| 7359 | aircraft rental |
| 7372 | educational courseware design and production |
| 7389 | trading stamps and motivational programs |
| 7812 | visual simulation |
| 8249 | aviation schools |
| 8299 | flying instruction |
| 8699 | auto owners assoc |

*Note:* This list does not include businesses in categories that do not have an SIC, like aircraft fractional ownership and office furniture rental. Also this list does not include the SIC of partly owned businesses like Coca-Cola and American Express.

# Buffett CEO Timeline

## THE FOUNDING YEARS

1836   Campbell Manufacturing founded

1870   Borsheim's jewelry founded in Omaha

1877   *Washington Post* founded

1879   Justin Boot founded

1880   *The Buffalo Evening News* founded

1883   H.H. Brown Shoe founded

1886   Coca-Cola Formulated

1888   Hathaway Manufacturing Co. founded

1889   Berkshire Cotton Manufacturing Co. founded

1891   Acme Brick founded

1893   Rose Blumkin born December 3

1906   Kirby cleaner invented

1912   Star Furniture founded

1914   Scott Machine Shop founded

1915   Helzberg Diamonds founded

1915   Scott & Fetzer formed

1917   World Book first published

1920   Campbell Hausfeld formed

1921   See's Candies founded

1928   Jordan's Furniture founded

1932   R.C. Willey founded

1936   GEICO founded

1937   Nebraska Furniture Mart founded with $500 (Mrs. B, age 44)

1940   National Indemnity founded

1951     FlightSafety founded with Ueltschi's $15,000 home mortgage
        Chuck Huggins joins See's Candies

1954     Berkshire Hathaway formed

1957     Dexter Shoe founded

1961     Tony Nicely begins GEICO career

1964     Executive Jet founded

1967     Warren Buffett begins managing Berkshire Hathaway

## THE ACQUIRING YEARS

1972     See's Candies acquired for $25 million

1973     *The Washington Post* partly acquired (15% for $11 million)

1974     Don Graham and Warren Buffett appointed to *The Washington Post* Board

1974     Ralph Schey begins Scott Fetzer career

1976     GEICO partly acquired

1977     *The Buffalo News* acquired for $34 million

1980     Lou Simpson begins managing GEICO's capital

1982     Ajit Jain begins Berkshire career

1983     Nebraska Furniture Mart acquired for $55 million (80%)

1983     Susan Jacques joins Borsheim's at age 23, earning $4 per hour

1984     Rich Santulli acquires Executive Jet

1985     Berkshire's original textile business discontinued

1986     Scott Fetzer acquired for $315 million cash

1989     Borsheim's Jewelry acquired

1991     H.H. Brown Shoes acquired

1991     Tony Nicely named GEICO CEO

1992     Lowell Shoe acquired

1993     Susan Jacques appointed Borsheim's CEO at age 34
        Dexter Shoe acquired for $420 million in stock

1995     Helzberg Diamonds acquired
        R.C. Willey Home Furnishings acquired

1996    Balance of GEICO acquired for $2.3 billion
        FlightSafety acquired for $1.5 billion
        Class B stock created, worth 1/30 of Class A stock

1997    Star Furniture acquired

1998    Executive Jet acquired for $725 million ($350 million cash and
        $375 million stock)

1998    Rose Blumkin dies August 9, at age 104

1999    Jordan's Furniture acquired

2000    Acme Brick acquired
        Justin Boot acquired
        Ralph Schey retires


*Note:* All of the acquired companies were founded on average in 1909
and 58 years before Warren Buffett started managing Berkshire Hathaway.

# Notes

## Chapter One   Introduction—The Warren Buffett CEO

1. Warren Buffett, "Chairman's Letter to Shareholders," 1987.
2. Warren Buffett, "Chairman's Letter to Shareholders," 1989.

## Chapter Two   Buffett CEO Selection

1. Terry Piper, letter to the author, June 27, 2001.
2. Warren Buffett, "Chairman's Letter to Shareholders," 1994.
3. Warren Buffett, "Chairman's Letter to Shareholders," 1991.
4. Warren Buffett, "Chairman's Letter to Shareholders," 2000.
5. Warren Buffett, "Chairman's Letter to Shareholders," 1981.
6. Warren Buffett, "Chairman's Letter to Shareholders," 1992.
7. Warren Buffett, "Chairman's Letter to Shareholders," 1995.
8. Warren Buffett, "Chairman's Letter to Shareholders," 2000.
9. Warren Buffett, "Chairman's Letter to Shareholders," 1998.

## Chapter Three   The Administrator—Tony Nicely, GEICO Insurance

1. Alan Breznick, "GEICO Revs Up to Try to Triple Its Market Share," *Washington Post,* March 30, 1998.
2. Warren Buffett, "Chairman's Letter to Shareholders," 1995.
3. Ibid.
4. Warren Buffett, "Chairman's Letter to Shareholders," 1980.
5. Roger Lowenstein, "To Read Buffett, Examine What He Bought," *Wall Street Journal,* January 18, 1996.
6. Stan Hinden, "The GEICO Deal: How Billionaire Buffett Bid at $70," *Washington Post,* November 6, 1995.
7. Lowenstein, "To Read Buffett. . . . "
8. Albert B. Crenshaw, "Premium Partners; Single-Minded GEICO Was Just Buffett's Style. Now They're Together for the Long Haul," *Washington Post,* September 18, 1995.

9. John Taylor, "Buffett Ends Long GEICO Waltz," *Omaha World-Herald,* August 26, 1995.

10. Crenshaw, "Premium Partners . . ."

11. Warren Buffett, "Chairman's Letter to Shareholders," 1996.

12. Warren Buffett, "Chairman's Letter to Shareholders," 1995.

13. Warren Buffett, "Chairman's Letter to Shareholders," 1996.

14. Warren Buffett, "Chairman's Letter to Shareholders," 1998.

15. Warren Buffett, "Chairman's Letter to Shareholders," 2000.

16. Noble Sprayberry, "Working Happy," *San Diego Union-Tribune,* October 18, 1999.

## *Chapter Four*   The Back-Up Capital Allocator—Lou Simpson, GEICO Insurance

1. Warren Buffett, "Chairman's Letter to Stockholders," 1995.

2. Devon Spurgeon, "Envelope, Please: Not One to Be Caught Unprepared, Mr. Buffett Makes His Plans Clear," *Wall Street Journal,* October 17, 2000.

3. David A. Vise, "GEICO's Top Market Strategist Churning Out Profits; Lou Simpson's Stock Rises on His Successful Ideas," *Washington Post,* May 11, 1987.

4. Suzanne Wooley with Joan Caplin, "The Next Buffett," *Money,* December 2000.

5. Ibid.

6. David Barboza, "Following the Buffett Formula; GEICO Chief May Be Heir to a Legend," *New York Times,* April 29, 1997.

7. Wooley with Caplin, "The Next Buffett."

8. Barboza, "Following the Buffett Formula."

9. James Clash, "The Next Warren Buffett," *Forbes,* October 30, 2000.

10. Warren Buffett, "Chairman's Letter to Shareholders," 1995.

11. Vise, "GEICO's Top Market Strategist Churning Out Profits."

12. *San Diego Union-Tribune,* May 11, 1997.

13. Barboza, "Following the Buffett Formula."

14. Vise, "GEICO's Top Market Strategist Churning Out Profits."

15. Warren Buffett, "Chairman's Letter to Stockholders," 1982.

16. Warren Buffett, "Chairman's Letter to Stockholders," 1986.

17. Vise, "GEICO's Top Market Strategist Churning Out Profits."

18. Brendan Boyd, "Investor's Notebook," Uexpress Online, www.uexpress.com, February 10, 2001.

19. Stan Hinden, "As Spring Blooms, So Do Annual Reports," *Washington Post,* April 26, 1993.

20. Wooley with Caplin, "The Next Buffett."
21. Barboza, "Following the Buffett Formula."
22. Spurgeon, "Envelope, Please."
23. Ibid.
24. Clash, "The Next Warren Buffett."

## Chapter Five   The Accidental Manager—Ajit Jain, Berkshire Hathaway Reinsurance Division

1. Warren Buffett, "Chairman's Letter to Shareholders," 2000.
2. Devon Spurgeon, "Envelope, Please: Not One to Be Caught Unprepared, Mr. Buffett Makes His Plans Clear," *Wall Street Journal,* October 17, 2000.
3. Anthony Bianco, "Warren: The Buffett You Don't Know," *Business Week,* July 5, 1999.
4. Warren Buffett, "Chairman's Letter to Shareholders," 1996.
5. Warren Buffett, "Chairman's Letter to Shareholders," 1990.
6. Warren Buffett, "Chairman's Letter to Shareholders," 1997.
7. Andy Kilpatrick, *Of Permanent Value: The Story of Warren Buffett* (AKPE, 2000), p. 245.
8. Warren Buffett, "Chairman's Letter to Shareholders," 2000.
9. Janet Kornblum, "Site Runs the Risk of a $1 Billion Grab," *USA Today,* October 25, 2000, p. 3D.
10. Warren Buffett, "Chairman's Letter to Shareholders," 2000.
11. Ibid.
12. Warren Buffett, "Chairman's Letter to Shareholders," 1989.
13. Warren Buffett, "Chairman's Letter to Shareholders," 1992.
14. Warren Buffett, "Chairman's Letter to Shareholders," 1994.
15. Warren Buffett, "Chairman's Letter to Shareholders," 1996.
16. Warren Buffett, "Chairman's Letter to Shareholders," 1999.
17. Andy Kilpatrick, *Of Permanent Value,* p. 238.
18. Spurgeon, "Envelope, Please. . . . "

## Chapter Six   The Natural—Rose Blumkin, Nebraska Furniture Mart (NFM)

1. Linda O'Bryon, Warren Buffett Interview, Nightly Business Report, April 26, 1994.
2. Robert Dorr, "Rose Blumkin, 1893–1998: Remembering Mrs. B," *Omaha World-Herald,* August 10, 1998.

3. Rich Rockwood, "Model of Success," www.focusinvestor.com
4. Dorr, "Rose Blumkin."
5. Barnaby J. Feder, "Rose Blumkin, Retail Queen, Dies at 104," *New York Times,* August 13, 1998.
6. Jim Rasmussen, "Omaha, Neb.-Based Furniture Store Owner Happy at No. 2," *Omaha World-Herald,* June 2, 1999.
7. Warren Buffett, "Chairman's Letter to Shareholders," 1983.
8. Feder, "Rose Blumkin."
9. Andrew Cassel, Interview with Rose Blumkin, December 14, 1989.
10. Linda O'Bryon, Rose Blumkin Interview, Nightly Business Report, June 1, 1994.
11. Dorr, "Rose Blumkin."
12. Rockwood, "Model of Success."
13. Dorr, "Rose Blumkin."
14. Cassel, Interview.
15. "The Life and Times of Rose Blumkin, An American Original," advertising supplement to the *Omaha World-Herald,* December 12, 1993.
16. Andrew Cassel, "Andrew Cassel Column," *Philadelphia Inquirer,* August 14, 1998.
17. Cassel, Interview.
18. Cassel, Interview.
19. "Life and Times."
20. Feder, "Rose Blumkin."
21. Cassel, Interview.
22. Feder, "Rose Blumkin."
23. Rockwood, "Model of Success."
24. Ibid.
25. Dorr, "Rose Blumkin."
26. Cassel, Interview.
27. Cassel, Interview.
28. Rockwood, "Model of Success."
29. Warren Buffett, "Chairman's Letter to Shareholders," 1983.
30. Linda O'Bryon, Interview with Blumkin.
31. Warren Buffett, "Chairman's Letter to Shareholders," 1983.
32. Cassel, Interview.
33. Feder, "Rose Blumkin."
34. Joyce Wadler, "Blumkin: Sofa, So Good; The First Lady of Furniture, Flourishing at 90," *Washington Post,* May 24, 1984.
35. "Life and Times."
36. Frank E. James, "Furniture Czarina: Still a Live Wire at 90, A Retail Phenomenon Oversees Her Empire," *Wall Street Journal,* May 23, 1984.

37. http://www.nebraskafurnituremart.com/pages/timeline.html "Factoids."
38. Cassel, Interview.
39. Feder, "Rose Blumkin."
40. O'Bryon, Warren Buffett Interview.
41. Rockwood, "Model of Success."
42. Cassel, Interview.
43. Andy Kilpatrick, *Of Permanent Value: The Story of Warren Buffett* (AKPE, 2000), p. 413.
44. Rockwood, "Model of Success."
45. Roger Lowenstein, *Buffett: The Making of an American Capitalist* (Doubleday, 1996), p. 247.
46. Linda O'Bryon, Warren Buffett Interview.
47. Ibid.
48. Warren Buffett, "Chairman's Letter to Shareholders," 1983.
49. Rockwood, "Model of Success."
50. Wadler, "Blumkin: Sofa, So Good."
51. Feder, "Rose Blumkin."
52. Linda O'Bryon, Warren Buffett Interview.
53. Dorr, "Rose Blumkin."
54. James, "Furniture Czarina."
55. Warren Buffett, "Chairman's Letter to Shareholders," 1984.
56. Cassel, Interview.
57. Associated Press, "Mrs. B, 96, Starts Over in Furniture Business," *St. Louis Post-Dispatch,* November 12, 1989.
58. Rockwood, "Model of Success."
59. Associated Press, "Mrs. B."
60. Cassel, Interview.
61. "Life and Times."
62. Larry Green, "At 96, Feuding Matriarch Opens New Business," *Los Angeles Times,* December 18, 1989.
63. Cassel, Interview.
64. Green, "At 96, Feuding Matriarch."
65. Feder, "Rose Blumkin."
66. "Life and Times."
67. Warren Buffett, "Chairman's Letter to Shareholders," 1992.
68. Kilpatrick, *Of Permanent Value.*
69. O'Bryon, Rose Blumkin Interview.
70. Robert Dorr, "Nearly 104, Mrs. B Retires: Gone From the Sales Floor but Not From Business, Mrs. B's Business," *Omaha World-Herald,* October 26, 1997.
71. Rockwood, "Model of Success."

72. Dorr, "Rose Blumkin."

73. "Life and Times."

74. Anonymous, "Mrs. B., Buffett in Cable TV Spot," *Omaha World-Herald*, February 8, 1995.

75. Green, "At 96, Feuding Matriarch."

76. Lowenstein, *Buffett*, p. 249.

77. Cassel, Interview.

## *Chapter Seven*   The Visionary—Al Ueltschi, FlightSafety International

1. Al Ueltschi, "The History and Future of FlightSafety International," The Wings Club Thirty-fourth General Harold R. Harris Sight Lecture, The Wings Club, May 21, 1997.

2. Ibid.

3. Id.

4. Id.

5. Id.

6. Id.

7. Id.

8. Id.

9. Id.

10. Id.

11. Id.

12. Id.

13. Id.

14. Id.

15. National Business Aircraft Association, "NBAA Honors FSI Founder," 1991.

16. Ueltschi, "History and Future."

17. Ibid.

18. Id.

19. Id.

20. Id.

21. Warren Buffett, "Chairman's Letter to Shareholders," 1996.

22. Ueltschi, "History and Future."

23. Berkshire Hathaway Press Release, October 15, 1996.

24. Ueltschi, "History and Future."

25. Associated Press, "Berkshire Chief Buys New York Company," October 16, 1996.

26. Paul Lowe, "Billionaire Buffett on Business Aviation," *Aviation International News,* 1999.
27. National Business Aircraft Association, "NBAA Honors."
28. FlightSafety brochure.
29. "Warren Buffett Buys FlightSafety for $1.50 Billion," *Aviation News,* 1996.
30. Andy Kilpatrick, *Of Permanent Value: The Story of Warren Buffett* (AKPE, 2000).
31. Mike Busch, "Simulator-Based Recurrent Training Product Comparison," *AVweb,* May 5, 1998.
32. Fleming Meeks, "The Pilots' Pilot (FlightSafety International) (The 200 Best Small Companies in America)," *Forbes,* November 13, 1989.
33. Judy Temes, "No Fancy Digs, Just Big Profits; Founder Keeps FlightSafety Lean, Shareholders Happy," *Crain's New York Business,* February 5, 1990.
34. Ueltschi, "History and Future."
35. Ibid.
36. Warren Buffett, letter to the author, April 10, 2000.
37. Jerry Wakefield, "Achievement: Al Ueltschi," [Kentucky] *State Journal,* 1979.

## *Chapter Eight*   The Innovator—Rich Santulli, Executive Jet

1. Anthony Bianco, "What's Better Than a Private Plane? A Semiprivate Plane," *Business Week,* July 21, 1997.
2. Ibid.
3. Ron Carter, "Stars in the Sky: Executive Jet Becoming Transportation of Choice of the Rich and Famous," *Columbus Dispatch,* December 12, 1999.
4. Joann Muller, "Gimmick Gives Industry a Lift; Fractional Ownership Moves Private Jets within Reach of Small Firms, Individuals," *Boston Globe,* August 3, 1997.
5. Warren Buffett, "Chairman's Letter to Shareholders," 1998.
6. Ron Carter, "Executive Jet Has Big Fan: Buffett," *Columbus Dispatch,* August 26, 1998.
7. "Flying Buffett," *Forbes.com,* September 21, 1998.
8. Carter, "Executive Jet Has Big Fan."
9. Ron Carter, "Executive Jet to Announce World-Record Order," *Columbus Dispatch,* June 13, 1999.
10. Carter, "Executive Jet Has Big Fan."
11. Warren Berger, "Hey, You're Worth It," *Wired,* June 2001.

12. Ibid.
13. Bianco, "What's Better Than a Private Plane?"
14. Buffett, "Chairman's Letter to Shareholders," 1998.
15. MedAire, Press Release, February 24, 2000.
16. Executive Jets, "NetJets U.S. Investment Summary, Year 2000," September 1, 2000.
17. Buffett, "Chairman's Letter to Shareholders," 1998.
18. John Edwards, "Billionaire Discusses Strategy for Picking Stocks," *Las Vegas Review-Journal,* October 19, 1998.
19. Roger Bray (?), "Supersonic Joys Shared Out: Business Travel High-Speed Aircraft," *Financial Times* (London), October 26, 1998.
20. The Sandman, The Motley Fool, "Executive Jet," May 17, 2000.
21. Paul Burnham Finney, "The Sonic Boom in Shared Jets," *Frequent Flyer Magazine,* March 2000.
22. Don Stancavish, "Woodbridge, N.J., Company Sells Time Shares of Aircraft," *Record* (New Jersey), October 29, 2000.

## *Chapter Nine*   The Disciple—Don Graham, *The Washington Post*

1. Barbara Matusow, "Citizen Don," *Washingtonian,* August 1992.
2. Ibid.
3. Jeffrey Toobin, "The Regular Guy," *New Yorker,* March 20, 2000.
4. Richard J. Cattani, "Kay Graham's Story As Told by Herself," *Christian Science Monitor,* February 18, 1997.
5. Andy Kilpatrick, *Of Permanent Value: The Story of Warren Buffett* (AKPE, 2000), pp. 276–277.
6. Toobin, "The Regular Guy."
7. Matusow, "Citizen Don."
8. Roger Lowenstein, *Buffett: The Making of an American Capitalist* (Doubleday, 1996), pp. 182–183.
9. Ibid.
10. Toobin, "The Regular Guy."
11. Lowenstein, *Buffett,* p. 185.
12. Toobin, "The Regular Guy."
13. Matusow, "Citizen Don."
14. Felicity Barringer, "Media Talk: Emphasizing Journalism to Stock Analysts," *New York Times,* December 11, 2000.
15. Matusow, "Citizen Don."
16. Audit Bureau of Circulation (March 91–March 01).
17. Toobin, "The Regular Guy."

18. Ibid.

19. Frank Swaboda and Howard Kurtz, "Donald Graham Is Named Post Co. President, CEO," *Washington Post,* March 15, 1991.

20. James Harding, "Inside Track: From Watergate to Web," *Financial Times* (London), December 17, 1999.

21. Toobin, "The Regular Guy."

22. Ibid.

## *Chapter Ten* The Third-Generation Family Successor— Irvin Blumkin, NFM

1. Jim Rasmussen, "Omaha, Neb.-Based Furniture Store Owner Happy at No. 2," *Omaha World-Herald,* June 2, 1999.

2. Warren Buffett, "Chairman's Letter to Shareholders," 1988.

3. Barnaby J. Feder, "A Retailer's Home-Grown Success," *New York Times,* June 17, 1994.

4. Ibid.

5. Steve Jordon, "Furniture Mart to Buy Iowa Company," *Omaha World-Herald,* September 14, 2000.

6. Feder, "A Retailer's Home-Grown Success."

7. Warren Buffett, "Chairman's Letter to Shareholders," 1997.

8. Warren Buffett, "Chairman's Letter to Shareholders," 1995.

9. Warren Buffett, "Chairman's Letter to Shareholders," 1997.

10. Warren Buffett, "Chairman's Letter to Shareholders," 1999.

11. Ibid.

12. John L. Ward, "Keeping the Family Business Healthy," Jossey-Bass Publishers, 1987.

13. Ibid.

14. Warren Buffett, "Chairman's Letter to Shareholders," 1984.

## *Chapter Eleven* The Retired Manager—Frank Rooney, H.H. Brown Shoe

1. Carol Beggy and Beth Carney, "Tee Time for Clinton to Be Delayed?" *The Boston Globe,* August 18, 1999.

2. Sheila McGovern, "Factory Closing Rocks Richmond," *Montreal Gazette,* October 21, 2000.

3. Warren Buffett, "Chairman's Letter to Shareholders," 1991.

4. Ibid.

5. Andy Kilpatrick, *Of Permanent Value: The Story of Warren Buffett* (AKPE, 2000), pp. 459–460.

6. Robert Preer, "Shoes, Jobs in Decline . . . ," *Boston Globe,* January 3, 1995.
7. American Apparel and Footwear Association, November 2000.
8. Preer, "Shoes, jobs in decline."
9. Kilpatrick, *Of Permanent Value,* p. 459.
10. Frederic M. Biddle, "Morse Sells Lowell Unit to H.H. Brown," *Boston Globe,* December 3, 1992.
11. Warren Buffett, "Chairman's Letter to Shareholders," 1992.
12. Warren Buffett, "Chairman's Letter to Shareholders," 1993.
13. Kilpatrick, *Of Permanent Value,* p. 463.
14. *Forbes,* October 10, 1994.
15. Kilpatrick, *Of Permanent Value,* pp. 463–464.
16. Ibid, p. 464.
17. *Business Week,* October 12, 1998.
18. Kilpatrick, *Of Permanent Value,* p. 465.
19. Warren Buffett, "Chairman's Letter to Shareholders," 1998.
20. Warren Buffett, "Chairman's Letter to Shareholders," 1993.
21. Warren Buffett, "Chairman's Letter to Shareholders," 1999.
22. Warren Buffett, "Chairman's Letter to Shareholders," 1991.
23. *Business Week,* July 5, 1999.

## *Chapter Twelve*   The Principled Manager—Bill Child, R.C. Willey Home Furnishings

1. E.K. Valentin & Jerald T. Storey, "R.C. Willey Home Furnishings: A Case Study," John B. Goddard School of Business & Economics, Weber State University, 1999.
2. Cover story, "The Berkshire Bunch," *Forbes,* October 12, 1998.
3. Warren Buffett, "Chairman's Letter to Shareholders," 1999.
4. Karl Kunkel, "Place Your Bets, Ladies and Gentlemen," *High Points,* July 2000.
5. Stephen W. Gibson, "R.C. Willey Got Its Humble Start Selling Refrigerators to Farmers," *Deseret News,* April 11, 1999.

## *Chapter Thirteen*   The Partner for Life—Melvyn Wolff, Star Furniture

1. Warren Buffett, "Chairman's Letter to Shareholders," 1997.
2. John Taylor, "Berkshire Adds Third Furniture Store to Stable of Companies," *Omaha World-Herald,* June 25, 1997.

3. Buffett, "Chairman's Letter to Shareholders," 1997.
4. Kimberley Wray, "Buffett's Galaxy Grows: Investor Inks Deal for Star Furniture," *Home Furnishings News (HFN)*, June 30, 1997.
5. Nina Farrell, "Made in the Shade," *High Points*, August 1998.
6. Ibid.

## *Chapter Fourteen*    The Shoppertainers—Eliot and Barry Tatelman, Jordan's Furniture

1. Andrew Edgecliffe-Johnson and Victoria Griffith, "Furnishing an Entertainment Revolution," [London] *Financial Times*, October 16, 1999.
2. Kimberly Wray, "Jordan's 'Bad Boys' Score Again," *Home Furnishings News (HFN)*, April 20, 1998.
3. Patti Doten, "A Matched Set," *Boston Globe*, January 25, 1999.
4. Arthur Lubow, "Wowing Warren," *Inc.*, March 2000.
5. Doten, "A Matched Set."
6. Lubow, "Wowing Warren."
7. Doten, "A Matched Set."
8. Lubow, "Wowing Warren."
9. Ibid.
10. Id.
11. Doten, "A Matched Set."
12. Warren Buffett, "Chairman's Letter to Shareholders," 1999.
13. Lubow, "Wowing Warren."
14. Kimberly Blanton, "Brothers Will Sell Jordan's Furniture," *Boston Globe*, October 12, 1999.
15. Lubow, "Wowing Warren."
16. Eric Convey and Tim McLaughlin, "Buffett Is Sold on Jordan's; Billionaire to Buy Furniture Chain," *Boston Herald*, October 12, 1999.
17. Blanton, "Brothers Will Sell Jordan's Furniture."
18. Lubow, "Wowing Warren."
19. Brian McGrory, "Doing Things the Right Way," *Boston Globe*, October 12, 1999.
20. Edgecliff-Johnson and Griffith, "Furnishing an Entertainment Revolution."
21. Warren Buffett, "Chairman's Letter to Shareholders," 1999.
22. Jessica Goldbogen, "The Fabulous Tatelman Brothers," *High Points*, December 1999.
23. Lubow, "Wowing Warren."
24. Patricia Resende, "It's Party Time for Employees," *Boston Herald*, February 26, 1999.

25. Lubow, "Wowing Warren."
26. Brian McGrory, "Barry, Eliot Go Against Tide," *Boston Globe,* May 11, 1999.
27. Lubow, "Wowing Warren."
28. McGrory, "Barry, Eliot Go Against Tide."
29. Lubow, "Wowing Warren."
30. "The Customer Is King," *Cabinet Maker,* August 4, 2000.
31. Doten, "A Matched Set."
32. "Retailer Entrepreneurs of the Year: Barry and Eliot Tatelman," *Chain Store Age,* December 1, 1997.
33. Doten, "A Matched Set."
34. Ibid.
35. Bella English, "Camp Comfort: Tatelmans Create Weeklong Refuge Where HIV-Infected Children Can Just Be Kids," *Boston Globe,* August 10, 2000.

## *Chapter Fifteen*   The Turnaround Manager—Stan Lipsey, *The Buffalo News*

1. Andy Kilpatrick, *Of Permanent Value: The Story of Warren Buffett* (AKPE, 2000), p. 410.
2. "Path to Billions Began with a Newspaper Route," *Buffalo News,* October 4, 1993, p. 1.
3. John Henry, "Buffett in Buffalo," *Columbia Journalism Review,* November/December, 1998.
4. Roger Lowenstein, *Buffett: The Making of an American Capitalist* (Doubleday, 1996), pp. 204–205.
5. Ibid.
6. Id.
7. Id., pp. 208–215.
8. Id., pp. 217–218.
9. Henry, "Buffett in Buffalo."
10. Warren Buffett, "Chairman's Letter to Shareholders," 1989.
11. Henry, "Buffett in Buffalo."
12. Ibid.
13. Id.
14. Warren Buffett, "Chairman's Letter to Shareholders," 1984.
15. Warren Buffett, "Chairman's Letter to Shareholders," 1983.
16. Warren Buffett, "Chairman's Letter to Shareholders," 1985.
17. Warren Buffett, "Chairman's Letter to Shareholders," 1989.

## *Chapter Sixteen*   The Loyalist—Chuck Huggins, See's Candies

1. Karola Saekel, "California's Sweetheart," *San Francisco Chronicle*, February 14, 1996.
2. Ibid.
3. Frank Green, "Candy Land; Working in See's Kitchen Is Sweet Job for Loyal Crew," *San Diego Union-Tribune*, December 12, 1985.
4. Laurie Ochoa, "Land of Milk and Toffee," *Los Angeles Times*, December 22, 1996.
5. Nancy Rivera Brooks, "After 70 Years, Success Is Sweet to See's Candies," *Los Angeles Times*, May 10, 1991.
6. Warren Buffett, "Chairman's Letter to Shareholders," 1999.
7. Warren Buffett, "Chairman's Letter to Shareholders," 1984.
8. Saekel, "California's Sweetheart."
9. Warren Buffett, "Chairman's Letter to Shareholders," 1983.
10. Warren Buffett, "Chairman's Letter to Shareholders," 1984.
11. Warren Buffett, "Chairman's Letter to Shareholders," 1985.
12. Warren Buffett, "Chairman's Letter to Shareholders," 1986.
13. Warren Buffett, "Chairman's Letter to Shareholders," 1988.
14. Warren Buffett, "Chairman's Letter to Shareholders," 1991.
15. Mary McNamara, "In Their Capable Hands," *Los Angeles Times*, July 19, 1999.
16. Saekel, "California's Sweetheart."
17. Gavin Power, "See's Seeks to Sweeten Profits by Closing Unprofitable Stores," *San Francisco Chronicle*, April 11, 1994.
18. Michelle Gabriel, "The Candy Man," *South Bay Accent*, February/March 1998.
19. Andy Kilpatrick, *Of Permanent Value: The Story of Warren Buffett* (AKPE, 2000), p. 403.

## *Chapter Seventeen*   The Professional—Ralph Schey, Scott Fetzer Companies

1. Warren Buffett, "Chairman's Letter to Shareholders," 2000.
2. Lynne Thompson, "Venture Idealist," *Inside Business*, October 1999.
3. Ibid.
4. Id.
5. John Ettorre, "Business: Sweeping the Competition," *Cleveland Magazine*, May 1993.

6. Kenneth N. Gilpin, "President Resigns at Scott & Fetzer," *New York Times,* September 7, 1984.
7. Roger Lowenstein, *Buffett: The Making of an American Capitalist,* Doubleday, 1996, p. 265.
8. Warren Buffett, "Chairman's Letter to Shareholders," 1985.
9. Ibid.
10. Id.
11. Robert Dorr, "Kirby Sales Tactics: Berkshire's Vacuum Unit Draws Unwanted Attention," *Omaha World-Herald,* October 11, 1999.
12. Warren Buffett, "Chairman's Letter to Shareholders," 1985.
13. Warren Buffett, "Chairman's Letter to Shareholders," 1986.
14. Warren Buffett, "Chairman's Letter to Shareholders," 1994.
15. Warren Buffett, "Chairman's Letter to Shareholders," 2000.
16. Ralph Schey, "Entrepreneurial Opportunity," *Cleveland Enterprise,* Summer 1991.

## Chapter Eighteen  The Appointed One—Susan Jacques, Borsheim's Fine Jewelry

1. Warren Buffett, "Chairman's Letter to Shareholders," 1997.
2. Mary De Zutter, "Borsheim's Chief Credits Friedman as Retail Mentor," *Omaha World Herald,* June 26, 1994.
3. Ibid.
4. Id.
5. Andy Kilpatrick, *Of Permanent Value: The Story of Warren Buffett* (AKPE, 2000), p. 452.
6. Warren Buffett, "Chairman's Letter to Shareholders," 1989.
7. Ibid.
8. De Zutter, "Borsheim's Chief Credits Friedman."
9. Kilpatrick, *Of Permanent Value,* p. 455.
10. Warren Buffett, "Chairman's Letter to Shareholders," 1990.
11. Online Career Center, "About Susan Jacques," *USA Today,* January 20, 2001.

## Chapter Nineteen  The Gem of a Retail Merchant— Jeff Comment, Helzberg Diamonds

1. Andy Kilpatrick, *Of Permanent Value: The Story of Warren Buffett* (AKPE, 2000), pp. 467–468.

2. "Helzberg to Merge with Berkshire Hathaway," *Jewelers' Circular,* April 1995.
3. Warren Buffett, "Chairman's Letter to Shareholders," 1995.
4. Jennifer Mann Fuller, "Warren Buffett to Buy Helzberg Shops," *Kansas City Star,* March 11, 1995.
5. Ibid.
6. Andy Kilpatrick, *Of Permanent Value,* p. 467.
7. Warren Buffett, "Chairman's Letter to Shareholders," 1995.
8. Fuller, "Warren Buffett to Buy Helzberg Shops."
9. "Helzberg to Merge with Berkshire Hathaway."
10. Marianne Wilson, "CEO Suits Up for Christmas," *Chain Store Age,* December 1, 1997.
11. Helen T. Gray, "By Applying Biblical Principles, Speaks Find Success in Business," *Kansas City Star,* November 7, 1997.
12. Kent Pulliam, "How About a Boat Ride in October?" *Kansas City Star,* September 25, 1999.
13. International Council of Shopping Centers, White Paper on Sales by Store Type, 1999.
14. Jeffrey W. Comment, Address to Jewelers' Charity Fund, Las Vegas, NV, June 4, 2000.

## *Chapter Twenty* The Newcomers—Randy Watson, Justin Brands; and Harrold Melton, Acme Building Brands

1. Warren Buffett, "Chairman's Letter to Shareholders," 2000.
2. Justin Industries, Press Release, June 20, 2000.
3. Gregory Winter, "Private Sector: Giving Buffett the Boots in a Corporate Farewell," *New York Times,* June 25, 2000.
4. Diana J. Kleiner, "Justin Industries," Handbook of Texas Online, February 15, 1999.
5. Ibid.
6. Id.
7. Irvin Farman, *Standard of the West: The Justin Story* (Texas Christian University Press, 1996), pp. 172–181.
8. Kleiner, "Justin Industries."
9. Farman, *Standard of the West,* pp. 174–175.
10. Ibid.
11. Edwin E. Lehr, *Colossus in Clay: Acme Brick Company* (The Donning Company, 1998), p. 145.
12. Ibid., pp. 147–149.

## *Chapter Twenty-Two*   Buffett CEO Evaluation and Compensation

1. Warren Buffett, "Annual Letter to Shareholders," 1988.
2. Warren Buffett, "Annual Letter to Shareholders," 1997.
3. Warren Buffett, "Annual Letter to Shareholders," 1994.

# Index